M Programming

M Programming: A Comprehensive Guide

Richard F. Walters
University of California, Davis

An Imprint of Elsevier
Boston • Oxford • Johannesburg • Melbourne • New Delhi • Singapore

Digital Press™
An Imprint of Elsevier

This book is printed on acid-free paper.

Library of Congress Cataloging-in-Publication Data

Walters, Richard F., 1930-
M programming: a comprehensive guide / Richard F. Walters.
p. cm.
Includes index.
ISBN-13: 978-1-55558-167-1 ISBN-10: 1-55558-167-6 (alk. paper)
1. M (Computer program language) I. Title.
QA76.73.M15W35 1997
005. 13'3—dc21 97-6513
CIP

ISBN-13: 978-1-55558-167-1
ISBN-10: 1-55558-167-6

British Library Cataloguing-in-Publication Data
A catalogue record for this book is available from the British Library.

The publisher offers special discounts on bulk orders of this book.
For information, please contact:
Manager of Special Sales
Elsevier
200 Wheeler Road
Burlington, MA 01803
Tel: 781-313-4700
Fax: 781-313-4802

10 9 8
Printed in the United States of America.

To Ed de Moel, Chair,
and the members of the
MUMPS Development Committee

Contents

Foreword

Initially, the books about M[UMPS] were published by local interest groups and were not for sale in the general bookstores. About 10 years ago, this changed when textbooks about M[UMPS] started to appear in the "regular" press in German, French, and Dutch. I was extremely happy when, around 1990, two new textbooks appeared which were in English, and were available in the general bookstores. One of those two was the first edition of Dr. Walters' *The ABCs of MUMPS*.

Of course, books about computer languages have one major disadvantage: it takes quite an amount of time to prepare the publication of a book and by the time a book is printed, the text in that book is already showing its age. The subject matter of computer languages evolves so rapidly that it takes only a couple of years for books to change from the "latest and greatest" to largely obsolete. The books about M[UMPS] that appeared five years ago are no exception in this context. Consequently, I was delighted when Dr. Walters told me he was working on a revision of "the ABCs." The M[UMPS] language has made a number of important leaps forward over the past five years, and the first edition of "the ABCs," of course, only describes the language as it was when that edition was published.

This new edition still describes the elementary building blocks of the M[UMPS] language. These haven't changed. But the importance of this new edition is that it also describes those new language elements that have been added over the past five years. Several of the commands and functions in the language have been extended to offer new capabilities, and a couple of completely new sections have been added to the language. The publication of this book is scheduled to occur only a couple of months after ANSI gave its final approval to the 1995 version of the standard for this language and I am happy to have been able to assist Dr. Walters in ensuring that as many as possible of the new additions to the language are covered in this book.

Thirty years have passed since a modest system in a lab of a university hospital was given the nickname MUMPS. This system has now evolved to a programming environment with international acceptance. Currently, many people still call the language by its original name, and probably equally many prefer to call it by the name M. Whatever name people use for the language, its strengths are still the same: the language offers access to a multiuser database, it offers all the flexibility of a programming language, it offers all the capabilities of a preprogrammed environment to enforce carefully defined access, both in the limiting sense of security requirements and in the extending sense of opening up sources of information for those who need it for their daily activities. The programming language can be used to maintain purely hierarchic databases, as well as purely relational ones, as well as any form or type of hybrid. Certainly, these capabilities are also available in the systems that can be found advertised in the popular software press. Unfortunately, most of these offer only some of these advantages, and those that have the capability to offer all the same benefits do so only if they are implemented in an environment that is tailored to fit. M[UMPS] still offers its advantages regardless of its environment, and will continue to do so.

The programming language was originally mainly used in hospital environments, and currently primarily finds its application in banking environments, stock exchanges, libraries, travel agencies, hotel administration, pizza delivery and, of course, diverse medical systems are still supported as ever before.

It is obvious to me that the M[UMPS] language is still thriving, and I am delighted to see continued updates in the literature about this language.

Ed de Moel
Chairman MUMPS Development Committee
November 1996

Preface

The first version of this book, *The ABCs of MUMPS* published in 1989 by Digital Press, covered all the features of the M Programming language, as it was then known, including elements that did not get incorporated into the standard until the next year. The text was aimed at novice programmers, unfamiliar with basic concepts of high-level languages in general and M in particular. Another text written by a close friend appeared at the same time and was aimed at experienced programmers.

Since the appearance in 1989 of these two texts, a great deal has happened. The language has evolved. New language elements make it virtually impossible to encompass the entire spectrum of programming in M and still maintain an approach suitable for introductory-level students. These features are important, and they belong in a standard reference on the language. John Lewkowicz, author of the second text alluded to earlier, has decided not to update his text, and there seem to be no other authors wishing to write an English introductory or intermediate text.

As a result, the new text which you are holding is a hybrid: Part I retains the introductory elements, little changed from the ABCs version with the exception of adding some new language features and a few exercises. It still has advice to experienced programmers as to the content of each chapter, so that those readers could decide whether to delve into the material covered in that chapter. In addition, we have added an entirely new section, Part II, which is aimed at people with programming experience in other languages. This section begins with an overview that may serve as a useful summary for Part I, and then moves into language elements that require programming experience to use effectively. Some of the slightly more complex language elements formerly included in *The ABCs* have been moved to this section to retain the novice focus of Part I.

As a result, we expect that there will be two general groups of readers using this text, with lots of people standing partway between the two. If you are new to programming, then a linear, start-from-the-beginning approach is recommended, making sure that you do some or all of the exercises at the end of Chapters 3–16. If you are somewhat more advanced, you may wish to review the chapter summaries, skipping those that seem familiar.

If you have programmed extensively before opening this text, by all means start with the Part II Overview, Chapter 19, which opens the advanced section. You will get the flavor of the language from that chapter, and you should be able to make appropriate decisions as to where to go next.

Acknowledgments

Writing a comprehensive text covering all new language elements was not an easy task. Although I agreed to take responsibility for the writing, I was painfully aware that my own background in the new features of M was deficient. Though I had served on the MUMPS Development Committee (MDC) for over 20 years, I had been forced by my university commitments to resign from that group a few years back. A great deal has happened since, and I needed help to unravel some of the more arcane passages in the new standard M language so as to make them comprehensible to programmers from other high-level languages.

Fortunately, help was available. Current MDC members graciously offered their assistance, and I accepted their offers with alacrity. They not only provided me with examples of code illustrating the new language elements, but in addition several MDC members offered to review portions of the text. As a result, all new sections of the text have been reviewed by at least one and sometimes two or three active MDC members, as noted in the acknowledgments at the end of this preface.

Although many people helped me with different parts of this revision process, a few stand out as being the major contributors. Ed de Moel, to whom (with the rest of the MDC) this book is dedicated, read every new chapter and helped me correct a good many misconceptions. Any errors that remain are mine, but he reduced the number and severity by his careful review and excellent suggestions. Roger Partridge, who was instrumental in the development of Error Handling in the 1995 standard, graciously shared with me both his tutorial notes from MTA courses and his guidance in reviewing that chapter. Gardner Trask, an MDC and MTA stalwart who helped develop the M Windows Application Interface (MWAPI), and Bill Yaksick, a close friend and consultant programmer using windows interfaces, contributed important examples and valuable comments on the windows chapter. Ben Bishop, another MDC member, helped me with the chapter on interface to other standards, most especially with respect to the interface between M and the Graphical Kernel System (GKS). Kate Schell, Vice Chair of MDC, provided advice on many elements of the standard.

To all of these people, my heartfelt thanks. Their very rapid turnaround of my requests for help made it possible for me to deliver the text to Liz McCarthy, editor for Digital Press, on time (well, almost). Liz's constant encouragement was a real confidence builder, and I am especially grateful to her for expediting the publication cycle of this text so that it could hit the bookstores early in 1997.

Writing, even "just" revising, a book has its penalties in time, and there are many around me who suffered because of the time spent on this text. I am particularly indebted to my wife, Shipley, for her understanding as the deadline approached. I am also grateful to the many students who were so understanding of my time commitments and understood when their equally important demands were sometimes temporarily set aside.

In short, this book, dedicated to Ed de Moel and the MDC, is a joint effort, even if only one author's name is on the cover. To all of the M community, so supportive in encouraging me to update the ABCs, my most sincere thanks. I hope that the final product reflects well on their confidence in the author.

Part I

M for the Novice Programmer

A Brief Introduction to Computers

1

The purpose of this chapter is to provide an introduction to computers that will set the stage for writing computer programs. Its goal is to present information that will enable a novice to understand a little more about what goes on inside a computer as it affects one's ability to control the operations of the machine. In other words, instead of describing what a computer can do for you, this chapter helps you to understand how a computer does things for you, and it sets the stage to allow you, the user, to tell the computer how to do new and different things for you – things that you yourself will tell it to do.

In order to make sure that each reader has the same understanding of basic concepts of computers, this presentation begins at a very primitive level in describing computers. However, if you have not programmed a computer before, you may do well to read the entire chapter, because the information is presented in a different way from conventional texts.

So relax, be patient, and see if you can find some elements in the next few pages that are new to you as you also learn what it is that we will be concentrating on in the remainder of the book: *writing programs to instruct the computer to do our bidding.*

> **Note to Experienced Programmers:** This chapter summarizes the principal components of computers and describes the concepts of hardware, software, operating systems, applications packages, and programming languages, both interpreted and compiled. Anyone with experience in programming will already be familiar with most of the material presented in this chapter and should skip directly to Chapter 2.

Basic components of computers

Human beings have used aids to help count and perform arithmetic since the beginning of recorded history. Fingers were used before that, and no doubt pebbles, sticks or other objects served similar purposes. A fascinating account of how our use of numbers evolved may be found in Karl Menninger's *Number Words and Number Symbols* (MIT Press, 1969). The abacus, developed in the Orient, appeared some time in the last few hundred years (more recently than most people realize). Mechanical calculating devices used by the ancient Greeks have been recovered from the floor of the Aegean Sea, and a number of interesting calculating aids were developed during the Renaissance and later in our pre-electronic history.

One of the important historical contributions shortly after 1800 was the invention of a loom that could be instructed to print complex patterns without setting the threads manually. This loom, called the *Jacquard loom* in honor of its inventor, revolutionized weaving and created one of the first dire predictions that automation would drive humans out of useful work. An important concept in that invention was the idea of a *set of instructions* stored on wooden paddles that were fed into the loom's insides to *program* the movement of threads to produce specific patterns. This invention contained the beginnings of what computers do. First, we have some *hardware* (in this case a loom), which is instructed how to behave by a *program,* in this case produced by externally stored codes that were fed into the loom to produce the *output* of a consistent pattern. A very few years later, an Englishman named Babbage conceived of a notion whereby the same sorts of *instructions* could be stored *inside* his "analytical engine" to perform calculations. From his work came the idea of a *stored program,* a fundamental concept in computers today. Unfortunately, the machine tools for constructing hardware in the mid-1800s were not sufficiently precise to turn Babbage's concepts into reality, and his work languished after several unsuccessful attempts.

Not much happened from the mid-1880s until World War II, by which time electronics had been discovered and advanced to the point where it was possible to perform electronically what Babbage had tried to do mechanically. The old vacuum tubes used in early computers were not too reliable, but they were all that was needed to take the fundamental concepts and implement them in "hardware" that would work, at least some of the time. Since the 1940s, the progress of computing technology has been truly staggering, as all of us know. A *Time Magazine* article on the "Man of the Year" in 1982 (actually they were describing the personal computer revolution) quoted one source as saying that if automobile manufacturing had progressed as computers had since 1940, a Rolls-Royce in 1982 would cost less than $10 and go over 3 million miles on a gallon of gasoline. The rate of decline in the cost of hardware has continued at almost the same rate since then, and experts predict that hardware costs will continue to go down until well after the end of this century. I recently heard an expert at a conference give the definition of "obsolete" as the computer he bought that day.

Despite all these dramatic improvements, the concepts that concern the reader of this text are basically the same, and we will concentrate on a few fundamentals that set the stage for the following chapters.

Computer hardware

The simplest way to think of a computer is to see it as consisting of three major components, as illustrated in Figure 1.1.

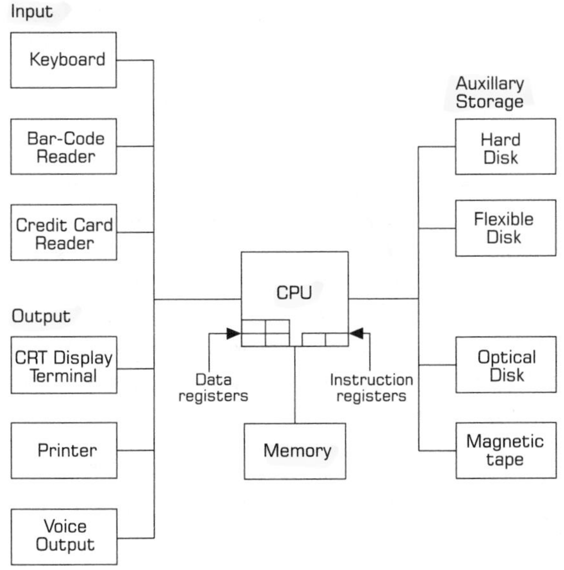

FIGURE 1.1: *Principal Components of Today's Computers.*

The left-hand side of the figure depicts a few typical *input* and *output* devices (there are many, many others besides those shown). The basic purpose of input devices is to convert to *machine-readable form* information or data from the outside world so that it can be manipulated inside the computer. Ultimately, the computer recognizes electronic pulses that are usually coded in a binary form – a string of numbers consisting of zeroes or ones which represent information that can be added, subtracted, compared, stored, or manipulated by other operations that may change it or generate new results. Users are by now familiar with keyboards, keypads at automated tellers, bar-code laser-scanners at grocery store checkout counters, and magnetic stripes on the backs of credit cards – all these devices are used for input, to enter some real-world information into a computer so that it can be used.

By the same token, we are also quite familiar with output from computers – printed letters that *had* to have been generated by a computer, not a human being (how else could we get the ridiculous errors that sometimes occur), screens that inform us, none too politely, that we entered our password (or PIN number) incorrectly, or even computer-generated "spoken" numbers from telephone information services. In each case, the need is to translate the information available inside the machine into a form that is comprehensible to us, the users.

The middle of Figure 1.1 shows two components: a *central processing unit* (CPU) and *memory*. It is here that the work is done in a computer. The CPU is an extremely complex device, even if today's CPUs are about the size of the last joint of your little finger. We will not try to describe CPUs other than to say that they bring pieces of information from memory into *registers*, where the information is manipulated; then the new information is stored once again in the computer's memory.

One point needs to be made about a computer's memory – it comes in two types, *read-only memory* (ROM) and *dynamic memory*, often referred to as *random-access memory* (RAM). (Actually, both ROM and RAM are random-access, but terms have a way of lasting even when they are not quite accurate.) ROM differs from RAM in two important respects. First, once information has been stored in ROM, it cannot be changed (hence the term *read-only*). Second, when the computer is turned off (power is shut off), the information stored in ROM remains unchanged. By contrast, information stored in RAM *can* be changed, but it does not get preserved when the computer is shut off. The size of RAM has increased dramatically in recent years: the first personal computers managed to get along with as little as 8K (8,000) bytes of RAM memory. Today's computers come with a minimum of 4M (4,000,000) bytes of RAM, and most have 16M bytes or more. (The older systems are no longer adequate to handle the programs used by today's computers.)

RAM and ROM are closely associated with the CPU, and information in the computer's memory can be moved back and forth very rapidly between these two components. However, since with RAM there is no way to preserve the information once the computer has been turned off, there is a need for another component – *auxiliary on-line storage*. These storage devices are used to store larger amounts of information than can fit into the memory of a computer, and they will retain the information even when power is shut off. The right-hand portion of Figure 1.1 lists a few devices in use today, but there are, of course, many others. The principal characteristics of these auxiliary storage devices are larger storage capacities than memory, slower access times (this fact is important in database systems), long-term storage of information, and in many cases, the ability to transfer the storage medium from one computer to another. Hard disks are not easily moved between computers, but the other forms depicted in Figure 1.1 are often used to transfer machine-readable information from one computer to another. Once again, the storage capacity of auxiliary devices, especially "hard disk" drives, has increased dramatically. In the 1980s, disk capacities were in the order of 10–20 M (10,000,000 – 20,000,000) bytes. Today a typical medium-level personal computer comes with a gigabyte (1,000,000,000) or more of disk storage capacity: about *five orders of magnitude* greater than the disks of the early 1980s!

Although we could consider many other components of computer hardware, the families described above will suffice to set the stage for our purposes in this text.

Software

If the term *hardware* can be used to describe the physical components of a computer system, why not use a general term, such as *software,* to describe their conceptual components? No reason not to, I suppose, although the term does not tell us much, and there is a great deal to be understood about this part of what makes computers work.

In our historical example, we referred to *instructions* as being one of the important components of the precursors of today's computers. However, an equally essential component has to do with what it is that the computer is to act on. In our loom example, the computer acted on threads that were converted into textile patterns. In Babbage's analytical engine, the idea was to work with numbers, which were used to compute other numbers. Simply put, a computer has to have *data* for the instructions to act on. Data is *input* (converted into machine-readable form), *manipulated* using a set of instructions, and *output* to human-readable form or stored on auxiliary storage devices for future reference.

We can say, therefore, that *software* consists of machine-readable bits of information which may represent either *data* or *computer instructions.* Both data and instructions can be stored in a computer's memory, input by users, stored on auxiliary devices, and output in various forms into human-readable form. Also, in electronic computers, both instructions and data are stored as binary numbers consisting of zeroes or ones. However, the computer treats these two pieces of software very differently. Instructions are copied into a special part of the CPU (*instruction registers*) where they are decoded and used to activate certain capabilities stored in the circuitry of the CPU. Data elements go into the CPU's *data registers*, where they are manipulated and (sometimes) returned to the computer's memory. The strings of zeroes and ones may look alike to us, but to the computer they represent different sorts of information and must be treated in different ways.

How does the computer manage to sort out the differences between instructions and data? The answer to this question could become quite complicated, but we will skim the surface to get across enough information to help us understand why programming languages such as M evolved.

Coding data for computers

Earlier we used the term *machine-readable form* to describe the encoding process required to convert external data to internal form. Several coding systems are used, but for our purposes, it is sufficient to consider only one: the American Standard Code for Information Interchange (ASCII). This code system groups together 8 binary bits into a *byte* and uses permutations of 7 of those bits to define 128 different codes. The complete list of ASCII characters is given in Table 3.1, but for the present, it is sufficient to realize that a coding scheme has been developed and accepted as a standard by all computer manufacturers, and this code makes it possible to convert both numbers and letters typed on a keyboard into a code 1 byte in length representing a specific character. When a computer user types a character, the keyboard recognizes which key is typed and transmits the appropriate code to the computer. Similarly, when output is called for, the printer or display screen used to output information examines the ASCII code and translates that into the appropriate character on the output device.

Computer instructions

Every family of computers has a clearly defined set of *machine instructions*, i.e., codes that perform a few basic operations. These codes are also combinations of binary bits similar to the ASCII character set described in the previous section. The codes differ from one computer to another, and they are too complex to describe in this text. However, it is helpful to consider what kinds of commands might be useful to tell computers what to do. The types of instructions that computers can recognize and execute fall into several different groups, roughly described as follows:

- *Input/output:* Instructions that read information in and out of memory from I/O or auxiliary storage devices
- *Arithmetic.* Instructions that add, subtract, or perform other simple operations on two pieces of data

- *Tests:* Instructions that examine one data element or compare two data elements and determine whether some condition is met (A typical test would be to see whether a number in one register is less than a number in a second register.)
- *Program execution flow control:* Instructions that halt execution and tell the computer to skip the next instruction or to branch to a different point to continue execution of instructions

Surprisingly enough, the most complex computer programs in existence can ultimately be broken down into instructions falling into these very few categories. Different CPUs have more or less complex instruction sets designed to provide faster execution of some tasks such as complex calculations, but the basic concepts all boil down to the same families of instructions. (The so-called RISC chips used in many computers today derive their name from *Reduced Instruction Set Chips*, a concept that increases the speed of performing the more common instructions used on computers.)

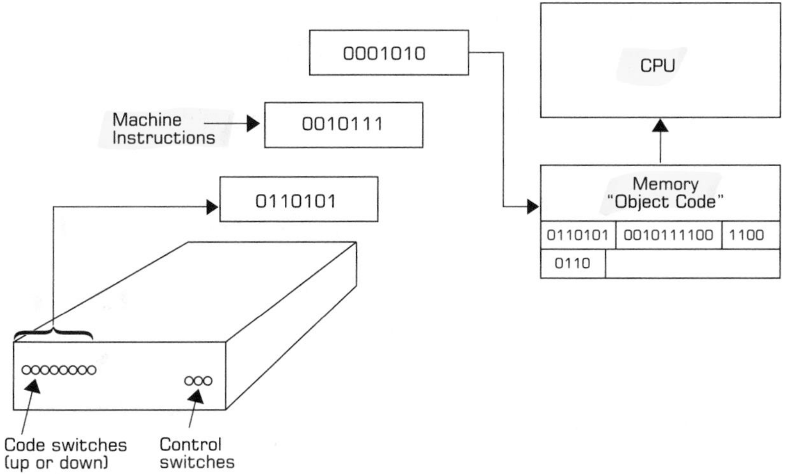

FIGURE 1.2: *Entering Machine Instructions Manually into a Computer's Memory for Execution*

Internally, each machine instruction is stored in a set of binary bits, and these bits cause the computer to perform exactly one such instruction. It is possible to enter these codes manually into computers. The early personal computers had switches on the front of the computer box to enable "hackers" of the 1970s to do exactly that; in fact, it was usually necessary to start up a computer by entering a number of these instructions into memory. The user would indicate where in memory the code was to go, set the switches for the code, and press an enter switch to store the code. The computer would automatically set the memory address to the next location, and the process would be repeated. In this fashion, the user created a *program,* consisting of several instructions, often used to *boot* the computer: to start it running in a useful way.

Figure 1.2 illustrates the manner in which such code would be stored in a computer's memory. The process was a form of *programming,* and the codes entered by the user could be executed directly by the computer. Such code is referred to as *object code,* the executable set of instructions actually used by the computer's CPU to do its work.

Machine-level programming is tedious business at best. It requires memorizing the zeroes and ones of each instruction, and humans are not good at remembering binary numbers. Early in the history of computing, it became apparent that something would have to be done to make the job of programming a little easier. The first approach to simplifying the task of programming was to write a program that would accept character-code input and, using a prescribed set of rules, convert the user's input into machine instructions. This program was called an *assembler.* The left-hand half of Figure 1.3 illustrates how an assembler works, taking one line of input from a user (generally typed on a keyboard or some other standard input mechanism) and converting it to one machine instruction.

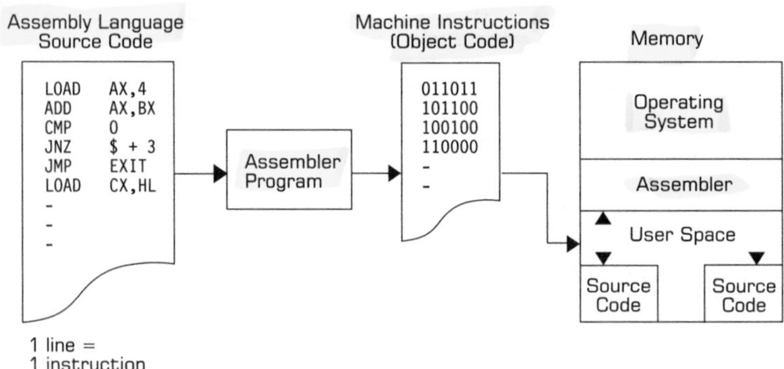

FIGURE 1.3: *Conversion of an Assembly-Language Program into Executable Object Code*

The beauty of using an assembler is that the programmer need not memorize strings of zeroes and ones; instead, some mnemonics, usually derived from English words, are used to represent the machine instructions. Very few programmers today are even aware of the exact binary codes used internally by machines, since assembly-language programming is about the most detailed information they will ever need to perform their jobs.

Operating systems: communicating with computers

Using an assembler adds one new layer of complexity to the process of using a computer. When a computer has an assembler available, somehow the user has to be able to gain access to the assembler and the assembler has to know where to find the user's *assembly program* in order to convert it to object code which can later be executed. In effect, it is necessary to have *another* program that can read the programmer's instructions about reading a set of assembly instructions to convert them to object code or, when that step is done, executing the object code.

The program that interprets user instructions about managing programs is called an *operating system.* In the previous section, we described the process of *booting* a system in order to start it on the path of performing useful functions. The term comes from "booting" a piece of machinery (or occasionally a live object) to make it run, and the analogy is valid, since booting a computer sets it on its way by loading a complicated program, called an *operating system,* into memory and then transferring control of the computer's execution to that program. The operating system usually resides on a disk or some other auxiliary storage device and loads into memory as a response to a boot program. Nowadays, the boot program need not be entered manually as in the 1970s. Instead, it resides in ROM and is automatically activated when the user turns on the computer.

An operating system is really just a program. However, it is the heart of the communication process between user and computer. Without an operating system, we would be back to entering machine instructions manually for everything we wanted to do, and no one would have any interest in using a computer at all. With the operating system, we can, by giving it different commands, get the computer to do any of a wide variety of tasks, including invoking an assembler to convert an assembly program into executable object code, running object code that has been filed on an auxiliary storage device, or in fact a whole host of other tasks that computers can perform today. On personal computers such as the IBM/PC family, the operating system is the program that displays a prompt such as:

```
C:\>
```

on the user's screen, waiting for the next command. When a user asks the operating system to convert an assembly-language program into executable code, the operating system transfers control to the assembler program, which reads the user's code, checks it for possible errors, converts it to executable code if it can, and then returns control back to the operating system. Thus, in effect, the operating system is acting as a traffic cop for all activities performed by the computer in response to the user's requests.

Programming in high-level languages

Although programming in assembly language is a big improvement over entering machine instructions manually, it is still a fairly primitive process. In assembly language, each instruction is converted into a single machine instruction and the user must think in terms of those instructions, which, as we saw earlier, are quite primitive. A programmer wanting to do something much more complex, such as solving a long mathematical formula, would have to translate the formula into the primitive instructions recognized by the computer. For example, if we wanted to do something like the following:

$$X = A \times B + (C/D) - (E \times F)$$

it would be necessary to break that single algebraic expression into many lines of assembly code so as to be sure that the steps were executed in the correct sequence.

For this reason, computer scientists devised one higher level of abstraction late in the 1950s: the concept of a *high-level language*. High-level languages are much closer to the English we use to converse with each other. (In fact, all high-level languages used today are based on the English language.) They represent at a more complex level a series of steps that can be visualized at the conceptual level without having to bother with determining the individual instructions necessary to implement those concepts. Two early high-level languages developed to solve different types of problems are COBOL (an acronym for **CO**mmon **B**usiness-**O**riented **L**anguage) and FORTRAN (an acronym for **FOR**mula **TRAN**slation).

From the user's point of view, both these languages operate in a manner similar to the lower-level assembly languages. The user writes a program and then asks the operating system to convert that program into executable code. The operating system loads into memory the appropriate *compiler*, a program written to translate high-level language statements into executable code, and transfers control to the compiler. The compiler sometimes does this operation in two steps, generating an intermediate set of assembly-language instructions which are then passed to an assembler, which finally creates the executable code (Figure 1.4). Today's compilers tend to skip the intermediate assembly step, but it doesn't hurt us in this review to realize that high-level languages *can* be converted to assembly language before they ultimately end up as object code. Either way, using a high-level language, the user is able to design a program at a level much further removed from the machine instructions, and therefore concentrate on concepts, not on machine-dependent factors.

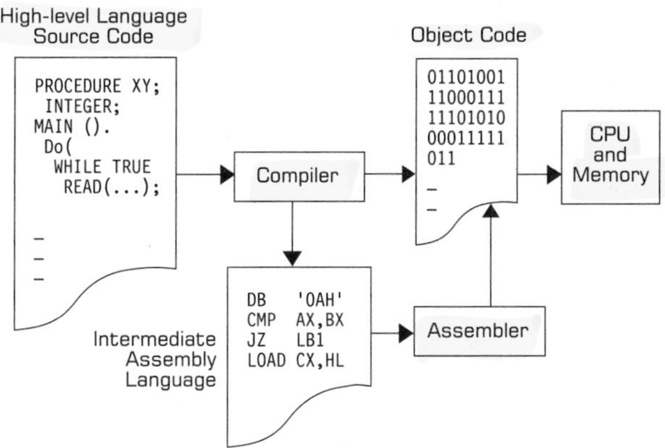

FIGURE 1.4: *Conversion of High-Level Language Source Code into Executable Object Code Using a Compiler*

Direct Execution of High-Level Language Statements: Interpreters

In all the methods just described, the actual execution of a user's program on a computer required two or more steps. Object code was created and then executed. However, in the world today it is often desirable to shorten this process, allowing a user to create code and have it execute immediately. Fortunately, there are some high-level languages that allow the user to type a line of instructions and immediately see the result. This type of high-level language is called an *interpreted language.* Figure 1.5 illustrates the manner in which an interpreter acts to execute each line of instructions as it is processed. Notice that no object code is generated or stored in memory; the interpreter processes a line and then goes on to the next without storing the executable code it created. Two languages that permit interpreted execution are M and BASIC. Their advantages are quicker response to the user who is typing instructions and hence a faster developmental process for writing programs.

Once programs have been written using any of the methods just described, they can be stored on auxiliary devices, such as disk, and later invoked by having the user instruct the operating system to *find* the program and *run* it. In the case of compiled and assembled languages, it is the object code that is retrieved for execution. In the case of an interpreted language such as MUMPS, it is the original source code which is read and executed, again without storing any resulting object code. (Many M implementations today allow users to execute instructions directly, but they compile stored programs to enable them to run faster.)

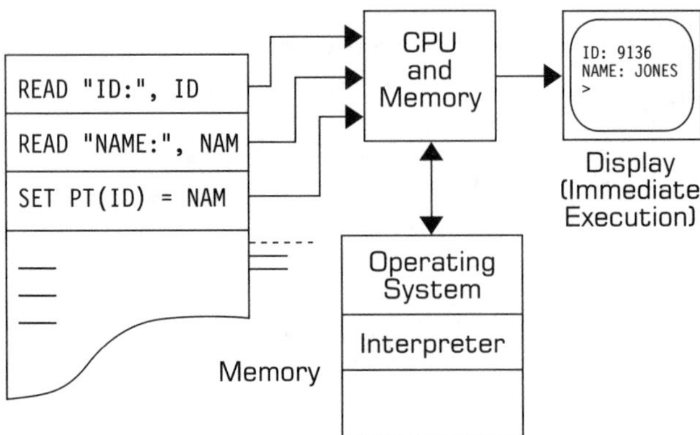

FIGURE 1.5: *Direct Execution of High-Level Language by an Interpreter*

The grammar of programming languages

Spoken languages have grammars that differ from one language to another. Latin and German tend to use word endings to convey meaning; English uses the sequence of words to accomplish the same purpose: "I look over the table," "I look the table over," and "I overlook the table" have three completely different meanings. In high-level computer languages, each one has its own grammar, but the manner in which those grammars are constructed may be quite different from one computer language to another.

However, just as spoken languages all have some forms of nouns, verbs, adjectives, and prepositions, so too computer languages have elements in common. Earlier in this chapter we noted that sets of instructions are used to accomplish such tasks as arithmetic operations, input/output, testing, and branching. The manner in which these tasks are accomplished in a computer language can be visualized as its grammar. The purpose of this text is to introduce the grammatical components of M in a way that will enable a novice or experienced programmer to use them to their best advantage, just as we are taught in school to write and speak more effectively.

Computer languages have many different elements. The nouns of computer languages may be *constants* or they may be named *variables.* The verbs may be *commands* or *functions.* The relational links used to explain the ways in which commands operate on variables and constants are *operators.* These components (as well as a few others introduced in later chapters) are linked together according to a fixed *syntax.* The syntax is similar conceptually to the grammatical rules of spoken languages, but usually it is a great deal stricter, since computers cannot handle ambiguity in instructions nearly as well as humans. As long as the syntax of an instruction is correct, it can be performed, even though the logic may still be imperfect.

In the remainder of this text, then, we will examine how the M language works – its grammar, its use of variables, the commands and operators available, and the syntax that ties these components together. The reader will learn that, in many ways, programming in M is extremely simple, that tasks which are very difficult to accomplish in other languages are made easy by the way M was designed. As a result, the reader should be able to use this language to solve real-world problems after completing only a few of the chapters that follow.

The many faces of computers: an overview of user–computer interaction

In this chapter we have reviewed briefly the concepts of stored programs and the different ways in which they can be used to allow computers to interact with humans. Let us summarize these concepts by considering what happens when a person decides to use a word processor to write a letter.

The first thing that the user is likely to do is to turn on the machine. At first, there is a whirring sound, but nothing happens for a few seconds. This phase of the interaction is with the *boot program* of the computer, which checks to be sure all is well and then looks around for some additional information. Usually, the computer searches the A: (floppy) disk drive first to find the boot program. The A: drive light goes on, indicating that the boot program is trying to read from that drive. If there is no disk in drive A, the A light still goes on for a second or two and then the hard-disk drive light goes on, indicating that since the information was not on drive A, it might be on the hard disk.

The information that the boot program is looking for is the *operating system,* a program that will control future interaction between the user and the computer. The operating system is loaded into memory, and it will display some information about itself: Perhaps it will ask the user for date and time, and then give a prompt, such as C:\>, which tells the user that the operating system is ready to accept instructions from the user.

When the user types the name of a *word processing package,* such as WP (for WordPerfect, one of the common commercial word processors today), the operating system looks on auxiliary storage devices to see if a program of that name exists. If it does, it loads the program and then turns control over to the program in question. From this point on, until the user exits the package, the word processing package interacts with the user, accepting its commands to create, edit, output, and/or store the letter.

At the end of an interactive session with the word processing package, the user may decide to make a backup disk of the letter just created. This process will be done by interacting with the operating system once again, using the correct commands to copy a file from one disk to another. If we analyze this typical interaction between user and computer, we can see that the user has actually communicated with several different entities within the computer's memory. The interaction can be summarized as follows:

User Action	Computer's Invoked Program
Turn on machine	Boot program, which loads:
Enter date, time	operating system
Invoke word processor package	Operating system, which loads:
Create and edit letter	word processor package
Exit word processor package	Word processor package, which returns to:
Create backup disk	operating system

One of the confusing things about computers is knowing exactly which of these many components is responding to a specific user entry. Sometimes the same command may be interpreted differently by different components, and unexpected results may occur. However, if the user remembers that there *are* different faces of the computer, the explanation may become apparent. It is essential *always* to know who it is, inside the computer, that you are talking to.

Summary

In this introductory chapter we have seen what goes to make up a computer and how the different components interact to execute user commands. The most important elements discussed are the following:

- The hardware consists of input/output devices, the central processing unit and its associated memory, and auxiliary storage devices.
- Software has two basic elements:
  - *Stored data:* Binary coded data that is usually stored using the ASCII character set, an 8-bit byte used to represent 128 different characters
  - *Machine instructions:* Binary codes that perform such functions as input, output, calculation, comparing, and branching to new instructions for continued execution
- Computer instructions are saved in stored programs, which are sequences of instructions used to tell the computer what steps to perform. These instructions come in several different forms:

- *Object code:* The actual codes used internally by the computer to execute a program
- *Assembly language:* A program using English-language mnemonics that free the programmer from remembering object code (One line of assembly language translates into one machine instruction.)
- *High-level language:* One of several languages that represent conceptually more sophisticated ideas

- High-level language commands are in two forms:
  - *Compiled:* Converted into object code by a compiler
  - *Interpreted:* Executed directly by an interpreter
- Control of a computer's interaction with the user resides with various programs:
  - *Boot:* A program that initializes the computer and loads the operating system
  - *Operating system:* A program that performs many different tasks at the user's request, including loading specialized programs
- A variety of specialized programs are available:
  - Application packages, which are in the form of word processors, database systems, spreadsheets
  - Assemblers, compilers, or interpreters, which permit the user to create new programs aimed at solving new problems

Note: In this text, we will concentrate on the characteristics of the *M Interpreter,* a program that provides exceptional flexibility in allowing the user to create new programs that can solve many problems in which a computer can play an important role.

Introduction to M 2

It is always helpful in learning about a new subject to have some background on its history. This chapter provides a brief summary of the evolution of the M programming language, which in many respects differs markedly from the manner in which other programming languages have evolved. The chapter also lists supplementary reading about M and its origins.

What is M?

In the computer world, the term *MUMPS* has been used to define a number of concepts related to a computer language that originated at Massachusetts General Hospital in 1967. The first letter of the acronym, *M,* stands for that hospital, and the remainder of the term represents the words *U*tility *M*ulti-*P*rogramming *S*ystem. In 1995, the new standard was adopted using the name **M**, with **MUMPS** as an alternate. We will use the term M in this text, but in this chapter, where there are historical associations with the name MUMPS, we will often use that term.

> **Note to Experienced Programmers:** Although this chapter contains no details about the syntax of the M language, it is useful in providing background information about why the language was conceived and what needs it was intended to serve. All readers, even experienced programmers, will find this information helpful in understanding the underlying objectives that led to the design of the M language.

M embodies three concepts. First, it is an interpreted, general-purpose computer programming *language* – "interpreted" because it may be executed directly without conversion to "object code," as required by compiled languages. In addition, the ability of M to process large dynamic data files directly within the language (unlike most other high-level languages) makes the term synonymous in part with *database management systems* designed solely for that purpose. Finally, since M was traditionally implemented on minicomputers as a single-language multiuser system, the term also has been used to refer to the dedicated *operating system* supporting the M environment. The first two uses, language and database management system, are inherent in every M implementation. The third feature, a dedicated operating system, is optional and is rare in today's M implementations.

The brief history of the language provided in the next section offers some explanation of the diversity of viewpoints (and many misconceptions) about M. Whatever the background, M is now one of a very few high-level computer languages accepted by the American National Standards Institute (ANSI), joining such better-known languages as FORTRAN, COBOL, and C. (There is also a standard version of BASIC, but it is so limited that all commercial implementations significantly extend the standard to the point that code is not portable from one machine to another.) M also has been adopted by the US government as a federal information-processing standard. M has been implemented on a variety of computers ranging from personal computers through minicomputers to large mainframes. It is widely known and used in Europe, Japan, and South America (especially Brazil). Its uses include a surprising predominance of business applications. M is gradually becoming better known in nonmedical academic and business circles, and its visibility is increasing as more manufacturers offer M implementations on their hardware.

A brief history of M

The computer industry got its start with "batch processing" computers, whose programs were read in via punched cards and processed sequentially, with output usually taking several hours to be produced. "Interactive computing," involving users seated at terminals and communicating directly with the computer, got its start in government-sponsored time-shared systems during the early 1960s under the pioneering leadership of the Rand Corporation and others. In late 1967, the Laboratory of Computer Science at Massachusetts General Hospital embarked on a development effort based on these early interactive prototypes. Their design was intended to create a system that would incorporate an interpretive language aimed especially at manipulating text-related data in a shared file environment and operating responsively on available minicomputers. One of the classic papers describing this effort

Figure 2.1: *Evolution of MUMPS*

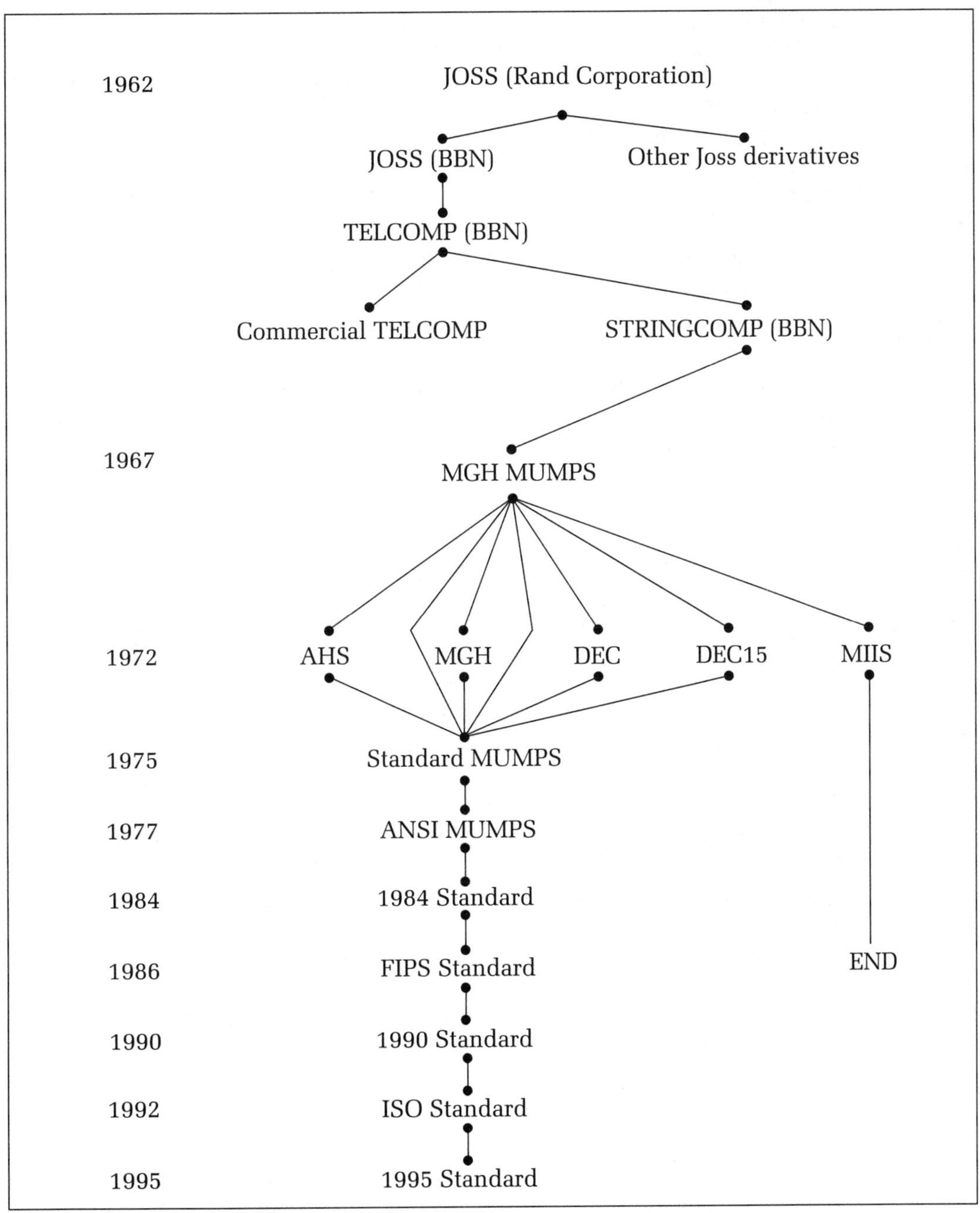

appeared in 1969 (Greenes et al., 1969). The language, which came to be known as MUMPS, succeeded in meeting the early design goals and gained rapidly in popularity in the medical community, both in clinical applications and in medical education. Its fame spread beyond the confines of the founding institution, and soon a number of dialects appeared, each modifying and expanding on the original MUMPS in ways that created incompatible versions. New applications were developed, some in the original language and others in various dialects available from private or commercial sources. As a result, use of the term *MUMPS* lost its specific meaning. By 1972, according to one study (Johnson, 1972), there were as many as 14 separate and incompatible operational or developmental versions of MUMPS.

Support provided by federal sources in the United States had helped create several innovative and promising applications of computers to medical research and education. However, the portability of these packages was jeopardized by the widespread language incompatibility between dialects. Accordingly, the National Center for Health Services Research and the National Bureau of Standards jointly sponsored an effort beginning in late 1972 to foster development of a new standard MUMPS language that would facilitate convergence of existing dialects. This effort involved the principal implementors and users of the extant MUMPS dialects, aided by administrative assistance from the National Bureau of Standards through its representative, Joseph T. O'Neill. It was conceived as a project of consensus, not fiat. The *MUMPS Development Committee* (hereafter referred to as the *MDC*), formed to guide the development of the new standard, adopted a formal constitution and bylaws to ensure impartial consideration of all viewpoints. Meetings were held several times a year starting in 1973, and by 1975, a new standard MUMPS language had been agreed on and adopted. This definition was submitted to ANSI for approval in early 1976, and following the canvass approval method, the language was approved by ANSI in September of 1977.

Voting membership in the MDC is based on active interest in the evolution of the language and regular attendance and participation in its meetings (held approximately three times a year in various locations in the US and abroad). Current membership includes implementors of the language, software vendors, large governmental agencies using M, some consultants, and a few academic institutions. International representation is active in helping define new components of the language, with regional MUMPS Development Coordinating Committees (MDCCs) contributing significantly to the process. At present there are MDCCs in Europe and Japan. Users who fail to maintain a regular attendance record lose their voting rights.

The process of programming language definition is a continuous one. All languages approved by ANSI are obligated to undergo periodic review to determine if the language should be retained, updated, or removed as a standard. The MDC is officially charged with the responsibility to perform these duties with respect to the M standard. This committee's activities include review of the existing standard, approving corrections or clarifications as necessary, and proposing revisions and extensions to the language to be included in the next standard. The normal review period for programming languages is supposed to be every five years. In practice, however, most languages are reviewed less frequently. In late 1983, the MUMPS Development Committee completed a revised standard and resubmitted it for approval to ANSI, again following the canvass process. After the normal review process was completed, ANSI approved the revised standard in November of 1984, giving it the title *ANSI/MDC X11.1–1984: MUMPS*. The 1984 standard incorporated several important new features that are described in this text. Subsequent revisions were approved by ANSI in 1990 and, most recently, in 1995. ANSI approval of M is based on the *canvass method*, a process whereby people who are or might be interested in the language's evolution may ballot on the validity of the proposed standard or changes incorporated in subsequent versions. This process involves submission of the standard for approval to a large number of individuals and organizations that might be affected by the standard. Provision is made for appeals, which, if they occur, further delay the approval process.

M was also approved as an international standard (ISO/IEC11756:1992), using the *fast track method*, which means that, instead of forming its own subcommittee or work group to study the standard, the ISO committee responsible for programming languages accepted the recommendation of its US members that the ANSI MUMPS X11.1–1990 be accepted as a standard. It seems likely that a similar process will be undertaken with respect to the 1995 standard, but that process had not yet begun as this text was being revised.

The MDC, in addition to preparing the 1995 M standard, considered a number of changes to the M programming environment that, in their judgment, were better submitted as separate standards. Accordingly, the review and approval process for the principal M standard (X11.1) was accompanied by requests for participants to vote on the approval of four other documents: X11.2, Open M[UMPS] Interconnect; X11.3, M[UMPS] GKS Binding; X11.4, M[UMPS] X Window System Binding; and X11.6, M[UMPS] Windowing Application Programmers Interface. These standards have also been approved and are implemented by several vendors at this time.

M is unusual among programming languages in that, from the inception of the standardization process (1973), a user's group was formed to support the M community. This group, formerly called the MUMPS Users' Group and now referred to as M Technology Association, meets annually in various cities around the US, publishes its own journal, provides administrative support for the MDC, and serves as an important focus for M-related activities (see the end of this chapter for contact information). There are also users' groups in Europe, Japan, and Brazil.

How to use this text

This text was written in two parts. The purpose of Part I is to introduce the M programming language to beginning users who are unfamiliar with other programming languages. *The ABCs of MUMPS*, which is the predecessor of this text, was designed solely as an introduction to M for novices. Other texts, notably *The Complete MUMPS*, by John Lewkowicz, offered guidance to M programming for intermediate and advanced programmers. With the evolution of the language, however, it is no longer appropriate to try to cover all aspects of the language at an introductory level. Several features of the language (e.g., Transaction Processing and Graphical User Interface design) are not subjects for the novice. For this reason, the current text has been revised to include Part II, aimed at experienced programmers, in which advanced programming components of M are presented. This part begins with an overview of the language for experienced programmers that allows them to move quickly past the more fundamental syntax of the language into those features that distinguish it from other high-level programming languages.

This text now serves three purposes. It is a general reference to the 1995 standard, containing descriptions of all the language elements found in the X11.1 standard and in the ancillary standards referenced earlier (ANSI X11.1, 11.2, 11.3, 11.4, and 11.6, respectively).

Experienced programmers should skip Part I of this text and proceed directly to Chapter 19: Overview of M. Material presented in that chapter will enable these readers to understand M's basic design as well as the features that make it different from other high-level languages. Guidelines for experienced programmers may be found at the beginning of all chapters in Part 1, in case they wish to review quickly some features covered in this section.

Novice programmers should proceed through Part I of the text, which has been designed to introduce concepts in a progressive fashion, each chapter building on the previous one. The beginning student will benefit most from reading this text in conjunction with the use of one of the several M implementations available. (Two vendors offer free single-user versions of M which are suitable for use with this text.) There are exercises at the end of Chapters 3 through 17 designed to reinforce some of the concepts presented. The beginning programmer is encouraged to use these exercises to gain more familiarity with language concepts. Programming can only be learned by doing, and these exercises provide that opportunity. The reader is strongly urged to work carefully through the problems using whichever version(s) of M may be available.

The text is designed to present cumulative blocks of information, each chapter building on concepts presented before. For this reason, a beginning programmer should make sure that the material in one chapter is thoroughly understood before proceeding to the next. This suggestion is particularly relevant to the material presented in Chapters 3 to 13. Chapters 14 to 17 contain material covering advanced elements of the language which are pretty much independent of each other. Chapter 18 provides a complete programming example that may be studied independently.

Some of the exercises at the end of the later chapters suggest designing small applications that may be of practical significance to the reader. You are encouraged to attempt these applications without assistance. However, suggested solutions are also found at the end of the text. These programs are not extensively annotated, but they may be entered into an M system if they are found to meet a reader's need.

For the experienced programmer who wants to learn about MUMPS

Experienced programmers should begin with the overview that appears at the start of Part II (Chapter 19). This chapter highlights the differences between M and other languages, and it points back to sections in Part I that may help clarify small points. In addition, programmers with specific interests in areas such as windows applications will benefit from obtaining the standard documents themselves (see below for further information).

Where to go for further information

The body of literature describing the M language is rapidly expanding. Articles covering different applications and features of the language may be found in many computer journals, especially those with a medical orientation, such as *MD Computing.* However, the most important source of M information may be obtained by writing

M Technology Association
1738 Elton Rd Suite 205
Silver Spring, MD 20903
(301) 431-4070 voice
(301) 431-0017 fax

Among the more important references available from this group are the standard itself, *ANSI/MDC X11.1–1995,* and the associated standards referenced earlier in this chapter. *M Computing,* published five times a year by M

Technology Association, is an excellent source of current information. Back issues are available from M Technology Association.

M has a number of sites on the Internet (see *M Computing*'s November, 1996 issue for many listings), with one of the most informative email addresses (for MTA) being `info@mcenter.com`

Web sites (a number are accessible through the Yahoo search engine) include the following:

- M Technology Resource Page: `http://www.mcenter.com/mtrc`
- MDC: `http://world.std.com/~demoel/mdc/`
- MUMPS of Georgia User's Group: `http://www.mindspring.com/~mga/`
- Bonnici's M Home Page: `http://www.geocities.com/SiliconValley/7041/`

The latter two addresses are well stocked with general information about the M community.

Summary

The history of the MUMPS language is unique in that its design stemmed from a need to address a particular field: medical information. It is also unique in its evolution from a single version through a period of several incompatible dialects back to a new standard, approved by the American National Standards Institute. The language continues to evolve under the guidance of the MUMPS Development Committee, and it has a large and active international users' group which has successfully promoted a number of public-domain application packages serving the medical community and business and commercial interests. Many of the language features of M differ from conventional compiled languages. These differences offer important advantages in many applications, making the language especially suitable for text-related processing. Some of the most unique language elements are

- Lack of declaration statements
- Use of a single data type (string)
- Incorporation of shared, persistent variables within the language
- Use of hierarchical, sparse arrays incorporating multiply nested integer, decimal, or string keys
- Powerful string manipulation language primitives
- Dynamic run-time code modification
- Support for non-English character sets

References

Greenes, R. A., Pappalardo, A. N, Marble, C. W. and Barnett, G. O. (1969). "Design and Implementation of a Clinical Data Management System," *Computers in Biomedical Research*, Vol. 2, pp. 469–485.

Johnson, M. E. 1972. *MUMPS: A Preliminary Study*. National Bureau of Standards and the National Center for Health Services Research and Development.

Basic Components of M

3

All computer languages are made up of *building blocks* that take on special meanings within the syntax of the language. For every programming language, it is necessary to indicate what character code sets are permitted, how numbers and text are to be identified and stored, and what other special terms are used to enrich the capability of the language to perform useful operations on data.

In M, the building blocks are generally simpler than in most other languages, yet the power of the language to manipulate text-oriented data is as great as that of many far more complex languages. In this chapter we will consider the key building blocks used in M:

- The *character set* recognized by M
- M's representation of *numbers*
- M's representation of *strings*
- M conventions in naming *variables*
- M auxiliary aids: *functions* and *special variables*

> **Note to Experienced Programmers:** Although much of the material in this chapter is probably familiar to individuals who have programmed in other languages, there are some important differences in M. A summary of these features is provided at the end of the chapter. The experienced programmer is advised to read this summary and, if necessary, review pertinent sections of this chapter that amplify the specific language features.

We will see that, compared with many other languages, M is much simpler in its use of these language elements.

Character set

The M language uses the 7-bit character code defined by the American Standard Code for Information Interchange (ASCII) and published in the American National Standards document X3.4–1968. This is the character set used for most personal computers and minicomputers, but it is different from the Extended Binary Coded Decimal Interchange Code (EBCDIC) used on IBM and many other large mainframe computers.

The ASCII character set, which is reproduced in Table 3.1, includes the 26 uppercase letters A through Z, the 26 lowercase letters a through z, the 10 numeric digits 0 through 9, and the 33 special printing characters (including the space character).

TABLE 3.1: *American Standard Code for Information Interchange (ASCII) Character Set*

Character Name	Code (dec)	Code (hex)	Character Name	Code (dec)	Code (hex)
		Nonprinting characters			
NUL	0	00	DC1	17	11
SOH	1	01	DC2	18	12
STX	2	02	DC3	19	13
ETX	3	03	DC4	20	14
EOT	4	04	NAK	21	15
ENQ	5	05	SYN	22	16
ACK	6	06	ETB	23	17
BEL	7	07	CAN	24	18
BS	8	08	EM	25	19
HT	9	09	SUB	26	1A
LF	10	0A	ESC	27	1B
VT	11	0B	FS	28	1C
FF	12	0C	GS	29	1D
CR	13	0D	RS	30	1E
SO	14	0E	US	31	1F
SI	15	0F	DEL	127	7F
DLE	16	10			

TABLE 3.1 (CONTINUED): *American Standard Code for Information Interchange (ASCII) Character Set*

Character Name	Code (dec)	Code (hex)	Character Name	Code (dec)	Code (hex)	Character Name	Code (dec)	Code (hex)
				Printing characters				
Space	32	20	@	64	40	‘	96	60
!	33	21	A	65	41	a	97	61
"	34	22	B	66	42	b	98	62
#	35	23	C	67	43	c	99	63
$	36	24	D	68	44	d	100	64
%	37	25	E	69	45	e	101	65
&	38	26	F	70	46	f	102	66
'	39	27	G	71	47	g	103	67
(	40	28	H	72	28	h	104	68
)	41	29	I	73	49	i	105	69
*	42	2A	J	74	4A	j	106	6A
+	43	2B	K	75	4B	k	107	6B
,	44	2C	L	76	4C	l	108	6C
-	45	2D	M	77	4D	m	109	6D
.	46	2E	N	78	r#	n	110	6#
/	47	2F	O	79	4F	o	111	6F
0	48	30	P	80	50	p	112	70
1	49	31	Q	81	51	q	113	71
2	50	32	R	82	52	r	114	72
3	51	33	S	83	53	s	115	73
4	52	34	T	84	54	t	116	74
5	53	35	U	85	55	u	117	75
6	54	36	V	86	56	v	118	76
7	55	37	W	87	57	w	119	77
8	56	38	X	88	58	x	120	78
9	57	39	Y	89	59	y	121	79
:	58	3A	Z	90	5A	z	122	7A
;	59	3B	[	91	5B	{	123	7B
<	60	3C	\	92	5C	|	124	7C
=	61	3D	]	93	5D	}	125	7D
>	62	3E	^	94	5E	~	126	7E
?	63	3F	_	95	5F			

In addition, there are 33 nonprinting control characters used in terminal I/O and other special functions. It is possible to write programs in M using uppercase or lowercase letters for commands. In some cases, the use of uppercase code only may be preferable. M also will accept lowercase characters, but there are some instances where these two alphabets are treated differently, as described later in this chapter.

Although M relies on the ASCII character set for its language syntax, there is no explicit restriction on the use of character codes beyond the decimal 0–127 set specified in the current definition of ASCII. The 1995 M standard sets the stage for use of other character sets to accommodate non-English languages, and it seems likely that as M evolves, users will be able to use other character sets quite easily. Despite this flexibility, the M standard is defined in terms of the ASCII character set, and this is not likely to change. Some implementations already permit use of non-ASCII character sets for data, string literals and variable subscripts and, in limited cases, for data manipulation. This matter is dealt with in greater detail in Part II of this text under the general subject of internationalization.

Numbers

M can be used to perform mathematical computations involving numbers. The simplest form a number may take is that of a positive integer. For example, 17, 245, 1967, and 100500789 are integers that are acceptable to M systems. Integers include whole numbers; that is, those that have no fractional component. An *integer* is defined as any whole number, optionally preceded by a positive or negative sign (+ or –).

Most computing languages distinguish between an integer and a real number. A *real number* is defined as one in which there is a whole number and a decimal fraction, such as 2.3, 7.5, or 100.500789. Real numbers are often used in calculations requiring a high degree of accuracy, in most division problems, and in other operations likely to generate a fractional result. For most purposes, M does not make any distinction between integers and real numbers, and computation mixing these two data types is permitted. There are some situations where M allows the user to distinguish between integers and real numbers, but for most applications the type of number used is unimportant to the language.

Because most computers are binary machines, accurate representation of decimal fractions may differ slightly from one machine to another in the least significant digits. Also, computers differ in the precise way that they handle fractions, so it is likely that dissimilar computers may produce results that differ slightly in the last digits printed. It is important to remember that such distinctions occur, since in some calculations, these small differences may be important.

People find difficulty in reading long strings of digits. In conventional publications, large numbers are usually broken up by commas to facilitate reading, so that the number one million is often written 1,000,000. This type of notation is not acceptable in M, nor is it allowed in most programming languages. Instead, a special notation used in scientific calculations has been adopted for use in the M language. This notation, called *exponential notation,* expresses the number raised to some power often by writing the number followed by E, then by the power of ten used. Here are some examples of exponential notation:

Conventional Notation	**Exponential Notation**
125	12.5E1 *(12.5 times 10)*
1389.468	13.89468E2 *(times 100)*
1000000	10.E5 or 1E6
172.4	17.24E1
0.0156	15.6E-3
.000000762	76.2E-8

Because this notation is useful in representing very large or very small numbers, it is used commonly for scientific computation.

In general, numbers represent a special case of character sets. In this text, we will refer to a set of characters satisfying the descriptions given above as a *numlit,* that is, a series of characters that can be interpreted as having numeric value. The following examples illustrate valid and invalid numlits:

Valid	**Invalid**
36	Thirty-six
29000	29,000
10E5	10×10^5
0.34	34/100 *(an expression, not a number)*
13.0E4	13.4 E4 *(spaces not allowed)*
10	E + 1 *(no number before E)*
5.25	$5.25
65	65%

Numeric ranges and precision

Digital representation of a fractional number is always finite; there can be no endless fraction, such as the decimal representation of 1/3. Computer languages must select some degree of accuracy for numbers used in computation. Standard M calls for 15 digits of precision in any number, integer or real. Thus the numbers:

123456789012345 and 1.23456789012345

are both valid, but a number such as:

99.12345678901234

would probably be retained as

99.1234567890123

with the least significant number rounded off. Although the M standard requires a minimum of 15 significant digits accuracy, some standard implementations provide for even greater accuracy. If the problems you are dealing with require such accuracy, you should check with the provider of your system to determine the accuracy on your own machine (or, using the examples at the end of the chapter, you might test the accuracy yourself). Since exponential notation permits representation of much larger and smaller numbers than can be expressed by conventional notation, a convention must be adopted to set boundaries on the size of the exponent that must be recognized by standard M.

ANSI/MDC X11.1–1995: M specifies that numbers between 1E-25 and 1E25 will be accepted by any implementation of the standard. Once again, many implementors offer ranges that exceed this minimum level. The accuracy of any number within the permitted range may still remain at nine significant digits.

String literals

Many uses of computers involve sorting and searching through natural-language words – names, addresses, text materials, etc. M is particularly suited to the manipulation of such strings of characters. In general, a *string literal* is any combination of the printing ASCII character set illustrated in Table 3.1. Thus all numbers defined in the previous section also may be considered as string literals (we will call a string literal *strlit* in cases where we wish to distinguish it from a *numlit*).

The convention used in defining strlits is to enclose them in quotation marks. Thus `"ABC"` is a strlit whose three characters are `A`, `B`, and `C`. Any string of numbers, alphabetical characters, or special printing symbols (including spaces) can be included in a string literal. The convention of enclosing a strlit in quotation marks is fine for every case except the one in which you wish to include a quotation mark in the string. However, the designers of the language, recognizing the need for this option, modified the convention to define two sets of quotation marks occurring together to mean a single quotation mark included in the strlit. When two sets of quotation marks occur alone (i.e., not within a strlit), they signify a null (or empty) string. A few examples of the definition and actual strlits are given below.

Definition	Actual strlit
`""`	*(empty string)*
`"XYZ"`	`XYZ`
`"John Doe"`	`John Doe`
`"a ""super"" party"`	`a "super" party`

Strings, like numbers, cannot be infinitely long, owing, among other things, to the storage capacity of the computer. Once again, therefore, limits on the length of strings have been placed in the M standard. The upper limit has been established as 255 characters in any single string, and any standard M implementation must handle strings of this length. Some implementors may have elected to extend these limits, but since it is not required, use of longer strings is discouraged for any programs that may be transferred to other machines.

Variables

It is common practice in algebra, for example, to substitute some letter (usually X in most textbooks) for an unknown quantity in an equation. Thus we may be asked to state the value of X in the equation $X = 13 + 22$. The value of such a named variable may be changed during execution of a program. This approach is valuable in many problems where a variable will take on different values under different circumstances. Computer languages provide various ways of defining such variables. In M, a variable may be given any name, provided that the first letter is a letter of the alphabet or the character % (percent sign, usually reserved for implementor-defined variables), and the remaining characters (up to eight in all) are either letters or numbers. Acceptable names might include X, NAME, %HGHT, or R2D2. Terms such as 25th or A*B are not valid names according to the preceding definition. Note that a variable name is never enclosed in quotation marks. This difference makes it possible to distinguish between names and strlits in a line of M code. The following examples illustrate valid and invalid variable names in M.

Valid	Invalid
XYZ	A*B
%X2	2ABC
R2D2	X2%
JDOE	J DOE

Although a variable name may be longer than eight characters, it is not a good idea to assign a long name to a variable that is often used in manipulating data. Standard M specifies that a name can be up to eight characters long; any letters in a name beyond the first eight characters are ignored. This restriction is changing: the next (post-1995) revision of the standard requires that at least 31 unique characters be allowed, and some implementations may already allow for longer names, but until the next standard is adopted, it would be well to check with your own implementation and keep the names short.

Many languages (such as FORTRAN, C, and Pascal) adopt special rules distinguishing integer variables, real variables, and other data types. M does not make any such type distinction in storing variables. Instead, M considers all variables as strings, even though it permits calculations on valid numbers stored as variables. This is an important feature distinguishing M from most other programming languages. It means that numbers inside a strlit may be used in calculations and then replaced in the string for subsequent storage or output. The practical applications of this feature are illustrated in later chapters.

Functions

In the preceding sections we described the basic building blocks of the M language – numbers, strings, and variables. The power of many languages, including M, is also dependent on special features that assist in the manipulation of these basic elements. One class of such operations is referred to as *functions*, and they are identified in M by their names, which always begin with a dollar sign ($). Examples of some of the important M functions are $FIND, $PIECE, and $SELECT, which allow the M programmer to reference strings of text in various special ways.

Special variables

The last components that we will consider are called *special variables*. Like functions, these elements are also identified by a name beginning with a dollar sign. However, special variables are used to provide a single value, such as the date and time ($HOROLOG) or the position of the cursor on a screen ($X and $Y). Special variables do not manipulate other variables in the way that functions do.

Summary

Like any computer language, M uses a specified character set, defines acceptable data types, provides for syntactical use of variable names, and has reserved terms for special variables and functions. In many respects, however, M treats these building blocks differently from other languages. The most important features of the M building blocks, as presented in this chapter, are as follows:

- M uses the ASCII character set for language syntax. Some extensions are permitted by the 1995 M standard to permit use of other character sets (see Part II of this text), but for beginning programming, this feature can be ignored.
- M has only one data type: string. Within this data type, however, it is possible to represent and perform numeric operations on integers, real numbers, and mixed numeric and nonnumeric variables. The M portability standard requires fifteen decimal digits of accuracy and permits for representation of numbers between 10 raised to the –25th power and 10 raised to the +25th power.
- M string literals may be composed of any printable ASCII characters and may be up to 255 characters in length.
- M allows variable names beginning with alphabetical characters or with the special character % (percent sign), followed by any alphanumeric characters, with a maximum length of eight significant characters used to distinguish between variables.
- M reserves special functions and variables to provide language-augmented manipulation capability. These special functions and variables are identified by a dollar sign ($) followed by reserved names, as described later in the text.

Interactive programming in M

One of the most important components of this text is the inclusion of some exercises at the end of the next several chapters. Even though the material from a given chapter may seem simple, the exercises will give you a chance to work through examples in an active sense, thereby reinforcing the written material presented earlier in each chapter.

This section helps you get started in working with a computer terminal (or personal computer) that has access to standard M. There are many different M systems available. Specific information about M vendors can be obtained by writing the M Technology Association (see information at the end of Chapter 2).

For now, all you will need is to find a system and to follow the instructions given below. You will need a little help to log on to your specific system, and this text does not attempt to tell you what user codes and passwords are accepted by the implementation you are using.

Log-on procedures in M

In order to use M on any system, you need to know how to *log on* to the system. On minicomputers with many users, this process includes typing your name and a password. On personal computers, it may only require typing the word MUMPS. Find out how to get into the M language on your system. However, if you are using a PC-compatible computer with Windows, it may suffice to click on the M (or DTM or MSM) icon to activate M. Other implementations may require you to enter an identification number and password. For details on your system, check your documentation or check with a friend who has already worked with the system.

Once you have logged onto M, you are ready to begin the exercises described below.

Using the SET command

In order to explore the different variations of data types, variables, and other features described in this chapter, you must know how to create a variable and how to write out its value. An M variable is created through the SET command, described more fully in Chapter 6. For the present, it is enough for you to know the following: When you see an M prompt (usually >), type a SET statement as follows:

```
>SET<space>X=3 <enter>
```

In other words, type SET, followed by a space, followed by a name of a variable, an equals sign, a value, and then type the <*enter*> key. In the remaining examples, we will use the following format:

```
SET X=3
```

omitting the M prompt and the special symbol for space and for enter at the end of each line.

In M, the space is an important element of the language syntax. When you type `SET X=3`, you *must* have one space between SET and X, but you *cannot* have more than one space. Nor are spaces permitted in the remainder of the command (between the variable name, the equals sign, and the value). If you follow this simple syntax, you will be able to use the SET command without difficulty.

Using the WRITE command

Just as you have learned to type `SET X=3` (or, in general, `SET varname=value`), you also may want to write out some values that have been previously stored or that are calculated with a SET statement. When you want to write a value, type

```
WRITE X
```

and the value will appear on the next line of the display. Again, use one and *only one* space between the WRITE and the name of the variable.

Terminating an M session: the HALT command

Whenever you are through, even temporarily, working with the M interpreter, it is important to *log off* the system. To do so, you must type HALT and hit the <*enter*> key. If you exit in other ways (unplugging the computer, hanging up the phone, or leaving the terminal without doing anything at all), the system will not know that you have left. Although nothing serious will happen to your M code at this stage, serious consequences could arise later on. Therefore, always remember to type HALT when you wish to exit M.

You are now ready to start programming in M. The exercises that follow will give you some practice in using the concepts described in this chapter. Since these exercises do not require programming solutions, there are no suggested answers at the end of the text.

Exercises

The only way to become proficient in any computer language is to write programs. The purpose of these exercises is to give you some practice in writing M code at the level covered to this point in the text. Using the procedures described in the previous section, *log on* to your M system and then follow the instructions given below.

Errors in M statements

In the exercises that follow, you will be asked to enter statements that will generate errors (so that you can tell the difference between an acceptable and an invalid use of the language). When your M interpreter sees an invalid statement, it will display a message such as

```
<SYNTX> or ILLEGAL COMMAND NAME
```

It also may redisplay the line you typed in with an asterisk below the place where the error was detected. Do not be concerned by this message. It is expected, since you are being asked to type in invalid syntax on purpose. You may continue to enter new SET statements, and the interpreter and you can forget that the error ever happened.

1. ***Numeric Variables*** As a first step in programming in M, here are some examples to test valid as well as invalid assignments of variables.

a. Type in the statements as shown. You should consider before typing each one whether you think it will be accepted as valid based on the material presented in this chapter.

```
SET X=27.12
SET X =3      (Note space after X.)
SET Y=1E5
SET A=1A5
SET B=20e3
SET C=10,000
WRITE X       (Which value of X will be produced?)
WRITE Y
WRITE A       (Why does this generate an error?)
WRITE B
WRITE C
```

b. Try a few more variations on setting variables equal to numbers until you feel comfortable with what is correct and what will generate a syntax error.

2. ***Limits of Valid Numbers***

a. Type in the following statements to see whether they are accepted and, if so, what values are actually stored in your computer.

```
SET X=111222333444555666777
WRITE X/2            (to see how many decimal digits of accuracy are
                     preserved in your system)
SET Y=123E25
WRITE Y
```

```
SET Z=123E-25
WRITE Z
```

b. If part a. works, try higher numbers after E. If not, try lower numbers. Some systems tested in writing this text permitted exponent (E) values as high as E100 and E – 30, so you should find out how your own system performs. Here are some additional suggested values for you to try.

```
SET A=-234E24
WRITE A
SET B=200E-25
WRITE B
```

3. ***String Variables*** Type in the following string values, being careful to count the number of quotation marks where several occur in a row.

```
SET D="SMITH"
SET E="SMITH", JOHN (Did you get an error? Why?)
SET F="DEERE, JOHN"
SET G="A/C*D"
SET Z="O'Keefe, Meritt, et al."
SET X="012xyZ"         (mixing numbers, uppercase, and lowercase)
WRITE X
SET A="That %$@*!CAT!"
SET Y="Please enter your name:"
WRITE Y
WRITE A
SET A="010"
SET B="10"
SET C=10.0
SET D=10
WRITE A
WRITE B
WRITE C
WRITE D                (Is there any difference between these values? Why?)
```

4. ***Variable Names***

a. Type in the following variable names, trying to anticipate before you do so which names might generate errors.

```
SET AbCd=1
SET aBC=2
SET %123=4
SET XY%=5
SET ANum1=6
SET TENFOUR=7
SET 10S="TENNIS"
```

```
SET AAABBBCC=8
SET AAABBBCCDEF=9
WRITE AAABBBCC
```
(What value did you get? Why?)

b. Try a few more variations until you are comfortable with the rules of naming variables.

Note: It is not easy to test the length of strings without using some additional M features. We will defer the string-length test until a later chapter, unless you really *want* to type in over 255 characters preceded and followed by quotes to see if it will work on your system.

Operations on Numeric Values

4

In Chapter 3 we learned that M recognizes only one type of data, a string, but that it can operate on numeric strings to produce valid numeric results. Since there is only one data type, a given variable can hold either numeric or text data, or both. Redefinition of a M variable, including changing back and forth between text and numbers, is perfectly acceptable in this language. You also learned that both types can be stored in the same variable at different times. This chapter introduces the types of operations that can be performed on numeric values; later, we will learn about other operations affecting strings as well as numbers. Most of the concepts used in M should already be familiar, since these ideas are really ones that you learned in elementary arithmetic.

Binary operators

M defines seven operators that are used to combine numeric values in different ways (shown in the table on the next page). The first four operators correspond to the four basic arithmetic operations used in everyday activities.

> **Note to Experienced Programmers:** The M arithmetic operators are similar to those of most other languages. However, it may be valuable to review the operation of the modulo operator (#), operator precedence (not like other high-level programming languages!), the $RANDOM function, and the $HOROLOG special variable, since these features differ from similar operators in many other languages.

Operator	Function	Operator	Function
+	Addition	\	Integer quotient division
–	Subtraction	#	Modulo, or remainder, division
*	Multiplication	**	Exponentiation
/	Division		

In their most common form, these operators are binary in nature; that is, they act on two values to produce a result. The following values illustrate typical M expressions with these operators:

Expression	= Result	Expression	= Result
4+7	= 11	9*6	= 54
18–6	= 12	10/2	= 5
3–4	= –1	4/3	= 1.33333333333333

The last example reinforces the point that M preserves fifteen significant digits. The quotient of 4/3 is a number of infinite length: 3333...; however, as noted earlier, M truncates this value to nine significant digits.

The next two operators have to do with different forms of division. Integer quotient division (\), as indicated by its name, returns only an integer value. Strictly speaking, the operator (\) returns only the integer portion of the quotient calculated by the more normal division operator (/). Modulo, or remainder, division is the complementary operation to integer division in that the value returned by the # operator is the remainder deleted by the integer division. Some examples of these operations on arithmetic values are illustrated in the following table (truncation may vary):

N	D	N/D	N\D	N#D
10	2	5	5	0
–8	4	–2	–2	0
6	–3	–2	–2	0
–6	4	–1.5	–1	2
1	3	0.33333333	0	1
–14	–6	2.33333333	2	–2
13	5	2.6	2	3
4	–3	–1.33333333	–1	–2

Most of these examples are self-explanatory (note that M can mix integer and decimal values in the same expression). The modulo operator, however, requires some clarification. For positive numbers, the result of a modulo operation is the familiar remainder from long division. Thus 13 divided by 5 gives a quotient of 2 and a remainder of 3 (the modulo result in the next to last line of the preceding table). A formal mathematical expression of the modulo relationship is given by the equation:

$$\text{Modulo } N/D = N - [D \times \text{floor}(N/D)]$$

where N is the numerator, D is the denominator, and floor(X) is defined as the largest integer less than or equal to X. Substituting the values from the last two examples given above, we obtain

$13 - [5 \times \text{floor}(13/5)]$
$13 - [5 \times \text{floor}(2.6)]$
$13 - (5 \times 2)$
$13 - 10 = 3$

Similarly, when $N = 4$ and $D = -3$, we obtain

$4 - [-3 \times \text{floor}(4/-3)]$
$4 - [-3 \times \text{floor}(-1.33333333)]$
$4 - (-3 \times -2)$
$4 - (6) = -2$

This second example illustrates the need for the use of the term floor(X), since −2 is a smaller (i.e., more negative) value than −1.33333333. Using this definition, you should be able to verify each of the relationships in the preceding examples, remembering that the sign of the result is always the sign of the denominator.

The final arithmetic operator, introduced in the 1995 M Standard, is the exponentiation operator **. Exponentiation is used to raise one number to the power of another: 3**2 is like saying 3 raised to the second power, or more commonly, 3 squared (9). Exponentiation can also be used to obtain roots of numbers, so that 16**0.5 will produce 4, since 0.5 is equivalent to the 1/2 power, or square root. Remember that the exact precision of exponentiation may be system-dependent. The actual result may vary from one machine to another even though the same vendor's M is used on both.

Arithmetic expressions and operator precedence

The arithmetic operators defined above may be combined in various ways to form *arithmetic expressions,* statements involving arithmetic values and arithmetic operators that may be evaluated to give a single numeric value. The preceding section gave examples of several simple expressions, each consisting of a single operator between two values. Expressions may, however, be considerably more complex. For example

1 + 2 + 3 + 4 + 5 + 6 = 21

is an expression that uses several values and several operators yet still gives a single result. As expressions become more complex, involving different operators, computer languages such as M must define rules for evaluating them in order to give consistent results. Consider the expression 3 + 5 × 2. As it is written, there are two possible interpretations, depending on which operator is evaluated first. The alternatives are clarified by rewriting the expression with parentheses, so that the meaning may be either (3 + 5) × 2 to give a result of 16 or 3 + (5 × 2) to give a result of 13. In M, as in other computer languages, you may use parentheses, controlling the sequence of operations to produce the desired result. However, this approach fails to tell us what happens if no parentheses are used in such expressions. M simply evaluates such expressions from left to right, taking each value and operator in sequence as it is encountered.

Note: This left-to-right precedence is not used in most other computer languages. In fact, different cultures teach different rules of precedence. In the US, we assume that multiplication and division take precedence over addition and subtraction, but we make no difference in precedence between multiplication and division. In some European countries, however, there are additional precedence rules that separate multiplication and division. Fortunately for us, we don't have to worry about this in M: the precedence is *always* simple left-to-right.

Thus our example is treated by the M language as if it had been written (3 + 5) × 2, or 16. Naturally, parenthesized expressions are evaluated first, so if you wanted the alternative interpretation, you would have to use parentheses to obtain it, that is, 3 + (5 × 2). If M saw this equation, it would evaluate the parenthesized value first, giving the final result of 13. Left-to-right evaluation appears natural and causes no problems for individuals unfamiliar with other computer languages. The experienced FORTRAN programmer, however, will immediately notice that the precedence defined by M is different from that for FORTRAN, which assigns higher precedence to multiplication and division than to addition and subtraction. Any explicit precedence sequence can be achieved in M by using parentheses, so you should use them freely if you have any doubts about a particular calculation.

We conclude this section with one final example illustrating the order of execution of a complex statement. In each line, the bold operation is the next one performed.

```
17 - 4/2 + (8*3)\6#2
    13/2 + (8*3)\6#2
     6.5 + (8*3)\6#2
        6.5 + 24\6#2
           30.5\6#2
            5#2 = 1
```
(final answer)

In all the previous examples, we have used numeric constants to keep the examples as simple as possible. M also allows us to use variables in arithmetic expressions. If, for example, the following assignments had been made to a set of variables:

A = 17 B = 4 C = 2 Y1 = 3 BCX = 6 X = 8

then the previous example could be rewritten

A – B/C + (X × Y1)\BCX #C

and it would be evaluated in precisely the same sequence as shown earlier, producing the same result. Any arithmetic expression may be composed of a mixture of arithmetic constants, arithmetic variables, and arithmetic operators together with parentheses required (or desired) to clarify the evaluation.

Unary operators

Two of the arithmetic operators (+ and –) also may appear in front of a single operand. In such a case, instead of being binary operators requiring two operands, they are referred to as *unary operators*. These unary operators are used especially in dealing with arithmetic variables, converting them from string to numeric form when there is any question about their string representation. The unary plus sign simply converts a string to its numeric equivalent; the minus sign changes the sign of such a conversion. If, for example, we have three variables $A = 0$, $B = 3$, and $C = -6$, the result of unary operations on these variables would be as follows:

```
+A = 0
-A = 0
+B = 3
-B = -3
+C = -6
-C = 6
```

Numeric interpretation

With one exception, these examples complete our discussion of arithmetic expressions. Remember, however, that a variable may contain either a numeric value or a string value. In an expression such as $A + 3$, the definition of addition requires that A have a numeric value. In general, you need not worry about this fact, since M incorporates a feature known as *automatic mode conversion* which means that if A contains a string value when the expression $A + 3$ is evaluated, M will convert the string to its numeric equivalent before evaluating the expression. Thus, if A has the string value "123", the result of A + 3 would be 126. The string conversion is based on the definition of a number, and M evaluates the string from left to right. If the left-hand portion of the string (after removal of any leading unary operators) forms a valid numeric constant, the string is interpreted as being that numeric value. If no valid numeric constant can be found at the beginning of the string, M assigns the value of zero to the numeric interpretation. The following examples show how numeric conversion works:

String	Value
"ABC"	0
"" *(null string)*	0
"123"	123
"–12"	–12
"+36.5"	36.5
"12ABC"	12
"3.1E–3"	.0031
"A12B36C"	0
"+ –0.362"	–.362
"9E2AB"	900
"01267"	1267

The last example deserves special attention, because of the use of ZIP-CODES in the US. As we all know, zipcodes in the northeastern part of the US begin with the digit 0, followed by four other digits. M would treat the zipcode 01267 as 1267 if it were preceded by a unary + operator. Later (in chapters 11 and 14), we will see that sorting in M can be affected by leading zeros. For now, it is useful to know that the unary operator can force interpretation of numbers like 01267 and 0.25 to be treated as numbers. In fact, one of the most common uses of the unary operators is to force a numeric interpretation of its operand. There are situations in M where a numeric value is absolutely required. In these situations, use of a unary plus will force M to perform a numeric interpretation. In the preceding examples, addition of the unary plus in front of each of those strings (or their variable names, if any) would produce the corresponding value shown in the table.

Arithmetic function $RANDOM

Standard M defines only one purely arithmetic function: $RANDOM. This function takes a single argument, an integer that must be equal to or greater than 1. Each time the function is called, it returns a pseudorandom integer within the range of 0 to (argument –1). Thus calling $RANDOM(100) returns an integer value between 0 and 99, $RANDOM(10) returns an integer between 0 and 9, and $RANDOM(1) returns only the value 0 (and hence is pointless). This function is useful in a number of arithmetic calculations where random values are required. Other functions (trigonometric, logarithmic, and the like) are not available as standard functions in M at this time, although most implementations provide utilities to perform these operations. The MDC is in the process of adopting a library of mathematical functions; these functions may be incorporated in the next revision of X11.1 (in the year 2001? no one knows for sure). See Chapter 25.

Special variable $HOROLOG

Although database languages such as SQL provide for dates to be entered and evaluated as days of a year, most high–level programming languages do not offer such a feature. M is unique in this regard, in that it provides one special variable that may provide useful information on both *date* and *time of day:* the $HOROLOG variable. This variable contains information about the current date and time which can be used to calculate things such as a person's age or the length of stay in a hospital or the time required to execute a program. Since the use of this variable requires more knowledge of the M language than has been presented up to this point, we will only note the availability of $HOROLOG at this time and defer a more complete discussion to Chapter 14.

Summary

The M language has the normal arithmetic operators found in other programming languages. There are, however, some features of the language that differ from conventions used in most other high–level languages. In general,

- M has seven binary arithmetic operators (+, –, *, /, \, #,**) to perform the functions of add, subtract, multiply, divide, integer divide, modulo, and exponentiation.
- The unary operators (+ and –) force left-to-right arithmetic interpretation of strings, including those which contain mixed alphanumeric characters.
- M normally follows a strict left-to-right precedence of arithmetic operators, with no hierarchical precedence. Parentheses may be used to override this inherent precedence.

- The function $RANDOM provides a random number generator within the language. Other functions are usually available as utilities from the different M vendors.
- M provides a special variable, $HOROLOG, which contains information about date and time. Details on the use of this variable are found in Chapter 14.

Exercises

With the addition of arithmetic operators to the toolkit you now have available you can begin to do some useful calculations in M. The purpose of these exercises is to help you become confident with these operators and to give you one potentially useful programming problem. A suggested solution for Exercise 4 is found in the back of this text.

1. ***Simple Operations with Two Variables*** Try these examples, making sure that you understand how each answer is calculated. Determine which examples generate errors and why.

```
KILL (Make sure no variables exist at outset.)
SET A=23
SET B=7
SET Y=-11
SET Z=-3
WRITE A*B
WRITE A/B
WRITE AB
WRITE A#B
WRITE Y/A
WRITE YA
WRITE Y#A
```

2. ***Complicated Operations with Multiple Variables and Parentheses***

```
WRITE A+Y*Z
WRITE (A+Y)*Z
WRITE A+(Y*Z)        (Are there any differences? Why?)
WRITE A/(Y+Z)*Z*Z    (Move the parentheses around to see what values
                      result.)
SET X=111222333444555
SET Y=999888777666555
WRITE X*Y
WRITE YX
WRITE Y#X (Did your system truncate these answers?)
SET C=456E20
```

```
SET D=321E-25
WRITE C*D
WRITE C*C  (These values may exceed the limits of your system.)
WRITE D*D
```

3. ***Operations on Numbers and Strings***

```
SET A=013
SET B="12QRS"
SET C="13.0"
SET D="E12"
WRITE A*2
WRITE B*A
WRITE A/(A/3)
WRITE C*D   (Which value caused the error? Try A × D, A × C.)
```

4. ***An Exercise in Calculating Time of Day*** Assume that 1,190,647 seconds have elapsed since the beginning of a month (any month will do). What meal might you be eating at that time of day? To solve this problem, SET TIME = 1190647 and then calculate values for DAY, HOURS, MINUTES, and SECONDS using the various numeric operators described in this chapter (Work it out on your own, then check the answer at the end of the text.)

Logical Operators, Comparisons

5

In the preceding chapter we considered arithmetic expressions that allow us to set the value of a variable or to perform calculations using variables as constants. In many computing applications, however, we need to test a relationship between two variables and take differing actions depending on the result of the test. All computer languages have some way to perform tests of this type. (In fact, the ability to test and then branch to different instructions based on the result is the real secret to the power of computers.) In M, there are several different types of comparisons and operations that can assist in this process. These operators will be considered in this chapter.

Arithmetic relational and string relational operators

Since M stores variables as strings, a distinction must be made between the value of numeric strings and other strings, since some numbers may be expressed in several different ways. The numbers 35, 3.5E1, and .35E2, for example, are all equivalent, but they are stored in different ways. To test numeric relationships, two operators are available:

> **Note to experienced programmers:** This chapter describes some conventional operators (>, <, =), but also several that operate on strings, as well as some different symbols for logical AND and OR operations. Check the summary at the end of the chapter, and if necessary review the descriptions of those operators that remain unclear.

Operator	Meaning
<	Less than
>	Greater than

When these operators are invoked, the variables are first converted to their numeric value and then the comparisons are made. (The use of an equals operator is discussed below.) For example, if `A=3` and `B=7`:

Expression	Evaluation
`A>B`	FALSE
`A<B`	TRUE

In addition to the two numeric relational operators, five additional string relational operators are used. They are:

Operator	Meaning
=	Equals
[	Contains
]	Follows
]]	Sorts after (this operator is covered in Chapter 11)
?	Pattern match (this operator is covered in Chapter 14)

Note: Because the sorts after and pattern match operators require more knowledge of string manipulation, their discussion is deferred to a later part of Part 1.

The first of these operators tests to see if two strings are equal. Note that this comparison is not numeric, so the numbers 35 and 3.5E1 are not evaluated as equal using this operator. If numeric equality is to be tested, the programmer must make use of the unary plus operator to force numeric interpretation. Thus, if `A="35"` and `B="3.5E1"`, then `A=B` is not true, but `+A=+B` is true, since numeric interpretation is forced. Programmers should take care in using this operator when numeric values are involved.

Since there is only one such form for each numeric value, the equals operator may be applied directly. If `A="33"+"2"` and `B=+"3.5E1"`, then `A=B` is true. The equals operator will work with numbers entered in the same manner, e.g., if all numbers are entered with no quotes and no leading or trailing zeros, they can be tested for equality without the unary plus operator. Calculated numeric results also can be tested for equality, since they are recognized as numbers internally. For example, if A = 3 and B = 7

Operator	Meaning
A+B	10
A*7	21
A*B	21
A*"7"	21
34*"2 " *(the digit two)*	68

The latter example illustrates again how M interprets a string from left to right and takes leading numeric values when need for arithmetic calculations.

The 'contains' operator '[' tests to see if a value contains another value. This operator works on the code values stored by M for strings, which is assumed to be the ASCII character set. (In Part II we will see that other character sets can be used, in which case the contains operator will compare those code values.) For example, if VAR = "ABC123", TEST1 = "BC1", and TEST2 = "C2" respectively, then some possible tests and results would be as follows:

Expression	Evaluation
VAR["A"	Evaluates as TRUE (the string "ABC123" contains the letter "A")
VAR[TEST1	Evaluates as TRUE (the string "ABC123" contains "BC1" even though it is not at the start)
VAR[TEST2	Evaluates as FALSE (although "C" and "2" are both in VAR, they do not occur together)

When we say that one variable follows another, we are testing its collating order, using the ASCII code values illustrated in Table 3.1 (again, other codes are allowed by M; see Part II). Using the three variables above,

Expression	Evaluation
VAR]TEST1	Evaluates as FALSE ("ABC..." comes *before* "BC...")
TEST1]TEST2	Evaluates as FALSE "B..." comes *before* "C...")
TEST2]VAR	Evaluates as TRUE ("C..." comes *after* "A...")

This operator, like many in M, follows a strict left-to-right, character-by-character process in order to determine whether a comparison is TRUE or FALSE. This operator is particularly useful when it is desired to sort names or other strings into an alphabetical sequence, since the letters of the alphabet are properly ordered in the ASCII collating sequence (see Table 3.1). Comparison is done on a character-by-character basis, from left to right.

However, there are some cases where this approach might seem intuitively unexpected. For instance:

Expression	Evaluation
`3]1`	TRUE
`30]10`	TRUE
`3]10`	TRUE(!)

The third example (`3]10`) is true because 3 follows 1, and the rest of the string is ignored.

When we say that a test of this sort evaluates as TRUE or FALSE, we mean that the result of a test such as those given above will return the value 1 if the test is true and 0 otherwise. These values, 0 and 1, are referred to as *truth values*.

Logical operators

In addition to the arithmetic and relational operators described in this and the preceding chapter, M allows for testing combinations of conditions using the following logical operators

Operator	Meaning
&	And
!	Or
'	Not (a single apostrophe)

The result of an AND test will be true only if both tests are found to be true. An OR test will return a true value if either condition is true. Given a situation where `X = "ABC"` and `Y = "DEF"`, we can demonstrate the combination of logical operators with some of the earlier expression tests as follows:

Expression	Evaluation	Expression	Evaluation
`"ABC"=X`	TRUE(1)	`X[Y!(X["AB")`	TRUE
`"AB"=X`	FALSE (0)	`Y]X&(Y["EF")`	TRUE
`X["AB"`	TRUE	`X]Y&(X["B")`	FALSE
`"AB"[X`	FALSE	`12>11!(X=Y)`	TRUE

Note that parentheses are required after logical operators in the last four examples to ensure proper interpretation with left-to-right evaluation. To illustrate this sequence, consider the following example and the manner in which M evaluates expressions of this type (expression components in bold are those evaluated at each step):

Evaluation of `X["Y"!(Y]X)&'1!(X["A")`

Expression	Evaluation of Bold Component
X["Y"!(Y]X)&'1!(X["A")	FALSE (0)
0!**(Y]X)**&'1!(X["A")	TRUE (1)
0!1&'1!(X["A")	TRUE (1)
1&**'1!**(X["A")	FALSE (0)
1&0!(X["A")	FALSE (0)
0!(X["A")	TRUE (1)
0!1	TRUE (1)

Notice that all comparison operators *except the first* require parentheses. The first portion of the expression, `X["Y"`, is evaluated in normal left-to-right form and requires no parentheses.

The NOT operator (`'`) is used to reverse the truth value of the affected expression. Thus `'(11 > 12)` would evaluate TRUE, but `'("ABC" = "ABC")` would evaluate FALSE (the reverse of their original truth values). The NOT operator may also be used in conjunction with the relational and logical operators. For example, if `A="ABC"`

Expression	Evaluation
11'>12	TRUE
'(11>12)	TRUE
A'="ABC"	FALSE
'(A="ABC")	FALSE

In general, `A ' relation B` has the same value as `' (A relation B)`.

Using the operators described above, complex combinations of relationships may be tested and a single true or false value returned.

Truth value interpretation

We saw in Chapter 3 how any string value can be interpreted as a number. In a similar manner, any value can be interpreted as a truth value. This interpretation is performed automatically (automatic mode conversion) whenever truth values are required, e.g., as the operand(s) of a logical operator. The truth value interpretation of a string value is performed by first taking the value's numeric interpretation. If this numeric value is zero, the truth value is FALSE (0). Otherwise, the result is TRUE (1). Thus, if `X="ABC"` and `Y="4F"`, then

Expression	Truth Value
`0`	FALSE (0)
`1973`	TRUE (1)
`'X`	TRUE
`X!Y`	TRUE
`X<2-1&Y`	FALSE

Summary

This chapter has introduced the M relational operators. Together with the arithmetic operators described in the previous chapter, they represent a powerful set of tools that permit the programmer to perform many tasks involving numeric, string, and logical relationships. The language elements covered in this chapter include the following types of operators.

- Numeric relational operators:

  < Less than
  > Greater than

- String relational operators:

  = Equals (may be used in numeric contexts)
  [Contains
  ] Follows

(the operators]] (sorts after) and ? (pattern match) are covered in Chapters 11 and 14, respectively)

- Logical operators:

  & AND
  ! OR
  ' NOT

Exercises

In the previous two chapters the commands SET and WRITE were introduced in their simplest form. We now add one variation of the WRITE statement, one that permits the user to determine whether an expression is TRUE or FALSE. The syntax of this form of the WRITE command is WRITE <*expression*>, with the result evaluated as logically true or false. To illustrate, assume that `A = "ABC"` and `B = "B"`. Some examples are

```
WRITE 2>1
WRITE A=B
WRITE "ABC"["A"&(B]A)
```

In each case, the response will be either a 0 or a 1, depending on whether the expression is evaluated to be TRUE or FALSE. With this new form of WRITE, we can investigate the logical and relational operators discussed in the last two chapters.

Note: Since there are no programming challenges in these exercises, there are no solutions provided in the back of the text.

1. *Relational Operations*

a. Check the following for truth value of each expression.

```
SET X1="ABC/DEF"
SET SLASH="/"
SET X2="A"
SET X3="DEFG"
WRITE X1[X2
WRITE X1]X3
WRITE (X1[X2)&(X1[SLASH)
WRITE X2]X3!(X3]X1)
```

b. Try some other variations of your own.

2. *ASCII Collating Sequence*

a. Try some variations using uppercase, lowercase, and numerics to see how they collate.

```
SET UPPER="ADAMS"
SET lower="john"
SET MIX1="Adams"
SET MIX2="jOHN"
WRITE UPPER]lower
WRITE lower]MIX2
WRITE MIX1]UPPER
WRITE MIX1]MIX2
SET NUM1="0121"
SET NUM2="120"
WRITE UPPER]NUM1
WRITE NUM1]NUM2
```

b. Continue by setting a variable that begins with a space to see where it will fall in the collating sequence. Check your results against Table 3.1.

3. ***Numeric Strings and Quoted Numerics***

a. M makes distinctions between values in quotation marks and values entered without quotation marks. Try the following examples, guessing before you type the WRITE statements what the results will be.

```
SET A1="010"
SET A2=10
SET A3=10.0
SET A4="10.0"
WRITE A1=A2
WRITE +A1=+A2 (How does this differ from the previous line?)
WRITE A2]A1
WRITE A3=A4
WRITE A3=+A4
```

b. Try some other variations until you are satisfied that you understand the differences between these representations of values.

Operations on Strings

6

In the previous two chapters we considered, first, arithmetic operators and functions and then logical and relational operators, including a few that acted on string relations. This chapter is concerned with the final group of (non-relational) operators and some functions used for string manipulation. With the coverage of the string operators, we will have introduced each of the major language elements: variables, constants, operators, functions, and commands. The remaining chapters expand on some of these elements, especially commands, but it is comforting to realize that there are no major new categories of language components to learn about.

Consider what operations might be performed on a string of text, in addition to using the contains, equals, or follows operators previously described. It might be desirable to determine the *length* of a string, to *find* or *extract* some substring from the text, to *concatenate* two strings together, to *insert* or *modify* a subfield *(piece)* of the text, or to *convert back and forth* between *character* and *ASCII* codes. We might also want to translate a string, replacing its con-

> **Note to experienced programmers:** One of the main strengths of the M language is its ability to manipulate text. This chapter contains most of the language elements that perform those functions. As such, it is probably the most important and most unique set of language concepts in this text. The experienced programmer will probably benefit by reviewing the entire chapter and its exercises. It would be well to begin with the summary at the end, which provides a useful guide to the language elements covered in the body of the chapter.

tents with some alternative form. M allows all these operations to be performed, in most cases using functions whose names are readily identified with the operations just described.

String operators

In Chapter 5 we described three relational operators that act on strings (saving]] and ? for Chapter 14). They were

Operator	Action Taken
`A=B`	Compares A with B for equality
`A[B`	Determines if A contains B
`A]B`	Determines if A follows B in the collation sequence

To this group of operators, we now add a fourth, represented by the symbol _ (underline). The purpose of this function is to append one string to the end of another, or to *concatenate* the strings. The following examples describe its use with literals and variables. Assume that `A="ABC"` and `B="MUMPS"`.

Expression Evaluated	Value Produced
`A_"DEF"`	`ABCDEF`
`A_B`	`ABCMUMPS`
`A_"s OF "_B`	`ABCs OF MUMPS`

This operator is particularly useful in constructing messages into which string variables are inserted. For instance, if a variable called `FIRSTNAM` had been set equal to the name of the user at the terminal, we might create the following string:

```
SET GREET="Hello, "_FIRSTNAM_". Welcome to M."
WRITE GREET
```

The resulting string would concatenate the three strings together, inserting the user's name in the middle. The string `GREET` could then be used to add a personal touch to the log-on message.

String functions

In Chapter 3 we described the $RANDOM function and its use in arithmetic operations. We now examine several functions that are useful tools for effective string manipulation.

$LENGTH function

One important characteristic of a string is its length, i.e., the number of characters it contains at a given time. $LENGTH determines the length of any string, returning a single number, which may range from 0 to 255, the maximum string length allowed in M. Here are some examples and their actions, assuming that `T="JOE_BROWN"`, `V="ABC;DEF;GHI"`, `DATE="9/5/55"`, and `X="TOWN"`:

Expression Evaluated	Value Produced
`$LENGTH("")`	0 *(empty string)*
`$LENGTH(T)`	9
`$LENGTH(V)`	11
`$LENGTH(DATE)`	6
`$LENGTH(T_X)`	13
`$LENGTH("THE END")`	7 *(a space counts as a character)*

Note that `($LENGTH(T)+$LENGTH(X))` is the same as `$LENGTH(T_X)`, provided that the total length does not exceed the 255 character limit of M strings. In other words, an expression, rather than a single string or variable, may be evaluated by the $LENGTH function.

There is another operation that is sometimes useful relating to the length of a string – that is, to determine the number of occurrences of a character (or group of characters) within a string. M provides this capability by a second variation of the $LENGTH function, this time using *two* arguments: the string to be tested and the character(s) to be searched for. Suppose, for example, that the variable SENTENCE was assigned the value `the quick brown fox jumps over the lazy dog`. In order to find out how many words are in this sentence, one could use $LENGTH as follows:

```
WRITE $LENGTH(SENTENCE," ")
```

The answer would be 9, which is *one more* than the number of spaces found in the variable (assuming it is written on one line), but which is the correct number of words in the sentence. The two-argument form of $LENGTH, then, returns a value one greater than the number of occurrences of the second argument in the first argument. Some other examples using the same variable are as follows:

Expression Evaluated	Value Produced
`$LENGTH(SENTENCE,"q")`	2
`$LENGTH(SENTENCE,"the")`	3
`$LENGTH(SENTENCE,"26")`	1

Note: If the string is not found, the value returned is 1, not 0. (The reason for this choice relates to use of another function, $PIECE, described later in this chapter.)

One very valuable application of the two-argument form of $LENGTH is in writing programs to take care of the "wraparound" problem with word processing: allowing a user to type continuously without pressing the <Enter> key and adjusting the text so that partial words at the end of a line are moved to the start of the next line). See Problem 5 at the end of this chapter.

$FIND function

The $FIND function determines whether and at what position a substring occurs within another string. It is often used when the location of data within a string is unknown. Some distinctive portion or even the entire field may be used as the second argument of $FIND, which, upon evaluation, indicates the position of the second argument within the string specified in the first argument. The result is an integer value that corresponds to the character position immediately *following* the occurrence of the second argument string within the first. For all instances where the second argument substring does not appear within the first argument string, a value of 0 is returned by $FIND because there is no position at which the value exists.

In the following example, we will assume that a variable named CITY has been assigned the value `SAN JOSE, CA 95150`. Using the $FIND function could produce the following results:

Expression Evaluated	Value Produced
`$FIND(CITY,",")`	10
`$FIND(CITY,"CA")`	13
`$FIND(CITY,"WA")`	0

Since San Jose is in California, there is no match for `WA` and the function returns a value of `0`.

However, it might happen that instead of San Jose, the city was CALISTOGA. In this case, `$FIND(CITY,"CA")` would return a value of 3, the position following the first occurrence of that string. It might therefore be useful to permit searching for a match starting at some position other than the first character in the string. $FIND provides this capability with a third argument that specifies the character position within the first argument string at which the search for the second argument substring is to begin. If we were to change CITY to the value `CALISTOGA, CA 95828`, we could obtain the following results:

Expression Evaluated	Value Produced
$FIND(CITY,"CA")	3
$FIND(CITY,",")	11
$FIND(CITY,"CA",12)	14

We have not yet discussed the construction of programs in M, but in the preceding example, it would be possible to create a variable that contains the value 12 derived from the second line and then use this value in the third line as follows:

```
SET START = $FIND(CITY,", ") (Note the space after the last comma.)
SET STATE = $FIND(CITY,"CA",START)
```

$EXTRACT function

The $EXTRACT function is employed primarily for the extraction of fixed-length subfields from composite strings. $EXTRACT can be used in several ways. The simplest form is a single-argument version that returns only the first letter of the variable evaluated. Thus `$EXTRACT("ABC")` is `A`. A slightly more powerful function is contained in the two-argument form, which is used to extract a single character from the variable identified by the first argument at the character position specified by the second argument. If, for example, we assigned to FNAME the value `Maureen` and to LNAME the value `Lily` we could obtain the following results:

Expression Evaluated	Value Produced
$EXTRACT(LNAME)	L
$EXTRACT(FNAME,2)	a
$EXTRACT(LNAME,$LENGTH(LNAME))	y

In this example, we have created an expression in which we want to know the last letter in LNAME, and by using the $LENGTH function as the second argument of $EXTRACT, we obtain the desired result. Note that two parentheses are required at the end of this expression. In other words, it is perfectly ok to *nest* functions inside each other.

In the three-argument form of $EXTRACT, the second and third arguments specify the initial and final character positions, respectively, of the desired field which is to be extracted. To illustrate, assume that a variable NAME has been given the value `de Moel, Ed` and that we want to *extract* the first name. The following steps could be used:

Expression Evaluated	Value Produced
`$FIND(NAME,", ")`	10 *(note that the string used is a comma followed by a space)*
`$EXTRACT(NAME,10,999)`	Ed

In the second operation it is possible to use a third argument that is greater than the largest value expected, and $EXTRACT will return only the valid characters in the target string. This example also could be converted into program statements by setting FIRST to the value of the $EXTRACT function.

If the $EXTRACT function attempts to retrieve a value beyond the end of the available string, e.g., `$EXTRACT(NAME,23,45)`, the value produced is a *null*. Similarly, if the third argument is smaller than the second, e.g., `$EXTRACT(NAME,17,10)`, an empty string is returned.

(A final use of $EXTRACT in conjunction with the SET command is discussed in Chapter 7.)

$PIECE function

The $PIECE function provides a useful method for separating subfields of a string that contains one or more delimiting characters. In contrast to $EXTRACT, which requires knowledge of the initial and final positions of the field to be extracted, $PIECE will search a string for a given delimiter regardless of its position in the string.

With $PIECE, all that must be known in order to retrieve a substring field is the relative placement of that field with respect to other fields and the delimiter used to separate these fields in the main string. The first argument of $PIECE is the string from which the subfield is to be retrieved, the second argument is the delimiter, and the third is the relative field position of the desired field. To illustrate, suppose we wanted to extract day, month, and year from a variable DOB with the current value `August/6/55`. Although the use of $FIND and $EXTRACT might serve to separate these values (remember, the length is unknown because both month and day can be variable in length), the $PIECE function makes the task a great deal simpler:

Expression Evaluated	Value Produced
`$PIECE(DOB,"/",1)`	`August`
`$PIECE(DOB,"/",2)`	`6`
`$PIECE(DOB,"/",3)`	`55`
`$PIECE(DOB,"/",4)`	`""` *(the empty string)*
`$PIECE(DOB,":")`	`August/6/55`

The first three examples are more or less self-explanatory. The fourth example indicates that an empty string is returned if no value exists that matches the function arguments. The final example, which could also be written `$PIECE(DOB,";",1)` returns the first piece of a string using the prescribed delimiter. If the delimiter does not exist in the string, the entire string is returned. (This example explains why the equivalent example of `$LENGTH(str, delimiter)` returns a value of 1 rather than 0: to be symmetrical with the $PIECE function in the same situation.)

Like $EXTRACT, another argument can be added to $PIECE to signify a range of fields to be extracted. To illustrate this use, assume that we have a list of authors in the variable AUTH, whose current value is `Greenes, RA^Pappalardo, AN^Marble, CW^Barnett, GO`. We could separate the primary author from the others with the following expressions using $PIECE (using the same strings defined above):

Expression Evaluated	Value Produced
`$PIECE(AUTH,"^",1)`	`Greenes, RA`
`$PIECE(AUTH,"^",2,99)`	`Pappalardo, AN^Marble, CW^Barnett, GO`

Furthermore we could make use of a nested $PIECE function to obtain the last names or initials of each author:

Expression Evaluated	Value Produced
`$PIECE($PIECE(AUTH,"^",2),",",1)`	`Pappalardo`
`$PIECE($PIECE(AUTH,"^",4),", ",2)`	`GO`

In the second example, we used two characters (comma and space) to restrict the answer to the initials without a leading space. It is not necessary to limit the delimiter to a single character, and as shown, two different delimiters may be used within a single string to create major and minor subdivisions of the text. As this example shows, it is relatively easy to retrieve subfields from larger data strings, thereby permitting the M programmer to store concatenated variables for subsequent decomposition. $PIECE is, in fact, one of the most useful string functions in the M language, performing a function that requires complicated special coding in most other computer languages. Many examples of its use are found in later chapters of this text.

Finally, let's consider the following example:

Expression	Result
`$PIECE("abcdef","/")`	`abcdef`

(As in the case of $EXTRACT, there is another variation of $PIECE which can be used in conjunction with the SET command. This feature is discussed in the next chapter.)

$ASCII function

Sometimes it is important to know the ASCII code representation of a particular character in a string. $ASCII provides this value, using two arguments, the first giving the string to be searched and the second giving the position of the character to be evaluated. If no second argument is used, the first character in the string is evaluated. The number returned by $ASCII will be a decimal integer between 0 and 127, the range of ASCII character codes. If we have two variables assigned values `XX="ABC123"` and `YY="Q:R!"`, then

Expression Evaluated	Value Produced
`$ASCII("A")`	65
`$ASCII(XX)`	65
`$ASCII(XX,4)`	49
`$ASCII(YY,2)`	58
`$ASCII(YY,4)`	33
`$ASCII("")`	−1

Note: Since all values between 0 and 127 are valid ASCII characters, the number −1 is used to represent the empty string.

The M language is used in many countries, most of which require special characters in addition to the ASCII character set. To accommodate these additional characters, M now provides for the optional use of an additional 128 characters, with the values 128 to 255. Since ASCII characters actually contain 8 bits, this extension remains within the 8-bit ASCII convention, but it permits special definitions of the values 128 to 255 to be adopted for use in languages in which these values are required. Extension of the standard to accommodate non-English languages is covered in greater detail in Part II of this text.

$CHAR function

The $CHAR function performs the inverse of $ASCII; it returns a character at the collating sequence position specified by its argument value. Argument values must be integers less than 128 (or 255 in the extended version) in order to avoid an error. Negative argument values are ignored. For multiple arguments, the characters that correspond to each argument are returned in the same order, as a single string:

Expression Evaluated	Value Produced
`$CHAR(72,73,89,65)`	`HIYA`
`$CHAR(77,65,-40,67,75)`	`MACK`
`$CHAR(-10)`	`""` *(the empty string)*

$TRANSLATE function

In Problem 4 of the exercises at the end of this chapter you will use a combination of $ASCII and $CHAR to convert a character from lowercase to uppercase, a useful function in many situations. However, the M language includes another function that makes this process even easier. $TRANSLATE is a function that provides for automatic conversion of characters according to a user-specified conversion table. Suppose we had a dictionary of terms, and we wanted to see if a variable called MATCH was in the dictionary. Since the variable might consist of a mixture of uppercase and lowercase letters, it would match only if it were converted to the same form as the dictionary, in this case all uppercase letters. In order to perform such a conversion, the following code would suffice:

```
SET MATCH = $TRANSLATE(MATCH,"abcd... (all letters)","ABCD...(all letters)"
```

The first argument is the variable to be transformed, the second is the set of individual characters to be replaced, and the third is the set of replacement characters, *matched in sequence with the characters to be replaced*. The example would convert every lowercase letter to uppercase, and a search could then be made for a dictionary match.

The $TRANSLATE function also can be used to convert several characters to the same character, to delete characters, or to perform other operations on strings. No matter how many times or in what sequence the letters occur in the string, $TRANSLATE will replace every occurrence of a character in argument 2 with its counterpart in argument 3. The following examples illustrate some of these options.

Expression Evaluated	Value Produced
`$TRANSLATE("04-06-51","-","/")`	`04/06/51`
`$TRANSLATE("5,432,111",",","")`	`5432111`
`$TRANSLATE("That %#&! Cat","%#&!","----")`	`That ---- Cat`

The first example illustrates substitution of one character throughout a string of text. The second is an example in which a character is deleted (thereby creating a valid number), and the last shows that multiple characters can be replaced by a single character.

Summary

One of the most powerful features of the M language is its ability to manipulate text information. In this chapter, the principal string operators and functions available in the language are described Among them are the following:

- Operators:
  [Contains (introduced in Chapter 5)
  ] Follows (introduced in Chapter 5)
  _ (underline) Concatenate
- `$LENGTH(string)`: Number of characters in a string
- `$LENGTH(string1,string2)`: Number of occurrences, plus 1, of `string2` in `string1`
- `$FIND(string1,string2)`: Position immediately past the first occurrence of `string2` in `string1`
- `$FIND(string1,string2,integer)`: Position immediately past the first occurrence of `string2` in `string1`, beginning at `integer`
- `$EXTRACT(string)`: The first character in that `string`
- `$EXTRACT(string1,integer)`: The character in `string1` at position `integer`
- `$EXTRACT(string1,integer1,integer2)`: The string of characters occurring in `string1` starting with `integer1` and ending with `integer2`
- `$PIECE(string,delimiter)`: The characters in `string` occurring before `delimiter`
- `$PIECE (string, delimiter, integer)`: The characters after the `integer-1` occurrence and before the `integer` occurrence of the same delimiter.
- `$PIECE (string, delimiter, integer1, integer2)`: The characters between the integer1 and `integer2` occurrences of delimiter in `string`
- `$ASCII(string)`: The code value of the first character in string
- `$ASCII(string,integer)`: The code value of the `integer` character in `string`
- `$CHAR(integer1,integer2, ...)`: The ASCII character represented by codes with values `integer1`, `integer2`, etc.
- `$TRANSLATE(string1,string2,string3)`: Replaces occurrences of characters in `string2` appearing in `string1` with characters in `string3`

Exercises

Now that almost all the string operators and functions have been presented, you should be in a position to solve much more complex problems than could be presented before. In the exercises that follow, you will be challenged to use groups of operators and functions in order to solve everyday string-manipulation problems. You are encouraged to complete these exercises and then to experiment with problems that you have encountered in trying to deal with strings or text. Solutions for these problems are found at the end of the text.

1. ***String Arithmetic*** Given the string:

   `BONMOT="This is the first day of your life as a M programmer"`

   find and WRITE the middle character in the string.

2. ***Some Easy String Modifications***

   a. Create a variable (using SET) called `NAME` with the form `<First MI. Last>` (`MI` being middle initial followed by a period). Then, using only SET, $FIND, and $EXTRACT, create three variables: `FNAME`, containing only the first name; MI, containing only the middle initial; and `LNAME`, containing only the last name (no extra spaces or punctuation). Next, using these variables, create a variable called `LASTFRST` that is the same name in the form `<LNAME, FNAME MI.>` (with punctuation added).

   b. Do the same steps, using $PIECE instead of $EXTRACT and $FIND.

3. Given that the variable `DATE="March 12, 1957"`, convert it to the form `Mar/12/1957`.

4. Use the SET command to store a single lowercase letter in the variable `X`. Then, using $ASCII and $CHAR, write a nested function to convert the letter to its uppercase equivalent. (You may want to study the table of ASCII characters in Chapter 2 to help you with this problem.)

5. Use the SET command to store a long sentence (at least 45 characters long) in the variable `SENTENCE`. Then assuming that you could only fit 30 characters on a line, use SET, $LENGTH, $PIECE to create two variables: `LINE1` with complete words that do not exceed the 30-character limit, and `LINE2`, which contains the remaining string (minus a leading space).

6. Create a form of the $TRANSLATE function that will accept the name of any month in mixed uppercase and lowercase format and convert it to uppercase. Use only those letters occurring in the 12 names of the months.

7. Using $TRANSLATE, convert the string `Richard` into `Dick`.

Introduction to M Commands

7

In the preceding chapters we learned some elements of the *vocabulary* of M, including operators, variables, and a few functions. Implicit in some of the material already covered was some introduction to the *syntax* of the language. Chapter 3 gave you enough information on M syntax to allow you to complete the examples in the early part of this text. In this chapter we will focus more on syntax, considering the concept of an M *command* and how that language element is used with the operators, variables, and functions described in previous sections. At the end of this chapter you will be ready to start writing complete M *statements,* and you will be well on your way to *programming* in M.

What is a command?

Consider the following three English sentences:

1. Stop.
2. Open the door.
3. Put the book on the table.

> **Note to Experienced Programmers:** This chapter covers the rudiments of command structures in M, using assignment and I/O statements (SET, KILL, READ, WRITE) as examples. The material is quite straightforward, although M does attach a syntactical significance to spaces that is not found in most other languages. In addition, the special forms of some of these commands might bear review. The summary at the end of the chapter, together with a review of the exercises, should tell the experienced reader if more detailed review is needed.

Each sentence is a command, telling someone to do something. In speaking to other human beings, we generally soften these kinds of orders by saying, "Please open the door," but when we do so, we introduce some shades of meaning that make the request a little more ambiguous. "Don't Stop!" may take two opposite meanings, depending on whether there is a pause between the two words.

When we tell a computer to do something, we want to be as clear and unambiguous as possible, so we use direct (hence impolite) terms to express our desires. Fortunately, the computer prefers this type of communication, since it would be confused by any other form.

With the exception of "Don't Stop!" the English sentences listed above are unambiguous commands, if we assume that only one door, book, or table is available. The first sentence is only one word long. It is simply a command to do something. In the second case, we are telling someone to do something with something. Finally, in the third sentence, we tell someone to do something involving two objects. We could devise considerably more complex commands but these examples will suffice for the moment.

A computer command is like a direct English command in many respects. Some commands are one word long, such as HALT, which you have already used to stop running the M language. Other commands require the computer to perform some action on one or more elements available at the time. In these latter cases, we say that the command has *arguments.* We have seen the use of arguments in the M functions already introduced. Just like a function, an M command may have no arguments, one argument, or more than one argument. And, just like functions, when multiple arguments are present, they are separated by commas.

M also uses spaces in a specific syntactical form that sometimes causes programmers (even experienced ones) some confusion. Here are the special rules governing the use of spaces in M commands:

1. An M command must be separated from its arguments, if any, by one and only one space (as noted earlier in the use of the SET command).
2. There can be no spaces within or between arguments (unless they are part of a quoted string).

In general, these rules are not troublesome, but as noted in some of the early examples in this text, they will generate syntax errors if they are not followed precisely. (One further rule relating to the use of spaces is explained in the next chapter, when we look at the structure of a command line.)

Although you have become used to the idea of the SET and WRITE commands introduced in earlier chapters, the material in this chapter shows you how to make much more creative use of these and other sample commands, setting the stage for actual programming.

SET command

In earlier chapters we saw that the SET command can be used to create variables and assign values to them. The exact syntactical form that we used was

```
SET <space> variable=expression
```

(no spaces allowed after the start of variable unless embedded in quotes)

This is the simplest form of the SET command, and it typifies M commands in general. The space (only one) is required, and no spaces can occur between the variable name and the equals sign or following the equals sign in the expression. Let us consider for a moment what M actually does when it sees a SET command. First, it recognizes that the command is the one called SET. Next, it evaluates the expression to the right of the equals sign to obtain a value. It then identifies the variable to which a value is to be assigned (the characters after the space and before the equals sign) and looks in the user's workspace (the portion of the computer's memory assigned to that user) to see if a variable of that name already exists. If none exists, it creates one, and then *assigns* it the value determined by the expression following the equals sign. However, if the variable already exists, M will *replace* the previous value with the new value.

The concept of variable names and contents can be likened to mailboxes. Each mailbox (variable) has a *name* on the outside, and *contents* (value) inside. The contents can change without having to change the name of the mailbox. There can be any number of mailboxes (limited only by computer memory restrictions) in an M session.

Consider the following statements:

```
SET X=3
SET Y=X+7
SET X=X*Y
SET X=X/Z (an invalid expression, since Z is not defined)
```

In the first case (assuming we started with no previous M statements), M creates a variable named X and gives it the value 3. The second line uses that value for X plus the constant 7 to form an expression, the value of which (10) is assigned to a (new) variable Y. In the following line, the expression X*Y is evaluated to produce the value 30. This value is then assigned to X, erasing the previous value (now you can see why the expression must be evaluated before it is assigned to a variable). In the final case, M would try to evaluate the expression X/Z and fail, since Z does not yet exist, and an error message would be displayed.

So far, other than knowing a little more about *how* M uses the SET command, we have presented nothing new. However, there are several additional forms of the SET command that make programming easier in many cases. One variation allows a programmer to assign the same value to several variables in one assignment statement. For example,

```
SET (X,Y,Z)=20
```

would assign the value 20 to each of the variables X, Y, and Z. Another option available allows several different variables to be defined without using multiple SET statements. The form of this variation is

```
SET X=5,Y=2,Z=X*Y,W=X>Y
```
(again, no spaces after the first X)

(The value of W=X>Y will be a truth value TRUE : 1, since X is greater than Y.) You can see at once that we could have written earlier exercises more concisely if we had used this form of SET instead of the multiple-line alternative:

```
SET X=5
SET Y=2
SET Z=X*Y
SET W=X>Y
```

Notice, too, that each value is immediately available for use in the next part of the multiple SET statement, so that it is perfectly all right to use X and Y in the last two assignments. In the last example, the value assigned to W is the logical result of the expression X>Y (1). In general, most M commands (including the WRITE command we used before) allow multiple expressions of this type.

SET $PIECE and SET $EXTRACT

The SET command may be combined with the $PIECE function to permit an interesting and somewhat more complex form of an assignment statement. The $PIECE function is usually employed to *retrieve* a value from an existing variable. However, in conjunction with the SET command, it also can be used to *assign* a value to a portion of a variable (even if that variable does not yet exist). To illustrate the value of this command, let us assume that we type in the following statement:

```
SET M="JAN/FEB/MR/APR/MAY/JUN/JUL/AUG/SEP/OCT/NOV/DEC"
```

Looking back at our handiwork, we see that we managed to misspell the abbreviation for March (an all-too-common event in the life of many programmers). Although the string-replacement functions in M are powerful, it is not all that easy to correct this line. The commands used to make the correction might be

```
SET A=$PIECE(M,"/",1,2),B=$PIECE(M,"/",4,12)
SET C="/MAR/",M=A_C_B
```

A typist who had trouble with the first line of text would in all probability have some difficulty entering these commands in an error-free fashion, and frustration might result. Using the SET $PIECE command, however, one could type

```
SET $PIECE(M,"/",3)="MAR"
```

which is not only much shorter, but is clearer and more explicit, avoiding the possibility of errors in the more complex approach. The result would be replacement of the third piece of M with `MAR`, and the remainder of the value would be unchanged.

SET $PIECE also can be used even if a variable does not yet exist. Suppose we use a special format to store an address, where the delimiter "^" separates strings that represent street address, city, state, and ZIP code (all stored in one variable, a common M convention). If we only know one element (the ZIP code) in a person's address, we might write the command

```
SET $PIECE(ADDR,"^",4) = 85718
```

The result would be that `ADDR` would now consist of the string ^^^85718 with the delimiters inserted to ensure that the ZIP code is placed at the proper piece of that combined variable. In this case, even though the variable did not exist before, it would be possible to store partial information pending collection of the other data items.

The same principle applies to SET $EXTRACT, which will replace a given character or set of characters in a string, or create a new variable padded with blanks to fulfill the specifications. Here are some examples (assume that `INIT="RFW"`):

Command	**Value Produced**
`SET $EXTRACT(INIT,2)="P"`	`RPW` *(my father's initials)*
	`DTW` *(my son's initials)*
`SET $EXTRACT(INIT,5,11)="RFW DTW"`	`RPW`<sp>`RFW`<sp>`DTW` *(add my son)*
`SET $EXTRACT(X,3,7)="Hello"`	<sp><sp>`Hello`

In the third example, since the new value begins with the fifth character, a space is added after the existing value so as to place the new string in its proper location. In the final example, two spaces precede the new string in a variable that did not previously exist.

KILL command

Once a variable has been defined using the SET command, it may be removed from the list of variable names and their values by using the KILL command. Like SET, KILL may be used in several ways. When used with a single argument, KILL removes that variable and its value from the list of values available to the programmer. KILL followed by two or more arguments removes each of the variables specified. Finally, KILL used without any arguments removes all of the variables available at the time. Thus

Code Executed	Effect Produced
`KILL A`	Variable `A` and its value are deleted.
`KILL B,C`	Variables `B` and `C` are deleted.
`KILL`	All variables are deleted.

Note: The last example erases *all* variables in the user's workspace. This is a potentially dangerous command, but it is useful in cases where the programmer wants to start a new problem with a clean slate.

Another form of the KILL command provides a comparable ability to clean up all unwanted variables, yet retain those which will be needed in the next problem. This version makes use of *parentheses,* as shown in these examples:

Code executed	Effect produced
`KILL (A)`	All variables except `A` are deleted.
`KILL (B,C)`	All variables except `B` and `C` are deleted.

Note: The last example is not a multiple-expression form (outside parentheses), and it is therefore not the same as `KILL (B),(C)`, which would delete all variables, since the first would erase all variables except `B` and the second would attempt to erase all variables except `C`, which has already been erased.

WRITE command (with format controls)

So far in this chapter we have learned how to create and erase variables with SET and KILL. As we saw in earlier chapters it is also possible to display the value of a variable using the WRITE command. As with SET, WRITE has several additional forms that provide us much more flexibility. The version we have used to date consists of writing out the value of a constant, variable, or the results of an expression, such as `WRITE NAME` or `WRITE 3*2`. WRITE also permits multiple expressions, including string literals that are not defined as variables. Suppose, for example, that we want to print on one line a person's name and date of birth, stored in the variables NAME and DOB respectively. The simplest WRITE command to perform this function would be

```
WRITE NAME," ",DOB
```

A more elegantly formatted version might be

```
WRITE "Name: ",NAME," Date of Birth: ",DOB
```

This example illustrates that variables and string literals can be mixed to create more pleasing forms of output. There are, in addition, other variations of the WRITE command that allow the user to specify *where* to place the WRITE message on the terminal's screen or page. The control character "!" appearing by itself (without quotation marks) in a WRITE statement will cause the remainder of the message to be printed at the start of the next line. Thus,

```
WRITE "Hello",!,"My name is ",NAME
```

will produce two lines of output, the second beginning with `My name is` and then concluding with the value assigned to the variable NAME.

Similarly, one can use the special character # to move to a new page on printed output or the top of the screen on a CRT terminal. Finally, the special character "?", followed by an integer, will position the message starting at the column specified by the integer. The command

```
WRITE #!!,"CLIENT",?10,NAME
```

executed on a CRT terminal will clear the screen, move the cursor to the top left position on the screen (invoked by #), drop down two lines (invoked by !!), write the word CLIENT, and then skip to column 10 and enter the current value of the variable NAME.

> **Note:** Commas are necessary between different expressions in WRITE statements, but they are not required when several format characters are used together (such as the #!! in the preceding example).

There is one final version of the WRITE command which, while not actually a part of the M standard, is used in many M implementations. This form of WRITE has no arguments, and it results in the M system displaying the names and values of all variables in the user's workspace. It is useful in debugging M statements, since the programmer may not remember all the variables that have been created. Examples of its use are given in the exercises at the end of this chapter.

$JUSTIFY function

The question mark format control character allows programmers in M to write a variable or string of text starting at a specified column. However, it is sometimes important to do more sophisticated page layouts, making certain that variables will fit on a given line or page and lining up columns of numbers or other values so that they are right-justified or otherwise consistent. M provides several additional aids to programmers to accomplish these tasks. The first of them is $JUSTIFY, which is used to perform right justification and adjust for uniform decimal point position in numbers.

The two-argument form of $JUSTIFY takes a variable as the first argument and the space it should occupy in an output line as the second argument. Suppose we have two variables, `X=186` and `Y=20`. Although we could work with $LENGTH to determine the size of each such variable, it is more convenient to use $JUSTIFY to make certain that each number is right-justified and properly aligned. The expressions that follow would line these numbers up right-justified on column 20 of a page:

Expression	**Output**
`WRITE !?10,$JUSTIFY(X,10)`	186
`WRITE !?10,$JUSTIFY(Y,10)`	20

$JUSTIFY(X,L) pads the string expression X on the left with spaces to a total length of L. If X is longer than L, the full value of X is returned, i.e., no information is lost.

A convenient way to create a string of 10 spaces would be

```
SET SPACES=$JUSTIFY(" ",10)
```

We could then use this variable in other output as follows:

```
WRITE !,NAME,SPACES,AGE,SPACES,SSN
```

thus avoiding the necessity of embedding 10 spaces between each variable.

The $JUSTIFY function also can be used to right-justify text strings, but its greatest use is with numbers. In the case of decimal values, a three-argument form of $JUSTIFY is used. `$JUSTIFY(X,10,2)` takes the numeric interpretation of `X`, rounds it to two decimal places, and pads the result to 10 characters. If required, $JUSTIFY provides the necessary rounding operation to fit the decimal portion of the number in the space available. The third argument of $JUSTIFY must be non-negative (a value of zero specifies that the number will be rounded to a whole number).

The following examples illustrate some uses of $JUSTIFY.

Expression	Output
`$JUSTIFY(3.716,10,0)`	`4`
`$JUSTIFY(.3716,4,2)`	`0.37`
`$JUSTIFY(3.716,10,1)`	`3.7`
`$JUSTIFY(3.716,4,2)`	`3.72`
`$JUSTIFY(3.716,10,4)`	`3.7160`
`$JUSTIFY(7,0,3)`	`7.000`

Note: In the case of a fraction less than 1, a leading zero is appended. Moreover, unlike the integer divide operator, $JUSTIFY rounds a number rather than truncating it. The output value 3.72 in the fourth example above illustrates this feature of the $JUSTIFY command.

$FNUMBER function

Although $JUSTIFY provides useful functionality in output format, especially of numbers, it does not fulfill all functionality required in common numeric output. Accordingly, the 1990 revision of the M standard included the new function $FNUMBER, which, together with $JUSTIFY, completes the most common output requirements of conventional numeric reports.

Presentation of numeric data often requires some special formats that have been adopted by convention to enhance the readability of long lists of numbers. One of the most important aids to readability is the inclusion of commas in long numbers. For instance, at this moment, the US national debt is in the range of three trillion dollars (give or take a trillion), or $3000000000000. This number, horrendous as it is, is not easy to read without the helpful commas that render it $3,000,000,000,000. $FNUMBER has a format option that specifies inclusion of commas for numbers with values greater than 1,000. If we had a variable `USDEBT` with the value $3 trillion, we could write the number with commas as follows:

```
WRITE $FNUMBER(USDEBT,",",0)
```

which specifies that the number is to be written without decimal values and with commas between groups of three digits for numbers greater than 1,000.

This function also provides for a number of other options which can sometimes be used in combination. The format functions available are as follows:

,	Put commas in long numbers.
+	Add a plus sign (+) to positive numbers.
–	Suppress the minus sign on negative numbers.
T	Place the sign (+ or –) at the end of the number.
P	Put negative numbers in parentheses.
<nn>	print <nn> digits after the decimal point

To illustrate some of the functionality of $FNUMBER, suppose we wish to maintain a balance sheet for a petty cash account in a small office. The following commands (excluding updating arithmetic statements) would generate output as shown:

M Command	Changes	Balance
`WRITE !?60,"$",$FNUMBER(CUR,"P",2)`		$11.53
`WRITE $FNUMBER(POSTAGE,"T",2)`	9.75–	
`WRITE !?60,$FNUMBER(CUR,"P",2)`		1.78
`WRITE $FNUMBER(COFFEE,"T",2)`	6.39–	
`WRITE !?60,$FNUMBER(CUR,"P",2)`		(4.61)
`WRITE $FNUMBER(KEYDEPOS,"T",2)`	3.00+	
`WRITE !?60,$FNUMBER(CUR,"P",2)`		(1.61)
`WRITE $FNUMBER(ADDIT,"T",2)`	25.00+	
`WRITE !?60,$FNUMBER(CUR,"P",2)`		23.39

This example includes a number of formats commonly used in ledger sheets and illustrates the versatility of the $FNUMBER function. Although it is possible to write M code that would accomplish these tasks, the code would be complicated, and the functionality of these format instructions is an important addition to the usefulness of the M language in accounting applications.

$FNUMBER also can be combined with $JUSTIFY to produce completely formatted output lines. Consider the need to report on current and cumulative salary, with the two figures appearing on one line. For example, consider the following command line:

```
WRITE $JUSTIFY($FNUMBER(SAL,",",2),10,2),$JUSTIFY($FNUMBER(CUM,",",2),25,2)
```

The preceding command will produce the following output line:

```
4,006.75    32,054.00
```

with the values right-justified as indicated and the appropriate formatting commas included in the output. There are many variations on the output combinations available through the use of $JUSTIFY and $FNUMBER, but these examples should suffice to illustrate their versatility.

$X and $Y special variables used with WRITE and SET commands

Another useful tool provided by the M language gives the user some feedback on the current position of the printing element or cursor on a line. Sometimes the user will not know beforehand exactly how long some variable such as NAME may be at output time. In this case, it would be nice, for cosmetically acceptable output, to calculate the position of the printing element so as to adjust accordingly. Two *special variables,* $X and $Y, are provided by M to give the user this information. $X indicates the position of the cursor or printing element on the current line of text, and $Y indicates the number of lines down from the top of the screen or page. With these two special variables available to us, it is possible to generate a neat output line even when variables take on different lengths. These two variables are automatically updated each time a character is written to the output device. When the format character '!' appears in a WRITE statement, $Y is incremented by 1 and $X is reset to 0. The exercises at the end of this chapter will illustrate some ways in which $X and $Y can be displayed.

A recent addition (in the 1995 M Standard) to the functionality of $X and $Y is the ability to use the SET command to adjust the values of these special variables. In designing a form to appear on a screen, for example, it might be useful to specify the precise location of a user prompt. This could be done by the following lines:

```
SET $Y=12,$X=20
WRITE "SSN: "
```

and the prompt for Social Security Number would appear beginning in column 20 of line 12. This opens up a whole new area of programming for windows, a subject that is treated in more detail in Part II of this text.

In addition to the formatting features just described, M offers some more sophisticated output functions associated with the WRITE command. These features are described in Chapters 13 and 14, which present advanced input and output characteristics of the M language, and in Part II, which deals with graphic control of windows systems.

READ command

Up to this point, we have introduced only one way in which variables may be created and assigned values – the SET command. However, it is often necessary in writing a program to request that a value be entered from the terminal as the program is executing. The M READ statement is the way in which keyboard entries can be accepted and assigned to variables. In its simplest form, READ with one argument will take a value typed by a user and store it, as in

```
READ X
```

When the user types in a value for X and presses the <*enter*> key, the variable X is created and whatever value was typed in is assigned to that variable.

There is a problem with this form of the READ statement: It does not tell the user what information is requested. For example, a series of READ statements might ask for NAME, AGE, and SEX, but the user would not know the sequence in which these variables were requested. To clarify this ambiguity, M allows prompts to be embedded in a READ statement, using the same formats as described earlier in the WRITE command. The following example illustrates a READ command with appropriate prompts:

```
READ !,"AGE= ",AGE,!,"DATE OF BIRTH (MM/DD/YY)= ",DOB
```

In this example, two variables are created, with each request appearing on a new line. Notice that the statements have a space after the prompt message in order to separate the prompt from the user input. In our example, the display device would advance one line, output the first message, wait for input for AGE from the user, and then advance another line and print the second message before awaiting input for the variable `DOB`.

These examples of the READ command provide sufficient flexibility to cover most input requirements. There are some more advanced input techniques available in M, but their description is deferred until Chapter 14.

Abbreviated forms of commands

M allows two ways of writing each command or function. The first is to write the entire word, such as SET, KILL, WRITE, READ, and so on. The second method is to write only the first letter of the command or the first two letters of functions. The commands and functions we have considered thus far may therefore be abbreviated as follows:

Command	Abbreviation
KILL	K
READ	R
SET	S
WRITE	W
$ASCII	$A
$CHAR	$C
$EXTRACT	$E
$FIND	$F
$LENGTH	$L
$PIECE	$P
$RANDOM	$R
$TRANSLATE	$TR

In the case of the function $TRANSLATE, it is necessary to use the first three characters ($TR), since another function, $TEXT, is also defined in the M standard (see Chapter 14).

Examples of the use of abbreviated commands are

```
R "Please enter today's date: ",DAT
W !!,"TODAY'S DATE IS ",?20,DAT
S A=3,B=A#2,C=A+1,R="XYZ"
```

Note: In their abbreviated form, single-letter commands may look like single-letter variables. The R in the last line above, for example, is a variable, not a command. M can make these distinctions by the syntactical position of the abbreviated command in context. Programmers often prefer to use single-letter commands because it is faster, and with very little practice, the code is easily read. In this text, however, we will stick to the full spelling of commands so as to minimize confusion.

Summary

M commands consist of the command name (or a single-letter abbreviation thereof) followed in some cases by a space and one or more arguments without separating spaces. The commands introduced in this chapter are as follows:

- ```
  SET var=expression[,var=expression . . .]
  SET (var,var . . .)=expression
  SET $PIECE(var,delim,integer)=expression
  SET $EXTRACT(var,start,end)=expression
  ```
  ```

- `KILL var[,var . . .]` removes named variables.
  `KILL (var[,var . . .])` removes all *except* named variables.
  `KILL (no arguments)` removes all variables in user workspace.
- `WRITE "string"` outputs `string` to display device.
  `WRITE var` outputs `var` to display device.
  `WRITE <format|var|string>[,< format|var|string> . . .]`

  Note: Format|var|string stands for format, var OR string. Compound write format controls for WRITE and READ are:

`!`	New line
`#`	New page/screen
`?nn`	Move to column `nn`

- `WRITE (no arguments)`: Nonstandard method of displaying variables.
- `$JUSTIFY(var,width)` right-justifies `var` to `width`.
- `$JUSTIFY(var,width,integer)` right-justifies `var` to `width` with `integer` decimals.
- `$X,$Y`: current position of cursor/print element in column `$X`, row `$Y`.
- `$FNUMBER(var,format,integer)` provides for increased flexibility of formatted output. The use of `integer` is similar to `$JUSTIFY`. Format controls (which may be multiple) include:

,	Put commas in long numbers.
+	Add a plus sign to positive numbers.
–	Suppress the minus sign on negative numbers.
`T`	Place the sign (+ or –) at the end of the number.
`P`	Put negative numbers in parentheses.
`<nn>`	Display `<nn>` digits after the decimal point.

- `READ var` obtains input from keyboard and assigns value to `var`.
  `READ "string",var[. . .]` issues prompt before obtaining user input.

  Note: M commands may be abbreviated to single-letter forms (e.g., S for SET), and functions may be abbreviated to double-letter forms (e.g., $P for $PIECE).

Exercises

With a formal introduction to commands, the reader should now be in a position to perform many complex operations typical of computer programs. These exercises are intended only to provide a brief introduction to some of the rich variety of options opened up by these commands. The reader is encouraged to explore other variations based on these exercises. Solutions for

Exercises 2 to 4 are found in the back of the book.

1. ***SET, KILL, and WRITE (with No Arguments)*** This exercise uses the nonstandard form of WRITE to determine what variables exist in the user's workspace. This version of the WRITE command exists in most M implementations. If your version does not have this feature, you may wish to find out how to display the names and/or values of variables in your user workspace on that implementation.

   a. Type in the lines listed below, and see what values are assigned to the variables by using the WRITE command.

   ```
   SET (A1,A2,A3)="86"
   WRITE
   KILL A2
   WRITE
   SET X=A1,Y="Hello",Z=Y_", old "_A1
   WRITE
   KILL△(Z)
   WRITE
   KILL
   WRITE
   ```

   b. Experiment with these variations until you understand the differences between the different versions of SET and KILL.

2. ***SET $PIECE, $EXTRACT, and READ with Prompt*** Write a series of M commands that will prompt the user to enter MONTH, DAY, and YEAR in a format that you specify in a prompt message. Then, using SET $PIECE, assign each value to the first, second, and third delimited portions of DATE, using "/" as the delimiter. Use SET $EXTRACT to modify the year.

3. ***Formatted WRITE Statements***

   a. Use a READ with a prompt to create a variable `GOODWORD` as user input. Assuming that you have an 80-column screen, write the value of this variable centered on the screen. (You will need to use some of the operators and functions described in previous chapters to accomplish this task.)

   b. Prompt the user to enter a title for a paper, storing it in `TITLE`. Set `PAGE` equal to some page number, and then write a header for a page that consists of the title on the left-hand side of a line and the page number at the far right of the same line. (Assume your page is 80 characters wide.)

4. ***$JUSTIFY*** Create five numeric variables named `N1`, `N2`, `N3`, `N4`, and `N5` using READ with appropriate prompts. Each number should contain

decimal fractions. Print them in a column rounded to two decimals and right-justified on column 40 of your screen.

5. ***$X, $Y, and WRITE*** In this exercise, you will get some values for $X and $Y. However, each one will represent the value *at the time the value was requested,* and each time a new line is issued by M, the values will change. Try some of these examples, to see what values you get.

```
READ !,"What do you think of M now? ",COMMENT
WRITE !!,COMMENT,$X," ",$Y
WRITE $X," ",$Y   (Note that the values are no longer the same.)
WRITE !!!?10$X,$X,$X (The values will run together.)
WRITE !,"The length of your comment is ",$LENGTH(COMMENT)," ",$X
WRITE #,$X,$Y     (Did your screen clear before displaying the values?)
```

See how many times you can write COMMENT (as you entered it) on one line without running out of space by checking $X after writing it once, twice, and so on. As you do so, you will probably realize that it would be nice to check this value and then go to a new line when it gets beyond a certain limit. This feature of M is introduced in the next chapter.

Command Lines and Conditional Tests 8

Chapter 7 introduced the concept of *syntax* in the form of single commands. In that chapter you learned how to write one M command properly, using variables and operators. At this point, your level of expertise has progressed to that of first-grade texts, where each sentence begins on a new line.

In this chapter we extend the concept of commands to permit the inclusion of several commands on one line. We will also start to look at some commands that interact with others, thereby increasing our ability to form more expressive instructions, such as those which may or may not be executed.

Format of a command line

So far you have learned how to take the "nouns" and "verbs" of the M language and to construct statements with the vocabulary already introduced. Next, we will turn our attention to the creation of groups of statements (commands) that link together to perform useful functions.

> **Note to experienced programmers:** This chapter discusses the format of command lines, and it presents three forms of conditional tests ($SELECT, postconditional expressions with commands and arguments, and the IF and ELSE commands). The conditional tests warrant special study, since they differ in important respects from conventions in other languages. The remainder of the chapter material should be straightforward, requiring only a review of the Summary.

The basic unit of an executable M program is a *command line.* This unit, in turn, is made up of the elements introduced in previous chapters: *commands* syntactically linking *variables, operators,* and *functions.* In addition, a command line may contain other elements (*labels* and *comments*) for procedural or clarification purposes. A command line may consist of a single command; the examples in the preceding chapter were valid command lines. However, a command line also may combine multiple commands. The length of a command line is limited not by the physical length of a line of text on a terminal, but by the M limitation of 255 characters to a string (since command lines are stored as strings).

In the exercises at the end of each of the preceding chapters, you learned to type M commands and see the results immediately. This mode of operation is referred to as *direct-mode execution.* Sometimes, however, it is desirable to create a set of commands that can be stored as a program and executed at a later time. In this way of using the M language, sometimes referred to as the *programming mode,* the commands are not immediately executed, but instead they are stored in the user's workspace in a form that will eventually be saved as a M *routine.*

The way in which M recognizes that what a user has typed is to be treated as a programming-mode entry is through a character known as a *linestart.* In most systems, the linestart is a <*tab*> key; readers should verify this element by checking their own implementation manual. The linestart must be present in any command line that is to become part of a program. Command lines that will be executed directly need not have a linestart. We will describe command lines in the programming mode so that readers will recognize command lines in M programs. In this chapter, we will omit the linestart in most of the examples.

A command line may contain, in addition to the linestart character, three different components: a *label,* one or more *commands,* and *comments.* Any (but not all) of these elements may be missing in a command line. A line that contains only comments (no commands) may be used for procedural or documentation purposes or even to improve readability of the code. The following is an example of a command line that contains all essential and optional elements for programming mode:

```
SSNO<tab>READ !,"Enter your Soc Sec No (nnn-nn-nnnn):",SSN ;get ID
```

A *label* is a name appended to the beginning of a line for reference purposes. Labels may either follow the rules for names of variables (i.e., begin with % sign or alpha character and be followed by alphanumerics), or they may be integers. Real numbers are not permitted as labels. Since a label must uniquely identify a specific command line, provision must be made to ensure that duplicate labels do not occur within a single M routine. The maximum length of a label is eight characters; additional characters will be ignored in determining the uniqueness of the label. A command line may have only one label (and that one is optional); the label, if present, must occur at the beginning of the line.

The only required part of a command line in programming mode is the linestart character This character (a tab in many implementations, a space in some others) separates the label field from the rest of the command line. Commands, if they are present, follow the linestart character. Comments may also occur after a linestart character or after the last command of a command line. A *comment* consists of a semicolon (;) followed by any free text the programmer wishes to add to help the reader understand the purpose of the command line. This feature permits internal documentation of M code so that its purpose and relationship to other blocks of instructions can be clarified. When the M interpreter encounters a semicolon, it will automatically ignore the remainder of that line. Therefore, a comment must always be at the end of any command line on which it appears. Sometimes programmers will write lines that consist only of comments or even just a semicolon to enhance program readability.

To illustrate the concept of a command line, let us consider a few examples. First, let us examine the following line:

```
START<tab>READ "ENTER WEIGHT (LBS): ",L SET K=L/2.2 WRITE K," KILOS"
```

This command line contains a label and three separate commands. The first command requests the user to enter his or her weight in pounds. It then calculates the equivalent weight in kilograms and finally prints out a message to verify the accuracy of that calculation. Notice that the line begins with a label followed by a single space or tab. Note also that single spaces separate the individual commands (commas have a different meaning in M syntax and cannot be used for this purpose). As presented, this command line is a complete miniature program, with input, calculation, and output.

> **Note:** Remember that a "line" may extend over more than one physical line of text, provided that the 255-character limit is not exceeded.

In the preceding chapter we cautioned about the significance of spaces within commands. It is now time to introduce two more rules affecting the use of spaces. In Chapter 7 we noted the following rules:

1. An M command must be separated from its arguments, if any, by one (and only one) space.
2. There can be no spaces within or between arguments (unless they are a part of a quoted string).

To these two rules, we add the following:

3. If an M command has no argument, then there must be *two spaces* between that command and the next command or comment on a command line.
4. M commands may be separated from each other by more than one space (for readability purposes).

Of these rules, the requirement for two spaces after a command such as ELSE or KILL (with no arguments) causes the most difficulties in writing programs. Later in this chapter we will examine several other commands that may (or must) be written without arguments, and we will again emphasize this point.

Another major point to bear in mind with respect to command lines is their left-to-right execution. The example given above would make no sense if this sequence were not followed, and as one might expect, all command lines are processed from left to right, just as the M operators are evaluated from left to right.

There are times, however, when a programmer may want to exercise some choice in the execution of a command The options permitting conditional execution are described in the next section.

Conditional execution of commands: introduction

One of the brilliant concepts developed early in the evolution of programmable computers is the concept of a *test* followed by a *conditional branch* in program execution depending on whether the test proves true or false. We have seen a number of operators and expressions that return values of TRUE or FALSE, but so far we have not described how a programmer might take advantage of these results.

A typical English conditional statement is "If it looks like rain, I'll take my umbrella." The implication is that the umbrella gets left behind if it does not look like rain (this may be a dangerous assumption in England, but it works pretty well in California). In computer programs, there are likewise many times when it is useful to say "If a condition exists, do the following."

Conditional execution can be accomplished in three ways in the syntax of the M language: through the use of the $SELECT function, using *postconditional expressions* following certain commands or their arguments, and using IF and ELSE. Each of these options is described separately.

$SELECT function

The $SELECT function selects, from a list of expressions, a single expression that is evaluated and whose value is returned. The evaluation of the expression is, like everything else in M, from left to right, and the *first* true expression is selected, ignoring all subsequent options. An optional expression at the end of the $SELECT function may be defined to accept any condition other than those previously described. Consider the problem of assigning grades to students taking a course with numeric exam results. The following statement will take care of all conditions, assuming TST is the test score:

```
SET GRADE=$SELECT(TST>89.5:"A",TST>79.5:"B",TST>69.5:"C",TST>59.5:"D",1:"F")
```

The value for TST will be checked against the expressions, one at a time, from left to right. If the value of TST is greater than 89.5, M stops there, assigns the grade of A, and no further checking is done. If it is lower than 89.5, M goes on to check the next option, and so on down the line. At the end of the list, the expression 1:"F" means that if all previous tests fail, then assign the grade F. Hence, anyone with a grade lower than 59.5 automatically receives an F grade. This final option is defined by the value 1 followed by a colon. It stands for "otherwise ..."

The $SELECT function must always have at least one true case or an error will result. When a situation arises in which the computer cannot do what it has been ordered to, the M system will indicate that an error has occurred. It always assumes (in its superior way) that the error is the fault of the programmer, and most implementations try to help him find the error with some message that gives a hint as to the type of error encountered. Error messages vary from one system to another, but it is nice to know that the computer is looking out for us and that it will point out those errors which prevent it from doing what we ask (even if these messages sometimes appear at embarrassing moments).

Let us examine a few additional examples of use of the $SELECT function. Again, let A=1, B=2, and C=3.

Code Executed	Result
SET RESULT=$SELECT(A>B:1,A>C:2,A<B:3)	3
SET RESULT=$SELECT(A=B:1,B=C:2,A=C:3)	Error
SET RESULT=$SELECT(A=B:2*C,A=C:A+B,1:0)	0
SET RESULT=$SELECT(A>B:A,A<B:C,A<C:B)	3 *(value of C)*
SET RESULT=$SELECT(A=C:"LB1",A<C:"LB2",1:"LB3")	LB2

Note: In the fourth example, two true cases are present. $SELECT chooses the first true expression as it proceeds from left to right.

Postconditionals on commands

In the $SELECT example, we saw that M chooses one assignment statement from a list of options provided by the programmer, depending on the value of the variables at the time of execution. Sometimes, however, it may be useful to avoid completely the execution of a command (an option not available with the $SELECT function). M provides the programmer with the capability of conditionally executing a command based on an expression that may be evaluated as either true or false. This operation is called a *postconditional.* If you were writing a program to simulate a blackjack game, you might assign any hand with a COUNT of 21 points the value of "BLACKJAK". To do so in M, one would write the command:

```
SET:COUNT=21 SCORE="BLACKJAK"
```

The added characters :COUNT=21 constitute the postconditional; the colon (:) indicates the presence of a postconditional expression, and COUNT=21 is the expression itself. When the command is executed, M detects the presence of the postconditional and suspends execution of the SET command temporarily until it has evaluated the postconditional expression. The SET command would be executed only if COUNT was exactly 21; otherwise, the statement would be ignored and execution would proceed to the next command or command line. The postconditional variation of the SET command also can be used in the multiple form:

```
SET:AGE>21 VOTEAGE="OK",DRINKAGE="OK"
```

or

```
SET:AGE>21 (VOTEAGE,DRINKAGE)="OK"
```

(In some states, these values could be true at lower ages, but the logic would be the same.)

The postconditional expression may be more complex than in the preceding example. It may in fact be any legitimate M expression. Postconditionals may be applied to all but three M commands: IF, ELSE, and FOR (covered in the next chapter). Combined with the WRITE command, postconditionals give flexibility in output depending on the circumstances specified. As one example, suppose you wish to process a large data set, monitoring progress as you go along. One way to monitor progress would be to write an output statement each time a data element had been processed. This approach would probably tell you more than you wanted to know, generating voluminous output on the terminal screen or printer. A better way might be to have the program write a message each time it had processed, say, 100 items. The output would be reduced a hundredfold, giving you adequate information about the processing without excessive output. If the number of items processed is defined by incrementing a variable N, the following command, inserted after N has been incremented, would generate the desired output every hundred iterations:

```
WRITE:(N#100=0) !,N," Items processed."
```

In this case, we also could use another form without the equals sign in the postconditional:

```
WRITE:'(N#100) !,N," Items processed."
```

Any value of the expression N#100 other than zero would be turned into a false statement by the NOT operator ('), and the statement would execute only once every 100 iterations. (We will see how to create such iterations in Chapter 9.)

Another variation on the use of postconditionals is their use in conjunction with arguments to certain commands. Since these commands have not yet been introduced, we will defer discussion of this form until the next chapter.

IF command and $TEST special variable

The third way in which to provide optional execution of a command line is by use of the IF command. This approach looks more like the umbrella-toting example described earlier. We used the word *IF* to describe the condition that must be fulfilled. M uses the IF command in the same manner. The syntax of the M IF command is of the form `IF <expression> <command line>`. In M, the range of the IF command is the rest of the command line to the right of the IF. For example, assume that we wish to perform a credit check on a transaction, where BALANCE is the current credit available on an account and DEBIT is the amount to be charged. One way of performing this verification would be as follows:

```
IF DEBIT<BALANCE SET AUTHORIZ="OK"
```

The value of AUTHORIZ could then be used in multiple other transactions required to transfer the funds from one account to the other. Upon execution of this command line, M will first determine whether the argument of the IF command is true. If the statement is true, AUTHORIZ is set to "OK" and other statements can use this information. To take another example, suppose we want to find the maximum of a set of numbers. If X=17 and Y=33, we might write the command line

```
IF X<Y SET X=Y WRITE "X has been reset to: ",Y
```

The IF argument in this case evaluates as TRUE and the SET and WRITE statements are executed. Remember that IF affects only commands that follow it on the same command line. Other commands on other command lines are not affected. The IF command does, however, change the special variable, $TEST.

There is one effect of the IF command that will happen whether or not the remainder of the command line is executed. Upon evaluation of an IF argument, $TEST is set to 0 or 1, depending on whether the argument evaluates as FALSE (0) or TRUE (1). $TEST is useful in extending the scope of the IF argument evaluation. Suppose that we have a number of actions to take depending on the truth evaluation of an IF argument. If these actions cannot all be placed on one command line, then without the $TEST special variable it would be necessary to repeat the IF argument on each successive command line. Consider the following example, which might be used in an interactive fictitious survey:

```
IF CITY="Hanover",ST="NH",OCCUP="Stud" WRITE !,"To a Dartmouth
...student:"
IF  WRITE !,"We would like to ask you a few questions."
IF  READ !,"What is your academic major ",MAJ
IF  READ !,"Do you live in a Dormitory? (Y/N): ",YESNO
IF  READ !,"How many miles from Hanover is your home?",MILES
```

(Notice the *two* spaces after the initial IF command on all but the first line.) In this example, the IF argument in the first line is tested, found to be true, and $TEST is set to 1 accordingly. Then the remainder of that line is executed. The use of commas between the expressions in the IF statement is equivalent to saying `IF CITY="Hanover"&(ST="NH")`, and so on, but it avoids the need to use parentheses. However, if *any* of the tests proved to be false, the WRITE statement would not be executed. Since the length of this IF command is rather long, it would be difficult to have to retype the same test for every question asked on subsequent lines. Therefore, the alternate form of IF is used, in which the IF command is followed by two spaces. The second space signifies the use of an IF without any arguments ("argumentless IF"). In this situation, M will examine the value of $TEST (set TRUE on the previous line) and, finding it true, will execute the remainder of the command line. Similarly, the next three lines also will be executed. This is a good example of the sensitivity of M to spaces within commands. If only one space were used, M would assume that the next word (e.g., WRITE on the second line) was a variable, not a command. However, it would be permissible to use *more* than two spaces after the IF to indicate more visibly the separation of the IF and the WRITE commands.

Note: $TEST is reset each time a conditional command is executed, in which case the action taken on the IF statement may not be the one expected. For instance, if the preceding dialogue had inserted a second IF statement to ask questions of dormitory residents, the original question would have to be repeated in order to be certain that the value of $TEST corresponds to the correct IF statement.

ELSE command

Sometimes it is desirable to do either one action or another, depending on the evaluation of an IF argument. The argumentless ELSE command allows us to do the exact inverse of the argumentless IF statement. In other words, ELSE examines $TEST, and if its value is zero, the remainder of the command line is executed. Using a different type of questionnaire typical of the "pat on the head" types of tutorials often found in elementary school programs, we might see the following:

```
WRITE !,"This part of the text deals with"
WRITE !?10,"1. Meaningless drivel",!?10,"2. Conditional execution"
WRITE !?10,"3 Sex"
READ !!,"Choose 1, 2, or 3 ",OPT
IF OPT=2 WRITE !!,"How very perceptive of you!, Please read on."
ELSE  WRITE !,"I suggest you take a cold shower, have some cof-
   fee",!,"and then reread Chapter 8."
```

(The exact questions may not appear in an elementary text, but you get the idea.)

Note: ELSE is always argumentless, requiring two spaces between ELSE and the next command.

Summary

- M command lines may be up to 255 characters long. In direct-execution mode, they may consist of a sequence of commands, each separated by one or more spaces. In programming mode, a command line consists of an optional label (alphanumeric, up to eight characters), a mandatory linestart (tab or space, depending on the system), an optional series of commands separated by one or more spaces, and optional comment text consisting of an initial semicolon followed by free text. If commands and comments are present on the same line, the comments must be separated by at least one space from command arguments or by two spaces from argumentless commands.
- M permits four forms of conditional execution:

- $SELECT examines a series of expressions in a list from left to right and, based on the first TRUE evaluation, performs the associated assignment to a specified variable.
- Postconditionals on commands are expressions that are evaluated prior to execution of the command. If the expression is true, the command is evaluated. Otherwise, the command is ignored.
- IF provides a conditional execution of a command line based on the truth value of the IF expression. $TEST is set to the result of that evaluation and may be used in subsequent argumentless forms of IF.
- ELSE also uses the value of $TEST to determine whether a command line will be executed, and does so if the $TEST is false.

Exercises

You are now nearly ready to start writing complete routines. In this chapter you learned how to write compound statements in the form of command lines, and you learned how to construct conditional execution commands. These exercises will give you an opportunity to use these new tools in a manner that comes close to writing full M routines. Suggested solutions for all these problems are found in the back of the text.

1. ***Command Lines*** Write, on a single command line, a query to determine the user's age, set the variable `VOTER` to `"Y"` or `"N"` depending on age being over 18, and if of voting age, ask if the user is registered. Use postconditionals to accomplish portion(s) of this problem.

2. ***$SELECT*** Get a user's input of age. Using $SELECT, set the variable AGEGRP to the appropriate value based on the user's input:

   Under 20: Juvenile
   From 20 to 64: Adult
   Over 64: Senior citizen

   Use a default value at the end of the options to select the final choice.

   Note: You can work from either end to solve this problem.

3. ***Text Subdivision with Conditionals*** Get a user response of all he or she remembers of the first sentence of Lincoln's Gettysburg Address, and assign it to the variable GTBRG. Depending on the length of the string typed in, do one or more of the following:

   a. If the length is over 30 characters, write the first 30 on line 1, write characters 31 to 60 on line 2, characters 61 to 99 on line 3 (if anyone goes further than that, ignore the remainder). Use IF and ELSE, plus some functions and operators introduced in earlier chapters, to solve this problem. In order to preserve your original text and still have separate variables for each line, use the variables `LINE1`, `LINE2`, and `LINE3` for each subdivided line that you create.

b. With the same variable, use the two-argument form of $LENGTH (along with other functions) to split the text in lines of 30 or less characters but include only complete words (in other words, solve the "wraparound" problem of word processing). Use the same variables, `LINE1`, `LINE2`, and `LINE3`, to solve this problem. (*Hint:* You will need to use $PIECE and $EXTRACT as well as the two-argument form of $LENGTH.)

Routine Structure and Execution Flow Control

9

In Chapter 8 we learned how to write a command line, making use of the line-start character (either a tab or a space, depending on your implementation). As we will see in this chapter, use of this character also determines whether the M interpreter will execute a command line as soon as it has been entered or store it in a routine that can be saved. When a command line contains a line-start character (either at the beginning of the line or following a label), the line is stored in the routine workspace. When no linestart character is encountered, M executes the command line directly; this mode of execution is referred to as *direct-mode execution*.

What is a routine?

In this chapter we introduce the commands that allow a user to execute stored routines using the *programming mode* of execution. (The exercises at the end of this chapter provide specific information on creating and saving routines.) In order to do so, we must first define the nature of a routine. A *routine* is a col-

> **Note to experienced programmers:** The constructs described in this chapter deal with M language flow control. M provides calling flow control (through the DO command) as well as unconditional branching (GOTO command). However, there are some other aspects of flow control that are different from other languages, including scope of conditional execution and access to local variables. Block structuring is also available. QUIT with a postconditional is used to terminate single-line execution in some cases. Because the M implementation of these features differs from that of other programming languages, it is recommended that this chapter be studied with some care.

lection of command lines, all of which are associated with a single name, the name of the routine. This name is treated as a label in an M routine and obeys almost the same character rules (alphanumeric characters only, but it must begin with a letter or % sign). A routine name is used for reference purposes: to store or retrieve the routine or to access it from other routines (as discussed in the next chapter). By general convention, M routines usually begin with a line that contains a label that is the same as the routine name followed by the author's initials and the date of the last revision and an abbreviated description of its purpose. We will use this *first-line convention* hereafter in the routines used as examples in this text. In addition, many programmers use a second line to insert a comment that provides a slightly expanded description of the nature of the routine.

The body of a routine consists of a series of command lines, which may or may not be labeled. Typically, a routine will contain several lines with labels interspersed with others having none. Comments are often added for clarification. An abbreviated example of the normal format of a routine is

```
TYPICAL ;RFW;4/87;DEMO RTN
   ;example of typical routine structure
   - command lines
   - ;optional comments
   -
LABL1  ;some programmers put no commands on label lines for ease of reading
   - commands
   - ;comments after commands
   -
LABL2  ;sometimes the purpose of small subsections is stated on label line
   - commands
   -
   QUIT
LABL3 ;
   -
   ;END OF ROUTINE
```

Execution flow control

Statements are usually executed in the sequence in which they appear within a routine. There are occasions, however, when it is desirable to modify the sequence of execution. Several different alternatives may be useful under different circumstances. The most common variations of sequential execution are as follows:

- Skipping a section of code completely under some conditions
- Branching to one of several code segments depending on conditions
- Repeated execution of a line or block of code

The repeated-execution option may be for a fixed number of iterations, or it may be indeterminate, depending on conditions at the time of execution. M permits all these variations in flow control. In previous chapters we saw how to choose whether or not to execute the remaining commands on a line by using IF and ELSE. In this chapter we will examine commands that provide much more flexibility in controlling the sequence in which commands are executed.

DO and QUIT commands

It is sometimes necessary to access one section of code numerous times in the execution of a routine. This situation arises when users want to perform a repetitive calculation or use a generalized prompt question with different specific segments. In other cases, there may be a need to execute one of several code segments, depending on the situation, and then continue with a series of statements that are always executed.

The DO command is the preferred way to handle execution of repetitive segments or optional segments that might be suitable for repeated execution. DO references a code segment that is terminated by a QUIT command. DO transfers execution control to the referenced label. At the conclusion of execution of the code section starting with that label (signaled by a QUIT command), control is transferred back to the next command after the DO statement. The following example, related to "lifestyle" types of questionnaires, shows how these two commands can be used in a repetitive manner:

```
PCTACTIV ;RFW; 9/78, UPD 5/87; TIME STUDY
   ;Converts hours spent in activities to %
   WRITE "We would like next some details of your weekday life."
   WRITE !,"Please enter the number of hours spent daily in each"
   WRITE !,"of the following activities",!
START ;
   SET TOTAL=0
   READ !,"Sleeping: ",V DO PCT SET SLPCT=Y
   READ !,"Watching TV: ",V DO PCT SET TVPCT=Y
   READ !,"Reading for relaxation: ",V DO PCT SET RDPCT=Y
   READ !,"Exercising: ",V DO PCT SET EXPCT=Y
   READ !,"Commuting: ",V DO PCT SET COMPCT=Y
   READ !,"Regular job: ",V DO PCT SET WRKPCT=Y
   IF TOTAL>24 WRITE !!,"Oops. You have described a ", TOTAL," hour day."
GOTO START
   WRITE !!,"That leaves ",24-TOTAL," hours for other activities."
   READ !,"Does that seem about right? (Y/N),: ",ANS
   GOTO:ANS["N" START
   WRITE !,"Thank you for your cooperation."
```

```
   QUIT
PCT SET Y=V/24,TOTAL=TOTAL+V
   QUIT
   ;END OF MODULE
```

In this routine, the two QUIT statements just before and after the PCT label serve two slightly different functions. In the case of the code segment beginning with PCT, QUIT returns control to the position immediately following the DO statement that invoked this segment (in other languages, such a segment would be called a *procedure*). In the case of the QUIT that immediately precedes the PCT label, execution control is returned to the command that invoked the routine. If the routine was called from direct mode (the way in which we have been programming until now in this text), control would return to the user, who could then type another command. In the next chapter we will see that this routine also can be invoked by another routine. Notice that if this QUIT were not present, execution would proceed right into the PCT segment, a situation that is not intended in this routine.

This example illustrates repetitive use of a calculation, using the same variables (V and Y) to communicate between the calculation procedure and the main part of the routine. The same type of control flow may be used to create more readable code, leaving options open for flexible execution sequences. Comparing this routine with the multiple GOTO example in the section that follows, we can easily see how much better the DO/QUIT approach is than GOTO in terms of clarity and ease of modification.

M syntax attaches an implicit QUIT at the end of a routine, even if a QUIT is not actually present. Therefore, if a DO calls a code segment near the end of a routine, the code will be executed sequentially either until a QUIT is encountered or else to the end of the program. Then, if no further command lines exist, control automatically transfers back to the command immediately following the DO statement. For example, if the QUIT command were not present in the next-to-last line of the preceding routine, an implicit QUIT would be invoked after M finished scanning the last line of the routine. Although this syntax is valid, it is very bad practice to rely on it, since other code segments might be added later, and the result of omitting the QUIT would be to continue into the appended code.

GOTO command

The GOTO command also offers a mechanism for branching from one portion of code to another. The principal difference between DO and GOTO is that there is no return to the portion of code containing the GOTO statement. For this reason, it is impossible to determine how transfer to a given code segment has been invoked. This uncertainty leads to many problems in program debugging; it is one of the main reasons why GOTO statements are discouraged in modern programming techniques.

We will illustrate the GOTO form of programming as a contrast to the DO/QUIT form described in the preceding section. Although it is useful in cases requiring unconditional transfer, it is often misused when that transfer is better done with a DO. Although GOTO is available and in some cases preferable, we discourage its use when a DO structure is feasible.

In some problems it is necessary to devise branches that bypass blocks of instructions. We have already seen that, using the extended IF command, it is possible to avoid execution of some command lines. However, this process is cumbersome when a large section of code needs to be skipped or when additional IF conditions that might affect the value of $TEST appear in the optional command lines. The preferable way to skip code segments is to use the GOTO command. GOTO <*label*> instructs the M interpreter to execute, as its next step, the command line associated with the <*label*> referenced. An example of such branching logic might be the following:

```
MEDHIST ;RFW; 3/87; RISK FACTORS
   ;get some history on patient's lifestyle
   WRITE !,"We would like to find out a little about your lifestyle."
   READ !!,"Are you a smoker? (Y/N): ",ANS GOTO:ANS'["Y" ALCH
   READ !?5,"How many packs/day do you smoke? ",PKS
   READ !?5,"and for how many years have you been smoking? ",SMKYRS
   ;<more info on smoking history>
ALCH;
   READ !!,"Do you consume alcoholic beverages regularly? (Y/N): ",ANS
   IF ANS["N" GOTO XRCSZ
   READ !?5,"Do drink 1)daily 2)weekly or 3)occasionally (1/2/3): ",FREQ
   READ !?5,"How many drinks in that period?: ",AMT
   READ !?5,"Do you drink liquor other than beer or wine? (Y/N): ",HRD
   <other alcohol questions>
XRCSZ ;ask questions about type of exercise here
```

It is easy to see that complicated branching questionnaires can be constructed using this technique (although using the DO construct to invoke those sections if a respondent answers positively is a much better method of programming this case). Incidentally, one of the more common uses of the M language is in the area of questionnaires, especially in obtaining patient histories and in education. Examining the DO/QUIT example in the preceding section, you also can see that, in this case, the use of DO is probably a better choice.

It might be possible to reconstruct this example by putting all the optional branches in a separate section of code. Although this technique leads to improved program readability, it may lead to real problems in program modification. Consider the following abbreviated alternate flow control structure:

```
MEDHIST2 ;RFW; 3/87; LIFESTYLE (BAD EXAMPLE).
   ;example of improper use of GOTO
   WRITE !,"We would like to find out a little about your lifestyle."
   READ !,"Are you a smoker? (Y/N): ",ANS GOTO:ANS["Y" SMOK
Q2 READ !,"Do you drink regularly? (Y/N): ",ANS IF ANS["Y" GOTO ALCH
Q3 READ !,"Do you exercise regularly? (Y/N): ",ANS GOTO:ANS["Y" XRCSZ
Q4 ; continue in same fashion
   -
   <other commands>
   GOTO <exit address> (We will discuss this option in Chapter 10.)
SMOK ;ask smoking questions
   -
   GOTO Q2
ALCH ;ask drinking questions
   -
   GOTO Q3
XRCSZ ;ask exercise questions
   GOTO Q4
```

At first glance, this might seem like a valid way to design a routine. However, it has several drawbacks. First, it doubles the number of labels that must be included in the routine. Next, it is very hard, on inspection, to map the program flow. The person reading this routine is forced to chase all over the routine to find out where execution branches under different conditions. Updating such a routine is difficult, partly because changes in flow control will probably require changing several labels. In addition, the exit from this routine is not at the end, so it must unconditionally transfer control to another location. This is a classic example of the worst type of "go to" programming that is preached against by computer science professionals. Finally, the code in such segments might be appropriate to access from more than one location in a routine. (In fact, one of the strengths of the DO command approach is that the code is reusable, an option that makes for more efficient code development.) It is impossible, using GOTO, to provide optional return branching without introducing extraordinarily convoluted conditional GOTOs at the end of such a code segment. GOTO flow control has its place, but this is clearly not the way to handle this example.

Postconditionals on arguments

In Chapter 8 we saw how commands could be conditionally executed through the use of postconditionals. The branching example in the section on the GOTO Command in this chapter also illustrated a postconditional used to control execution flow with that command. However, the DO and GOTO commands also permit use of postconditionals at the argument level. The following example, a hypothetical menu driver for a tutorial course, illustrates using postconditionals with arguments and also shows where GOTO and DO might be used together to accomplish reasonably efficient code. In this case, the user is asked to pick a choice, after which the program returns to the menu to offer the user another choice. While this is not elegant code, it illustrates several execution flow control options: DO with a postconditional operator, and GOTO.

```
MENU ;RFW; 10/96;
   ;illustrating a valid use of the GOTO command
   READ !,"Which lesson are you are working on: ",lesson
   WRITE !,"Tutorial Options.",!
   WRITE !?5,"1. Answer Pre-lesson questions."
   WRITE !?5,"2. Do the lesson."
   WRITE !?5,"3. Answer post-lesson questions."
   WRITE !?5,"4. Quit."
retry READ !,"Please respond with a number between 1 and 4: ",ans
   IF ans<1!(ans>4) GOTO RETRY
   QUIT:ans=4
   DO pretest:ANS=1,lesson:ANS=2,posttest:ANS=3
   GOTO Menu
pretest;
   (code for pretest here)
   QUIT
lesson;
   (code for lesson here)
   QUIT
posttest;
   (code for posttest here)
   QUIT
   ;END OF PROGRAM
```

In this case, the postconditional operator is used with each of the arguments following the DO command. GOTO is used in two cases: to repeat a prompt if the user types an invalid entry; and to return to the top of the menu driver after an option has been completed. It would be difficult to program this without using GOTO, although it might be done. This is a case where I believe GOTO is appropriately used.

FOR command

The DO/QUIT command pair works well to perform repetitive code segments that require several command lines. There is another repetitive execution command in M that permits repeated execution of one line of code – the FOR command. FOR has two main syntactical forms. In the first, the arguments form a list of repeated values separated by commas. To illustrate, suppose we have the following interactive reservation system available on a dialup telephone line:

```
RESERVE ; HF; 7/81; RESSYSTM
   ;Offer reservation options, up to two options per call.
   WRITE !,"Welcome to Golden Pond Resort Reservation System."
   WRITE !,"Currently, we have one-week reservations available for:"
   WRITE !?10,"1. June 29",!?10,"2. July 20",!?10,"3. July 27"
   WRITE !?10,"4. August 10, and",!?10,"August 24"
   READ !!,"Please select the number of your first choice: ",OPT1
   READ !!,"Now select your second choice: ",OPT2
   FOR INDX= Opt1,Opt2 DO LISTRES
CONFIRM ; Ask if caller wants to make reservation
   -
   WRITE !!,"Thank you for calling"
   HALT
LISTRES ;display accommodations for INDX week
   <commands>
QUIT
```

This (slightly contrived) example illustrates a use of the FOR command where, before the user makes a final selection, several different executions of the reservation list are presented. M looks at the argument list after the FOR and assigns INDX the value of each in turn before executing the DO command. After the routine returns from LISTRES, M assigns the next (and all subsequent values) and repeats the execution until the list of choices is exhausted.

This syntax of the FOR command has some uses, but a more powerful version takes the form

```
FOR INDX=A:B:C... <command>
```

which M interprets as: "Beginning with an initial assignment of the value A to INDX, perform the rest of the command line. Then increment A by B and repeat the command line. Continue incrementing by B until the value of A exceeds C, then terminate the FOR loop."

The FOR loop is a powerful execution flow control sequence available in M, and we will see it appear in several variations in M routines throughout the remainder of this book. As an initial example, suppose we want to post the average grade for an exam taken by a class. A routine to generate that number might read as follows:

```
AVG ;RFW; 5/87; AVG GRADE
   WRITE !,"This program calculates the average of a set of grades."
   READ !!,"How many grades do you wish to enter: ",NUM
   SET SUM=0
   FOR N=1:1:NUM READ !,"Enter next grade: ",GRAD SET SUM=SUM+GRAD
   SET AVG=SUM/NUM
   WRITE !!,"The average grade for ",NUM," scores is: ",AVG
   READ !!,"Would you like to calculate another average? (Y/N): ",ANS
   QUIT:ANS'["Y"  GOTO AVG
```

In this example, the value of a new grade is obtained the number of times specified by the user and the final result is printed as calculated. The index value N is not used in the calculations (although it is legal to do so). In this example, the user does not have to define each value before the FOR loop is initiated, making the command line considerably more flexible than the parameter list approach described earlier.

There is another variation of the FOR loop that is even more flexible: using an open-ended FOR loop with a postconditionalized QUIT statement. Using this variation, the AVG routine just listed could be modified as follows:

```
AVG2 ;RFW; 5/87; AVG GRADE (2nd version)
   WRITE !,"This program calculates the average of a set of grades."
   WRITE !!,"Enter grades till done, then hit return key with no value."
   SET SUM=0
   FOR N=1:1 READ !,"Next grade:",GRAD QUIT:GRAD=""  SET SUM=SUM+GRAD
   SET N=N-1; (decrement N to equal number of grades entered)
   SET AVG=SUM/N
   WRITE !!,"The average grade for ",N," scores is: ",AVG
   READ !!,"Would you like to calculate another average? (Y/N): ",ANS
   QUIT:ANS'["Y"  GOTO AVG2
```

In this version, the opening message does not ask for a total number. Instead, the user is notified that a null answer (typing the <*enter*> or <*return*> key without typing any value) will terminate the FOR loop. The QUIT:ANS'["Y" (followed by *two spaces*, since QUIT has no arguments) will terminate the FOR loop. At that point, the value of N, the index used in keeping track of the number of times the FOR loop has been executed, is set at one greater than the last valid number. Hence, in order to calculate the average, the SUM must be divided by N-1, and that is also the value printed in the result.

It is easy to see that this form of the FOR loop can be used to create highly flexible execution flow control. A word of caution: writing such a FOR loop command line usually entails a rather long string of text. Most M programmers, when typing in this type of command, are concentrating on the concept, not the syntax. As a result, the most common error made is to omit the second space after the postconditionalized QUIT. This syntax error will cause an execution abort when the missing second space is detected, and the user who is working in direct mode (see the exercises at the end of this chapter) must retype the entire line. It is easy to say "Don't forget the two spaces," but it's even easier to do just that.

The use of FOR with an open-ended index is common in M routines. Often the counter, or index, is used simply to represent an indication that the FOR loop is to be repeated, and it is not used in the commands in the remainder of the command line. M allows the use of a degenerate form of the FOR loop in which there are no arguments for the FOR command. This version allows the command `FOR I=1:1` to be replaced by `FOR<sp><sp>` followed by the remainder of the command line (since there are no arguments, two spaces are required between the FOR and the remaining commands on that line.) A FOR loop of this type must contain a conditional QUIT or GOTO or the loop would run forever.

Block structuring

The M language exercises flow control through the concept of a command line, which can be up to 255 characters long. Although this approach is easy to understand, it has some drawbacks. First, as illustrated by several of the examples in this text, a "line" of many characters cannot always be reproduced on one physical line of a program printout. The convention adopted in this book is to continue the command line on a second line, indenting and inserting three dots at the start of a continuation line. In later chapters we will see some rather long command lines, some requiring more than one continuation line (e.g., the application examples in Chapter 18). While command lines of this length are permitted, they are hard to read and harder still to follow.

The second drawback of the command-line flow control concept relates to the overall structure of a computer program. Computer scientists have for many years advocated the concept of "structured programming," in which flow control is made more obvious through the internal design of the program. Using a structured approach makes program maintenance easier and highlights the flow control of a program. The "bad" example given earlier in this chapter of GOTO flow control in obtaining a patient's smoking and other history is the worst version of poor program structure, but even the normal DO flow control structure leads to separation of the module from its calling location. While this modular separation may be desirable in some cases, in others it is unnecessary, a result of trying to restrict command line length or improve readability.

The manner in which block structuring is achieved in M is by extension of the DO command to permit a syntax with no arguments. Conventional DO statements must identify a label or routine to which flow control is transferred. In the argumentless DO syntax, control continues on following lines which are identified by an *additional period and linestart character*, one for each level of nesting. A simple example would be the following:

```
MEDHIST3 ;RFW;12/87; RISK FACTORS(BLOCK STRUCTURE EXAMPLE)
;example of block structuring
WRITE !,"We would like to find out a little about your lifestyle."
READ !!,"Are you a smoker? (Y/N): ",ANS
IF ANS["Y" DO
. READ !,"How many packs a day? ",PKS
. READ !,"and for how many years? ",PKYRS
. <other smoking questions>
READ !!,"Do you consume alcoholic beverages regularly? (Y/N): ",ANS
IF ANS["Y" DO
. READ !,"Do you drink 1) daily 2)weekly or 3)occasionally? ",ALFRQ
. READ !,"How many drinks in that time period?",ALAMT
. <other alcohol questions>
READ !!,"Do you exercise regularly? (Y/N): ",ANS
(etc.)
```

Comparing this example with MEDHIST as it appeared earlier in this chapter shows that the principal differences are the lack of GOTO structure and the lack of labels required by the GOTO for each subsection. Also, the code relating to each positive answer is easily identified as a subset related to that question, with indentation to increase the visual separation of that module.

Structured blocks can be nested within outer structured blocks. When such nesting occurs, each level of nesting is identified by a period, so that a line nested two levels deep would begin with two periods. To illustrate, consider the following example:

```
XYZCO ;RFW; 12/87; COMPANY DATABASE
   ;create description of company
   WRITE !!,"Please help us update the XYZ company database."
   FOR I=1:0 DO  QUIT:DEPT=""
   . READ !,"Enter name of next department to be defined: ",DEPT
   . QUIT:DEPT=""
   . READ !,"Enter location (Building and Floor): ",DLOC
   . READ !,"Enter current annual budget: ",DBUDG
   . READ !,"Enter dept manager employee number: ",DMGR
```

```
.  FOR J=1:0 DO  QUIT:DEMP=""
.  .  READ !,"Enter employee number: ",DEMP
.  .  QUIT:DEMP=""
.  .  READ !,"Enter employee's job classification: ",DEMPCL
.  .  READ !,"Enter employee's room number: ",DEMPLOC
WRITE !,"Thank you for your assistance."
QUIT
;END OF ROUTINE
```

This example shows nesting two levels deep. It is again easy to read and follow. Each section of the data entry is controlled by a DO that is terminated by a null entry or the end of the questions for that section. The readability of indented code can be retained by limiting the number of commands on each line, since it is no longer necessary to group multiple commands on the same line. In the block-structured mode, a GOTO may be used to access a label at the same level of nesting, but it cannot reference a label outside that level. The use of GOTO is not recommended in this situation.

These examples illustrate the M approach to block structuring. The alternative approach (found in many programming languages) of using BEGIN and END has been proposed for M, but it has not been adopted by the MDC.

HALT and HANG commands

In the introduction to M programming found in Chapter 3, we pointed out that in order to exit the M language, it is necessary to type "HALT". This is another form of execution flow control. It is essential to exit M in this manner because there may be some house cleaning that M must do before logging an individual off – such operating system requirements as making sure that all data that have been used during the session have been properly stored or that any inadvertent omissions on the part of the user to instruct the system about saving routines have been identified and resolved.

HALT is a command that performs these functions. It stops all execution and returns control to the operating system. HALT can have no arguments, nor can any commands following HALT on the same command line be executed (unless HALT has a postconditional). It is a comforting feeling for the programmer to know that there is a way of escaping (short of unplugging the computer) from the situation at hand. For example, in a tutorial session, a student may on occasion be presented with the following question:

```
READ !!,"Would you like to stop now? (Y/N): ",ANS
HALT:ANS["Y"
```

Note: In many examples provided in this text we use a *contains* operator rather than an equals sign to check the user's response. This approach will make the correct decision even if the user happened to type YES, YUP, AYE, or a number of other unconventional answers.

Although HANG may sound somewhat more drastic even than HALT, it is in fact a far more innocuous command. HANG permits the user to suspend operations for a specified number of seconds and then continue. The M interpreter will silently count the appropriate time and then proceed to execute the next statement. Like most M statements, HANG may be modified with a post-conditional statement. To illustrate, suppose we had developed a tutorial that asks a student to respond with the result of a series of calculations. A portion of this tutorial might look like the following:

```
Q73 ;circumference
   SET RAD=$RANDOM(10)
   WRITE !,"What is the circumference of a circle with a radius of ",RAD
   READ !?20,"Circumference = ",ANS
   IF ANS'<(3*RAD*2)!(ANS'>(3.2*RAD*2)) WRITE "OK" GOTO Q74
   WRITE !!,"Not close enough. The formula for a circle is 2*pi*r,"
   WRITE !!,"where r is the radius and pi is 3.14"
   HANG 5 WRITE # GOTO Q73 ;try again after 5 seconds
Q74 ;next question
```

This example will present a random number for radius between 1 and 9, check the response for a close enough value, and give some tutorial hint before returning to the question with a new random value generated. The 5-second pause allows the student to look at the tutorial prompt, then writes a "form feed" (which on some devices will erase the screen), and starts over. There are many situations where such pauses would be helpful. Another common occurrence that is helped by the HANG command is in displaying text on a screen. Inserting a HANG 10 (pausing, not surfing) command after every 15 lines or so would allow the reader to check over the output before scrolling earlier material off the screen. HANG only accepts integer arguments (i.e., it will pause a specific number of seconds). Use of noninteger values may be truncated to the integer component, but since the result is not defined, it is better to use only integer arguments for the HANG command.

Summary

- M accepts input from a user in two modes:
  - *Direct mode:* Each command line is executed as typed.
  - *Programming mode:* Command lines are stored in a workspace for future execution.

In programming mode, it is essential to include the linestart character (a tab or space, depending on the system). The linestart must appear after a label (if any) and before the commands or comments. M stores such command lines in the user's workspace and asks for a new line of user input.

- Execution flow control of commands is normally *sequential*. However, it is possible to modify execution control in the following ways:
  - Skipping code segments by use of the GOTO <*label*> command
  - Branching to input-selected code segments, using GOTO <*label*>
  - Repetitive execution of code segments, using DO and QUIT
  - Repetitive execution of command lines, using FOR

  Note: FOR may accept a specified parameter list for repeated execution of the remainder of a command line, or it can use a counter, incremented by a number until a specified terminal value is reached. An open-ended repetitive FOR loop should be terminated by a postconditionalized QUIT command.

- M also permits modification of flow control by use of the HALT command, which terminates execution of that user session and restores stored variables to a standby condition, available for a new user.
- Finally, M permits temporary suspension of all execution by using the command `HANG nn`, where `nn` is an integer representing the number of seconds of delay before execution is to resume.

Interactive programming in Mumps

Learning to use the programming mode

Up to now, all command lines you entered have been written in *direct mode,* which meant that every line you typed was executed immediately. In this chapter you learned that it is possible to type in command lines in *programming mode,* which results in their being stored in the user workspace assigned to you when you logged on to the M system.

The M standard does not define programming mode in a form that requires all M systems to be identical. In order to use programming mode effectively, you should seek some help from your manuals, M system representative, or a local M guru who knows about these things and about your system.

Many M implementations offer a screen editor to facilitate programming. If such an editor is available, you should definitely use it, since it will take care of most of the problems of code generation and maintenance more or less automatically. If there is no screen editor, you should check your implementation's documentation to find out how to create, edit, save, and revise a routine. A few of the most common conventions used in most commercial implementations today are the following:

Functions required for programming in M

- Linestart: Most implementations use a <*tab*>, but some also permit a space. Use a tab to be safe.
- Print: ZPRINT will print the routine in your workspace for all M implementations (even though it is not part of the standard). `ZPRINT <label>+offset` will print a specific line.
- Saving a routine: Many implementations have utilities for saving and loading routines. Typically they are give names such as `%rsave` and `%rload` (the names of routines are case-sensitive). Check your documentation. ZREMOVE (or ZDELETE) works in most implementations to clear the workspace.

To run a routine that you have created in workspace, type `DO <label>`. While the routine remains in workspace, this command will suffice. If the routine is already stored on disk, it is necessary to type `DO ^ <routine-name>` in order to retrieve the routine from disk and execute it. The caret (^) identifies the name as the name of a routine. The name of the routine is usually the name as it appears on the first line. Routine names are case-sensitive: `DO ^MYTEST` and `DO ^mytest` would try to find two different routines.

In order to gain some confidence, try typing in the following sequence of code. (We will identify the tab key by *<tab>*.) The standard prompt in M is the greater than bracket '>'. Characters typed by the user in the following sequence are printed in **boldface.**

```
>TEST<tab>;try a test routine
><tab>READ !,"Enter a number: ",N
><tab>WRITE !,"That number squared = ",N*N
><tab>QUIT
><tab>;END OF ROUTINE
>ZPRINT (This should list the routine as you have entered it.)
>DO TEST

Enter a number: 7
That number squared = 49

>ZSAVE TEST
>ZREMOVE        (Remove the routine from your workspace.)
>ZPRINT         (You should get nothing.)
>DO ^TEST       (Retrieve routine from disk.)

Enter a number: (The routine will execute as before.)
```

Exercises

1. ***Skipping Code Segments*** This exercise gives you practice in using the GOTO statement.

a. Write a routine called `SENIOR` (using GOTO statements) that does the following:

- Ask the user to enter his or her `AGE`.
- If the age entered is not greater than `64`, skip to a label `CONTINUE`; otherwise, ask if member of senior citizen club.

- If member, skip to CONTINUE; otherwise, ask for phone number for contact.
- After CONTINUE label, put in a QUIT statement to end program.

b. Once you have created this routine, try running it a few times to be sure it does what you want under the several different answers given by the user.

2. ***Conditional Branching*** Remove the routine written for Exercise 1. Create a new routine (using argument-level postconditionals) that does the following:

   - Welcome user to "Dog's World" veterinary clinic waiting room; ask if pet is dog, cat, or other.
   - If dog, branch to label DOG; then branch to EXIT.
   - If cat, branch to label CAT; then branch to EXIT.
   - If OTHER, ask for type, issue a message "to be added soon" and branch to EXIT. EXIT section should perform normal quit and indicate end of program.

   This routine need not be complete in terms of questions asked for cats or dogs, but the framework should be there. In those sections, a WRITE statement indicating that execution control was transferred there would be a good idea.

3. ***Repeated Execution Using DO and QUIT*** This problem gives you the opportunity to create a game of chance that may be fun (provided no real money is used). You are to create a coin-tossing game with the following outline:

   - Name the routine TOSSPOT.
   - Allocate $10 to the variable PURSE at the outset, to be used for betting.
   - At a label BETS: ask the user to place a BET which cannot be more than the current value of PURSE.
   - Transfer control to a label FLIP, where the program asks for a choice of HEADS or TAILS.
   - Using $RANDOM(2), get the value of the coin toss, and assign a value to WIN accordingly.
   - Return from FLIP code segment to main body of routine.
   - Add or subtract BET from PURSE.
   - Inform player of result.
   - If PURSE is not depleted, give the player an option to quit or continue. Branch accordingly.

   Test this routine until you are happy with it, then perhaps you may want to try it on friends. You may want to write down the routine for future reference (or get help from someone as to how to print or save the routine).

4. ***Repeated Execution of a Command Line Using FOR*** Write a short routine called `WORDS` that does the following:

   - Using an open-ended FOR loop, ask user to type in a sentence (any sentence) or null (just return) to exit. If null, QUIT line. On the same line, if the user did type in a sentence, transfer to a code segment labeled `CALC` (using DO).
   - When user wishes to exit, QUIT program (on next line).
   - In the `CALC` code segment, calculate total length of sentence (number of characters) and number of words (by counting spaces).
   - Return control to FOR loop line after writing out result of `CALC`.
   - Run the program a few times to see that it works properly with several different inputs.

Program Structure 10

Routines are collections of command lines that are stored by the M interpreter in such a way that they can be retrieved and used as a unit. Routines are given names, and by convention, the first line of each routine contains its name, the author's name or initials, the date of creation, and a brief description.

The final step in creating a computer solution to an information-handling problem is to link routines together so as to form *packages,* which are collections of routines that together fulfill a common purpose. By use of the DO/QUIT combination, it is possible to create a modular solution involving a series of routines, each solving a limited portion of a problem. GOTO also may be used for transfer of control between routines, though it offers less structured flow control between routines.

DO/QUIT and GOTO commands used with routines

There are two ways to access routines that have been previously stored. These involve the use of the DO and GOTO commands described in the previous chapter, with one additional feature: the name of a routine is preceded by a caret (^), which prints on some terminals as an up-arrow.

> **Note to experienced programmers:** This chapter expands on execution control flow introduced in Chapter 9 by describing interroutine flow control. Execution flow control is quite similar to comparable constructs in other languages. The exercise section introduces the concept of saving routines and using nonstandard system editors.

To illustrate the design of an M application package using a DO/QUIT structure, consider the problems associated with entering a customer sale from a computer-supported checkout counter. To make our problem simpler, assume that only one item at a time is considered. When a sale takes place, it affects a number of other functions in a store, each of which might be linked through a single M application package. A partial list of some of the functions that should take place when a sale is entered into such a system includes the following:

1. Identify the item by its registered number.
2. Check the item's current cost against various options (sales, and so on).
3. Determine total cost, including taxes or special add-ons.
4. Determine method of payment offered by customer.
   a. If a cash payment, determine money received and calculate change from cash register.
   b. If a personal check, verify that name on check is not on bad credit list.
   c. If other credit, verify the card, credit balance, and so on, as appropriate.
   d. If a store charge account, check account for authorization and status.
5. Print a sales slip and credit slip.
6. Update the status of the cash register.
7. Credit the department and salesperson; record commission.
8. Update gross sales for the day.
9. Add to the transaction file for the day.
10. Update inventory; check for reorder level algorithm.

This list, admittedly incomplete, gives some idea of the potential for generation of a rather complex total system that can fully justify the point-of-sale types of registers now used in many stores. Analyzing the functions just described, it would not be difficult to design a series of program modules, each of which would perform a group of related functions. One design might be as follows:

- `DPMAIN` Identify transaction type; call appropriate subcategory (Not all options are shown below.)
- `DPSALE` Using subsidiary routines: check item number; check payment; complete transaction; update inventory; credit department; return to `DPMAIN`
- `DPITMNO` Check item number, set bonuses, discount parameters
- `DPPMNT` Using subsidiary routines, authorize payment type:
  - `DPCASH`: for cash transactions
  - `DPCHK`: for personal checks

   ○ DPCHG: for credit transactions
- DPDEPT Credit department, salesperson; update daily sales
- DPINV Update inventory
- DPTRANS Enter transaction in transaction log

This outline illustrates the manner in which different modules could serve the intended purposes. Examination of the subdivision shows that some components might be called from other branches (inventory and department credit, for example). The package described is a rather complex one, but for purposes of this illustration, an outline of the routines involved is shown below.

```
DPMAIN ;RFW; 5/87; TRANSACT SYS
   ;process sales, credits, bill pmnts, inquiries
   - prompt for transaction type
   --
   QUIT:OPT="EXIT"
   DO:OPT="SALE" DPSALE
   IF VALID="NO" WRITE !,"Sale Not Authorized"
   GOTO DPMAIN; recycle for next transaction
   ;END OF ROUTINE

DPSALE ;RFW; 5/87; SALE TRANSACT
   ;called by DPMAIN
ITEM DO ^DPITMNO QUIT:VALID="NO"
PMNT DO ^DPPMNT QUIT:VALID="NO"
   DO ^DPCRDT
   DO ^DPINV
   QUIT
   ;END OF ROUTINE

DPITMNO ;RFW; 5/87; CHECK ITEM
   -- check to see that item number is valid
   QUIT:VALID="NO"
   -- establish discounts, bonus, other parameters
   QUIT
   ;END OF ROUTINE

DPPMNT ;RFW; 5/87; CHECK PMNT TYPE
   ; first, get type of payment offered (DPTYP)
   DO DPCASH:DPTYP="CASH",DPCHK:DPTYP="CHK",DPCHG:DPTYP="CHG"
   (note: VALID is set to "YES" or "NO")
   QUIT
DPCASH ;
   -- set parameters
   DO ^DPCOST QUIT
```

```
   DPCHK ;
   -- set parameters
   DO ^DPCOST QUIT

DPCHG ;
   -- set parameters
   DO ^DPCOST QUIT
   ;END OF ROUTINE

DPCOST ;RFW; 5/87; CALC ACTUAL COST
   ; called by DPPMNT
   -- using parameters, calculate cost, sales tax etc
   QUIT
   ;END OF ROUTINE

DPCRDT ;RFW; 5/87; COMPLETE ACTUAL SALE
   ;called by DPSALE
   DO ^DPDEPT
   DO SALE^DPTRANS
   -- print sales slip, credit card info
   QUIT
   ;END OF ROUTINE

DPDEPT ;RFW; 5/87; CREDIT SALE TO DEPT
   ;called by DPCRDT
   -- credit department, salesperson, update cash register status
   QUIT
   ;END OF ROUTINE

DPTRANS ;RFW; 5/87;ADD TRANSACTION TO LOG
   ;log all transactions to database.
   ;called from numerous entries. entry point varies
PAYMENT ;entry point if bill payment to be recorded
   -- enter account, amt paid, etc.
   QUIT
SALE  ;entry for item sale (as in this example)
   -- enter type of sale, dept, other info available
   QUIT
   ;
   -- other entries for other types of transactions
   QUIT
   ;END OF ROUTINE

DPINV ;RFW; 5/87; UPDATE INVENTORY
   ;called by DPSALE, and by other routines.
   -- deduct from inventory quantity sold,
   -- check on need to reorder
```

```
QUIT
;END OF ROUTINE
```

This sequence illustrates the general manner in which routines may be linked together, and it also shows the general manner in which package structure is internally documented by noting how a routine is invoked. It might be worthwhile to study the execution flow and relate it to personal experiences in dealing with point-of-sale transactions supported by programs of this type.

One feature not previously referenced is illustrated in the routine DPTRANS. M permits interroutine execution flow to go to labels *within* a routine, using the syntax

```
DO LABEL^ROUTINE
```

which transfers control directly to that label. Since the routine DPTRANS will be used to record many different types of transactions during daily operations, entry points specific to each provide a more useful form of execution flow control. This approach avoids the alternative of testing at entry to determine which type of transaction is involved and transferring accordingly.

The action of `GOTO ^Routinename` is the same as if one used the same command to reference a label within a routine. The transfer of control is to the top of the routine indicated, and each command in that routine is executed according to the statements encountered. This structure is useful when the material to be covered in each branch of the package is large, distinct from other branches, and more easily maintained as a separate routine. Use of the GOTO structure also seems reasonable when it is unlikely that the user will wish to follow more than one branch during a single session. Consider the following outline form of an M package designed to facilitate data collection for an insurance agency.

```
INSMAIN ;RFW; 5/87; CLIENT DATA
   ;Entry point for INS package
   READ !,"Please enter name (Last, first): ",CLIENT
   -- next, get address, phone number etc.
   ;
   WRITE !!,"Thank you. Now, would you like to insure your"
   WRITE !?10,"1. Home",!?10,"2. Rental Property"
   WRITE !?10,"3. Automobile",!?10,"4. Or other"
   READ !!,"Please enter a number from 1 to 4",OPT
   QUIT:OPT<1!(OPT>4)
   DO ^INSHOM:OPT=1,^INSRENT:OPT=2,^INSCAR:OPT=3,^INSOTH:OPT=4

INSHOM ;RFW; 5/87; HOME INF.
   ;called from INSMAIN
```

```
   ;get all details on home
   ----
   QUIT

INSRENT ;RFW; 5/87; RENTAL INF
   ;called from INSMAIN
   ;get all rental info
   QUIT

INSCAR ;RFW; 5/87; CAR INF
   ;called from INSMAIN
   ;get specifics on car(s)
   ----
   QUIT

INSOTH ;RFW; 5/87; OTHER INF
   ;called from INSMAIN
   ;get type of unit, info
   QUIT
```

This example illustrates several features characteristic of M application packages. A package of M routines should usually have a consistent set of names. Typically, this convention involves using the same first two or three letters for every routine that is included in the package. In this case, "INS" is used to link all routines in this package. The individual routines in an M package are generally structured to perform one or more closely related functions, as illustrated in this example. The first line convention is followed for each routine, but in addition, it is usually appropriate to indicate in the second line the routine's relation to others in the package. In this case, the subsidiary branches are all identified as being called from the main routine, which is identified as the entry routine for the package. A QUIT appears in each routine, which is a convention that prevents invalid flow control if the routine is modified. The result of executing the QUIT in each case would most likely be returning the user to direct-entry mode, since there are no DO commands in this example. In order to invoke this package from direct mode, the user would type `DO ^INSMAIN` *<return>*, and M would transfer control to that routine, first loading it into execution space from disk.

Not shown in this outline example is one other feature that also improves the maintainability of such packages. Variables used in packages are also often given uniform identifiers such as having common first letters and identifiable mnemonics. This technique makes it easier to identify and track variables associated with a given application, and it also reduces the chance of inadvertent overlap in names between two different applications.

This example follows the general approach illustrated by the postconditionalized argument example in Chapter 9, but in this case there are no GOTO statements (we assume that the user is familiar with the routines and will not want to run them a second time).

From these examples it is possible to construct many different forms of complex execution paths. M does not encourage the use of large individual routines, since modular code is easier to write and maintain. Programmers in other languages sometimes wonder how it is that M can run efficiently in relatively small user partitions (typically around 4 to 8 kilobytes per user). This modular structure is a partial explanation of that capability.

M does not require that all routines to be used by a given program be in the computer's memory at the start of execution. Instead, the interpreter will load the routines as they are required. In some implementations, the routines are accessed from disk each time they are invoked. Other implementations maintain buffer areas for routines, thereby reducing the number of disk accesses. The net effect is that the user may design programs that are arbitrarily large or complex, provided that each routine is small enough to be loaded as a single unit. This feature of M tends to promote modularity, a program characteristic that facilitates modification and maintenance of complex programs.

In addition to the routines created as a part of a package, most M implementations also provide *system utilities,* routines whose names often begin with a percent sign (%), to perform standard functions required in many applications. One such routine, common to many M implementations, is %DATE. In the preceding example, there are several places where calculation of the date might be useful. Having the ability to include the command DO ^%DATE anywhere in a package serves this function without requiring separate packages to have their own date management routine.

Summary

Execution flow control can be used to control the sequence of command execution within a single M line, within a single routine, or between several routines. In this chapter we introduced the way in which M controls execution between routines.

- M uses DO/QUIT and GOTO to permit execution flow control to pass between routines in an M package. The syntax of such control is expressed by

```
DO ^ROUTINE
GOTO ^ROUTINE
```

or

```
DO LABEL^ROUTINE
GOTO LABEL^ROUTINE
```

where the caret (^) precedes the name of a routine.

- The modular structure characterizing most M applications leads to creation of numerous small routines, each performing a specific function.
- Utility routines for special purposes are included with every M version.

Exercise

The functionality described in this chapter opens the door for creating large and complex routines. In order to give you some experience in this type of design, this exercise describes a package with a limited scope that could be expanded into a much more comprehensive application.

Creation of Payroll Package You are to design a limited payroll system that will accept, for one individual, employee number and amount earned for a month, and then calculate the actual amount deducted, paid to the employee, and other auxiliary actions. This problem is limited in scope to illustrate concepts only. It would require expansion to serve any real-world function. Assume that you have the following variables:

Variable	Description
MONTH	month of transaction
PREMPNO	employee number
PRSAL	amount earned this month
PRSSEC	Social Security withholding
PRSSCUM	cumulative Social Security
PRSTATE	state withholding
PRSTCUM	cumulative state withholding
PRFED	federal withholding
PRFEDCUM	cumulative federal withholding
PRHLTH	health insurance deduction
PRCHAR	charitable deductions
PRCURDED	total deductions this month
PRNET	net due to employee
PRCUM	salary to date

In your design, create the following routines:

PRMAIN	The main entry for your package
PRINIT	Sets all above variables to zero if month is January
PRDEDUC	Calculates deductions, cumulatives
PRWRCK	Writes "check" (output to screen) for employee

With this information, write a package that will

a. Ask the month (be sure to enter January, so as to be able to initialize variables used).

b. Get employee name and salary earned that month.

c. Using the auxiliary routines listed, deduct 18 percent for federal tax, 5 percent for state tax, 8 percent Social Security, $120 for health insurance, and $25 for charities.

d. Print a check stub itemizing all values.

e. Print a "check" with the amount remaining.

Note: Use $JUSTIFY to line up the figures in your output.

Local Arrays

11

Up to now. we have been concerned with simple variables, those which have a one-to-one association between the variable name and its value. Simple variables serve us well in many situations, but sometimes we need a way to manipulate a larger collection of data, such as a list of employee names. While it might be possible to devise a new simple variable name for each employee number or name, doing so would make programming output an extremely awkward process. M, like most other programming languages, solves this problem by including, as part of the language, arrays—and arrays are what we will study in this chapter.

What is an array?

An *array* is a type of variable that has a simple name, but one that may also have many values associated with it. Consider the way in which apartment dwellers are grouped. For the apartment complex named Tranquil House, for example, we may have the following names and addresses:

> **Note to experienced programmers:** The M concept of sparse hierarchical subscripted arrays is unique in programming languages. This chapter covers the concept of subscripts for such a structure, and as such it probably warrants more study than most elements of the M language. The language elements used to trace data structures and values ($ORDER, $DATA) are also unique to the M language and require special attention. Experienced programmers are advised to study the Summary, look at examples in the text, and try the exercises at the end of this chapter.

Apartment No.	Name
1	Lilly
2	Reynolds
3	Hanson
4	Brown
5	Piccone
6	McIntyre

Ideally, we would like to retain individuality for each tenant, yet be able to identify these individuals as living in one apartment complex. When it is necessary to make reference to one individual value out of the collection, a *subscript* is added to the name, serving to identify the particular value desired. Since most computer terminals lack the ability to print subscripts one-half line below the regular text, M (like most languages) encloses the subscript in parentheses immediately after the name. With subscripted variables, our apartment address list might appear as follows:

```
SET TRANQUIL(1)="Lilly",TRANQUIL(2)="Reynolds",TRANQUIL(3)="Hanson"
SET TRANQUIL(4)="Brown",TRANQUIL(5)="Piccone",TRANQUIL(6)="McIntyre",
```

We might even create a program to identify the tenants of Tranquil House as follows:

```
APTADDR ;RFW; 4/96; GET NAMES IN APT
   READ !,"Please enter number of Apartments in complex: ",APNO
   FOR I=1:1:APNO WRITE !,"Enter Tenant name in ",I READ ":",NAM SET
   ...APTHOUS(I)=NAM
   WRITE !!,"Thank you."
   QUIT
```

Note: In this example in order to use the index number I in the prompt message, it is necessary to use a WRITE statement, since the READ cannot incorporate existing variables in its prompt (to avoid confusion with the variables being input). This example illustrates an important use of the FOR loop in creating sets of variables stored under one name with subscripts for each subsidiary value.

Multiple subscripts and sparse arrays

The apartment example just described uses only a single subscript to identify the apartment number in a building complex. However, M allows us to use more than one subscript, creating a hierarchical structure that is considerably more powerful. To extend the apartment example, consider a street on which there are many apartment houses, each with several apartments. In this case, instead of using the name of the apartment house (such as Tranquil House), the U.S. Postal Service would probably require a street number. If we wanted to extend the tenant-identification program of the preceding section to cover such an example, we might rewrite the entry program as follows:

```
APTROW ;RFW; 5/96; GET TENANT NAMES
   ;Get Street number of each apartment complex, then tenant names.
   READ !,"Enter Street Number of Apartment (Null to quit): ",APSTR
   IF APSTR="" WRITE !,"Thank you." QUIT
   READ !!,"How many Apartments at this address? ",APNO
   FOR I=1:1:APNO WRITE !?10,"Enter tenant name for Apt: ",I READ NAM
   ...SET APTROW(APSTR,I)=NAM
   GOTO APTROW ;Cycle back for next apartment unit
   ;END OF ROUTINE
```

The result of running this routine might be to create a variable array with the following values:

```
APTROW(1267,1) = "Lilly"
APTROW(1267,2) = "Reynolds"
APTROW(1267,3) = "Hanson"
APTROW(1267,4) = "Brown"
APTROW(1267,5) = "Piccone"
APTROW(1267,6) = "McIntyre"
APTROW(1273,1) = "Barnett"
APTROW(1273,2) = "Zimmerman"
APTROW(1273,3) = "Covin"
APTROW(1276,1) = "DeMoel"
APTROW(1276,2) = "Salander"
APTROW(1276,3) = "Partridge"
APTROW(1276,4) = "Beaman"
```

This example deserves a little additional study. Notice first that the street numbers do not begin with the number 1, incrementing serially from that point. Instead, the first number is a four-digit value, and the subsequent street numbers do not follow with the next available value. Instead, there are empty numbers (just as street numbers rarely include every number). However, M uses the actual street numbers to index the array. In most programming languages, this form of indexing would require that space be set aside for (in this case) a matrix with 1276 rows and 6 columns (the maximum number of apartments in one unit). In other words, for languages other than M, use of the actual street numbers would require at a minimum 7656 locations to store the names of tenants. However, in this example, only 13 names have been specified, so the remaining 7643 locations would be empty.

The apartment index just illustrated exemplifies what is called a *sparse array,* one in which many of the possible values that could be used to fill in such an array are empty. Sparse arrays are extremely common in real-world data; the apartment example is a good one, but it is by no means unique. Conventional languages require that such arrays be defined to cover all possibilities. Such arrays are declared ahead of time, warning the computer that space must be reserved for this array and specifying how much space to reserve. Such an array is referred to as a *dense array,* meaning that every subscripted value is provided for in the storage assigned to that program.

M differs from this approach in two important ways. First, there is no requirement that arrays be dense; instead, M permits sparse arrays in which only those variables which have been assigned values occupy space in the symbol table. Second, it is not necessary to specify this storage space ahead of time. M will, upon encountering a new variable, create the variable and assign the designated value. The use of sparse arrays thus conserves space and eliminates the need for declaration statements that reserve space that may never be used.

There is an even more important concept that the use of sparse arrays permits which is not generally feasible in other languages. The fact that an actual street number is used as an index means that subscripts may take on a meaning beyond reserving storage space in a dense array. Other languages might modify the structure defined above by creating a dense matrix with one row for each apartment complex and a column for each apartment (reserving space for the largest possible number per complex). However, the index of the apartment number would be an integer beginning with 1 and incrementing to the total number of apartment complexes. A *separate* dictionary would be required to associate the street number with the integer in such an array. By contrast, M has real-world information (the street number of the apartment) stored in the index Subscript) values of its arrays.

This ability to use subscripts to contain useful information beyond internal addresses is one that has been much more fully exploited in the M language, as we will see in the next section.

Noninteger subscripts in M

To extend the concept of sparse arrays, taking advantage of the ability to use subscripts to contain useful information, let us add one more level to our apartment address example. The routine listed in the preceding section did not allow the user to identify the *name of the street* on which the apartments were located. To remedy this situation in M, we might create yet another level of indexing, as shown below.

```
APTS ;RFW; 5/96; IDENTIFY ALL APTS
   ;get street name, then for each street, get apthouse number and tenant
   WRITE #,"This routine is used to get all apartment dweller names"
   WRITE !?10,"in a city you will be asked for the"
   WRITE !?20,"Street Name, then, for each street, for the"
   WRITE !?20,"Street Number of the Apartment. Finally, for each"
   WRITE !?20,"Apartment, you will be asked to enter the"
   WRITE !?20,"Apartment Number and the tenant's name"
   WRITE !!,"The street names, street numbers and apartment numbers"
   WRITE !,"need not be entered in order"
STREET ;
   READ !!,"Enter name of next street (null to quit): ",APSTRNM
   QUIT:APSTRNM=""
STRNUM ;
   READ !!,"Enter street number of apartment unit (null to quit): ",APST
   GOTO:APST="" STREET
   FOR I=1:1 READ !,"Enter apartment number (null to quit): ",APN QUIT:
   ...APN=""  DO APNAME
   GOTO STRNUM
APNAME ;
   READ !,"enter name of tenant: ",APNAM
   SET APTROW(APSTRNM,APST,APN)=APNAM
   QUIT
   ;END OF ROUTINE
```

This example illustrates several new features, and we can explain them by giving a possible response to one set of queries. From the way in which this routine is constructed, it might be possible to have the following value:

```
APTROW("Stratton Rd","189","C5")="Range"
```

Notice that there are three types of subscripts: a street name (including a space between `Stratton` and `Rd`, an integer, and a mixed alphanumeric (`C5`). It might also have been possible to use a decimal value in such a subscript sequence. However, the presence of text information in subscripts is a feature unique to the M language. Close examination of the routine used to generate such a value shows that it does not use the I index in the FOR loop and that entry of any numeric or text value could be accepted, even for the street number. Incidentally, since there is no need to specify more than one apartment, this routine could be used to collect information for single-unit residences as well. In fact, it could create an index for an entire town!

Another important feature of this routine is that the user need not enter streets, street numbers, or apartment numbers in any specific order. The amazing thing, though, is that the M language somehow places the numbers in order when they are stored, and the user will never have to worry about how it is done. We will see how this property is utilized later in this chapter. To illustrate some of the ways in which one can take advantage of the ability to use noninteger subscripts, consider the following possibilities:

- **Patient visit information**
  All visit information for patients could be stored according to their identification number and the date of the visit, followed by the specific item:

```
PT(ID,Date,LABTST1) = the result of a specific lab test
PT(ID,Date,DX1) = the name of a specific problem treated that day
PT(ID,Date,DX1,MED1) = the medication prescribed for that problem
```

- **Coded dictionary**
  Code numbers are often used to abbreviate reporting of standard items (diseases, traffic code violations, and so on). In order to be able to store the full text description of such dictionaries, one might use a structure such as the following:

```
DXCODE(521.5)="Congestive Heart Failure"
CITCODE("86.A.3")="Drunk and Disorderly in Public"
```

- **Outline for notes**
  The hierarchical system, taught to all school children for outlining notes, includes use of roman numerals, capital letters, arabic numerals, lowercase letters, and so on. These indices are used to various depths, depending on the subject matter. An outline for a report might include some of the following headings:

```
REP2("II","B","3.")="Insecticide Use in Wheat Production"
REP2("IV","D","5.","a","(3)")="Crop Yields in Saskatchewan"
```

In these few examples, the power of string subscripts and hierarchical sparse arrays stands out clearly against any alternative form of indexing. M, because it incorporates these features as a part of the language, is able to handle complex programming tasks associated with groups of text-related information in ways that greatly simplify the programmer's task.

Data retrieval in sparse arrays: $ORDER function

The power of sparse arrays and noninteger subscripts brings with it a new problem not found in dense matrices with integer identifiers. Because a subscript may take on any of a large number of values, it is impossible to predict with certainty what the next subscript will be. It is not even clear how the subscripts should be "ordered" in their storage in memory or on disk. Specifically, there are four questions that must be answered if one is to understand completely the structure and values in a sparse array:

1. What specific subscripts occur at a given depth in the hierarchical structure?
2. Does the variable identified by that subscript contain a value?
3. If a variable exists, what is its value?
4. Does a given element in a sparse array have descendants (i.e., subscripts at a lower level in the hierarchy)?

To illustrate, the example routine that created APTROW earlier in this chapter contains the following subscript and value:

```
APTROW(1267,4)="Hanson"
```

In this example, let us consider only the variable APTROW(1267). As defined, there is another subscript (for another street number) that follows 1267 (1273). However, there is no data value for APTROW(1267). There might be, if we wished to attach a name (Tranquil House) to the apartment at that address, but as it stands, the node is simply a pointer to a lower value. We have therefore dispensed with the second and third questions (since no value exists, we cannot identify it), and it remains only to verify that there are indeed subscripts below APTROW(1267), one for each apartment in the building. We are able to obtain these answers only because we have printed the list for examination. The programming challenge is to find ways in which we can obtain these answers *automatically,* regardless of what values may exist. M provides the tools necessary to accomplish these objectives, and in this section and the one following we describe their operation.

Let us begin with the question of finding, in order, all subscripts at a given level. We will start with a different example, an engagement calendar that also contains reminders for birthdays, anniversaries, and the like. In "outline" form, the hierarchical structure would look like this:

```
Year
.      Month
.        .        Day
.        .         .     Time
.        .         .     Time
.        .         .      ...
.        .        Day
.        .         .     Time
.        .         .     Time
.        .        ...
.      Month
.        .        Day
.        .         .     Time
.        .         .     Time
.        .         .      ...
```

The array repeats itself for every month, day, and hour for which there is information to be recorded. Notice that (thank goodness) not every day need be present and also that the appointment hours need not cover every hour of every day. This, then, is a typical sparse array, one that we want to fill in only as information is needed.

The structures can also be expressed as a tree, as shown in Figure 11.1. From the tree structure it is a little easier to visualize the ordering problem.

FIGURE 11.1: *A Hierarchical Tree of Dates*

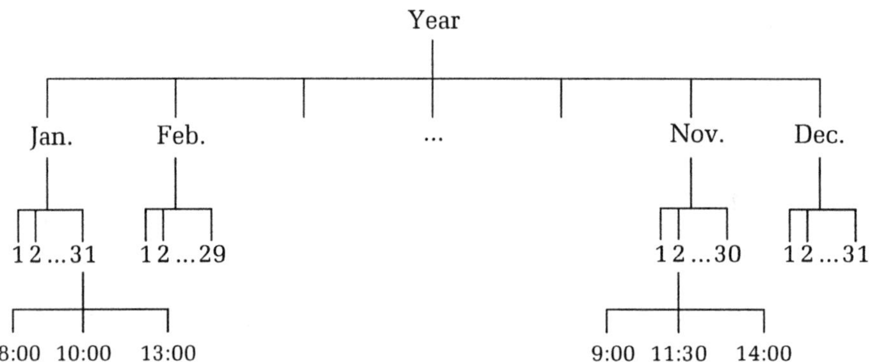

To illustrate with some specific examples, let's assume that we have the following sample information:

```
CAL(96,3,12)="Bday:DTW"
CAL(96,5,15)="Bday:BSH"
CAL(96,6,6,"09:00)="Mr. Covin"
CAL(96,6,6,"11:30")="Mr. Salander"
CAL(96,6,6,"12:15")="Lunch: Development Committee"
CAL(96,6,6,"14:30")="Dr. Orthner"
CAL(96,6,8,"07:00")="EAL fl 723: Atlanta"
CAL(96,8,6)="Bday:LWT"
CAL(96,8,6,"09:27")="Mr. Timson"
CAL(96,8,6,"10:15")="Ms. Lilly"
CAL(96,8,6,"16:45")="Ms. Ogden (+ dinner)"
CAL(96,8,30)="Anniversary"
```

This abbreviated list of entries will serve to give us some practice using the tools M provides to "browse" through such a file. This structure can be visualized in a tree type of format, as in Figure 11.2.

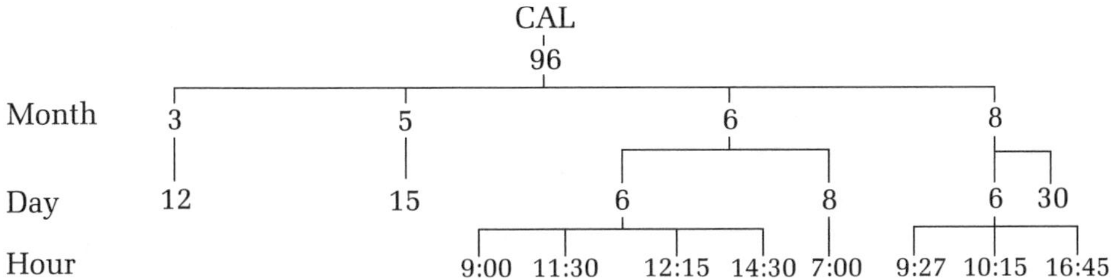

FIGURE 11.2: *A Sparse Array Showing the Tree-Type Structure Used in Multiple Subscripted Variables*

The first question we would like to address is: What months in 1996 are scheduled on the calendar. To answer this question, we use the ORDER function provided by M. `$ORDER(var(subscriptlist))` returns the next available subscript at the level specified. In order to obtain the first value, we use a *seed value* of `""`. Since the months are at the second layer in this hierarchical tree, we would use the following form of the ORDER function:

```
WRITE $ORDER(CAL(96,""))
3
```

This statement instructs M to find the first subscript underneath the year 1996, which in our example is 3 (March). To find the next subscripts in order, the following statements would give us a complete list of months so far included:

```
WRITE $ORDER(CAL(96,3))
4
WRITE $ORDER(CAL(96,4))
6
WRITE $ORDER(CAL(96,6))
8
WRITE $ORDER(CAL(96,8))
(Nothing is written.)
```

In other words, $ORDER returns the next subscript in order and terminates by returning a null value when no further subscripts exist.

Another example might be to ask the question: When and with whom are my appointments for June 6? This could be formulated into a FOR loop as follows:

```
SET X=""
FOR I=1:1 SET X=$ORDER(CAL(96,6,6,X)) QUIT:X=""  WRITE!,X,?10,CAL(96,6,6,X)
```

And the result would be

```
 9:00 Mr. Covin
11:30 Mr. Salander
12:15 Lunch: Development Committee
14:30 Dr. Orthner
```

In this sequence of M commands, we begin with a seed value for X of null and then loop through $ORDER, obtaining each value under the date of June 6. Each time the loop is processed, M checks to see if the value of X is null. If not, it writes the value of X (the next time entered), skips to column 10, and writes the appointment information. This line of code typifies one of the most common command lines found in M, since it is often necessary to traverse a set of subscripts in order to obtain their values.

Notice the two spaces after the postconditionalized QUIT. The second space is essential (and it is often left out by hasty programmers). We will see many other lines in the remainder of this text that resemble this general structure.

One important additional point should be made about the use of $ORDER. Notice that the only subscripts returned were those under the date of June 6. The appointments for other days were not listed, even though they are at the same hierarchical level. This response is due to the fact that the subscripts in the $ORDER list are specific for June 6, and $ORDER recognizes the end of subscripts for that date.

In this example we were able to obtain two pieces of information: the next subscript at a specified level and the data value for the variable defined by that subscript list. We now turn to the other questions raised at the start of this section.

Searching by depth and value existence: $DATA function

The calendar example gives us a chance to explore the other methods for searching a hierarchical tree-structured data list. Supposing we want to know what birthdays or anniversaries are in our file. We could use $ORDER to find all days listed. However, if we were to write the command

```
WRITE CAL(96,6,6)
```

we would get an error message informing us that no variable exists for that level. In other words, even though a date exists, there is no reminder of some special event for that date.

In order to avoid getting an error in such a situation, we can use the $DATA function, which will return a 0 if no value exists, and a 1 if a value exists. For example,

Expression	Value Produced
`$DATA(CAL(96,5,15))`	1
`$DATA(CAL(96,8,24))`	0

In the first case, a birthday reminder exists, whereas the second date has not yet been defined. When we use $DATA in this form, however, we do *not* get an error message for the August 24 date. We can therefore use this function to determine whether a value exists, and if so, we can write it out.

The second purpose of $DATA is to determine whether there are descendants in the hierarchical tree. This function is returned in the tens digit of the $DATA function. If descendants are present, the tens digit is set to 1, otherwise it is left at 0. To summarize all possible values for $DATA (combining both the data existence and the descendant information), we obtain the following matrix:

	Value Does Not Exist	Value Exists
Has no descendants	0	1
Has descendants	10	11

A few values from our example will illustrate the different options of $DATA:

Expression	Value
`$DATA(CAL(96,1))`	0 (not defined)
`$DATA(CAL(96,3,12))`	1 (defined)
`$DATA(CAL(96,6,6))`	10 (not defined, descendants)
`$DATA(CAL(96,8,6))`	11 (defined, descendants)

One useful way to consider the $DATA functions is the following guidelines:

1. Testing for a $DATA value less than 1 indicates whether the node exists at all.
2. Testing for a $DATA greater than 1 indicates if the value has descendants.
3. Testing for $DATA modulo 10 (`$DATA(ref)#10`) indicates whether the node has a value.

Used together, $ORDER and $DATA can provide a programmer with the capability of traversing a complete hierarchical tree of any complexity. To obtain the actual values at a particular node, one can use a WRITE statement, provided that $DATA of that node returns a value of either 1 or 11 (meaning that a value exists).

Sorting in M: the collating sequence for subscripts

If we examine these tools and the M hierarchical structure more carefully, we learn that *sorting* is not required in the M language, provided that subscripts are created to define the key that is to be sorted. As noted in the description of the routine listed earlier to obtain all apartment addresses for a town, the order in which routines accept data is not important in subscripted mode, since M automatically sorts them in their correct order. There is, however, one area in which M flexibility might lead to ambiguity. In our examples we have used integer, decimal, and alphanumeric subscripts. It would be a simple matter if subscripts were restricted to numbers or to alphanumeric characters, but the rules for these two types of strings are different. In the case of alphanumeric characters, the simplest rule to follow is to use the ASCII code representation as the collating sequence. The table of ASCII codes (Table 3.1) defines every printing character and can be used for sorting strings that consist of numbers, punctuation, special characters, and spaces, as well as uppercase and lowercase characters.

In the case of numeric values, however, the ASCII collating sequence will not work, partly because of the use of decimal points in numbers, which changes the place value meaning of digits that precede or follow it. In addition, if one were to store a number in scientific notation (e.g., 5E8), it would not fall in the proper numeric position with numbers represented in conventional notation.

For these reasons, M defines two collating sequences for subscripts. The first is numeric values, which can include integers or decimal values, *but it does not include numbers with leading or trailing insignificant zeros* (e.g., 007 or 1.00). After numbers of the class defined above have been separated and collated, the remaining values are stored in ASCII collating sequence. The definition of a *canonic number,* i.e., one without meaningless leading or trailing zeros, may appear to cause some confusion at first, but there is an easy way around it. For example, it is often necessary to sort addresses by ZIP Code (sometimes it can save large amounts of postage). However, New England ZIP Codes beginning with 0 collate *after* other ZIP Codes using the M definition. The solution is simple: Use a unary + operator to force arithmetic interpretation. If we had a variable `ZIP="01267"`, used as a subscript in the expression `MAIL(ZIP)="BH^MW^FS"` (the initials of people with that zipcode), we could force the subscript to be interpreted as a number by saying `MAIL(+ ZIP)= . . .`, and the codes could then be sorted in order. In practice, these problems arise rarely, but it is nice to know that such solutions exist. (Another solution would be to append a space to the ZIP Code, which would force its interpretation as an alphanumeric string.)

The problem of canonic numbers and their collation can be further illustrated by the following list of subscripts:

```
X(.5)
X(1.3)
X(1.150)
X(XYZ)
X(011)
X(12)
X(X Y Z) (Note spaces between letters)
X(110)
X(150)
X(1.725)
X(150.0)
```

Using the command lines

```
S Z=""
F I=1:1 SET Z=$ORDER(X(Z)) QUIT:Z=""  WRITE !?10,Z
```

we would obtain the following result:

```
.5
1.3
1.725
12
110
150
011
1.150
150.0
X Y Z
XYZ
```

Although this sequence may seem unusual at first, the leading or trailing insignificant zeros in the numbers following 150 (itself legitimate) provide the answer to the result printed.

The fact that M *has* such a collating sequence associated with subscripts can be utilized in many applications. Sorting becomes an implicit function associated with creating a sparse array indexed according to the key that is to be sorted, and M takes care of the rest. (A T-shirt available from the M Technology Association Office reads "M means never having to say you're sorting.")

As powerful as M's collation is in its present form, there are ways in which it could be improved. Non-English languages require special characters, even if they use ASCII as a component of their alphabet (such as western European languages). The codes for these characters do not appear in a numeric sequence that provides alphabetic collation. Even in English, upper and lower case letters are separated in the ASCII code sequence, and hence words like COBOL, California, and calculator would not sort correctly (unless $TRANSLATE were used to convert them either to upper or lower case). This is an issue that the MDC has wrestled with. A partial solution is described in Part 2 of this text. As you get more familiar with M, you may want to follow this important evolutionary trend of the language.

KILL as used with arrays

The KILL command (Chapter 6) also may be used to delete arrays. However, the meaning of a KILL command acquires greater flexibility when used with arrays. The following examples should serve to illustrate the point. Consider the example of the street addresses and apartments given earlier.

Expression	Value Produced
`KILL APTROW(1267,4)`	Only Apt 4, address 1267 deleted
`KILL APTROW(1273)`	All apartments at address 1273 deleted
`KILL APTROW`	The entire variable deleted with all subscripts

The second and third examples are especially important, in that they delete not only the value mentioned, but all subscripts stored in the tree below that value.

Summary

This chapter has introduced the concept of subscripted "sparse" arrays that characterize M. The key features described are as follows:

- M does not require declaration of arrays. Array values are created dynamically, and they can be "sparse." Only defined values occupy space in the computer's memory.
- M allows multiple subscripts, separated by commas, to define a hierarchical data structure of arbitrary depth and complexity limited only by conventions of portability requirements (currently, the total number of characters in the subscript fields must be less than 128).
- M permits the use of integers, decimals, and strings in subscripts. Strings may consist of any printing ASCII characters (control characters are not allowed).

- M stores subscripted variables according to a collating sequence that separates canonical numbers (those integer or decimal values without meaningless leading or trailing zeros) from all other ASCII strings, the latter being sorted according to the ASCII code value of each character.
- In order to search a sparse hierarchical structure, M provides the functions $ORDER, which returns the next subscript at a given level, and $DATA, which provides information about the existence of values at hierarchical nodes as well as the presence of descendants below the specified node.
- The use of a FOR loop with $ORDER provides an effective means for obtaining all subscripts at a given level of a hierarchical data structure.
- The KILL command can be used to remove entire arrays or individual items. Removal of a node in the middle of a tree also removes all descendants below that node.

Exercises

The hierarchical M array structure is one of the most powerful and unique features of the language. Individuals familiar with languages that require declarations for predefined arrays often find this concept disturbing, yet it is clear that the approach lends itself to many new forms of data representation that are more natural for storing real-world data than the traditional matrices of other languages.

In these exercises, we introduce only a few examples of the use of M tree-structured data. Other chapters will continue to build on this concept, which lies at the heart of the power of the M language. In order to give some practice in developing a potentially useful package, the following exercises build on a single problem – that of creating a student grading system.

1. ***Creation of a Grade File*** Write a routine that will ask for a student `ID` and for a `GRADE` (expressed as a score between `0` and `100`). The `ID` should consist of the first letter of the student's last name followed by three digits. The `ID` should be used as a subscript for the variable `STDN`, and the `GRADE` should be assigned to that `ID`.

   The routine should end entry of student `ID`s and `GRADE`s when the user types a <*return*> with no new `ID` (null entry).

   The routine should keep track of how many students were entered, as well as the `MIN` and `MAX` values entered for `GRADE`. At the end of the entry process, the routine should list the student `ID`s and their `GRADE`s in collating sequence order and display how many students were entered, as well as the `MIN`, `MAX`, and `AVG GRADE` received.

When you execute this routine, be sure that you enter the same grade for several students (e.g., two or three students with 75, a few with 80, and so on). You will need this condition to solve the next problem. You should enter about 20 or so IDs and GRADEs.

2. ***Creating a Histogram of Grades*** Using the information obtained in Exercise 1, create a new array DIST which has an entry for each *different* grade received. To create this array, use $ORDER to go through the STDN array and obtain each grade. The DIST variable will be created with a value of one asterisk for each time a grade of that value is encountered (see sample output below). For each grade, using $DATA(DIST(GRADE)), determine if a value has been entered from a previous grade. If not, create the value DIST(GRADE) and assign it a value of one asterisk. If the value has been previously encountered, append another asterisk to the first (use the concatenate operator). When the last grade has been processed, use $ORDER to print out the grade and the number of asterisks for that particular value. The output should look something like this:

```
Histogram of Grades

60 *
68 *
72 **
75 ***
78 ****
80 ***
84 *****
87 *
88 **
90 *
92 *
97 *
```

3. ***Creating a Sorted List of Students*** Using the array STDN, present, one at a time, the ID values to the user and ask for a name in the form <last, first>. Create a new array called STDNAM which has the student's name as the subscript and the ID as the value. Then list this array in alphabetical order, with the ID first and then the student's name, as follows:

```
A786  Addams, Charles
C322  Capp, Alfred
S198  Schultz, Charles
S056  Stevenson, Robert
T455  Trudeau, Gary
```
etc.

Global Variables

12

In Chapter 3 we introduced the concept of a *variable*, an entity that holds a value. This concept was expanded in Chapter 11 to include the notion of *arrays*. Arrays provide a convenient method of grouping associated values in clusters with common relationships. Now we want to introduce the principle of variables that will be retained by the M system after the user has signed off. The variables described up to this point belong to the class called *local variables*. M uses the term *local* in a somewhat special sense, in that local variables are limited both in their accessibility and in their lifetime. M local variables may only be referenced by a single user during a single session; they cease to exist when he or she signs off, and they may not be accessed by other users even though they are logged in at the same time. The reader has perhaps experienced some frustration with exercises in earlier chapters, in that each time a new session is terminated, the variables created in that session are erased, and if they are needed later, they must be regenerated. This notion of

Note to experienced programmers: The M language is unique in defining *persistent, shared variables* that are directly referenced with M commands, stored on disk, and available to all authorized users as soon as they are created by any user. M uses the term *global variables* to identify these variables, and it reserves the term *local variables* for temporary variables created during a single interactive session and erased at the conclusion of that session. Local variables are not available to other users, and they are not retained. The concept of global variables (identified by a caret (^) in front of the name) is unusual and requires some adjusting in programming style. Other elements covered in this chapter include the use of abbreviated syntactical reference forms for identifying global variables (the *naked syntax*).

the meaning of *local* conflicts with the use of the term in some other programming languages. Users familiar with other systems such as Pascal or FORTRAN should take note of the distinction.

What is a global variable?

Since one of the main benefits of the M language relates to its use of persistent, shared files, some means must be found to define variables that may be stored on disk and shared by many users after the user session that created or modified them. No other high-level programming language has this capability; the variables created by a program in C, for example, are destroyed when the program terminates. Other languages have to use cumbersome, nonstandard ways of opening files and accessing them. M, on the other hand, accommodates these requirements through the use of *global variables.* (Note: Most other programming languages use the terms 'local' and 'global' in a different way, since none of these languages provide persistent data. We use the terms here using the M definition. We will refer again to this distinction in discussing the NEW command in Chapter 16.)

Global variables have the same general properties as local variables, but they may be shared by multiple users and they are stored by the M system until they are explicitly killed. The most common way in which global files are retained is on some mass storage device, such as a magnetic disk. The physical characteristics of such devices may affect the manner in which they are accessed, but from a logical point of view their nature remains constant. As you become more familiar with your system and your own needs for shared global files, you may wish to learn more about the implementation features of your system's global files, so that you can make efficient use of these files in your own programs.

Global variables are distinguished by the presence of a caret or up-arrow (^) in front of the variable name. For example:

```
SET X="Aardvark"
```

creates a *local variable* that will be destroyed when the user session terminates (poor aardvark!). However,

```
SET ^X="Aardvark"
```

instructs M to create a *global variable* which will be stored on disk and available for subsequent use by anyone with access to the globals created by that user. (Most implementations create groups of users, so that multiple applications can run on the same system.) In all other respects, global variables follow the same rules of formation defined in Chapter 11 for local variables: they may be subscripted or nonsubscripted, and if they are subscripted, they may have an unlimited number of subscripts (providing the line length is not exceeded). Generally speaking, global variables may be used interchangeably with local variables. They return similar results as local variables when used with $DATA and $ORDER, and they obey the same rules when referenced in SET and KILL commands.

There are, however, three situations in which global variables may not be used:

- As the control variable in a FOR command
- As a subargument in the parenthesized form of the KILL command
- As arguments in the NEW command, parameter passing, and extrinsic functions (see Chapter 16)

If we take a moment to review the examples and exercises of the previous chapters, we can see immediately that modifying those routines by substituting global variables instead of local variables would be far more valuable if the information were to be retained.

> **Note:** There is one important caution that should be mentioned at this point. When an M global variable is created in an interactive session, it is stored temporarily in a *buffer* in the computer's main memory. A buffer is an intermediate storage space for data that will eventually be written out to disk. Since, however, disk access is slow, all M systems and most operating systems provide buffers to improve system performance. The only danger with the use of buffers is the possibility that the data may *not get written* to disk, thereby being lost at the end of a user session. The two ways in which this undesirable event might happen are (1) a hardware failure or power loss, and (2) termination of a user session without typing `HALT` at the end. When M sees the HALT command, it checks all the buffers used by that session and ensures their being written to disk prior to terminating the session. If a user fails to type `HALT` the system is unaware of the need to preserve these variables.

The danger of losing information stored in temporary buffers is even more important when existing global variables have been modified during a session, since there may be important indexing attributes stored in buffers that must be dumped out to disk if the global file is to retain its data integrity. M globals are usually stored as B-tree files, which have a unique and complicated structure that requires accurate storage of pointers as well as data information.

The main point, then, is to emphasize that typing `HALT` at the end of a user session is extremely important when global variables have been set or modified during that session. Failure to do so may result in corruption of the global file, a situation that requires expert intervention to correct.

Additional commands and functions for dealing with global variables

Since M permits users to store persistent data, it makes sense to provide some additional ways that these data elements can be manipulated. In this section, we will point out a number of language elements (two commands and several functions) that can make M's persistent data storage even more flexible and powerful. These language elements make little sense in dealing with local variables, and hence they are applicable only to globals.

Copying globals: the MERGE command

Suppose we had a global variable with the following structure:

```
^Pat
 .    ID
 .    .    Date
 .    .    .    Visit#
 .    .    .    .    Problem
 .    .    .    .    .    Lab Test
 .    .    .    .    .    .         Result
 .    .    .    .    .    Medication
 .    .    .    .    .    .         Dosage
                          Instruc-
 .    .    .    .    .    tions to
                          patient
```

This is a common form of a medical record, in which laboratory procedures, medications, and patient instructions are grouped by the "problem" to which they relate. Such a global would be large, depending on the number of patients in the database (our university hospital has over 1 million patient names on file). If someone wanted to study a particular problem for one patient, it would be necessary to make many accesses to the database in order to obtain that information. A partial solution would be to copy a part of the large database into a temporary file, thereby reducing the size of the global accessed. The MERGE command is particularly useful for this purpose. For instance, one could type

```
MERGE ^TEMP(278946)=^Pat(278946)
```

which would cause the *entire* set of records for that patient to be stored in a temporary global called TMP. This file could be further reduced to those visits dealing with a specific problem (say, problem number 7) as follows:

```
SET ID=278946,(date,visit,prob)=""
FOR  SET date=$ORDER(^TMP(ID,date)) QUIT:date=""  DO
  . FOR  SET visit=$ORDER(^TMP(ID,date,visit)) QUIT:visit=""  DO
  . . FOR  SET prob=$ORDER(^TMP(ID,date,visit,prob)) QUIT: prob=""  DO
  . . . IF prob'=7 KILL ^TMP(ID,date,visit,prob)
```

(continue)

The same type of logic could be used to restrict the temporary database to specific date ranges, using an internal form of date storage that corresponds to $HOROLOG's first component (the number of days elapsed since Dec. 31, 1840). The point is that the MERGE command can allow useful subtrees of an M global to be copied into another global, thereby facilitating processing of data more efficiently.

Extended search functions: $GETand $QUERY

The functions $DATA and $ORDER provide powerful search functions in traversing local or global variables. However, there are two pieces of information that they do *not* provide. The first is the actual *value* of a variable. If one wants to get this information, one must either WRITE the variable or perhaps assign the value to a new variable (if it is to be manipulated).

The second piece of information not provided by $DATA and $ORDER is specific reference to a new level of the hierarchical reference. We will deal with these two programming problems separately below.

$GET function

To provide a more direct way of getting the value of a local or global variable, the function $GET was added to the standard in 1990. `$GET(var(subs))` returns the value of the specified variable. The `var` may be either a local or global variable reference. If the variable does not exist, $GET returns the empty string, *but it does not return an error.* This latter distinction avoids the necessity of checking the value of $DATA in referencing variables that may or may not exist.

To consider an application of this function, suppose that we want to create a cross-reference, by ZIP Code, of individuals in an address list. Assume that the new name to be added is stored in NEWNAME and that all names are stored in a global variable ZIP with the ZIP Code as the subscript and each name appended, separated by a caret (^). Such an approach would generate a list of the following type:

```
ZIP(20037)="SCAMC^GWU^Georgetown U^"
ZIP(20709)="MTA Office^Silver Spring^"
```

with each ZIP Code reference containing the names of individuals or groups with that postal code. In order to create such a cross-reference, the following code would be required if only $DATA were available:

```
IF '$DATA(^ZIP(VAL)) SET ^ZIP(VAL)=""
SET ^ZIP(VAL)=^ZIP(VAL)_NEWNAME_"^"
```

The first line is required, since the second line would generate an error the first time a new ZIP Code is encountered. If the $GET function is used, the code is reduced to

```
SET ^ZIP(VAL)=$GET(^ZIP(VAL))_NEWNAME_"^"
```

This line of code is not only shorter, but it avoids the necessity of having to be certain each time that a variable exists. Programmers often fail to consider this possibility, and though the code works in most cases, errors can arise when undefined variables are referenced.

$QUERY function

The second functional tool that is not provided by current functions in M is the ability to get information directly about the next lower subscript in an M hierarchical structure. With $ORDER and $DATA, it is possible to write a routine that will traverse an entire global variable. However, this is a rather difficult programming task, requiring sophisticated techniques and the use of indirection (described in Chapter 15) if the routine is to be truly general purpose. Most implementors have utilities that perform this function, often achieved by adding nonstandard language extensions (see Chapter 14). Since it is often necessary to obtain information about a global file in a more convenient form than that available through the $ORDER and $DATA functions, $QUERY was approved as a standard means of providing programmers with this increased functionality.

The calendar example given in the introduction to the $ORDER function in Chapter 11 provides a good example of the utility of this function. In that example, we created the following variables (which we will now assign to a *global* array instead of the *local* array used in that chapter):

```
^CAL(87,3,12)="Bday:DTW"
```

```
^CAL(87,5,15)="Bday:LWT"
^CAL(87,6,6,"09:00")="Mr. Covin"
^CAL(87,6,6,"11:30")="Mr. Salander"
^CAL(87,6,6,"12:15")="Lunch: Development Committee"
^CAL(87,6,6,"14:30")="Dr Orthner"
^CAL(87,6,8,"7:00")="EAL fl 723: Atlanta"
^CAL(87,8,6)="Bday:LWT"
^CAL(87,8,6,"09:27")="Mr. Timson"
^CAL(87,8,6,"10:15")="Ms. Lilly"
^CAL(87,8,6,"16:45")="Ms. Ogden (+ dinner)"
^CAL(87,8,30)="Anniversary"
```

In Chapter 11 we showed how $ORDER could be used to traverse *one level* of that tree, describing how to determine which months were represented with one line of code and then, in a separate example, searching for the hours scheduled in a given day. However, that section presented no general way for examining the entire calendar. If we want to write a routine that allows a user to maintain a personal calendar of the type displayed, we would have to use nested loops, one for each level of the calendar (year, month, day, time). The routine would get convoluted, mainly because of the limitations of the available standard functions.

The $QUERY function provides the solution to this problem:

```
$QUERY(global variable(subscripts))
```

returns the next subscript having a data value, using a depth-first search technique. To illustrate, consider the following line of code, assuming there are no other entries to our global variable `^CAL`. The command line

```
WRITE $QUERY(^CAL)
```

would generate the following result

```
^CAL(87,3,12)
```

the first subscript under that global variable name. Notice, though, that the value returned is the *complete reference*, not just the subscript Moreover,

```
WRITE $QUERY(^CAL(87,3,12))
```

would produce

```
^CAL(87,5,15)
```

Notice that there is no result for `^CAL(87,5)` because there is no value at that subscript level. This function eliminates several knotty programming problems. First, it obviates the need to create a separate FOR loop for each separate level of subscripting. Second, it eliminates the need to use $DATA to test either whether a subscript has a data value or has descendants. Since the $QUERY function only returns the next subscript with a value, $DATA will always be either 1 or 11, and it is no longer necessary to use that test.

$QUERY returns the entire global reference, including the name of the global variable, so it can be used directly to retrieve the intended value. In Chapter 15 we will see how this example can be further extended (by the use of indirection) to traverse an entire tree, including both subscripts and values. (We will also learn about three new functions for global manipulation: $NAME, $QLENGTH, and $QSUBSCRIPT; these functions are also best understood when used with the indirection operator and hence their discussion is deferred to Chapter 15.) The combined features of $DATA, $ORDER, $GET, and $QUERY give M programmers a powerful set of tools with which to traverse and manipulate hierarchical M global variables.

LOCK command

(The LOCK command, available to permit multiple users to share the same data without interfering with each other, is an important feature of M. It is also somewhat advanced, and for this reason, discussion of LOCK will be deferred to Part II of this text, where it is found in Chapter 21.)

Naked references to global variables

M's references to long subscripts may sometimes be cumbersome even though they are useful. For example, suppose we have a global with a person's name as the first subscript, and we wanted to use separate subscripts for street address and so on. Using the standard form of the global reference, our command lines might look like this:

```
SET^CLIENT("Lilly, M.","STR")="1738 Elton Rd"
SET^CLIENT("Lilly, M.","CITY")="Silver Spring"
SET^CLIENT("Lilly, M.","STATE")="Maryland"
SET^CLIENT("Lilly, M.","ZIP")="20905"
```

The chances of typing the full subscript reference correctly will diminish with the number of times it has to be repeated. An additional, shorthand, form of global variable reference is also provided in the M language. This form, referred to as the *naked syntax,* allows the programmer to refer *implicitly* to the most recent previous global reference, modifying only the last subscript. In the preceding example, we could perform the same functions by modifying the commands as follows:

```
SET^CLIENT("Lilly, M.","STR")="1738 Elton Rd."
SET^("CITY")="Silver Spring"
SET^("STATE")="Maryland"
SET^("ZIP")="20905"
```

The syntax of the naked reference involves omitting the *name* of the global variable and all subscripts except the last one. M automatically inserts the missing information to complete the assignment statement. The shortened reference defines an imaginary string called the *naked state*, which consists of the global name, the left parenthesis, and the subscripts up to but not including the last.

Naked references also may use multiple subscripts, so that the command line

```
SET^A(1,2)=5,^(2,3)=13
```

results in ^A(1,2,3) being set equal to 13.

Naked references are used to keep code concise and to make the job of typing command lines easier. This form of reference may, however, be a bit tricky, so it should be used with caution. Remember that the naked state is defined by the last executed global reference, not necessarily the one that precedes it in the routine. One common error that can arise occurs when a routine is modified, inserting a global reference between two lines without realizing that the insert changes the naked reference of the line following the inserted line. For this reason, when routines are being developed, it is always good practice to use full global references. A better approach would be to assign the value of the reference to a variable name and use that name in programming. Special language features supporting this latter approach are described in Chapter 15.

As another example of a potential problem with the use of naked references, consider the following sequence of instructions. Assume that we wish to test for the existence of ^A(I) and, if defined, create ^A(I,J) = J for values of J from 1 to 100. The following command line might appear to be a reasonable solution:

```
IF $DATA(^A(I)) FOR J=1:1:100 SET ^(I,J)=J
```

However, when this sequence of instructions is executed, we will create a global file with 101 levels (subscripts), since each execution of the naked syntax will increase the length of the naked state by one subscript. The resulting global will be

```
^A(I,1)=1
```

```
^A(I,I,2)=2
^A(I,I,I,3)=3
```

In fact, the correct code to accomplish the desired task is

```
IF $DATA(^A(I)) SET ^(I,1)=1 FOR J=2:1:100 SET ^(J)=J
```

The use of naked syntax is erroneous if the naked state is not defined. The naked state is undefined in the following cases:

- At user sign-on, i.e., before any global references have been made
- After any unsubscripted global reference

Summary

This chapter introduced the concept of global variables, values that may be shared by multiple users of an M system and are stored, usually on disk, for extended time periods. Local variables, on the other hand, are used during individual interactive sessions, may not be shared by users, and are not retained after the user who set them signs off the system.

- M global variables are identified by a caret (^) preceding the name of the variable.
- Globals can be manipulated using most of the same commands that apply to local variables (e.g., SET and KILL).
- M functions such as $EXTRACT, $FIND, $LENGTH, and $PIECE can all be used with global variables, as can $ORDER and $DATA. The MERGE command copies entire globals or specified subtrees of globals. In addition, M offers two functions specific to globals: $GET, which retrieves the value stored at a subscript, and $QUERY, which performs a depth-first search of an entire global tree.
- M permits an abbreviated form of reference to global variables known as the *naked reference,* which uses the most recent previous global reference to establish all but the last subscript in such a reference.

Exercises

The use of globals makes it possible to store values generated by M routines on disk after a session has been terminated. This capability is a useful option in many situations, including some of the exercises listed in previous chapters. In order to take advantage of this language feature, you might want to modify one or more routines written in earlier chapters to create global variables where local variables were used before. To do so, the best way is to enter an edit program provided by your system and select the variables that you might want to store for future reference; then, for every reference of that name, insert a caret (^) in front of the name.

Most M implementations give you ways in which you can determine what globals are currently stored on disk. Some systems have utilities such as %GD (`DO ^%GD` will give the desired result) to serve that purpose. In UNIX-based systems, %gl is available for the same purpose. Find out from your system's manual or support person how you can obtain such a list on your implementation.

1. ***Modification of Previous Example*** One good example would be to take the variable `STDN` in the Exercises in Chapter 11 and substitute `^STDN` for that local variable. Try it; then see if the variable is stored for future reference by running the routine(s), logging off when a list of students and grades has been entered, and then logging on again and running only the list portion of the routine. (The other files in that exercise can be retained as local arrays.)

2. ***Creation of a Dictionary*** Write a routine that will allow a user to create or update one or more dictionaries of terms. The global variable should have the following structure:

   `^DICT(AREA) =` *<area definition for a set of terms>*
   `^DICT(AREA,TERM) = DEF` *(the definition of a word or term)*

   Your program should ask first for AREA. If it is a new area, get a one-line definition. Then, within that area, store each TERM, using the TERM as the second-level subscript, and obtain a DEF(inition) of that term. Use a null entry for TERM to proceed to LIST (see below).

   LIST should give the user the option to display the sorted list of terms for that AREA dictionary. If the user wishes the values displayed, list each term on a new line, with the definition starting in column 20 on the same line. Enter values for one dictionary (as few or as many as you wish). Exit the program; then invoke it again, entering terms for a second dictionary. Exit again; then append at least one new and one modified definition for either dictionary. Display the results to verify correct action in each case.

External Communication: Files and Devices

13

Up to this point, all the interaction described in this text has dealt with the use of a terminal interacting with an M interpreter, whether the terminal was a keyboard and screen attached to a personal computer or one linked to a multiuser system. Often, however, the need arises to communicate with other elements of a computer system. A user may wish to

- Send output to a printer, graphics plotter, or special-purpose display
- Connect, via an external communications port, to a remote computer
- Create files that can be read by other languages or by a systems editor
- Read or create a file stored on magnetic tape
- Any other of many activities requiring use of resources beyond the terminal and M system itself

This capability is essential in transferring data and M routines from one location to another, sending messages to individuals at remote locations, and interfacing with other languages. As more M implementations permit multi-language access, this form of communication is becoming increasingly important.

> **Note to experienced programmers:** M provides for communication with external files and devices through the OPEN, USE, and CLOSE commands and the $IO special variable. These constructs are conceptually different from those of other high-level languages in that they provide access to resources usually requiring lower-level system calls. The summary and exercises provide most of the necessary information for experienced programmers, but the conceptual differences are subtle, perhaps warranting review of the body of the chapter as well.

M allows for this type of communication in ways that are sometimes not appreciated even by experienced M users. The features described in this chapter deal with elements that are not fully standardized, partly because the configuration of different systems is so variable that precise standardization is not feasible. However, the primitive commands and functions that support communication with external resources are standard, and we will concentrate on their general capabilities, giving a few examples that may have some minor nonstandard elements.

Devices in M

In order for an M user to be able to interact with an external resource, three steps are necessary:

1. Gain access to the resource.
2. Use the resource as desired.
3. Release use of the resource so that others can access it.

The way that M identifies external resources is to assign them *device numbers.* A device number is an integer that is recognized by the M implementation as having certain characteristics, such as the following:

Device type	Parameters
Printer	Page width, page length, font, graphics controls, etc.
Magnetic tape	Density, blocking, record size, fixed/ variable length, etc.
Disk file	Name, type, sequential/random, append, access codes, etc.
Communications port	System identifier, rate, parity, stop bit, etc.

These incomplete examples illustrate the difficulty of attempting to standardize such characteristics. M links this type of characteristic to a device by attaching *device parameters* to the identification of each device when its use is requested.

All M systems make use of devices of the type just described. In each implementation, the number and characteristics of the devices may vary. To use one example for purposes of illustration, UCD MicroMUMPS offers the following devices:

Device	Device Type
0	User console
1	Printer
2	Disk file (MSDOS type)
3	Disk file (MSDOS type)
4	Disk file (MSDOS type)
5	External communications port

Note: This implementation is out of date, in that features incorporated in the last two revisions of the standard are not included. It still serves as a useful vehicle for learning about the language at a novice level, and its use of devices is simple enough to serve as a good example in this context.

The device number in the case of a printer or a communications port is fairly self-evident. However, in the case of the disk-file devices, the integer values of the device (2, 3, or 4) are only identifiers which can subsequently be used in M to access specific files. Further identification is required to specify which files are attached to which devices. A user wishing to take advantage of the printer or communications port would need to make certain that the operating system calls setting up those devices have been done. Once the devices are available, M uses three commands to allow a user to access these devices: OPEN, USE, and CLOSE. These commands are described in the sections that follow.

OPEN command

Before any device or file may be referenced in an I/O operation, the device or file must be assigned to the user. There are two reasons for this approach. First, M must know which devices are to be accessed in a routine, and the device numbers must be related to specific physical entities. In addition, since M implementations usually support a number of simultaneous users, this provision is required to permit sharing of resources in an orderly manner. Assignment of a device to a user is accomplished by executing the OPEN command. Each argument list of the OPEN command consists of three parts, only the first of which is required:

- An expression that serves to identify the device or file to be opened
- One or more expressions, called *device parameters,* that provide information necessary to describe the device or file
- An expression that indicates the maximum amount of time the program should spend attempting to obtain the device or file (This expression is referred to as the *timeout.*)

Because the nature of I/O operations is highly dependent on the particular device and implementation of M, the ANSI standard does not define the interpretation either of the identifier expression or of the device parameter expression. The examples in the preceding section illustrate one set of devices. Other systems will make use of these and other device numbers with different meanings. For specific details on your installation, consult your system documentation.

When a program issues an OPEN command, M attempts to give that program exclusive "ownership" of the requested item, thereby preventing other users from accessing the same device. Upon encountering an OPEN request, execution of further code in the user's instruction sequence is suspended until ownership is obtained. If there is a timeout specified (the third part of the OPEN argument), control will return to the user's instructions if that time limit is exceeded. If ownership is obtained within the designated time, the special variable $T is set TRUE, indicating a successful OPEN. If ownership cannot be obtained within the time limit (i.e., some other user already has opened the device and it is therefore not available), the $T special variable is set FALSE. The user can therefore test this variable to determine if he or she has obtained ownership. If no timeout is present, $T is not affected. However, the OPEN will only return when ownership has been obtained.

The use of the OPEN command is illustrated by the following examples taken from the UCD MicroMUMPS environment:

`OPEN 1` *(No parameters: M assigns the printer to the user.)*
`OPEN 5` *(No parameters: M assigns the communications port to the user.)*
`OPEN 2:("A":"DOSFILE TXT")` *(File* `DOSFILE.TXT` *on drive* `A` *is opened.)*
`OPEN 1:10` *(If printer not available,* `$T` *returns* `FALSE` *after* `10` *seconds.)*

Other systems and devices require different parameter lists, but these examples illustrate the type of parameters used in one implementation.

It is often necessary to have two devices available at the same time. Suppose, for instance, that a user wishes to read a file from disk, perform some transformations on the data, and then output the results to a printer. In the UCD MicroMUMPS environment, the command initiating this process would be

```
OPEN 1,2:("C":"DATAFILE.TXT")
```

which would open the printer and an external disk file named `DATAFILE.TXT`. Notice that it is possible to list several devices in a single OPEN command.

Once a user has gained access to one or more devices, they will be available for use in M programs, as shown in the next section.

USE command and $IO special variable

Once a device or file has been opened, a user must indicate which device to reference with READ and WRITE statements. Since the user always communicates with M via a terminal, opening another device creates an ambiguous situation unless a way is found to identify the specific device intended. The ambiguity lies in the fact that once a secondary device is open, the READ and WRITE commands are not explicit as to which device is to be acted on. M resolves this ambiguity through the USE command, taking advantage of a special variable referred to as $IO, which is defined as the *current device* and is the single device referenced at any given time by READ and WRITE commands. Initially, the current device is the terminal, and the special variable $IO is set to 0 (the default value when a user logs on). In order for the program to change the current device, it must execute a USE command.

To illustrate by continuing the example begun in the preceding section, the expanded routine might read as follows:

```
 OPEN 1,2:("C":"DATAFILE.TXT") ;get access to printer, disk file
LOOP;
 USE 2 READ RECORD ;get a record from the DATAFILE.TXT file
 QUIT:RECORD=[EOF] ;terminate loop when end of file reached (see note)
```

<*commands to modify the contents of* RECORD>

```
 USE 1 WRITE RECORD ;output to printer
 USE 0 WRITE RECORD ;also display on terminal
 GOTO LOOP
```

Note: EOF differs in different operating systems. One useful technique is to terminate when a READ returns an empty string or one whose length is 0.

In this example, three devices are utilized in the same routine: one to obtain the record to be read from an external disk file, the second to output the manipulated data to a printer, and the third to confirm the action taken by displaying the same result on the user terminal. This latter step is often a useful safeguard, since sometimes the logic of data manipulation may be incorrect and the result may not be immediately available to the user, e.g., when a printer is located in a different room.

Each time the USE command is invoked, M resets $IO to the requested device. This variable may be interrogated to determine the identifier of the current device, as illustrated in the next section.

CLOSE command

When a resource has been opened by a user, it is restricted from use by others as long as the user retains it. For a shared printer, this restriction may prove to be an impediment to effective operations. It is incumbent on users to release the devices they no longer use so that others may OPEN and USE them as required. The release of a device is accomplished by the CLOSE command.

To illustrate, let us consider a common problem encountered in many operations where a user may or may not wish to save output to a printer. The following code demonstrates a typical scenario involving such a situation and using UCD MicroMUMPS notation:

```
READ !,"Would you like output to go to screen or printer (S/P)?: ",OUT
IF OUT["P" OPEN 1 USE 1
WRITE !!,... (Output commands will go to device 1 if specified.)
IF $IO=1 CLOSE 1 USE 0
WRITE !!,"Done",!!
```

This example typifies use of the CLOSE command as well as the interrogation of $IO to determine whether a CLOSE is required.

The CLOSE command also can appear with additional parameters besides those used to identify the device. Suppose, for example, that a disk file had been opened for use as a scratch file, to be subsequently deleted. This situation would differ from one in which the disk file was intended to be retained for future use, e.g., in transferring data to another system.

M allows the use of parameters with the CLOSE statement, but it reserves to implementors the specifics of the meaning to be attached to such parameters. In UCD MicroM, for example, the CLOSE command with an argument of 1 for an MSDOS file writes the file, closes it through MSDOS calls, and returns control to the M interpreter, whereas a CLOSE 0 erases the scratch file without saving it. Other systems each have their own conventions. This example serves to illustrate the potential value of parameters used with the CLOSE command.

Once the functions of OPEN, USE, and CLOSE are understood, it should become clear that M permits communication with external files and systems in a manner that is both open-ended and powerful. Implementors have introduced parameters that permit random access of remote files, special parameters to control I/O characteristics of selected devices, and other features that expand the utility of the M system. Although these functions cannot be standardized for all systems, their availability in one form or another on most systems ensures a greater flexibility to this language than is usually attributed to it.

The OPEN, USE, and CLOSE commands are extremely useful in M. It is an important assumption, in a multiuser environment, to ensure that any commonly used devices (such as printers or tape drives) are immediately returned to general availability when their use is terminated by a single user. The M standard provides the tools for implementing this desirable situation, but it requires discipline and operations supervision to make sure that access to shared resources is not abused by users.

Summary

M operates with variables and routines that are specific to the M environment, including *global files* and M *routines* whose location may be transparent to the user. This chapter defines some of the tools used in accessing external files of several types.

- **OPEN <device number>:<UCI/path specifications>:<timeout>** attempts to gain access to a device identified by the first argument of the OPEN command using parameters described in the (optional) second argument and trying for a number of seconds specified by the (optional) third argument of the OPEN command. More than one device may be open at one time, but no device opened by one user can be shared with another. The term *device* may refer to a hardware resource, such as a communications port or printer, or to a disk file, with name and format characteristics described in the second set of arguments in the parameter list.
- **USE <device number>** directs output for the READ and WRITE commands to the devices in question. Since the variety of I/O devices will vary considerably from one implementation to another, M does not reserve the meaning of any integers attached to a M system.
- **CLOSE <device number>:<parameter list>** is the complementary command of the OPEN command. In general, it releases a device previously restricted by an OPEN command to a single user, and it also may be used to determine whether a particular device is available within a given time period. The parameters used with CLOSE identify the status of the target file and indicate whether it is to be closely monitored in its formative time period. A normal M exit through the HALT command closes all user devices.

Exercises

In this chapter, the use of external files and devices has been described. These features of the M language are introduced to illustrate concepts that allow this type of operation in all M implementations. The reader is cautioned, however, that many features described in this chapter are not standard and that they may vary from one implementation to another.

1. ***Redirected Output*** Using the routine created to solve Exercise 2 in Chapter 12 (the dictionary problem), modify the routine such that the user will be asked after the label LIST whether the user wishes to send output to the screen or the printer. Execute the remainder of the code in conformance with the user's wishes; then CLOSE all devices not essential to the user's short-term needs.

2. ***Use of Multiple External Files*** Write an M routine that creates a global file named ^STATE containing names of STATES (ST) and their CAPITALS (CAP). Using a FOR loop, write the contents of this file out to an external sequential file named STATES.DAT in alphabetical order of STATE. Once the file has been created, close it and save it for future reference. (If you have access to the file from the operating system, e.g., MSDOS, type the file to be sure that it exists as intended.)

   Using the file created by this process, read into a new global named ^CAPITAL the names of all capitals entered in the STATE file with the state as a value: ^CAPITAL(CAP)=ST. Open a second external disk file named CAPS.DAT, and write out the contents of the capital-sorted global file.

   Using the two files STATES.DAT and CAPS.DAT, open each in order and output their results, formatted to produce attractive output, on a hard-copy printer device. Close the STATES.DAT file before opening the CAPS.DAT file, and make sure that the CAPS.DAT file output starts on a new page of the printer output.

14 Some Special Features of Standard M

We have considered nearly all the standard features of the M language up to this point. There remain a few language elements that do not readily lend themselves to inclusion in previous chapters. Some are advanced concepts that added unnecessary complication at an introductory level, whereas others do not fit into the organization of the previous chapters. This chapter deals with these features: extensions to the READ and WRITE commands, pattern match, $HOROLOG, and $TEXT, language features that provide additional tools helpful in editing and running M routines.

Extensions of READ and WRITE

Chapter 7 gave a formal introduction to the READ and WRITE commands. In that chapter, the forms most commonly used in M programming were described. There are, however, some extensions to these commands that take advantage of features not covered prior to Chapter 7. In this section we cover advanced forms of these commands that extend their power to cover a broader range of input and output.

> **Note to experienced programmers:** This chapter contains a collection of miscellaneous advanced language elements, including extensions to the READ and WRITE commands, the very powerful and somewhat complex pattern match operator, and some other features that do not fit readily into earlier chapters. The Summary should suffice to introduce most of the elements described. Review of the pattern match operator is recommended in addition.

The first extension is an option that permits the READ or WRITE to receive or send only a single character. This feature is valuable in cases where a routine may wish to check the first character typed and then branch accordingly without waiting for further input or where output of special characters is required to invoke special features of devices such as cursor control on video screens.

The single-character READ is indicated by prefixing the variable name specified in the READ argument with an asterisk, as in

```
READ *XYZ
```

This command specifies that the first character received from the current device is interpreted immediately, without waiting for an <*enter*>, according to a set of rules defined by the implementor, and an integer value corresponding to the character entered is returned. The integer value is the ASCII character code number of the key typed (Table 3.1). Conversely, the command

```
WRITE *XYZ
```

causes the integer value of XYZ to be converted to a single character according to the implementation's defined rules, and this value is then transmitted to the current device. This variation of the WRITE command is sometimes useful in performing special functions on output devices or implementing special communications protocols.

To illustrate the single-character READ, consider a menu driver that asks the user to invoke control characters to move the cursor up and down the screen. In order to give a partial example, we will assume that a terminal is in a waiting room with a display inviting the user to select one option. Since the user may not be trained to press the <*enter*> key, the single-character read allows the routine to continue without requiring that key to be entered:

```
WAIT WRITE #!!!?30, "While you are waiting, would you like information on"
   WRITE !?35,"1. New Tax Laws on Deductions"
   WRITE !?35,"2. Capital Gains Changes"
   WRITE !?35,"3. Tax Rate Changes"
   READ !!?30,"Pick a number: ",*NUM
   SET NUM=$SELECT(NUM=49:1,NUM=50:2,NUM=51:3,1:0)
   IF NUM=0 WRITE !,"Please type a number between 1 and 3" HANG 3 GOTO WAIT
   DO DED:NUM=1,CAPGAIN:NUM=2,RATE:NUM=3
   GOTO WAIT
```

Notice that the value returned from the READ *NUM is the decimal code ASCII value of the character typed. In this example, we converted the code to its character value before continuing. This routine will respond immediately to the first character entered by the user. In order for the error message to remain on the screen long enough for the client to read it, a pause (HANG 3) is inserted in the execution flow.

The single-character WRITE is particularly valuable when a user wishes to execute screen control functions. In the case of cursor positioning, for example, it is important to output the correct character sequence and then pause at that location for the next action. Different terminal devices use different code sequences, but most terminals have a way in which the cursor can be positioned at a given row and column. The following code is used to position a cursor at row 6, column 10 on a VT100 terminal. DY is set to the row value, and DX is set to the column position. First, the value of 48 must be added to the X and Y offsets, so that a control character will not be one of the values output to the screen (with a possible unwanted side effect):

```
SET DY=6+48,DX=10+48
WRITE *27,*91,DY,*59,DX,*72
```

At the conclusion of the WRITE statement, the cursor would be at the desired location, waiting for the next step in the routine. The first character of the WRITE statement, *27, is the ASCII Esc (escape) character; since many terminal control sequences begin with this character, the control sequences are sometimes referred to as "escape sequences." From these two examples, one can gain an appreciation of the potential uses of the single character variations of READ and WRITE commands.

There is a side effect of this form of the WRITE command: The values of $X and $Y will be unpredictably affected by the use of special nonprinting character sequences. The M standard does not define the effect of WRITE *VAR on $X and $Y, and implementors have adopted different actions when encountering this situation. For this reason, the M standard lets users modify $X and $Y to reflect the appropriate position on the screen. In the preceding example, the appropriate command would be

```
SET $X=10,$Y=6
```

Another variation of the READ command allows a fixed number of characters to be input by a READ statement. It is a common practice in data entry to limit the size of a given field to a certain number of characters. The normal flexibility of the M language is, in this case, too permissive; some means should be found to restrict the user to a specified field length. This capability is inherent in the following form of the READ command:

```
READ ZIPCODE#5
```

This variation of the READ command uses the pound sign (#) as a format control which specifies that the field named ZIPCODE cannot be more than five characters long. Of course, if the user wants to change to the expanded nine-digit code, this statement would need to be modified (to 10 characters since there is a dash between the fifth and sixth digits of the extended ZIP Code).

In order to prevent a READ operation from waiting indefinitely for a response from some device, it is possible to place a *timeout* on the READ command, as described in other commands, such as the OPEN command. The time limit is specified in seconds and is appended to the READ argument. Thus the command line

```
READ !,"WHAT IS YOUR ID?",ID:10
```

gives the respondent 10 seconds to enter the appropriate identification number. At the end of this time, only those characters already entered will be returned by the M system. The special variable $TEST will be set to reflect the result of the timeout. In the case of a single-character READ as described above, the result will be an integer specified by the implementation. If no single character is received, ID is assigned a value of −1.

Pattern match operator

In addition to the string operators described in Chapter 6, M has one other string operator: the *pattern match* operator. This feature represents a more advanced form of string comparison than those described in earlier chapters. Its value in many forms of input verification and error checking make it an important tool in many applications.

In some situations, it is valuable to test whether an input string such as a patient name, inventory number, date, or some other coded entry is entered according to system specifications. If, for example, we wish to make sure that date is entered MM/DD/YY with the slashes included, we would like to find a convenient method for testing the validity of the data entry. With the tools thus far described in M, it would be hard to verify that a user-typed value was correctly formatted, since it would be necessary to check each character. However, the pattern match operator provides us with a direct evaluation of the string that obviates the necessity of a character-by-character comparison of every position in the input string. The test of the data string is made by evaluating it against a special data element called a *pattern*. The expression

```
VAR?pattern
```

returns TRUE if the value of VAR "matches," or is in the form of, the pattern.

The question mark (?) serves as the MUMPS pattern match operator, testing whether a variable matches a specific pattern. Likewise,

```
VAR'?pattern
```

returns TRUE if the value of VAR does not match the pattern.

To understand this concept, we must understand the variations possible within the definition of a pattern. A pattern is a sequence of pattern elements, each of which is composed of a pattern code or string literal preceded by a multiplier count.

There are seven basic codes that may be defined within a pattern. They are:

- N The 10 numerics
- A All uppercase and lowercase alphabetic characters (including those with diacritical marks)
- U All uppercase alphabetic characters
- L All lowercase alphabetic characters
- P The 33 punctuation characters
- C The 33 ASCII control characters (including DEL)
- E The entire ASCII character set

Note: In order to permit processing of non-English languages which contain special characters with diacritical marks [é è ê], the 1995 Standard permits all alphabetic characters to be included in the pattern operators A, U, and L.

In addition, specific characters or strings may be identified by enclosing them in quotation marks. Using these definitions, we might verify a date as being in the desired MM/DD/YY format by describing this pattern as

```
2N1"/"2N1"/"2N
```

In this description, the numeric elements 2N are separated by slashes, and only one occurrence of each slash is permitted between each number pair. Notice that this form would not accept a date entered as 4/6/51 because the pattern of 2N is not observed in the month and day portions. Such limitations are common in many other languages and are a source of annoyance to users who legitimately believe that a one-digit code should be acceptable.

M handles this situation by allowing a *range* of values with the pattern operator, using the following syntax:

```
1.2N1"/"1.2N1"/"2.4N
```

This would allow one or two digits for the month or day, and from two to four digits for the year (an increasingly important option; the four-digit form may again become necessary. The period in this syntax could be translated as "between" the values on either side. If only the period (without bracketing numbers) is present, it defaults to "between 0 and infinity." This use of an indefinite range permits the pattern match operation to be adaptive, searching for an appropriate decomposition of the input string.

Consider the following examples:

Specification	Meaning
`X?1"ME".E`	X begins with "ME" and is otherwise unspecified
`X?.E1"ME".E`	X contains "ME" (same as X["ME")
`X?.E1"ME"`	X ends with "ME"

To test for a patient name in a last-name, comma, first-name format, the specification

```
PAT?1A.A1","1A.A
```

requires that there be at least one alphabetic character in both last and first names, that they be of indefinite length but composed only of uppercase and lowercase alphabetic characters, and that they be separated by a comma. If we want to permit (but not require) spaces after the comma and before the first name, we could use the pattern

```
PAT?1A.A1","." "1A.A
```

which would make it possible to have zero or more spaces after the comma.

Although use of single patterns such as those illustrated above is helpful, sometimes it is desirable to check for more than one pattern in a single matching sequence. To increase the versatility of pattern matching, M allows for composite codes to be specified. Thus, for example, AP selects either alphabetic characters or punctuation marks (as does PA), and LN selects lowercase and numeric characters (as does NL).

The usual assumption with names is that they consist only of alphabetic characters. However, this is not always the case. Consider the following list of names:

- Watson-Williams
- O'Kane
- van der Winkle

These names would not match any pattern that did not allow for spaces, apostrophes, or dashes (all of which happen to be punctuation characters in the pattern match code book). The pattern 1A.AP would accommodate all these variations of last names.

There is yet another powerful extension to M's pattern match operator, incorporated into the 1995 standard. Sometimes, a pattern may be acceptable if either of two options is used. Dates represent a common situation in which it is important to match for patterns, but valid dates may take different forms. For example, a date may be written "12-31-96" or "12/31/96". In order to permit alternate patterns, M uses parentheses to group alternatives. A check for valid dates of the type given above might be

```
?1.2N1(1"-",1"/")1.2N1(1"-",1"/")2.4N
```

With these and other more complex variations of the pattern match operator, and with the contains operator described earlier, it is possible in M to provide extremely sophisticated data input verification by using relatively short M commands. This flexibility tends to make M database systems far more complete in input error checking than those written in other languages.

$HOROLOG special variable

The $HOROLOG special variable was introduced in Chapter 4, but that introduction was necessarily brief and incomplete. We can now return to this variable, since we have presented additional language elements that allow us to explain it more fully.

In many computer applications it is valuable to have access to the date or even the time of day. Bills, reports, transactions, and many other documents are routinely dated. Some transactions that may take place several times during a day need in addition to record the time of day. Programmers sometimes want to know how long it takes for a certain section of code or activity to be completed in order to evaluate the performance of the system or the code itself. Many computers can accommodate this type of requirement by providing an *external clock*, a device that keeps track of the time of day, often to the nearest fraction of a second. For systems with an external clock, M offers the $HOROLOG function to provide date and time information.

$HOROLOG returns a string that contains two numbers separated by a comma. The form is D,S, where D is the day (using a formula described below) and S is the number of seconds elapsed in that day at the time the function is called. $HOROLOG supplies the date and time in one variable. Thus, if you were to issue the command WRITE $HOROLOG, you would get a value that looks like this:

```
56908,57876
```

which would translate into October 22, 1996, at about 4:05 P.M., the date and time when this sentence was added to the text. In order to allow the first part, D, to be completely generalizable for any day, month, or year, $HOROLOG provides this day as a single number that represents the number of days elapsed since the first day of January 1841 (the designers presumed that most M applications could operate within the period 1840 to the present without difficulty). Thus Christmas Day 1977 has a D value of 50032.You may wish to check this by remembering that every four years (including one leap year) has a total of 1,461 days, except for the year 1900, which was not a leap year (three out of four century years omit leap year to keep our calendar in synch with the sun. The year 2000 is an exception, since there will be a February 29). It is not particularly convenient for us to remember this type of calculation, so we reproduce below an M routine that can be used to calculate the date from the $HOROLOG D value given by your M system. This routine is taken from the *MUMPS Programmers' Reference Manual* (p. 98).

```
HOROLOG ;DS; 5/81 MM/DD/YY.
   ;calculate year month and day from $HOROLOG
   SET H=$HOROLOG>21608+$HOROLOG,LEAPYRS=H\1461,Y=H#1461
   SET YEAR=LEAPYRS*4+1841+(Y\365),DAY=Y#365
   SET:DAY=0 DAY365, YEAR=YEAR-1
   SET MO=1 IF Y=0 SET DAY=366
   FOR I=31,YEAR#4=0+28,31,30,31,30,31,31,30,31,30,31 QUIT:DAY'>I SET
   ...DAY=DAY-I,MO=MO+1
   WRITE MO\10,MO#10,"/",DAY\10,DAY#10,"/",YEAR
```

This is an advanced M program, but it is a good example of the use of M programming techniques. In the third line, the command

```
SET H=$HOROLOG>21608+$HOROLOG
```

can be translated into the following set of statements. First, $HOROLOG is evaluated as a number, which automatically takes the numeric value up to the comma, or the years component. In order to make things come out exactly even in terms of leap years, this expression creates a temporary variable, H, which is one day more than $HOROLOG's D component if the date is after February 28, 1900 (i.e., if there are more than 21,608 days in $HOROLOG). The expression `$HOROLOG>21608` will evaluate to 0 if it is not true and evaluate to 1 if it is true. Hence a date greater than 1900 will add 1 to $HOROLOG and store that in the variable `H`. Quite a lot to put into that one expression, isn't it?)

In order to determine how many leap years there are, the routine uses an integer divide of the new value `H` by the figure 1,461, which is 365 days times 4 plus 1. The routine then creates a new value `Y` which is the remainder when

H is divided by 1,461 or, in other words, the number of days since the last leap year.

The YEAR is calculated by taking the base year, 1841, adding to it the number of leap years times 4, and then adding the number of years since the last leap year (Y\365). Thus the expression

```
SET YEAR=LEAPYRS*4+1841+(Y\365)
```

takes care of all but one case (December 31 of the last year). The days in the current year are obtained by obtaining a modulo remainder from dividing Y by 365.

We are now almost ready to calculate the month and day. First, we set the month equal to 1 (January of the first post-leap year), and then we take care of the special case of December 31 in a leap year.

The next line adds the appropriate number of days for each month, using a FOR loop in which each month is subtracted from DAY until the next value of I (i.e., the next month) is larger than the remainder. The expression

```
YEAR#4=0+28
```

is similar to the first expression in this routine, saying, "take the truth value of the expression 'year divided by 4 equals 0' and add it to the number 28" (i.e., if a leap year, add the twenty-ninth day).

The last line uses first integer divide and then modulo to write out month and day. If the month is greater than 10, then MO\10 has a value of 1; otherwise, a zero is written. This form ensures the insertion of a leading zero in the output when the month or the day is less than 10. The rest of the output format is straightforward.

It is not all that difficult, once you have taken the routine apart expression by expression, but it does take some careful planning to put this much into such a short routine.

The second part of $HOROLOG gives the seconds since the start of the current day. You may recall having had to work with seconds in an exercise at the end of Chapter 4. That example was a little more complicated than needed in MUMPS, since the second part of $HOROLOG will be reset to 0 at the start of each new day. The actual values used to obtain hours, minutes, and seconds are:

```
SET TIME=$PIECE($HOROLOG,",",2) ;get the second portion of $HOROLOG
SET SECONDS=TIME#60
SET X=TIME\60 ;get the number of minutes since midnight
SET HOURS=X\60,MINUTES=X#60
```

This form will leave the hours in a military format (i.e., running from 1 to 23 hours). You will have an opportunity to modify this routine to develop A.M. and P.M. values in the exercises at the end of this chapter.

$TEXT function

MUMPS has a special function that allows a user to access lines in a routine and assign that text to another variable. This function, called $TEXT, is useful in editing routines, but it also can be used in programming, as illustrated below. The editing function is beyond the scope of this text; however, the programming use is an important tool that can make many forms of interactive programming much easier to generalize and hence much more flexible.

The purpose of $TEXT is to return to the user a command line, as specified in the argument of the function. The identifying argument of $TEXT permits identification either of a labeled or an unlabeled line by providing an offset from a line having a label. For example, if we were to use $TEXT on the routine HOROLOG from the previous section, we might obtain the following examples:

Expression	Value Produced
TEXT(HOROLOG)	HOROLOG; DS; 5/81, MM/DD/YY
TEXT(HOROLOG+1)	;calculate year, month and day from $HOROLOG
TEXT(HOROLOG+4)	SET MO=1 IF Y=1460 SET DAY=366,YEAR=YEAR-1

In other words, M will return the complete line, including label, commands, or comments, as referenced by the label+offset argument of the $TEXT function.

To see how $TEXT might be used to simplify programming, let us consider a routine created to obtain demographic information, as shown below:

```
ADDRESS ;RFW; 5/87; DEMOGRAPHY V. 1.
   get demographic data. conventional approach
   WRITE !,"Please enter name, street address, city, zip and state"
   WRITE !,"as prompted. To quit, type return with no value for name."
   START FOR I=1:1 QUIT:$DATA(^NAM(I))=""  ;go to end of list
   READ !,"Name: ",N GOTO FINISH:N=""
   SET ^NAM(1,1)=N
   READ !,"STR: ",N SET^NAM(I,2)=N
   READ !,"CIT ",N SET^NAM(I,3)=N
   READ !,"ST: ",N SET^NAM(I,4)=N
   READ !,"ZIP: ",N SET^NAM(I,5)=N,I=I+1 GOTO START+2
   FINISH WRITE !,I," ENTRIES NOW IN GLOBAL FILE NAM."
```

```
QUIT
;END OF ROUTINE
```

This version of the routine will do the job as specified. However, it only collects one name at a time and is completely specific for the one set of data which it was originally designed to collect. The problem with this approach arises when one wishes to make additions or deletions to the information to be collected. Suppose, for example, that one wished to change the input to exclude street address and add sex, Social Security number, and date of birth. In addition to having to modify the actual file itself (assuming old records are to be retained), the input program must be changed to reflect the new input and storage structure. These changes will occur throughout the section from START to FINISH. Using $TEXT, the routine design can be modified to accommodate changes more readily

```
ADDRESS2 ;RFW; 5/87, Demographic Data V. 2
   ;Collect demographic data. Open-ended approach
   WRITE #!?10,"We would like to obtain some client data."
   WRITE !!?10,"Please enter information as requested."
   IF $DATA(^NAM(0))=0 SET ^NAM(0)=0 ;count of names in file
INPUT ;
   SET I=^NAM(0)+1 READ !!,"Please enter client name (null to quit): ",N
   IF N ="" WRITE !!,I-1," Names now in file." QUIT
   SET ^NAM(I)=N,^NAM(0)=I
   FOR J=1:1 SET PROMPT=$PIECE($TEXT(LIST+J),";",3) QUIT:PROMPT=""  DO IN1
   GOTO INPUT
IN1 ;
   WRITE !,PROMPT READ DATA SET ^NAM(I,J)=DATA QUIT
LIST ;list of prompts for data input
   ;;Soc Sec No:
   ;;City:
   ;;State:
   ;;ZIPcode:
   ;;Date of Birth:
   ;;Sex:
```

Note: The double semicolons in the lines after LIST are inserted to be certain that these text lines are retained in the program. Some implementations of M remove all extraneous comment lines before saving the routine. When, as in this case, the comment lines are actually used in the routine, the two-semicolon convention instructs these implementations to preserve the line.

This approach requires only that the list of prompts be at the end of the routine. (A more sophisticated version could be written that looks for another terminator, thereby permitting the text to be in the middle of the routine.)

When the loop in line INPUT+4 finds a null value, the list terminates and execution flow returns to the start of a new client name. The only place where changes need to be made in the future are in the texts of the lines following the LIST label.

In subsequent chapters we will explore in greater detail the power of this form of data inclusion in M routines. However, this example will suffice to illustrate the way in which programs can be made significantly easier to update.

Up to now, we have assumed that the routine addressed by the $TEXT function is in the user's workspace. This function has been extended, however, to permit reference to a line in any routine. For example, if a user wants to look at the line following the label INPUT of the routine ADDRESS2 without loading it, typing

```
WRITE $TEXT(INPUT+1^ADDRESS)
```

and M will display the following result:

```
SET I=^NAM(0)+1 READ !!,"Please enter client name (null to quit): ",N
```

In this manner, routines can access text from other routines. In the examples given above, the text is embedded in the routine. However, it might make more sense to have routines that consist entirely of text in order to separate large databases from general-purpose drivers. One example of the use of this approach would be if an M routine were to be used in more than one natural language, e.g., English and German. The appropriate text for each language might be stored in different routines, and the driver routines could then access the appropriate one for a given country.

Summary

M offers a number of features relating to manipulating text and dates which extend the capabilities described in preceding chapters. Among them are:

- READ *CHAR allows a single character to be read from a terminal without waiting for the <*enter*> key to be pressed.
- WRITE *CHAR outputs a single character to the output device.
- READ X#nn limits the length of X to nn characters.
- The M pattern match operator is used to check for various types of character patterns in a variable. Options include

  A Alphabetic characters

  U Uppercase alphabetic characters only

  L Lowercase alphabetic characters only

N Digits
P Punctuation
E Any ASCII character
C ASCII control characters
String literals in quotes

Ranges may be specified by `n.n` (pattern), where `n` can be missing or any integer(s).

- $HOROLOG is a special variable of the form D,S, where D is the number of days since the first second of December 31, 1840 and S is the number of seconds since midnight of the current day.
- $TEXT is a function that can be used to return the value of a line of text in a routine in the workspace.

Exercises

This chapter contains a number of features that enhance the flexibility of M in programming certain applications. These exercises are intended to convey the flavor, not the full scope, of these features.

1. ***Extended READ Variations*** This problem starts you on the way to creating a formatted screen data-entry program. One of the utilities required in such data entry is the ability to move from one field to another. Although we will not be able to create all the functions associated with entry form movement (which requires knowledge of exactly where the fields are located on a screen), the screen-move utility is a good place to learn about using `READ *VAR`.

   Create a routine named `SCREEN` that uses the following control characters to perform screen manipulation functions:

   <tab> Move to next field

   <-> Move to previous field

   <#> Specify field number (nn)

   < ^ > Move to top of form

   <@> Move to bottom of form

   Use the `READ *CTL` form of the READ command to get a single character typed in by the user, then branch to appropriate places in your routine based on that input. Call the input variable `CTL`, match it with the ASCII code number for the characters listed above, and branch to subroutines named `SCTAB`, `SCBACK`, `SCNUM`, `SCTOP`, or `SCBOT`, respectively, for the functions listed above. Within these subroutines, write an output statement identifying which subroutine is invoked, then branch back to the READ command line.

2. ***Extended WRITE Variations*** Create a second routine that allows you to perform some screen control functions on your screen. In the list that follows, the specific commands for PCDOS screens are listed in parentheses. If you are working on other systems, check your manual to see what control-character sequences are required.

   Note: The ESC character is ASCII 27.

   CLEAR Clear the screen and home cursor to top left (`ESC"[2J"`: in other words, output the ESC character, then `"["`,`"2"`, and `"J"`)

   BOLD Output characters in intense (bold) mode (`ESC "[1m"`)

   DIM Output characters in subdued (normal) mode (`ESC "[2m"`)

   CURS Move cursor to position `DY` (row) and `DX` (col) (on IBM PC:

   ```
   ESC "["DY[row] ";" DX, "H")
   ```

   Note: You also may wish to add features of selective erasing to end of line or screen.

   Using `DO label^SCREEN`, test the functions you have created to be sure that they work. Separate the individual functions with QUIT commands. Be sure that you have defined `DX` and `DY` before calling the `CURS` subroutine, and follow that call with a WRITE of some text so that you can see where the cursor moved (otherwise, it will return to the next line without outputting any characters).

3. **Pattern Match** It is not possible to explore complete variations of the pattern match. Here are a couple of items you might try:

   a. Match input for Social Security in usual manner.

   b. Match input for telephone (area code in parentheses, dash before the last four numbers).

   c. Match for English postal codes, e.g., WZ1 02L (the first letter uppercase, the remaining alphabetic or numeric, with one space between groups).

4. **$HOROLOG** Write a routine that, given a date, will calculate the value for the first part of $HOROLOG for that date. Use the routine to enter a date, then calculate the number of years (plus fraction of a year expressed in `n/365`) between that date and the present.

5. **$TEXT** Change the example given in Chapter 11 entitled `APTS` to move all the prompt messages for input to text at the end of the routine.

15 Indirection: Dynamic Reference Modification for Execution Control and Data Management

The power of today's computer is dependent on a number of features. Two of the most fundamental are the ability of computers to store data in memory and the related but different ability to store instructions in memory. These features are found even in programmable calculators, where data are stored in "registers" and programs are stored in a separate area of memory reserved for that purpose. Today's general-purpose computers allow the use of the same memory locations either for data or for programs, but most computer languages make a very clear distinction between the two. M is different (so is LISP, to cite one other high-level programming language with a comparable feature), in that it allows programmers to store *executable code* as data. The features that make this possible (the XECUTE command and the indirection operator) are described in this chapter.

Overriding the distinction between code and data: the XECUTE command

The M language allows some cases where the usual distinction between code and data can be overridden. In this language feature, M resembles the lan-

> **Note to Experienced Programmers:** Since dynamic execution flow control is unknown in most compiled languages (there is a comparable feature in LISP), it deserves careful study for all levels of programmer experience. The concepts may be learned easily, but their effective use requires a good deal of practice. For these reasons, it is recommended that everyone read this chapter in its entirety.

guage LISP, a language usually thought of as belonging to the "artificial intelligence" field of computing. There are two ways in M that code can be treated as programming elements. The first of these is the XECUTE command. (The initial E of "eXECUTE" has been eliminated without changing the pronunciation so as to avoid possible confusion with the M ELSE command, since M allows for single-letter abbreviations of commands.)

The XECUTE command is used to treat the data stored in an M variable value as a complete M command or command line. To illustrate, we will reproduce a partial user dialogue with the M interpreter. User input is in boldface type.

```
> READ !,"Type an M command line: ",CMD
Type an M command line:SET Z=3 WRITE !,Z*2
> WRITE !,CMD
SET Z=3 WRITE !,Z*2
> XECUTE CMD
6
>
```

This dialogue illustrates the storage of a command line as an M variable. If the variable is written out using the WRITE command, it will appear as any M variable. However, if the M interpreter is instructed to XECUTE the command line, the code is executed and the appropriate result appears.

The XECUTE command can be used to create M code that can generalize certain operations, simplifying program development. Suppose, for example, that we want to develop a code segment that will allow a user to perform mathematical operations on two variables. Such a situation might arise if, in a statistical package, a transform was required before a data set is to be analyzed. A highly simplified version of such a routine might be the following:

```
MATH1;mathematics example;RFW;10/96
READ !,"Enter the first number: ",VAR1
READ !,"Enter the mathematical operator: ",OP
READ !,"Enter second number: ",VAR2
SET CALC="SET X="_VAR1_OP_VAR2
XECUTE CALC
WRITE !,X
```

Running this program would result in the following result (user input in boldface type):

```
>DO ^MATH1
```

```
Enter the first number: 39
Enter the mathematical operator: *
Enter the second number: 3
117
>
```

This example is of course greatly simplified, but the power of this type of code generation is evident from this example. In fact, some general-purpose M packages, such as the public-domain Veterans Administration FILE MANAGER package, utilize precisely this technique to customize their package for different database operations.

This type of programming uses what is often called *dynamic code modification*, because the exact action taken cannot be determined until the user types in the values and the operator to be used. Compiled languages generally cannot deal with dynamic code modification. M can, even though most implementations of M are "mostly compiled," that is, that most code can be safely compiled and when an XECUTE command is encountered, the M interpreter must be available to complete the execution of that command based on the data stored in related variables (in this case, VAR1, VAR2, OP, and X).

Indirection operator

The second way that M allows data to be treated as code is the *indirection operator* @. Indirection can be used in two ways. The first is a way in which M uses the *value* stored in a variable as the *name* of a second variable. It is sometimes thought of as a *pointer* to another variable. This use is referred to as *name indirection*. An example in which an M variable is referenced through the indirection operator follows:

```
DEPOSIT;add funds to acct;rfw;10/96
READ !!,"What is your account number: ",acctno
;insert some checks for valid entry here
READ !?5,"Enter amount to be deposited: ",amt
SET @acctno=@acctno+amt
WRITE !,acctno," has now been increased to ",@acctno
```

The variable acctno is just a name in a program, and it is not the place where the user's money should be deposited. Instead, the program should find the account number to which acctno is *pointing*, and increment that account by the user-specified value amt. This is a good example of indirection as a means of permitting a program to be generalized. In computer terms, the code is *dynamically modified* to refer to a location not known until the user types in the account number.

The second way in which the indirection operator can be used is at the *argument* level, referred to as *argument indirection*. In this case, the reference is to more than a single variable. To illustrate, suppose that in the first example we used an entry to a routine that was not the name of the routine itself. In other words, consider the following:

```
SET ROU="ENTRY^ROUTINE"
DO @ROU
```

This example is almost like the first one in the chapter, but the reference is now to a complete argument rather than to a single level. Either is quite acceptable in the M language.

Another example illustrating the argument-level use of indirection is

```
SET X1="A=3*2"
SET @X1 WRITE A
6
```

In this case, because the indirect reference includes a complete argument, the value is correctly referenced and the variable A is created. However, it is not permissible to use indirection for a *partial argument*. Hence the statement

```
SET @X1+3
```

is not valid, because the argument has been augmented by an additional expression and thus is no longer complete. Argument indirection is in many respects similar to name indirection, and its use is similar, with the exception that more complex forms can be substituted.

As a further, more complicated example of argument-level indirection, we return to the menu driver example from Chapter 14 in the section describing $TEXT. The next example builds on the program ADDRESS2, using techniques that are borrowed, with permission, from Brown and Glaeser's *A Cookbook of MUMPS* (see Chapter 18 for another variation of this general menu driver). This version of the address program has been expanded to a package in which separate routines are used to collect different types of information from the client.

```
address3  ;modified from Brown and Glaeser;RFW;10/96
          WRITE $PIECE($TEXT(OPT),";",3)
start;
          READ !,"Enter your choice ('?' for help): ",j I j="" QUIT
          IF j["?" DO list GOTO start
          IF j?1.N,j'=0,$TEXT(opt+j)'="" WRITE " ",$PIECE($TEXT(opt+j),";",4)
          ...GOTO DOIT
```

```
            IF j'?1.N FOR i=1:1 SET x=$PIECE($TEXT(opt+i),";",4) QUIT:x="" IF
            ...$EXTRACT(x,1,$LENGTH(j)=j WRITE $EXTRACT(x,$LENGTH(j)+1,99) SET j=i

GOTO DOIT
            DO list GOTO start
DOIT ;
            SET x=$TEXT(opt+j) DO @$PIECE(x,";",3) GOTO menu
list ;
            WRITE !!,"Choose one of the options by number or unique first letter:
            ...",!!
            FOR i=1:1 SET x=$TEXT(opt+i) QUIT:x="" WRITE i,".",?4,$PIECE(x,";",4),!
            QUIT
opt         ;;Get Client Information
            ;;^addr;Address information (work and home)
            ;;^phone;Phone/fax numbers (work and home)
            ;;^email;Electronic mail addresses
            ;;^dob;Date of birth, etc.
```

(Some lines are too long to print on one physical line of this textbook; they are continued on the next line, preceded by three periods (i.e. '...').

This example has a number of interesting concepts that can enhance its user-friendly nature and improve its efficiency and reusability. $TEXT is used to allow output text to be placed at the end of the routine after the label opt. The user is presented with title information and then an open-ended option; programs like this are used by people familiar with the options, so it not usually necessary to spell them out. However, the help option '?' is also there if needed, which will execute the subroutine after the label list before returning to get the user's choice. list extracts the fourth PIECE of each prompt line after opt (i.e., the text after the third semicolon) and prints it after the number representing its line position after opt (remember that some M implementations require two semicolons to preserve comment lines in M routines).

The user can either enter a numeric choice or choose by selecting a unique first letter or letters. If the choice is numeric, the prompt text is displayed after the number. If the user types one or more letters, the fourth line after the label start will present the remaining letters after the user's entry. For example, if the user types Phon, M matches those four characters with the first four characters of each prompt after the label opt then displays the fifth through '99th' (i.e., the end of the line) characters of the prompt, thereby completing the message.

Indirection is used in the subroutine labeled DOIT. The variable x is assigned the value of the third piece of the option line selected, which in the case of option 2 would be ^phone. The DO @x instructs M to use that option as an indirect argument reference, so the command is executed as `DO ^phone` in this case.

This program can be adapted very easily to other menu choice programs, since it is only necessary to change the text after `opt` by substituting the appropriate prompts and associated routine names. It would be hard to find a better example of reusable code.

The next form of indirection is more complex and also more powerful in its potential for application. In this form, the indirection operator is applied to *subscripts.* In modifying M to include this form of indirection, it was necessary to extend the syntax of the operator to accommodate partial subscripts, a change that makes use of the indirection operator a little more difficult to understand. To illustrate the use of *subscript indirection,* let us assume that we have defined the following variables:

```
SET MDC("CHAIR",1992)="Salander"
SET MDC("CHAIR",1996)="DeMoel"
SET YEAR="1996"
SET REF="MDC(""CHAIR"")"
```

In the subscript use of indirection, it is required that *two* uses of indirection be made. The first contains an indirect reference to the name and any initial subscripts, and the second contains an indirect reference to the last subscript in parentheses. Using the preceding values, the following command would produce the results shown:

```
>WRITE @REF@(YEAR)
DeMoel
>
```

Notice that the parentheses are required for the second, but not the first, use of the indirection operator.

Although this form of indirection may appear complicated, it proves quite useful when one attempts to traverse completely a global file without writing complicated code sequences to take care of arbitrarily deep levels of subscripting. The code required to perform this task is too advanced for this text, but suffice to say that by using forms of `$ORDER@REF@(FIN))`, with provision for descending to the next level, it is possible to traverse any combination of multiple levels and subscripts in a global tree.

This example may very well serve to point out an important warning with respect to the use of indirection. It is a powerful tool, but it can easily be misused in programming. Examples that are reasonably self-contained, such as the menu driver illustrated earlier (and further expanded on in Chapter 18), are readily understood. More obscure references are to be avoided in all cases where more direct references will suffice. Programs using indirection may execute differently, depending on run-time conditions. They are hard to debug and even harder to maintain. For this reason, indirection should be used with great caution, and one should avoid it unless its use is either clear (as in the menu driver example) or it is without question the best way to achieve a given solution.

Extensions of global reference functions using indirection: $QUERY revisited

In Chapter 12 we covered a number of M functions that help in accessing global variables stored in the M tree format. There are a number of additional capabilities in M that help this process, most of them relying on the use of indirection, and hence delayed until we could present that concept. Let's look at the function $QUERY, for example. As explained in Chapter 12, $QUERY can provide a depth-first traversal of an M global variable. However, in order to make use of this in a program, indirection is required. Let's pick up the example used with $QUERY in Chapter 12, which looks like this:

```
^CAL(96,3,12)="Bday:DTW"
^CAL(96,5,15)="Bday:BSH"
^CAL(96,6,6,"09:00")="Mr. Covin"
^CAL(96,6,6,"11:30")="Mr. Salander"
^CAL(96,6,6,"12:15")="Lunch: Development Committee"
^CAL(96,6,6,"14:30")="Dr. Orthner"
^CAL(96,6,8,"07:00")="EAL fl 723:Atlanta"
^CAL(96,8,6)="Bday:LWT"
^CAL(96,8,6,"09:27")="Mr. Timson"
^CAL(96,8,6,"10:15")="Ms. Lilly"
^CAL(96,8,6,"16:45")="Ms. Ogden (+ dinner)"
^CAL(96,8,30)="Anniversary"
```

In order to write a program that will traverse this tree completely, we have to use indirection, so that the variable in the program *points* to ^CAL. Here is one version of such a program:

```
treelist;search global tree;RFW;10/96
SET key="^CAL"
FOR SET key=$QUERY(@key) QUIT:key=""  WRITE !,key,?30,@key
;end of program
```

Executing this program would result in the following:

```
^CAL(96,3,12)          Bday:DTW
^CAL(96,5,15)          Bday:BSH
```

```
^CAL(96,6,6,"09:00") Mr. Covin
^CAL(96,6,6,"11:30") Mr. Salander
^CAL(96,6,6,"12:15") Lunch: Development Committee
^CAL(96,6,6,"14:30") Dr. Orthner
^CAL(96,6,8,"07:00") EAL fl 723:Atlanta
^CAL(96,8,6)         Bday:LWT
^CAL(96,8,6,"09:27") Mr. Timson
^CAL(96,8,6,"10:15") Ms. Lilly
^CAL(96,8,6,"16:45") Ms. Ogden (+ dinner)
^CAL(96,8,30)        Anniversary
```

This function replaces some particularly arcane code written by M experts to perform complete tree traversals and makes it possible to do the same thing without becoming really expert at M programming!

Indirection used with the pattern operator

A final use of the indirection operator relates to employing it with the pattern match operator. This form may be useful when one of several different patterns is to be selected and then used in a single-pattern match. Consider the case of ZIP Codes, which may now be either five or nine digits. Here is a series of commands that would test for either form:

```
ZIP1SET ZPAT="5N"
READ !,"Enter ZIP code: ",ZIP
SET:$LENGTH(ZIP)=10 ZPAT="5N1""-""4N"
IF ZIP'?@ZPAT Write !,"Invalid ZIP Code" GOTO ZIP1
```

This code first establishes a pattern of 5 digits, but if the user's input is 10 characters, then the pattern is changed to the standard 5-digit, 1-hyphen, 4-digit format and the input is checked accordingly. Hence both 5- and 10-digit ZIP Codes are verified.

There are numerous cases where a pattern can be adjusted to a specific case. Sometimes these patterns can even be built based on user-supplied specifications. Some of the database packages in M allow experienced programmers to submit pattern codes to be used for verification of data entry, store the patterns as variables, and use indirection to adjust the input routine to take advantage of the specific patterns supplied. In this manner, far more extensive and specific error checks can be performed on data at input time, enhancing the quality of the database.

Summary

The M language, being interpretive rather than compiled, allows the creation of data elements that consist of executable code. The forms of indirection allowed in M are the following:

- The XECUTE command takes the value of a data variable and treats it as code.
- With the indirection operator @, `SET @X=3` takes the variable identified by the current value of `X` and sets it to the value 3. The @ operator may be used at the name level (the example cited earlier), the argument level (representing a complete argument), or, in a special syntax, the subscript level (using the format `@REF@(LSTSUB)`, where parentheses are required and `LSTSUB` represents only the last subscript in a complete reference to a local or global variable).
- By using the @ operator with pattern match, patterns can be stored as data and referenced via the indirection operator.

Exercises

1. ***Use of XECUTE Command*** Write a routine `SALUPDT` that reads in

   `ID` (employee ID number)
   `SAL` (employee current salary)
   `CHG` (dollar figure to be added or subtracted)
   `OP` (+ to add, – to subtract)

   and create a command line that performs the desired salary change, XECUTE it, and print out a statement summarizing the action taken.

   Note: Be careful that you distinguish between string literals and the actual values when you create the executable line.

2. ***Indirection Operator (@) with Menu Options*** Adapt the `^address3` routine so that it gives the user an opportunity either to run one of three games or to quit. The games are

   `DUNGEON` (Dungeons and dragons)
   `ADVEN` (Adventure)
   `LIFE` (Life matrix)

   Obtain the user's choice, using a set of prompt messages by employing a $TEXT retrieval of lines with the format

   ```
   ;;^DUNGEON;1. Dungeons and Dragons
   ```

   The third PIECE (using ";" as the delimiter) is the name of the routine to be executed; the fourth PIECE is the prompt to be displayed to the user.

Begin the routine by displaying all options, and ask the user to type the number of the prompt line. Then, using indirection, DO the appropriate label. If the user specifies an invalid choice or null response, QUIT. Create dummy routine entries for the labels, write the name of the label to the screen, and return via a QUIT to the main driver portion of the routine. (This is a relatively easy exercise, given the example presented earlier in this chapter, but it should convince you of the modularity and reusability of this code.)

3. ***Subscript-Level Indirection*** Write a routine named `CRCAL` that will prompt for three-letter names of each month and then for the number of days (use a non-leap year). From this input, create an array named `^CAL` (for calendar) with the subscript values in the following form:

```
^CAL("JAN")=31
^CAL("FEB")=28
^CAL("MAR")=31
```

   Use this routine to create the array. Then create a routine `CALENDAR` that asks the user for a three-letter abbreviation of a month and then returns the number of days. Use name-level indirection to perform this function, i.e., store the entire name (with subscript) before using the indirect operator. Output the number of days in the appropriate month and return to ask for another month, with a null answer terminating the exercise.

4. **Pattern-Level Indirection** The British and Canadians use a form of postal code that has the following format:

   One or two letters followed by two digits and/or letters

   A space

   Three alphabetic and/or numeric characters

   Create a short routine `PATTERN` in which the variable `P` contains the appropriate pattern to match the British postal code; then use this value to check user input. Be sure you try such variations as WC1 02L, SWT2 5GK, and ZKED F01.

Access Control of Local Variables

16

M uses the terms 'local' and 'global' variables in a different way from most programming languages. M provides persistent data (i.e., globals, stored on disk); other languages do not have this feature. Another distinction, which may seem self-evident to M programmers, is that *all* local variables in an M user's workspace are available to all routines run in that workspace. This is a useful concept, but it is unlike other high-level programming languages which assume that each routine ('procedure' in many of those languages) has its own 'local' variables that are not shared with other routines unless explicitly stated.

There are times when the M solution is advantageous, but there are also times when it could be a disadvantage. This chapter describes a way in which the universal access to local variables can be controlled.

Note to experienced programmers: Since the language elements discussed in this chapter are treated slightly differently in M from their uses in other languages, it is recommended that experienced programmers study this chapter carefully. In most computer languages, "local" variables are those used within the scope of a procedure or routine called by another procedure. In M, all local variables are available to all executing routines in the user's partition. M does, however, allow programmers to create environments in which local variables have limitations to the scope of their applicability, either by inclusion or exclusion to the local environment. This functionality is accomplished through the NEW command, extrinsic functions, and parameter passing.

Scoped variables

In M, a *local variable* is defined as one created during an interactive session and not retained after the session terminates. This definition contrasts with the M use of the term *global variable,* which is a shared variable created during an interactive session for long-term storage (on disk) and available to multiple users. In M, local variables are available to all routines invoked by a user (either directly or as a result of routines invoking other routines) during an interactive session. Some other languages have a different approach to variables, restricting their access to individual procedures and passing values back and forth between such procedures or subroutines by explicit techniques of identifying which variables are to be transmitted.

There are advantages and disadvantages to each method of use of local variables. In the current form of M, programmers need not be concerned with making local variables available to utility packages or other routines, since, by implication, all routines can manipulate all local variables. There are, however, two dangers to this approach. First, if a utility routine uses variables that inadvertently have the same names used by other routines running in the same user partition, the values of those multiply defined variables may change in unexpected ways. In addition, users may be unfamiliar with the specific names used in a utility routine to calculate a value. For example, a utility date calculation routine may require that the value to be adjusted have the name %DATE, but the user who is unaware of this requirement will not be able to take advantage of this general-purpose utility.

For these two reasons, the MDC devised a set of commands, functions, and syntax modifications to existing commands that enable users to create variables with limited applicability, or *scoped variables.* These language elements, incorporated into the M standard in 1990, permit the forms of variable scoping and parameter passing available in most other languages.

Restriction of the scope of applicability of local variables can be accomplished in three ways. Variables can be declared to be *included* within a new environment. They also can be declared to be *excluded.* Finally, one or more variables can be explicitly passed to a local environment, where they may or may not have the same name. The M approach to each of these alternatives is described in the sections that follow.

NEW command

Since M does not yet have built-in features for arithmetic operations such as logarithms and trigonometric functions, most M implementations provide M utilities to fill the gap. Suppose, for example, that a user wished to calculate the square root of a number. The following utility will give a reasonably accurate value for the square root of a number X:

```
SQRT  ;Y is set to the square root of X on return
      SET Y=0 QUIT:X'>0
      SET Y=X+1/2
L     ;
      SET F=Y,Y=(X/F+F)/2 GOTO L:Y<F
      QUIT
```

This routine makes use of three local variables: X, Y, and F. It is uncertain whether these variables might be used by routines that invoke this function. If we assume that the user is aware that Y is used to return the answer and X is the value for which the square root is to be calculated, we are still uncertain as to whether there might be a variable F in the calling routine. To make certain that there is no possible side effect other than the use of the communicating variables X and Y, we can invoke the NEW command as follows:

```
SQRT  ;Y is set to the square root of X on return
      NEW F
      SET Y=0 QUIT:X'>0
      SET Y=X+1/2
L     ;
      SET F=Y,Y=(X/F+F)/2 GOTO L:Y<F
      QUIT
```

Addition of the NEW F command at the beginning of this routine ensures that, within the scope of the routine, F will assume a new value. Furthermore, when the routine is exited by a QUIT command (either on line 3 or at the end of the modified routine), the latest value of F in the routine is erased and the value of a variable named F, if any, in the calling routine is restored. Notice that removal of the temporary variable F is automatic when the routine terminates with a QUIT. It is not necessary to use a second command to explicitly kill the value of F and restore the previous value.

In the past, M utilities have often been coded using special variables beginning with a % sign (indeed, this is one reason why the % sign was permitted as a starting character for M variables). This technique works best when % variables are restricted for use only by systems programmers. Even so, it is often true that scratch variables are employed in utilities, and their values may affect the operation of a calling routine.

There is a second alternative to the problem posed above. We noted that the square root utility used the NEW command to "mask" or conceal the value of the variable F in the calling routine. Suppose that instead of calculating the square root, we wish to calculate the sine or cosine of a value X. The following partial routine can be used to perform these calculations:

```
SIN   ;Y=SIN(X) ;with the answer Y expressed in Radians
      SET F2=X DO C
      QUIT
COS   ;Y=COS(X) ;with the answer Y expressed in Radians
      SET F2=X+1.570796 DO C
      QUIT
C     ;
      IF F2>-1.570796 SET F2=3.14159265-F2
      IF F2>3.14159265 SET F2=F2-6.2831853 GOTO C
      SET F4=F2,Y=F2,F8=1.F6=-1
      FOR F5=3:2:11 SET F8=F8*(F5-1)*F5,F4=F4*F2*F2,Y=F4/F8*F6+Y,F6=-F6
      SET Y=+$JUSTIFY(Y,1,5)
      KILL F2,F4,F6,F8 QUIT
      ;END OF ROUTINE
```

This utility requires several local variables in the process of developing the correct algorithm. A programmer responsible for maintaining this type of utility might want to be sure that the routine was protected from all possibility of modifying variables from calling routines, leaving open the option to introduce new variables in the utility as the need arose. The NEW command has another form to provide this capability:

```
SIN   ;Y=SIN(X), with the answer Y expressed in Radians
      NEW (X,Y)
      SET F2=X GOTO C
COS   ;Y=COS(X) with the answer Y expressed in Radians
      NEW (X,Y)
      SET F2=X+1.570796
C     ;
      IF F2<-1.570796 SET F2=3.14159265-F2
      IF F2>3.14159265 SET F2=F2-6.2831853 GOTO C
      SET F4=F2,Y=F2,F8=1,F6=-1
      FOR F5=3:2:11 SET F8=F8*(F5-1)*F5,F4=F4*F2*F2,Y=F4/F8*F6+Y,F6=-F6
      SET Y=+$JUSTIFY(Y,1,5)
      QUIT
      ;END OF ROUTINE
```

In this form, the NEW command creates a new environment in which *only* X *and* Y are available from the calling routine. All other values are saved temporarily and then restored when the utility is exited via the QUIT command. Using this form of the NEW command, the programmer can create as many temporary variables as required, knowing that they will be killed implicitly at the end of the routine. (In fact, note that the KILL command is no longer used in the second version of this utility.) Since this routine has two entries (SIN and COS), the NEW command is repeated, but it would not be possible for it to be executed twice, given the flow control of the routine.

At first glance, it might seem that these two forms are almost equal in merit. In the first, the specific variables to be used in the local calculation are identified and protected from the calling environment; in the second, only those which are used for communication with the calling routine are available for the local utility. In fact, however, the second form, which masks all variables except those explicitly identified, is much more costly in its use of system resources and may in fact result in slower execution, since there may be many other local variables that must be preserved prior to execution of the utility. For this reason, the parenthesized form of the NEW command is not recommended in routines where speed is likely to be a factor.

DO command with parameter passing

The NEW command is a useful way to communicate with utilities, as illustrated earlier. However, there remain some limitations to its syntax, in that, despite the ability to restrict the scope of local variables, it is still necessary to have some information about the names of variables used in such utilities in order to make effective use of them. Sometimes packages developed independently may use parameters with names that relate to the package rather than to the utility invoked for special functions, such as those described in the previous section. Furthermore, it is often useful to be able to transfer not only variables, but entire arrays to be used in a general-purpose utility.

Many computer languages provide a mechanism whereby a calling program can pass parameters to the invoked procedure using a syntax such as `CALL SUBA(X,Y,Z)` in which `SUBA` is the name of the procedure invoked and `X`, `Y`, and `Z` are parameters used by that procedure. The DO command now offers this feature (as adopted in the 1990 Standard).

In the extended version of DO, the syntax has been changed to permit addition of parameters associated with the command. One example, based on the need to use a date utility, would be as follows:

```
<preceding lines in a calling routine>
DO ^%DATE(DT)
<routine continues>
```

In this example, a variable, `DT`, has been created by the calling routine. The value stored in the variable `DT` is passed to the routine `%DATE`, which has a variable attached to the name: `^%DATE(D)`. The names of these two variables need not be the same. If they are not, `DT` will retain its original value after `^%DATE(D)` has been executed and control returns to the command after DO ^%DATE(DT) in the calling routine. To illustrate, let's assume that DT is a number derived from the first component of the function $HOROLOG, and that we want to display the actual date on the screen. The value of this variable (DT) is passed to a utility routine called %DATE(D), which will take that value, convert it to a standard format, and output it on the display device. The value of the variable D created by %DATE is *not* available to the calling routine. In fact, it is implicitly KILLed (i.e., it has an implicit NEW invoked so that, when %DATE terminates, D is KILLed).

There is nothing further that needs to be done by the calling routine, nor will it need to use the value of D. The utility routine that accepts this procedure call will look much like a normal M routine with the exception of the first line:

```
%DATE(D) ;rfw; 6/96; calculate and print date.
   SET %H=D>21608+D+1460,%L=%H\1461,%YR=%H#1461
   SET %Y=%L*4+1837+%yr\365),%D=%YR#365+1
   SET %M=1 IF %YR=1460 SET %D=366,%Y=%Y-1
   FOR %I=31,%Y#4=0+ 28,31,30,31,30,31,31,30,31,30,31 QUIT:%D'>%I,
...SET%D%D-%I,%M=%M+1
   SET:%D<10 %D="0"_%D
   SET %M = $EXTRACT("JANFEBMARAPRMAYJUNJULAUGSEPOCTNOVDEC",%M*3-2,%M*3)
   SET D=%M_" "_%D_", "_%Y
   WRITE !?10,D;the date is displayed on the screen
   KILL %H.%L,%YR,%Y,%M,%D,%I QUIT
   ;END OF DATE UTILITY
```

This routine, which is almost identical to one illustrated in Chapter 14 has a different first line from routines described up to this point. Notice that a single parameter, D, is included in parentheses after the name of the routine (no spaces between the name and the left parenthesis). Notice, too, that the name of the variable in this utility need not be the same as that used in the DO ^ROU(var) call that invokes the procedure. This feature makes it possible to invoke such a routine with any parameter name, provided that, in a sequence of parameters, the ordering of the variables is the same in the calling and invoked procedures. For instance we might wish to modify the square root function illustrated earlier m this chapter as follows:

```
SQRT(X) ;Y=square root of X
<continue with remainder of routine>
```

In this form, the calling procedure can use any name for the value for which the square root is to be calculated. The returning value, however, will still be Y, and this value cannot be included in the parameters following the DO command.

The reason for the exclusion of the result in the parameter calls of the DO ^SQRT(VAL1) for this example is based on the manner in which the utility routine uses values included in its parameters. When a DO uses the name of a variable in the form shown, the value is passed to the invoked routine *without* being attached to the name of the variable. In the preceding examples, the DO parameters used to invoke the utility are passed *by value* to the utility. In other words, the value of VAL1 is obtained, and that value (but not the name VAL1) is used to seed the square root utility. It is assigned the name X inside the utility. However, the variable X is treated in a special manner. All variables named as parameters (i.e., enclosed in parentheses after a routine name) are automatically restricted by an implicit NEW command on their name before the body of the routine is executed, and the values of those variables are KILLed when the routine is exited.

Since, in this form of DO with parameters, dates are passed to the invoked utility by value and KILLed upon exit, the parameters can be passed in one direction only. Using this form of the DO command, it is possible to pass constants or the values of either local or global variables (provided they are not array references). The following examples illustrate forms that might be used to reference the %DATE or SQRT utilities listed earlier:

```
DO ^%DATE(53493)
DO ^SQRT(^Z)
DO ^%DATE($PIECE($HOROLOG,",",1))
DO ^SQRT(X(12))
```

In the last example, a value in an array is used, but it is first converted to its actual value and then passed to the SQRT utility.

In many cases, the need arises to establish a two-way communication between the calling and the invoked routine. For instance, it might be preferable to modify %DATE to return values for year, month, and day, so that the output could be used by the invoking routine. The extensions to standard M also permit this form of parameter passing, using the following type of syntax:

```
<preceding lines of routine>
SET DT=56908
DO ^%DATE(DT,.YR,.MO,.DA)  ;(Note the periods before YR, MO, and DA)
WRITE !,"The date of this event was ",MO," ",DA,", ",YR
```

And the utility %DATE would be modified as shown below:

```
%DATE(D,%Y,%M,%D) ;rtw; 6/87; calculate and print date.
   SET %H=D>21608+D+1460,%L=%H\1461,%YR=%H#1461
   SET %Y=%L*4+1837+%yr\365),%D=%YR#365+1
   SET %M=1 IF %YR=1460 SET %D=366,%Y=%Y-1
```

```
FOR %I=31,%Y#4=0+28,31,30,31,30,31,31,30,31,30,31 QUIT:
...%D'>%i  SET %D=%D- %1,%M=%M+1
SET:%D<10 %D="0"_%D
SET %M=$EXTRACT("JANFEBMARAPRMAYJUNJULAUGSEPOCTNOV
...DEC",%M*3-2,%Mt3)
KILL %H,%1,%L,%M,%Y
QUIT
;END OF DATE UTILITY
```

In this example, the invoking call uses two forms of referenced data in the parameter list. The value DT was SET in the line preceding the DO command, but YR, MO, and DY (identified by leading periods) were not previously defined. The utility %DATE has been modified to add the names %Y, %M, and %D to the parameter list and to remove the KILL of these variables at the end of the routine. If the command lines shown were executed, the result would be

```
The date of this event was OCT 22, 1996
```

This example illustrates several points. First, it is possible, by using a preceding period, to pass the *reference to a name* of a variable to a procedure invoked by a DO with parameters. That variable need not be defined when the DO is executed; the values will be inserted and the variables automatically SET when the utility is completed and control returns to the calling routine. In addition, it is possible to include *references to values* as well as names in a DO parameter list. Finally, the names in the invoked procedure need not correspond to the names of the variables in the calling procedure; transfer of values is done automatically upon exit of the invoked routine.

This form of parameter passing also may be used with arrays. Suppose we wanted to have a utility that gives a cross-reference of an array of terms by the value of each array element rather than its subscript. To illustrate, suppose we have the following array:

```
ID("123-98-0001")="Partridge, Roger"
ID("961-88-2003")="Trask, Gardner"
ID("726-77-1429")="Bishop, Ben"
ID("762-35-1984")="Yaksick, Bill"
```

We could use the $ORDER function to list these individuals in order of their Social Security number, but if we wanted to create an alphabetical list, we would need to write a special routine to do so. Since this is the type of alphabetical cross-reference that is often needed, it might be useful to write a general-purpose utility, as shown below:

```
XREF(ORIG,CROSS) ;RFW; 6/87; CROSS REFERENCE UTILITY
   SET %I=""
   FOR %I2=1:1 SET %I=$ORDER(ORIG(%I)) QUIT:%I=""  DO CROSREF
   QUIT  ;exit routine
CROSREF ;
   SET %I3=ORIG(%I),CROSS(%I3)=%I
   QUIT
   ;END OF UTILITY
```

To illustrate use of this routine with the examples shown (assuming the values of ID have already been set), the following commands could be employed:

```
   DO XREF(.ID,.NAM)
   SET X=""
   FOR I=1:1 SET X=$ORDER(NAM(X)) QUIT:X=""  WRITE !,X,?20,NAM(X)
```

And the output would be

```
   Bishop, Ben         726-77-1429
   Partridge,Roger     123-98-0001
   Trask, Gardner      961-88-2003
   Yaksick, Bill       762-35-1984
```

In this example, an array of arbitrary length could be used for input, and a second array (not previously defined) would be generated as the result.

These examples illustrate the flexibility of the DO command with parameter passing. There remains one limitation in the use of the pass-by-reference variation: It is not possible to use either a global reference or specific subscripted array references (e.g., a portion of a local array but not the entire array) or a multiply subscripted array. These restrictions are imposed to simplify the syntax of the parameter passing and to eliminate the possibility of referencing global arrays whose creation could be hampered by external factors.

Extrinsic functions

Taken together, the NEW and DO commands with parameters offer a broad range of possibilities for scoping of variables and development of more controlled code segments than are possible in the current version of standard M. There remains one additional feature that would add flexibility to the language: the ability to invoke a function with parameters. The MDC concluded that addition of *extrinsic functions* to M would facilitate inclusion of many utilities that might be implemented in ways that would improve execution of M, especially in problem solving requiring advanced arithmetic computation.

There would be no restriction on the language in which these functions might be written—assembly language, a special-purpose language, or any other mechanism that provides an efficient solution to a specific problem.

In preceding sections of this chapter we introduced the value of creating utilities to calculate square roots or trigonometric functions, and we showed that the NEW and DO language extensions can be used to create such general-purpose programs. In these two specific cases, however, the desired result is a single value, such as might be returned by a *function*. It would be nice, for example, to say something like "set Y equal to the cosine of X." Extrinsic functions provide this capability.

A reference to an extrinsic function is identified in an M command line by a name that begins with *two* dollar signs, e.g., `$$SQRT(X)`, `$$DATE(DT)`, `$$AVG(Z,N)`. We could use this syntax in the square root example by saying

```
SET X=2,DEF=$$SQRT(X)
```

in which case the value of `DEF` would be set to `1.414....` The utility `SQRT` would require slight modification as follows:

```
SQRT(X) ;Y is set to the square root of X on return
NEW F
SET Y=0 QUIT:X'>0 Y ;note one space before Y
SET F=Y,Y=(X/F+F)/2 GOTO L:Y<F
QUIT Y
```

In this modification, `X` is used as input to the function and `Y` is the value returned. Communication with the utility is via the calling parameters (there could be several). However, the final result is a single value that must be appended as an argument following the QUIT command exiting the function. (This is the only case in which the QUIT command may have an argument, and only one argument is allowed.) In other respects, the function remains much as shown before. Notice that it is possible to use NEW declarations in such a routine, as was suggested earlier in this chapter.

It is the intention of the MDC to propose a number of standard extrinsic functions. Once established, it will be the prerogative of implementors to execute these functions in ways that might be most efficient. In other words, the implementors may (and probably will) take standard extrinsic function calls and write special utilities that take advantage of machine code and other techniques to permit faster execution than by conventional M routines. Math functions would be particularly benefited by this approach, since most computers have hardware math coprocessors or comparable elements that execute many times faster than interpreted code.

Summary

The 1990 revision of the M language permit syntax that limits the scope of local variables and provides for parameter passing and the use of extrinsic functions. The language elements adopted in the 1990 standard are as follows:

- The NEW command permits explicit reference to variables that are to be used in an M routine with the syntax `NEW A,B,C`, where `A`, `B`, and `C` are variables created anew within the routine and KILLed when control returns from the routine to its calling location.
- The NEW command also permits implicit exclusion of all except variables within the scope of a local routine using the syntax `NEW (A,B,C)`, in which all existing variables *except* those identified are masked from the routine and variables other than those named will be created for the duration of the execution controlled by that routine and then KILLed when the routine is exited via a normal QUIT.
- The DO command is extended to permit identification of parameters to be referenced in execution of a called routine. `DO ^ROU(A,B,C)` passes those parameters to a called routine, but this function does not return new values for `A`, `B`, and `C` because these parameters were passed by value.
- Routine header lines have been modified to permit reference to parameters passed by the extended form of DO described earlier. A routine name of the form `ROU(X,Y,Z)` accepts parameters from such a DO command, but it does not change the values of the variables in the calling routine.
- A second form of the extended DO permits passing by reference local variables and arrays: `DO (.A,B,.C)` transmits the variables `A` and `C` by name and the variable `B` by its current value. Changes performed on the equivalent variables in the called routine are also made on the variables or arrays in the calling DO arguments. Only those references preceded by a period are modified in this syntax.
- M also permits use of an *extrinsic function*, which accepts arguments from a calling reference (identified by two leading dollar signs; e.g., `$$SQRT(X)` refers to an extrinsic function `SQRT`) and returns a single value identified by an argument following the QUIT command.

Exercises

The features described in this chapter are available in almost all commercial implementations at this time. If you are working on a version that permits use of these commands, you may find the following exercises useful in creating one or more utilities to help you perform some functions that are often required in the M environment.

1. ***Arithmetic Mean*** Create a routine that uses the array `X(I)` defined *external* to the routine to calculate the average, using the NEW command to create variables whose use is limited to that routine. In your routine, use SUM, N, and MEAN to calculate the values. Write out your answer within the routine and then return to the calling routine. For purposes of checking, use the following array:

   ```
   X(1)=7
   X(2)=13
   X(3)=4
   X(4)=11
   X(5)=14
   X(6)=9
   X(7)=6
   ```

   When you have completed creating these variables and running the routine, write out the values of SUM, N, and MEAN to make certain that the values calculated in your routine no longer exist.

2. ***Date Utility*** Given a date (`DT`) in the form `mm/dd/yy`, write a utility that calculates the value of the date portion of $HOROLOG. Assume that the date is later than 1901. Use a DO command with the argument of `DT` to access the utility, which accepts `DT` as an input parameter from the calling routine. Your utility should write out the value of the date in $HOROLOG format (first part) before returning to the calling command. Test your routine with the value `06/19/87`, which should return `53495`.

3. ***Date Extrinsic Function*** Create a second version of the date utility generated in Exercise 2 that calculates the $HOROLOG value but returns it as described in the extrinsic function section of this chapter. Test the function by executing it with a `WRITE $$DATE(variable)` command (use `6/19/87` again) to be certain that it returns the anticipated result.

Implementation-specific Components of M

17

Chapter 9 introduced the concept of *direct* and *program modes* of interaction available in the M language. The exercises at the end of Chapter 9 also provided a brief introduction to some of the editing commands necessary to create, save, and restore M routines. In this chapter, the concept of direct-mode execution is presented in the context of implementation-specific features of the M standard.

An interpretive language differs from a compiled language in that there are two ways that the language can be invoked. The first is in the so-called *direct mode,* in which each command typed by the user is executed as soon as it is completed. Throughout most of this text, the examples illustrate direct execution of commands. However, as we saw in Chapter 9, when creating a routine, the direct mode is used to enter routine command lines, which are then stored. To invoke these stored routines, the user types `DO ^<routine name>`, and M finds the routine on disk, loads it into the execution area, and proceeds to execute commands as specified in the routine. This mode of execution is called *program mode,* because the user does not have to enter each command manually.

> **Note to Experienced Programmers**: This section introduces the availability of language extensions and implementation-specific features available in M but not standard across all implementations. The details of each implementation will differ and should be described in documentation provided by the vendors. This chapter describes principles, not specifics, of these language elements and may be useful for that reason.

Direct-mode execution does not exist in compiled languages. Users write programs using operating system editors, compile them with the regular compiler, and then invoke them by using the appropriate operating system call. The direct-mode actions are in the operating system, not the language.

Since M has both direct and indirect execution environments, it was necessary in defining the language to provide some mechanism for incorporating these features. The developers of M were reluctant to dictate the precise details of the way in which direct mode would run on every machine, so they chose to leave the details of direct-mode execution undefined, allowing for implementation-specific differences. It was necessary, however, to place some limits on the manner in which specific implementations might invoke direct-mode commands, the most important restriction being to prevent conflict with the remainder of the language.

In addition to this unusual language characteristic, there also exist some language elements which are formally identified but whose exact actions or complete specifications are partially or completely implementation-specific.

This chapter introduces commands, special functions or variables, and other components of the M language that fall into the implementation-specific category. The underlying philosophy behind these language elements is described, and some effort is made to indicate the emergence of a consensus on the use of some such features (a long-term goal of the MDC is to standardize many of these language elements). One area in which standardization *has* occurred is Error Handling. Chapter 24 in Part II of this text discusses the new ways in which many components of error handling have been standardized. There remain, however, some nonstandard error handling features in most implementations, as noted later in this chapter.

Because of the variety inherent in the specifics of this chapter, there are no exercises to provide practice with the different language elements described. Readers are encouraged to explore the appropriate functions using documentation provided for their system.

Commands with implementation-specific components

Some of the language elements already introduced have nonstandard features. For instance, Chapter 13 introduced the OPEN, USE, and CLOSE commands, which refer to devices that have names or numbers selected by the implementor and are not necessarily consistent even between different installations by the same vendor. There are many options pertaining to different types of devices (files, printers, special displays, tape drives, disk drives, and so on), and it would not be possible to define exhaustively all such features. New devices appear regularly, often requiring new parameters. For all these reasons, it seemed prudent to permit some flexibility in allowing differences in the arguments associated with such I/O devices. The variations will continue to exist between different classes of devices, and these variations will require flexibility in the language.

Commands with implementation-specific interpretations: BREAK and VIEW

The M language standard currently defines two commands in a very general sense, without specifying exactly what they should do. These commands are BREAK, used to suspend execution, and VIEW, intended to provide machine-specific information. Although they are incompletely defined, they are useful concepts, and almost all M implementations take advantage of the availability of these two commands. Their use and significance are discussed in the next few paragraphs.

BREAK command

Often programmers are mystified by the failure of a routine to perform as intended. Careful inspection of the program flow control, the logic used to name and manipulate variables, and all other avenues for isolating the presumed "bug" have been exhausted. At this point, one useful technique is to execute the problem code, setting stopping points at which the contents of certain variables and other parameters might be examined to see if they conform to the expected logic. The BREAK command is intended to assist in this type of program testing and review.

There are two desirable forms of interrupting execution, corresponding to the direct and indirect modes of execution. However, a difference exists in that a user, watching a routine execute, may wish to interrupt its execution at some unanticipated moment, or alternatively, suspend execution at a predetermined point in the program. To begin with let's examine the predetermined interruption provided by the BREAK command.

As defined in the M standard:

BREAK provides an access point within the standard for nonstandard programming aids. BREAK without arguments suspends execution until receipt of a signal, not specified here, from a device.

The arguments available to the BREAK command also are not specified. One might think that this specification is of little value. In practice, however, BREAK has been implemented in ways that closely relate to the editing and debugging environment of each implementation, so its open-ended definition has proved a valuable characteristic.

To illustrate one way in which the BREAK command might be used, let us examine a routine that is capable of misbehaving, "run it" with varying input, and then use BREAK to determine the nature of the programming logical inconsistency. The following example is in fact taken from one encountered by the author in adapting the programming example of the next chapter for use in this text.

```
SET STUD="Weis, George" ;initialize with fictitious name
SET CRS(STUD,1)=95 ;an equally fictitious grade
<some irrelevant lines>
READ !?10,"Delete student from file? (Y/N): ",YN
IF "Yy"[YN KILL CRS(STUD) WRITE !,STUD," has been deleted."
<continue on with routine execution>
```

The purpose of the READ statement is to ask the user if the student identified is to be removed from the file. Here are some answers that the routine would provide for this portion of the code (user responses are in **boldface**):

- *Example 1*

```
Delete student from file? (Y/N): Y
Weis, George has been deleted.
<program continues>
```

- *Example 2*

```
Delete student from file? (Y/N): N
<program continues without deleting name>
```

- *Example 3*

```
Delete student from file? (Y/N): (User hits <enter> key.)
Weis, George has been deleted.
<program continues>
```

This perhaps surprising result indicates that the programmer has left open some sort of option in which the wrong action might be taken, as in the third example above. In order to isolate this problem, we will modify the code to insert a break at an appropriate point and then analyze the results:

```
SET STUD="Weis, George" ;initialize with fictitious name
SET CRS(STUD,1)=95 ;an equally fictitious grade
<some irrelevant lines>
READ !?10,"Delete student from file? (Y/N): ",YN
BREAK
IF "Yy"[YN KILL CRS(STUD) WRITE !,STUD," has been deleted."
<continue on with routine execution>
```

Having inserted the BREAK command on a separate line (to facilitate its subsequent removal when the problem has been corrected), we will execute our example again on a hypothetical system:

- *Example 4*

```
Delete student from file? (Y/N):", (null answer given)
**BREAK***
WRITE !,"the value of YN is now ",YN (A null value is written out.)
```

By interrupting execution at this point, we are able to see that, in fact, YN is empty. We are now forced to ask ourselves why an empty value will match the string "Yy". If we do more testing and checking we may find out that an empty value will correctly evaluate as TRUE in matching for a string such as "Yy". This result is because the string "Yy" implicitly also contains the empty string, so a null response will return a TRUE test (a fact not always taken into account in this type of test). Armed with this new piece of information, we modify our program as follows:

```
SET STUD="Weis, George" ;initialize with fictitious name
SET CRS(STUD,1)=95 ;an equally fictitious grade
<some irrelevant lines>
READ !?10,"Delete student from file? (Y/N): ",YN
BREAK
IF $LENGTH(YN),"Yy"[YN KILL CRS(STUD) WRITE !,STUD," has been deleted."
<continue on with routine execution>
```

In this version, an empty answer will give a $LENGTH of 0, and hence the IF test returns a FALSE answer. Running this code segment again, we find that Mr. Weis is not removed when an empty response is given, and we can edit the code to remove the BREAK.

This simple example illustrates how BREAK can be used in program mode to halt at a predetermined point in routine execution in order to examine the status of variables modified by the routine up to that point. Sometimes in the process of detecting errors it may be necessary to set several break points. In this case, many implementors allow addition of an argument that is displayed at the time the BREAK command is executed, such as, for example,

```
***BREAK*** routine XYZ, breakpoint 2
```

which would appear if, at that location, the BREAK were set as

```
BREAK "routine XYZ, breakpoint 2"
```

There are many different ways that implementors use BREAK, but all provide for it in one way or another. As shown later, most use a companion function, ZGO, to return to normal execution. We will return to that command in a later section of this chapter. The second interrupt option useful in program development is the ability to suspend execution at some unplanned point. Suppose a user had written the following command line:

```
FOR I=1:1 WRITE I,""
```

If this line were executed, it would go into an infinite loop, writing 1, 2, 3, 4, etc., until *something* happened to stop it. That *something* might have to be resetting the computer, turning it off, or some other equally drastic command if there is no *direct-mode* BREAK functionality available. Fortunately, most M implementations provide for a BREAK initiated by typing a `<ctrl-C>` or some such character. Since `<ctrl-C>` is a common interactive break key in many languages, this one is often used in M.

A key that halts execution and returns the user to direct mode is useful for programmers, but it may be dangerous to permit naive users with no programming experience to use such a key. Therefore, all M implementations have a way in which the BREAK key can be disabled until a separate command is issued to restore its functionality. This feature of M is also not standardized, but it is universally present in M implementations.

A common syntax for BREAK, used in many different implementations, is to have the form BREAK 1 (BREAK with the argument 1) used to *enable* the BREAK function and BREAK 0 used to *disable* the function. With this approach, it is possible to leave BREAK statements in routines and run them in uninterrupted form for further debugging. Sometimes disabling the BREAK function is a good idea for users, whereas programmers may wish to retain BREAK commands in the code for systems maintenance reasons. Because of its utility, the use of arguments 0 and 1 for BREAK has achieved widespread agreement among implementors. The BREAK command and BREAK key have been implemented with many additional features, but these examples will serve to illustrate the general functional need and manner in which it is used.

VIEW command

VIEW is another standard command with implementation-specific arguments. The standard states that VIEW is provided to give the implementor a means of examining implementation-specific information. For example, the implementor might use VIEW to permit the programmer to "dump" some portion of memory in order to examine data or code as a debugging aid or to look at the structure of global files on disk. A general summary of the way in which VIEW is used by different implementors is as follows:

1. To modify contents of memory (DT, MSM, ISM)
2. To examine and modify contents of global blocks (MSM, ISM)

As implied in this list, there are some implementations in which VIEW has not been defined. The use of VIEW to alter contents of memory or globals requires considerable expertise, so this capability is usually reserved only for those users who are trained and authorized to do so.

Extending the M standard: Z-commands

The developers of standard M believed that a need exists to permit orderly extension of the language. There are several reasons for this need. First, as noted earlier, certain functions affecting direct-mode execution must be provided in a complete implementation. Actions relating to creating, storing, and modifying routines are one example. Debugging functions and utilities (of which BREAK is one example) are another.

In order to allow for these capabilities without destroying the consistency of the standard commands, the M language allows implementors to add commands that are prefixed with the letter Z. It is understood that any such commands may be incompatible from one system to another. However, a review of the manner in which Z-commands have been implemented does reveal a certain measure of consistency between implementations. Table 17.1 is intended to give a partial summary of Z-commands as implemented by a few well-known M vendors. The table omits many commands that are unique to a single implementation, and it indicates where functional equivalents may be available on an implementation, perhaps through quite different mechanisms. This table should be taken as a guideline, since implementations change and the Z-command area is one of the most changeable of all M features.

The following abbreviations are used to identify vendors listed in Table 17.1:

OpenM: InterSystems' M for Windows 95, Windows NT
DTM: InterSystems' Data Tree M for Windows 3.1, DOS
MSM: Micronetics Standard M (Windows 3.1 Windows 95, Windows NT, UNIX)
DSM: InterSystem's DSM for OpenVMS VAX 6.5, OpenVMS Alpha 6.5, Digital UNIX 1.0
ISM: Intersystems Open M for UNIX, OpenVMS Alpha 6.1, OpenVMS VAX 6.9
PFCS: PFCS Corporation (UNIX)
GT.M: Greystone Technology Corporation (UNIX)

(Specific UNIX platforms are not listed above. For details contact individual vendors.)

TABLE 17.1: *Z-Commands as Implemented on Selected M Systems Today*

Name	Purpose	MSM	DSM	DTM	ISM	Open M	PFCS	GT.M
▪ **Editing:**								
ZDELETE	Delete rou.	f	Y	Y	f	f	u	f
ZEDIT	Scrn. editor	f	Y	Y	Y	Y	u	Y
ZINSERT	Insert line	Y	Y	Y	Y	Y	Y	f
ZPRINT	Print routine	Y	Y	Y	Y	Y	Y	Y
ZLOAD	Load routine	Y	Y	Y	Y	Y	Y	f
ZREMOVE	Delete lines/rou.	Y	Y	Y	Y	Y	Y	f
ZSAVE	Store routine	Y	Y	Y	Y	Y	Y	Y
ZWRITE	Disp. loc var.	Y	Y	Y	Y	Y	Y	Y
▪ **File management:**								
ZFLUSH	Flush buffers	Y	--	--	--	--	--	f
ZJOURNAL	Transact Journal	f	Y	Y	Y	Y	--	f
▪ **Error handling and debugging†:**								
ZCLEAR	Clear stack	f	--	--	--	--	--	f
ZDEBUG	Debug	f	Y	Y	Y	Y	--	f
ZESCAPE	Ret. to dir. mode	f	Y	--	--	--	f	f
ZETRAP	Error trap	f	--	--	--	f	f	f
ZGO	Resume exec.	Y	Y	Y	Y	Y	f	f
ZQUIT	Clear stack	f	Y	Y	Y	Y	f	f
ZSTEP	Single step	f	Y	Y	Y	Y	--	f
ZTRACE	Trace exec.	Y	--	Y	Y	Y	Y	f
ZTRAP	Error trap	f	Y	Y	Y	Y	f	Y

† Error handling has been partially standardized. See Chapter 24. Some variations in usage in these commands.

f: Functional equivalents exist.

u: Uses UNIX for equivalent functions.

From the table we can see that most implementors have addressed problems of routine management, file management, and error management, and many also include additional utilities to serve a variety of purposes. The reader is cautioned, however, that the use of the same Z-command in two systems may produce different results. In general, it is not wise to make use of Z-commands in routines that may be transferred to other implementations.

Special variables and functions with implementation-specific meaning: $JOB, $STORAGE, and $VIEW

Just as the BREAK and VIEW commands have implementation-specific meaning, M also provides for two special variables and a special function whose meaning may differ from one system to another: the special variables $JOB and $STORAGE and the function $VIEW. These language elements are considered briefly below.

$JOB is a special variable that returns a positive integer that uniquely identifies the M process. In other words, it is a job number that is assigned to you when you begin an M session. It remains constant throughout that session and uniquely identifies you so that your activity may be separated from that of other users. It is often used as an initial subscript in global scratch files to separate individual users' areas. By definition, $JOB will have no consistent interpretation between systems, nor even from one execution session to another. However, it is a valuable reference variable when several jobs are running simultaneously on a given system. See also Chapter 21 for the use of the special variable $SYSTEM.

$STORAGE was designed to provide information about the *workspace* available at any time during an interactive session. The concept of workspace implies an architecture for M implementations in which each user has an area of memory assigned at log-on time, and this space is available for use in editing and executing routines, creating local variables, and for the housekeeping "stacks" used to manage execution of routines. Although the concept is valid in many systems today (dedicated M minicomputers, certain microcomputers), it has a far less clear meaning when M is implemented under general-purpose, virtual-memory multiprogramming operating systems. In these cases, there is effectively no real meaning to the "storage space" available, since it is virtual and open-ended.

The use of $STORAGE, then, depends on whether the implementation is in fact limited in terms of the local workspace that can be assigned to a given user. In such systems, $STORAGE returns a number that gives the amount of space available for use at any time. The number will decrease as routines are expanded or as local variables are created or expanded, and it may serve as a useful guide to a programmer wondering whether the current implementation will run into limits affecting program execution. Most systems allow some user control in setting the size of the user's workspace. The current portability requirements of the M standard indicate that the workspace used to store routines and local variables should be at least 10 kilobytes in size; however, in recent meetings of the MDC, limits of 10,000 characters each for routine and local variable space have been proposed.

Since the significance of $STORAGE depends on the specific implementation, the reader is referred to vendor manuals for further details of each version.

The $VIEW function is similar to the VIEW command in that it is also used to examine machine-dependent information. The argument is unspecified.

Generally, this function is used to return one specific piece of machine-dependent information for each argument. In general, those implementations which define VIEW also make use of $VIEW in the modification of memory or global blocks.

Further extensions of M: variables and functions

In addition to the functions and variables defined earlier as having implementation-specific meaning, M also permits the use of the Z-syntax to allow implementors to create additional new variables and functions. The variety of terms used by different vendors is considerable, but, as in the case of extended commands, there are some consistent threads that occur across many different implementations (see Table 17.2).

TABLE 17.2: *Z-Functions as Implemented on Selected M Systems Today*

Name	Purpose	MSM	DSM	DTM	ISM	Open M	PFCS	GT.M
▪ **Global files:**								
$ZVERIFY	Integ. chk.	Y	Y	Y	Y	Y	f	f
▪ **Miscellaneous:**								
$ZC	CRC checksum	Y	--	Y	--	--	f	f
$ZDATE	Date function	Y	Y	Y	Y	Y	f	Y

f: Functional equivalent available.
Note: Some additional functions (e.g., bit manipulation) also available on some implementations.

In addition to the special functions listed in Table 17.2, some systems use Z-functions to define math capabilities, and others provide M routines to perform math. Several implementations have special functions associated with error processing. Some provide assistance in traversing routine directories. These capabilities are sufficiently disparate that they to not lend themselves to inclusion in Table 17.2.

The special variables defined in different systems (also identified by a leading $Z) are too varied to summarize in a table. They include features related to version numbers, information on the current routine in workspace, directory pathways, and some I/O status information. This increased diversity is to be expected, in that the special variables are likely to be more closely related to a given implementation and hence more diverse.

Summary

M defines certain commands, functions, and variables in a general way, reserving their exact definition to the implementors. The language features thus defined include:

- Commands:
  - BREAK—Used to interrupt execution
  - VIEW—Used to provide information on memory status, global structure, or other system-specific information
  - Z-commands whose names as well as functions are implementation-specific
- Special functions:
  - $Z-functions whose names and purpose are implementation-specific
- Special variables:
  - $JOB—Used to identify job currently executing
  - $STORAGE—Used to define remaining space available in user workspace
  - $VIEW—Used in conjunction with VIEW to manipulate memory or global reference information
  - $Z-variables whose names and uses are implementation-specific

Note: These language extensions have been adopted with some uniformity between implementations but they are not universally compatible and they should not be used in programming M routines designed for export to other implementations.

Exercises

Because of the diversity of options available in implementation-specific features discussed in this chapter, it is not appropriate to attempt formal exercises that cover many different versions. Instead, you are urged to review your user manual to locate the definitions and purposes of each of the language extensions implemented on your version.

In particular, you should find the answers to the following questions:

1. How is BREAK implemented? Are there differences between the use of BREAK with and without arguments? How does one return to execution following interruption via the BREAK command?
2. What Z-commands are available? It might be well to attempt to group these commands by related function (editing, file management, and so on).
3. What provisions are made for handling errors? This investigation may lead to a study of the classes of errors identified as well as the methods for recovering from such errors.
4. How does the implementation allow the user to review local variables?

5. Does the implementation provide for special features associated with traversing a global tree? If so, how do they work?

6. By answering these questions, you should be more familiar with your system and hence able to design and develop new applications more effectively.

18 An Applications Example: a Course-grading Package

The previous chapters introduced the basic concepts of M – those that are most likely to be used by beginning and intermediate programmers. In this chapter we will introduce an example of a package written in M. The example selected is one that handles the administrative details of grades for a class. This example was chosen because it is one familiar to all readers, with enough complexity to permit use of several different language elements and yet be self-contained. The author has used these programs for several years, and although the version listed in this chapter has a few extra components to complete the package, it is one that has been tested by use.

The intent of this example is to illustrate how a package can be designed and coded in M. Although the goal is a relatively simple one, it includes components that require careful structural design and modularization. In this example, we will discuss the design of routines and files used for the system and then present and discuss each of the modules that form the package.

> **Note to experienced programmers:** This real-world example is typical of many applications written in M. It illustrates the design process used in creating M applications, and it demonstrates the ease with which functions such as menu drivers and database management can be coded in M. As you study this chapter, begin by reading the Overview and Design section; then try to visualize how this problem might be addressed in another programming language. Compare that design with the M solution that follows. As you proceed, ask yourself how some of the coding problems might be solved in another language. The insights gained from this approach should help you to understand why it is that M has been acclaimed as an effective program for a wide variety of applications.

Overview and design

Grading a class should not be all that difficult. An instructor needs to decide what components will go to make up the total grade, determining how each is to be scored and how much weight to assign each, and then, having determined who is enrolled for the course, assign grades as they are completed. The grading package should take care of alphabetizing the student names, calculating simple statistics for individual assignments and tests, summing up the total scores, and presenting the results for review by the instructor and students.

This simplified definition of the task seems to call for a straightforward data structure, and might fit into one routine. However, in this case, we want to generalize the package to allow it to be used for any course and to allow for editing at several levels. The addition of these elements makes the design more complicated, necessitating a re-evaluation of the program design and file structure.

To begin this process, let's define the separable functions that go into the course-grading process. A partial list of these activities is as follows:

1. Define course (name, term and year, grade components, and weighting factors)
2. Identify students (name, ID number)
3. Enter scores for individual assignments or tests
4. Edit scores
5. Edit names
6. Report results of individual assignments or exams
7. Produce final grade summary
8. List all courses in file

These component functions could be lumped into one rather large routine, but it makes more sense to create several modules, each responsible for one or two of the functions in the list. Since there are several different activities associated with the package, it also makes sense to have a master program that will call the other routines in the package.

From this analysis, we can create the following set of modules:

- Main menu driver
- Initialization
  - Course initialization
  - Course listing
- Data entry

    - Student names
    - Grades
- Editing
    - Student names
    - Grades
- Reporting
    - Single assignment
    - Final summary

The modules listed may eventually be grouped into programs (e.g., reporting functions may be easier to combine). In addition, there may be additional utility modules required to complete the routines in this package. However, this design gives us a clearer picture of the activities that must be defined and coded.

Next, it is necessary to define the file structure that will be used to store the information. Since the package is to be generalized, this structure should accommodate multiple courses with multiple options in grading assignments and weighting. It is quite possible that a search for courses will be done by number, year, or term, so these items will require separate subscripts. Although it might be preferable in the long run to have a separate file for student name and ID number, we will not use a separate file in this design.

The basic file design proposed is as follows:

File design for ^COURSE

Subscript level	**Last subscript**	**Subscript value**	**Data value**
^COURSE(	CRSNO	Course number	—
.	YR	Year offered	—
..	Q	Quarter offered	Title of course
...	0	Total number of assignments/exams	
...	1	Title of assignment 1	—
....	0	Weighting of assignment 1	—
...	2	Title of assignment 2	—
....	0	Weighting of assignment 2	—
(etc.)			
...	n	Title of assignment n	—
....	0	Weighting of assignment n	—
...	Name	Name of first student	ID number

File design for ^COURSE (Continued)			
Subscript level	**Last subscript**	**Subscript value**	**Data value**
....	1	Student's grade in assignment 1	—
....	2	Student's grade in assignment 2	—
(etc.)			
...	Name	Name of next student	ID number
....	1	Student's grade in assignment 1	—
....	2	Student's grade in assignment 2	—
(etc.)			
		Name of next student	
...	Name	*(etc.)*	

This design keeps all values in one global name, which is easier to maintain, and it contains all the necessary information for a self-contained grading system. Other designs involving multiple files for additional course information, student identification, and so on would be preferable in a complete student record system, but this structure will serve the desired purpose.

Naming conventions

Before embarking on the actual coding for individual components of the package, it is wise to settle on some naming conventions to be used throughout the package. As noted earlier, the global used for data storage has been given the name `^COURSE`. In order to relate the routine names to this global, all routines will start with the three letters `CRS`. The main menu driver will be called `CRS`, and it will in turn call other routines. The routines used in the package are the following:

`CRS`	Menu driver for other routines
`CRSDEF`	Routine used to define a new course
`CRSLIST`	Routine used to list all courses in global
`CRSSTUD`	Routine used to enter names, IDs of students
`CRSGRNTR`	Routine used to enter grades for assignment
`CRSGREDT`	Routine used to edit grades
`CRSTDNM`	Utility used to look up student name on partial match
`RSSTMOD`	Routine used to correct name spelling or ID number
`CRSREPT`	Routine to report grades (one assignment or total)

This list includes some routines called by others (CRSLIST, CRSTDNM), whereas the remainder are called by the main menu driver.

The local variables also should have some consistency in the names used. The following naming conventions were chosen for this package:

- **Basic identifiers**
  - CNO Course number
  - YR Year of course offering
  - Q Quarter offered (F, W, S, SM are the four values recommended)
  - NAM Student name (may be array)
- **Secondary identifiers**
  - OPT User input option for menu driver
  - ST Students with scores reported for assignment
  - TMAX Highest score for an assignment
  - TMIN Lowest score for an assignment
  - TNAM Temporary student name in report generator
  - TSUM Sum of scores for an assignment
  - TMP Array used to store grade histogram
  - TTL Title of course, title of each assignment
  - WGT Weight of assignment in final grade
  - YN Yes/no response variable
- **Indexing variables**
  - C Course loop index for listing all courses
  - LNCNT Line count for paging output report
  - N1,N2,N3 Indexes for name searches
  - PAGE Page count for output report
  - Q Quarter loop index for listing all courses
  - T0 Index of total number of assignments
  - T1 Index for assignment number
  - TN Index for reporting by student
  - TOUT Output device indicator
  - TX Index for listing one student's grades
  - Y Year loop index for listing all courses

Having settled on these names, we are ready to begin with the design of each module.

Menu driver

Designing a menu driver is a task that must be performed many times in M applications. The functions of all menu drivers are similar, and design of a driver that can be adapted easily to a new application is a worthwhile goal.

In this case, the menu driver is one adapted from a general-purpose driver written by Brown and Glaeser (*A Cookbook of M,* published by Comp. Computing, Inc., Houston, Texas, 1985, pages 8+9). It was adapted for another purpose in Chapter 15, and in this case, it required minor modification for this application, and the author has used it for numerous other packages. A listing of the routine follows:

```
CRS;RFW;9/96;MENU DRIVER, GRADE PACKAGE;
   ;
   KILL  SET SD=";"
   WRITE #!?20,"Course grade package",!!
   READ !,"Are you creating a new course file? (Y/N): ",YN
   IF $LENGTH(YN),"Yy"[YN DO ^CRSDEF GOTO CRLOOP
   READ !?5,"Enter course number: ",CNO
   READ !?5,"Enter year: ",YR,!?5,"Academic term (F/W/S/SM): ",Q
   IF '$DATA(^COURSE(CNO,YR,Q)) WRITE !!,*07,"Course not in system" DO
   ...^CRSLIST GOTO CRS
   WRITE !!,^COURSE(CNO,YR,Q)
CRLOOP ;
   READ !!,"Select option (? for help, null to quit): ",OPT
   QUIT:OPT=""
   IF OPT["?" DO LIST GOTO CRLOOP
   IF OPT?1.N,OPT'=0,$TEXT(OPTS+OPT)'="" WRITE " ",$PIECE($TEXT
   ...(OPTS+OPT),SD,4) GOTO DOIT
   IF OPT'?1.N FOR I=1:1 SET X=$PIECE($TEXT(OPTS+I),SD,4) QUIT:
   ...X=""  IF $EXTRACT(X,1,$LENGTH(OPT))=OPT WRITE $EXTRACT
   ...(X,$LENGTH(OPT)+1,99) SET OPT=I GOTO DOIT
   WRITE !," Invalid entry. type '?' for help",! GOTO CRLOOP
   ;
DOIT ;
      SET X=$TEXT(OPTS+OPT) DO @$PIECE(X,SD,3) GOTO CRLOOP
LIST ;
   WRITE !!,"Choose one of the following options by number or unique
   ...first letter(s): ",!!
   FOR I=1:1 SET X=$TEXT(OPTS+I) QUIT:X ="" WRITE I,".", ?4,$PIECE
   ...(X,SD,4),!
      QUIT
OPTS  ;list of routines and menu prompts accessed by package
      ;;^CRSSTUD;IDENTIFY STUDENTS BY NAME AND NUMBER
      ;;^CRSGRNTR;RECORD GRADES FOR ONE ASSIGNMENT/EXAM
```

```
;;^CRSREPT;PRINT GRADE SUMMARY
;;^CRSSTMOD;CHANGE STUDENT NAME
;;^CRSGREDT;EDIT GRADES
```

There are a number of techniques used in this driver that bear special mention. The first lines (CRS–CRLOOP) are specific to this package, since there must be opportunities to initialize a new course, and in all cases, any further action requires definition of the course to be addressed.

The lines of code between CRLOOP and DOIT are very close to those used by Brown and Glaeser, and they contain some interesting programming techniques. Notice that line CRLOOP+1 simply asks the user to select an option without displaying the options available. The first time a user encounters this package, use of the "?" response will provide the option list. For experienced users of the menu driver, there is no need to present these options, since the user will already be familiar with the main components. Hence the choice is made not to list options unless requested.

If a user wishes to see a list of options, the section of code between LIST and the end of the program provides this function. The options are listed in the text at the end of the routine, separated from the names of the routines invoked by the delimiter ";" which is given the name SD at the start of the driver (line CRS+2). The list appears as follows:

```
1. IDENTIFY STUDENTS BY NAME AND NUMBER
2. RECORD GRADES FOR ONE ASSIGNMENT/EXAM
3. PRINT GRADE SUMMARY
4. CHANGE STUDENT NAME
5. EDIT GRADES
```

Notice that numbers have been added before each option (using the index variable I of the FOR loop). When the list is complete, the user is once again asked to select an option, using either the number or the first unique letter(s) of the option desired. Routine line CRLOOP+4 processes numeric values entered by the user, checking to make certain they are within range, and if so, writing out the text of the option selected. It then transfers control to the DOIT section (described later) to carry out the user's request.

The following line (CRLOOP+5) checks for unique letter(s) of user input matching text in the options available. If the user types only one letter (which in this case is sufficient), this command line prints out the remainder of the option found (the WRITE $EXTRACT()... portion of the line) and transfers control as before. If two options begin with the same letter and only one letter was used (e.g., if there were options EDIT GRADE as well as EDIT STUDENT NAME), the first option to match the user input would be selected. This is a minor limitation to the approach taken here (the user may wish to consider how to avoid this limitation), but it was avoided in this package by having unique initial letters.

The line DOIT uses indirection to go to the routine pointed to by the user's selection. The third PIECE of the identified line of text contains the name of the routine to be accessed, and the command DO @$PIECE(X,SD,3) uses indirection to transfer control to that routine. Following completion of this option, the program returns control to the menu driver. (As noted earlier, some M implementations discard comment lines unless they begin with two semicolons; hence the text lines after OPTS use this convention so that the routine will run without change on all M implementations.)

It is not difficult to see how this program could be easily adapted to serve as a menu driver for other applications. It would be necessary only to change the introductory lines and then change the text following the label OPT, inserting a routine for transfer of control and a prompt appropriate to that function. There are ways that the driver could perhaps be improved: There is no check for lowercase entries by the user, and as noted above, multiple prompts beginning with the same letter(s) might cause selection errors. However, this routine is functional and simple.

Listing available courses

Before going into the options selected by the main portion of the menu driver, we will examine the course-listing routine:

```
CRSLIST ;LIST AVAILABLE COURSES.RFW.7/96
   ;list all available courses in global
   SET (C,Y,Q)=""
   FOR J=0:0 SET C=$ORDER(^COURSE(C)) QUIT:C=""  DO YEAR
   WRITE !!,"End of courses currently on file" QUIT
YEAR;
   FOR J=0:0 SET Y=$ORDER(^COURSE(C,Y)) QUIT:Y=""  DO QTR
   QUIT ;end of one course title
QTR;
   FOR J=0:0 SET Q=$ORDER(^COURSE(C,Y,Q)) QUIT:Q="" WRITE !,C,?15,Y,?
   ...20,Q,?25,^COURSE(C,Y,Q)
   QUIT
   ;END OF ROUTINE
```

This is one way in which a global tree can be traversed nested three levels deep. Since it is known that the courses must all appear in this global traverse, it is not necessary to search for unknown descendants at different levels of the tree. Notice that the exit to this routine is near the middle, just before the label YEAR. Notice also that although the same index is used for each level of nesting, the values of the index are not used and the index is not incremented. This routine is in other respects unremarkable.

Definition of course content and students

The routine CRSDEF is relatively simple and straightforward, as shown by the listing that follows:

```
CRSDEF :RFW; 7/96; DEFINE NEW COURSE
   ;Asks for course name, qtr/yr. then for title, wt of each grade
   WRITE !,"Course Management Program",!!
   WRITE !?5,"Enter course number:" READ CNO
   READ!?5,"EnterYear(2Digits): ",YR,!?5,"EnterQuarter(F/W/S/SM): ",Q
   IF $DATA(^COURSE(CNO,YR,Q)) WRITE !!," Course already exists" QUIT
   READ !!?5,"Enter title of course: ",TTL SET^COURSE(CNO,YR,Q)=TTL
   ;get name, weighting for each course grade component
   WRITE !!,"Program will now accept title and weighting factor for
   ...each",!?5,"gradable assignment or test in class."
   SET T1=0
G1 ;
   SET T1=T1+1
   READ !!?5,"Enter title of assignment/exam (null to quit): ",TTL
   IF TTL="" SET^COURSE(CNO,YR,Q,0)=T1-1 QUIT
   SET^COURSE(CNO,YR,Q,T1)=TTL
   READ !?5,"Enter weighting value assigned to grade: ",WGT
   SET^COURSE(CNO,YR,Q,T1,0)=WGT
   GOTO G1
   ;END OF ROUTINE
```

The entry of title and weighting is in accordance with the structure previously defined. There are no items in this routine that present any novel approaches in coding, so we can proceed to the next section, that of defining student names and ID numbers:

```
CRSSTUD ;ENTER STUDENT NAMES. RFW 6/96
   WRITE !!,"This program used to enter student names.",!!
   SET T1=0
S1;enter students names
   READ !?5,"Enter next student name (last, first) [null to quit]: ",NAM
   ...QUIT:NAM=""
   READ !?5,"Enter student id#: ",ID
   SET^COURSE(CNO,YR,Q,NAM)=ID GOTO S1
   ;END OF ROUTINE
```

Once again, this is a straightforward routine with no special features requiring comment. Notice that the name is entered in a last name, first name order so that they will be stored in proper alphabetical order. The use of conventional uppercase and lowercase names (e.g., "Brown, David") makes printed reports more pleasing to the eye, but it is not essential in this file structure to do so.

Entering grades for assignments

The next function that must be performed is to enter grades for students. In this activity, one could use two approaches: ask the user to identify each student or present the names in alphabetical order. Here is a listing of the grade-entry routine:

```
CRSGRNTR ;ENTER GRADES FOR ASSIGNMENT/EXAM.RFW.5/87
   SET T0=^COURSE(CNO,YR,Q,0)
   FOR T1=1:1:T0 WRITE !,T1,?5,^(T1)
   READ !!!?5,"Select number of assignment/exam for which grades are to
   ...be entered: ",T2
   IF T2>T1 WRITE !,"Invalid number",QUIT
   SET N="A"
   FOR ST=1:1 SET N=$ORDER(^COURSE(CNO,YR,Q,N)) QUIT:N=""  DO GETGRAD
   QUIT
   ;
GETGRAD;
   WRITE !,"enter grade for ",N," : " READ GR
   SET^COURSE(CNO,YR,Q,N,T2)=GR
   QUIT
   ;END OF ROUTINE
```

This routine makes use of the index value listing the total number of assignments to print out the available list of assignments. Having checked to make sure that the grade in question is valid, the routine then starts with the *names* stored at the fourth level of the global ^COURSE (since assignments are in numerical order before student names). This is done by setting the seed value of N to A, which is past any numerical entry that might appear at that level. Then, in the line CRSGRNTR+6, the routine loops through each student alphabetically, recording the grade received. The FOR loop refers to a separate line of code to obtain the actual grade simply because of the length of code required to prompt the user, get the grade, and assign it to the proper storage location.

If a student's name appears for whom there is no grade for the given assignment (this happens with annoying regularity in the real world), the user simply enters a null and continues. This approach is preferable to asking the user to name students for two reasons: First, it is more efficient, saving the user the problem of typing the student name or ID number. Second, it serves as a check on the list of students enrolled, (which also changes more than might be wished), so that students who suddenly appear on a grading sheet can be subsequently enrolled and missing students can be checked for possibly having dropped the course or failure to turn in an assignment.

Editing: grades and student names

All too often in this world carefully recorded grades are changed. Students exhibit great creativity in finding reasons why their assigned grades should be modified, late assignments accepted, or extenuating factors taken into account. Kind-hearted teaching assistants and faculty sometimes are persuaded, and a grading package must be able to accept these irregularities and correct the appropriate score. The routine to accomplish this task is listed below:

```
CRSGREDT ;EDIT GRADES.RFW 8/96
   ;gets student name, prints values to date, picks one to change
   WRITE !!,"This program allows you to edit any grade for any student"
   WRITE !!?5,"The grade components for this course are:",!
   SET TO=^COURSE(CNO,YR,Q,0)
   WRITE "Item: " FOR TI=1:1:TO WRITE ?TI*11," ",^(TI)
   WRITE!,"Weight:" FORTI=1:1:TO WRITE?TI*11+5,^COURSE(CNO,YR,Q,TI,0)
CSTUD ;enter student name, find match
   READ !,"Enter start of last name of student (null to quit): ",NAM
   QUIT:NAM=""
   D ^CRSTDNM
   QUIT:N3=0
CPICK ;Right student
   WRITE !!,"Grades for ",NAM(N3)," are: ",!!
   FOR TI=1:1:TO WRITE ?TI*11,TI
   WRITE ! FOR TI=1:1:TO IF $DATA(^COURSE(CNO,YR,Q,NAM(N3),TI))
    ...WRITE ?TI*11,^(TI)
CHANGE;
   READ !,"Type number of grade to be modified (0 to exit): ",TI
   GOTO:TI>TO CHANGE
   IF TI'?1.N!(TI=0) GOTO CSTUD
   IF $DATA(^COURSE(CNO,YR,Q,NAM(N3),TI)) WRITE !,"Current value is:
    ..."^( TI)
   READ !?5,"Enter new value: ",VAL SET^(TI)=VAL
   GOTO CPICK
   ;END OF ROUTINE
```

This routine begins by listing the names of assignments available in the course, using a format statement ?TI*11 + 5, which translates into skipping 11 spaces for each assignment, starting in 5 spaces from the left-hand margin (line CRSGREDT+5). In addition, the following line prints the weights assigned to each gradable assignment.

The next portion of the routine, starting with the line CSTUD, is used to find the name of the desired student. Upon reflection, the need to find a student's name is a function required not only to edit grades, but also, as we will see shortly, to change student names or ID numbers. Hence, after the user has typed in the desired partial student name (a few letters usually will suffice), the routine calls on a separate utility to locate the student name (line CSTUD+3):

```
CRSTDNM ;FIND STUDENT NAME RFW;6/96
   ;NAM is entry. N3 returns 0=not found, 1=found, Nam(1)=value
   SET NAM(1)=$ORDER(^COURSE(CNO,YR,Q,NAM))
   IF NAM(1)="" SET N3=0 QUIT
TMP WRITE !,NAM
   IF NAM(1)'[NAM W "No match for ",NAM READ !,"Enter name: ",NAM GOTO
   ...CRSTDNM
   FOR N1=2:1 SET NAM(N1)=$ORDER(^(NAM(N1-1))) QUIT:NAM(N1)'[NAM
   SET N1=N1-1 FOR N2=1:1:N1 WRITE !,N2,?15,NAM(N2)
   IF N1=1 SET N3=1 QUIT  ;only one matching entry
   READ !!?5,"Pick number of desired name (0 if not listed): ",N3
   IF N3>0&(N3'>N1) QUIT
   SET N3=0 QUIT  ;no match
   ;END OF ROUTINE
```

This utility bears some study. At entry, NAM is the value typed in by the user wishing to find a student name (it might be Jon, Pa, or even M to get students with last names starting with these letter combinations). The third line of this routine returns the value of the first matching student name, if any. Lines 5 through 8 then proceed to find all names matching the search, quitting when a non-matching name is found and storing the results in a temporary array. If there is only one name that matches, the value is returned. Otherwise, the user is asked to identify the number of the student in the list of matching names, and that value is returned to the calling routine.

This utility works well, relieving the user of having to type an exact match. In fact, for most cases in moderate-sized classes, a single letter will retrieve a manageable list of names. However, the match used in line 5 will match if any letter in the name matches. For instance, if the user types M and the first name of a student whose last name is Nager, Maria, that name will match, since it contains a capital M. This is a minor inconvenience, well worth it because it relies on the contains operator instead of a complex pattern search that requires more computer time to perform.

Returning to the main edit program, once the student name has been selected through the utility just described, the routine presents current scores for that student and asks for a change, looping until all corrections have been made. The remainder of this code is more or less self-explanatory.

The second edit routine allows a user to modify student names. Often it is necessary to add or delete a student, and sometimes a student name or ID number may be incorrectly entered (especially if one must rely on handwritten input information). The routine used to accomplish this task is listed below.

```
CRSSTMOD ;CHANGE STUD NAME.RFW 9/96
   READ !,"Would you like a list of students (Y/N)? ",YN
   IF $LENGTH(YN),"Yy"[YN DO ROSTER
   SET TO=^COURSE(CNO,YR,Q,0)
NXTSTUD ;
   READ !,"Enter start of last name of student (null to quit): ",NAM
   QUIT:NAM=""
   DO ^CRSTDNM
   QUIT:N3=0
   SET NAM=NAM(N3)
   READ !!?5,"Delete student from file (Y/N)? ",YN
   IF $LENGTH(YN),"Yy"[YN WRITE *7 READ ?5,"Are you sure (Y/N)? ",YN
   ...IF $LENGTH(YN) KILL:"Yy"[YN ^COURSE(CNO,YR,Q,NAM) GOTO NXTSTUD
   READ !!?5,"Change name for student (Y/N)? ",YN
   IF $LENGTH(YN) GOTO:"Yy"'[YN ID
   READ !,"Enter corrected name for student: ",NEWNAM
   FOR T1=1:1:TO IF $DATA(^COURSE(CNO,YR,Q,NAM,T1))
   ...SET ^COURSE(CNO,YR,Q,NEWNAM,T1)=^COURSE(CNO,YR,Q,NAM,T1)
ID ;
   SET:'$DATA(NEWNAM) NEWNAM=NAM
   WRITE !,"Current ID is: ",^COURSE(CNO,YR,Q,NAM)
   READ !?5,"Change ID number (Y/N)? ",YN
   IF $LENGTH(YN),"Yy"'[YN SET ID=^COURSE(CNO,YR,Q,NAM) GOTO ID2
   READ !!,"Enter new ID number: ",ID
ID2 ;
   SET ^COURSE(CNO,YR,Q,NEWNAM)=ID
   KILL ^COURSE(CNO,YR,Q,NAM)
   GOTO NXTSTUD
ROSTER ;
   SET NAM="A"
   FOR I=1:1 SET NAM=$ORDER(^COURSE(CNO,YR,Q,NAM)) QUIT:NAM=""  WRITE
   ...!,NAM,?20,^(NAM) IF 1#20=0 READ !!," type Q to quit, any other key
   ...to continue ",X QUIT:X="Q"
   QUIT
   ;END OF ROUTINE
```

This routine begins by asking if the user wishes a list of students (to check for possible additions, modifications, or deletions). A positive response transfers control to the label ROSTER at the end of the routine, listing students one screen at a time (20 lines, as determined by 1#20=0 in line ROSTER+2).

The section asking the user to identify a student name is similar to that in the previous edit routine, using the same utility. Once found, the option exists to delete the student name (verified with a second request for confirmation), and if not, it allows the user to modify the student's name and/or ID number, as shown in the remaining lines between NXTSTUD and ROSTER.

Reporting grades

The final section of this package deals with generating reports. This function is accomplished by the following routine:

```
CRSREPT ;LIST GRADES RFW. 10/96
 ;list and summarize individual or all courses
 WRITE !!,"This program will list one grade or all grades and totals"
 WRITE !?5,"for course assignments and tests."
CR2;
 WRITE !!,"Report for ",CNO,?15,^COURSE(CNO,YR,Q)," ",Q,"Quarter,19", YR
 WRITE !!9.5,"The grade components for this course are:",!
 SET TO=^COURSE(CNO,YR,Q,0)
 WRITE !,"Item No:" FOR TI=1:1:TO WRITE ?(TI*11+9),TI
 WRITE !,"Item:" FOR TI=1:1:TO WRITE ?TI*11+5,^COURSE(CNO,YR,Q,TI)
 WRITE !,"Weight:" FOR TI=1:1:TO WRITE ?TI*11+5,^COURSE(CNO,YR,Q,TI,0)
 WRITE !!,"Pick item number to be listed or A for ALL:" READ TN
 IF TN["A" SET TN=TO+1
 QUIT:TN=0  GOTO:TN>(TO+1) CR2
CR3 ;summary for single assignment/test
 WRITE !,"List by:",!?5,"N (Name)",!?5,"I (ID # (last 4 digits only))"
 WRITE !!?10,"type N OR I: " READ TOUT GOTO:"IN"'[$EXTRACT(TOUT) CR3
 SET (TST,TMAX,TSUM)=0,TMIN=999999,TNAM="AA"
 ;
 KILL TMP
 FOR ST=1:1 SET TNAM=$ORDER(^COURSE(CNO,YR,Q,TNAM))QUIT:TNAM=""  DO CR4
 SET ST=ST-1
 GOTO CR5
 ;
CR4 ;process one student record
 IF TN>TO SET TMP=0 FOR TST=1:1:TO IF $DATA(^COURSE (CNO,YR,Q,TNAM,TST))
 ...SET TMP=TMP+(^COURSE (CNO,YR,Q,TNAM,TST)*^COURSE(CNO,YR,Q,TST,0))
 IF TN>TO SET^COURSE(CNO,YR,Q,TNAM,TN)=TMP
 ELSE IF $DATA(^COURSE(CNO,YR,Q,TNAM,TN)) SET TMP=^COURSE (CNO,YR,Q,
 ...TNAM,TN)
 SET TSUM=TSUM+TMP SET:TMP>TMAX TMAX=TMP IF TMP>0 SET:TMIN>
 ...TMP,TMIN=TMP
 IF TMP>0 IF '$DATA(TMP(TMP)) SET TMP(TMP)=""
 IF TMP>0 SET TMP(TMP)=TMP(TMP)_"*"
 IF TMP=0 SET ST=ST-1 ;don't count missing grade in avg
```

```
 WRITE "." QUIT
 ;
CR5 ;output report
 READ !,"Output to (P)rinter or (S)creen? (P/S): ",TO GOTO:"PS" '[TO CR5
 IF TO="P" OPEN 1 USE 1
 WRITE #,"COURSE REPORT FOR ",CNO," ",Q," QUARTER ",YR,!!
 IF TN'>TO WRITE ?10,"REPORT FOR ",^COURSE(CNO,YR,Q,TN),65."Page 1"
 ELSE  WRITE ?10,"REPORT FOR TOTAL COURSE ",?65,"Page 1"
 SET PAGE=1,LNCNT=4,TNAM="AA"
 FOR TST=1:1 SET TNAM=$ORDER(^COURSE(CNO,YR,Q,TNAM)),TNM=TNAM
 ...QUIT:TNAM=""  SET:TOUT="I" TNM=$EXTRACT(^(TNAM),8,11)
 ...DO TP1:TN'>TO,TPALL:TN>TO
 WRITE !!!,TST," Students in class; ",ST," had scores reported"
 WRITE !?10, "Avg = ",TSUM/ST," Top score: ",TMAX," Low score: ",TMIN
 SET TN="" FOR TO=1:1 SET TN=$ORDER(TMP(TN)) QUIT:TN =""
 ...WRITE ,TN,?10, TMP(TN) SET LNCNT=LNCNT+1 DO:LNCNT>59 TPAGE
 WRITE #
 USE 0 QUIT ;end of report
 ;
TP1 ;output one grade
 WRITE !,TNM,?30,^COURSE(CNO,YR,Q,TNAM,TN)
 SET LNCNT=LNCNT+1 IF LNCNT>59 DO TPAGE
 QUIT
 ;
TPALL ;print all grades for each student
 WRITE !,TNM,?20 FOR TX =1:1:TN WRITE:$DATA(^COURSE(CNO,YR,Q,
 ...TNAM,TX))^COURSE CNO,YR,Q,TNAM,TX),?(22+(TX*6))
 SET LNCNT=LNCNT+1 DO:LNCNT>59 TPAGE
 QUIT
TPAGE ;
 SET PAGE=PAGE+1,LNCNT=4
 WRITE #,CNO," ",Q," QUARTER, 19",YR,?65,"page ",PAGE
 WRITE !!! QUIT
 ;END OF ROUTINE
```

This routine, necessarily longer than the others, contains a few sections that are of general interest, along with many lines that simply control output format.

The opening lines are similar to other portions of code in this package, listing all assignments for the course and then asking the user to identify either the single assignment number or the final scores for reporting purposes. If the user selects all, the target subscript number, TN, is set to one more than the total scores recorded in the course grade file (line CRY+8).

The section beginning with label CR3 begins processing individual student records. First, the user is asked if the output is to be listed by student name or by the last four digits of the students' ID numbers (to protect confidentiality, the list is still alphabetical but no names appear). Line CR3+3 initializes some values used in the report, and line CR3+4 clears out any values in the array TMP that might remain from earlier reports written by this routine. The FOR loop in line CR3+5 processes each student's results in turn, keeping track of how many students were processed.

Section CR4 actually processes each student record. There are several places in this section where the routine checks, using $DATA, to see if a score is present and, if not, takes appropriate action. The processing of the final score involves adding the student's score to the sum (to calculate average), checking to see if it is a minimum or maximum score, and reducing the count of valid students' scores if none is reported for the current student. In addition, a matrix is created in the variable TMP, with an asterisk for each student score reported for a given grade (lines CR4+5 through CR4+7). Finally, to assure the user that something is going on, each time a student record is processed, a period appears on the screen (line CR4+8).

The output portion of the report generator begins at label CR5. The user is asked to select output to screen or printer, a header label is printed, and then depending on whether a single score or the course summary is desired, the program outputs the appropriate code (using TP1 or TPALL, respectively). The output routine keeps track of the number of lines printed and at appropriate intervals goes to a new page and prints a new header line. When all student records have been processed, the report summarizes with a simple statistical summary and a matrix of scores 4 lines (CR5+8 through CR5+10).

A number of the output techniques (header pages, line counts, generalized formats for scores, optional name or number) could be adapted for many different report forms. The matrix generation lines also might be useful in creating similar histograms for other types of data.

This completes the discussion of the routines used in this package. The overall design, file structure, naming conventions, and coding conventions used are representative of one style of programming that lends itself to easy code maintenance. Other programmers may find many ways in which to improve this package, but for the purposes of this text it illustrates a number of features alluded to in previous chapters and demonstrates a consistent approach to a well-known practical problem.

A sample run of the course-grading package

Although it is helpful to see program listings, the most useful way to review a package of this sort is to see it in action. In this section we display output generated by the use of the package in a fictitious course setting. User responses are printed in **boldface** to distinguish them from system messages Some comments interrupting the interactive dialogue are printed in *italics*. It is assumed that the user has entered M and typed **DO ^CRS.**

```
                  Course Grade Package
Are you creating a new course file (Y/n): Y
Course Management Program

   Enter course number: ECS188
   Enter Year (2 Digits): 87
   Enter Quarter (F/W/S/SM): S

   Enter title of course; M PROGRAMMING

Program will now accept title and weighting factor for each gradable
assignment or test in class.

   Enter title of assignment/exam (null to quit): PROG1
   Enter weighting factor assigned to grade: 1

   Enter title of assignment/exam (null to quit): PROG2
   Enter weighting factor assigned to grade: 1

   Enter title of assignment/exam (null to quit): PROG3
   Enter weighting factor assigned to grade: 1

   Enter title of assignment/exam (null to quit): MDTRM
   Enter weighting factor assigned to grade: 2

   Enter title of assignment/exam (null to quit): FINAL
   Enter weighting factor assigned to grade: 2

   Enter title of assignment/exam (null to quit):

Select option (?for help, null to quit): ?

Choose one of the following options by number or unique first letter(s):

1. IDENTIFY STUDENTS BY NAME AND NUMBER
2. RECORD GRADES FOR ONE ASSIGNMENT/EXAM
3. PRINT GRADE SUMMARY
4. CHANGE STUDENT NAME
5. EDIT GRADES

Select option (? for help, null to quit): IDENTIFY STUDENTS BY NAME
   ..AND NUMBER
This program is used to enter student names.

   Enter next student name (last, first) [null to quit]: Wilcox, Jerry
```

```
   Enter Student id#: 762-57-8910
   Enter next student name (last, first) [null to quit]: Tucker, Steve
   Enter Student id#: 769-12-8573
   Enter next student name (last, first) [null to quit]: Johnson, Steve
```

<This process continues to enter ten names.>

```
   Enter next student name (last, first) [null to quit]:

Select option (? for helps null to quit): 2 RECORD GRADES FOR ONE
   ...ASSIGNMENT/EXAM

1  PROG 1
2  PROG2
3  PROG3
4  MDTRM
5  FINAL

Select number of assignment/exam for which grades are to be entered: 1

   Enter grade for Bowler Jack : 18
   Enter grade for Diamond, Jon : 19
   Enter grade for Giere, Wolfgang : 16
   Enter grade for Johnson, Larry : 17
   Enter grade for Johnson, Steve : 18
   Enter grade for Pohl, Mary : 19
   Enter grade for Shima, Yoshi : 20
   Enter grade for Tucker, Steve : 16
   Enter grade for Wilcox, Jerry : 17
   Enter grade for Wolber, Dave : 18

Select option (? for help, null to quit): 5 EDIT GRADES

This program allows you to edit any grade for any student.

The grade components for this course are:

   Item: PROG1    PROG2    PROG3    MDTRM    FINAL
   Weight:  1        1        1        2        2

      Enter start of last name of student (null to quit): J

   1  Johnson, Larry
   2  Johnson, Steve

   Pick number of desired name (0 if not listed): 1

   Grades for Johnson, Larry are:
```

```
1  2  3  4  5
17

Type number of grade to be changed or entered (0 to exit): 1

Current value is : 17

      Enter new value: 19

Grades for Johnson, Larry are:
1  2  3  4  5
19

Type number of grade to be changed or entered (0 to exit): 0

   Enter start of last name of student (null to quit):
```

<At this point, there is a break in interaction. Other grades are entered, and more information is now available.>

```
Select option (?for help, null to quit): PRINT GRADE SUMMARY

This program will list one grade or all grades and totals for course
assignments and tests.

Report for ECS188 M PROGRAMMING S Quarter, 1987
Item No:         1       2       3        4      5
Item:          PROG1   PROG2   PROG3    MDTRM  FINAL
Weight:          1       1       1        2      2

Pick item number to be listed or A for ALL: 4

List by:
N        (Name)
I              (ID # (last 4 digits only))
Type N or I: N..........
```

<Dots appear as each student is processed.>

```
Output to (P)rinter or (S)creen? (P/S): P
```

<New page starts here.>

```
COURSE REPORT FOR ECS199 S QUARTER 87

                                 Report for MDTRM
Bowie, Jack                            18
```

```
Diamond, Jon                        17
Giere, Wolfgang                     19
Johnson, Larry                      16
Johnson, Steve                      17
Pohl, Mary                          14
Shima, Yoshi                        17
Tucker, Steve                       18
Wilcox, Jerry                       19
Wolber, Dave                        18

10 Students in class; 10 had scores reported
     Avg = 17.3 Top score: 19; Low score: 14

14    *
15    *
16    *
17    ***
18    ***
19    **

Select option (? for help. null to quit):
```

<At this point, the user asks for a report for the entire course, listing students by ID number.>

```
         COURSE REPORT FOR ECS188 S QUARTER 87

REPORT FOR TOTAL COURSE                          Page 1

7324       18    19    15    18    16    120
1283       19    18    15    17    18    122
2396       16    20    16    29    16    122
0362       19    16    14    16    15    111
6109       18    17    15    17    17    118
3241       19    18    16    14    16    113
7524       20    18    14    17    17    120
8573       16    15    16    18    18    119
8910       17    19    17    19    17    125
2950       18    17    13    18    16    116

10 Students in class; 10 had scores reported
     Avg = 118.6 Top score: 125; Low score: 111

111   *
113   *
116   *
118   *
119   *
```

```
120  **
12   **
125  *

Select option (? for help, null to quit):

>
```

This summary of interaction between the user and the CRS package was transcribed from an actual session. Although not all options were exercised, there are enough examples to illustrate the general flavor of the package and to show how relatively straightforward user interaction is.

There are many ways in which this package could be improved. The package assumes that all course grades will fit on one line and makes no provision for larger numbers of assignments. There are no ready options for editing course definition (names and weights of assignments, and so on). There are no retrievals for extracting results of a single student in several courses. These options could be added, but it would be more likely that they would become part of a much more complex registrar system that is beyond the scope of this text to design.

Summary

This example was presented to illustrate typical M techniques of design and development. During the course of transferring the code from a working version used by the author, numerous minor changes were made in the routines, a sure sign that a package is rarely ready for export when it is in production in one location. It is hoped that the reader may gain some insight into how M packages are designed and, even more, how relatively complicated problems can be simply solved in the M language.

Part II

M for the Experienced Programmer

19 Overview of M for Experienced Programmers

Part I presents the basic features of M for beginning programmers. This material is summarized in a brief overview for the experienced programmer who has worked with one or more other programming languages. The features described are cross-referenced to other sections of this book for supplementary information.

In order to make it easier to distinguish the characteristics of M that separate it from other high-level programming languages, we present first the general features of the language, then we review the unique features of M, followed by a section describing the features of M that are found in a few other languages.

Basic features of M

M is an interpreted language which can be executed one command line at a time in direct mode or by use of stored programs in indirect mode. Although the language is interpretive, all commercial implementations of M use some form of compilation or pseudo-compilation to increase performance. Since the language contains some features that require run-time code modification, it is necessary to retain the capability to invoke the language interpreter at run time under some dynamic conditions.

Like many other programming languages, M has been approved as a standard both by the American National Standards Institute (ANSI) and the International Standards Organization (ISO). ANSI approval as standard X11.1 was first granted in September, 1977, with subsequent revisions accepted in 1984,

1990, and 1995. This text describes features included in the 1995 version. ISO approval was granted in 1992, based on the ANSI 1990 standard; the 1995 ANSI standard is being submitted to ISO for approval at the time of this writing. The language is maintained by the MUMPS Development Committee, referred to as MDC in this text.

Since M is a standard, it is available on many platforms, including UNIX, VMS, various forms of DOS, and Macintosh systems as well as many others. Code written for one operating system or hardware system will run without change providing that only standard features have been used. Most implementors include some language extensions, mainly in support of systems interaction. These nonstandard elements are easily recognized in the code by the distinguishing first character notation: a leading "Z" in a command, function, or special variable denotes a nonstandard feature available without losing compliance with the language standard.

M was originally designed in the late 1960s to meet the needs of a hospital information system, with features supporting manipulation of shared textual databases in a responsive interactive environment. These features made the language attractive for many other applications, and M is now widely used in banking, containerized shipping, library systems, and a wide range of international (non-English) applications.

Despite the attractive features of the language (summarized in the following sections) and the fact that it has been approved by both ANSI and ISO as a standard language, M is not widely known or taught in computer science departments in this country. One of the chief reasons for the lack of attention to M in computer science programs stems from the fact that M was originally implemented on dedicated computer systems running an operating system that supported only M, with the most widespread versions running on Digital Equipment Corporation PDP-11 and comparable sized minicomputers. Microcomputer versions of M were not developed until the late 1970s, and dedicated operating system implementations of M dominated the market until the mid-1980s. Despite this inattention to the language by most computer science programs, M continues to play a major role in many commercial application fields today.

Features of M common to most programming languages

All high-level programming languages possess many common elements, even though the syntax of the individual languages may vary. It is helpful, therefore, to review the features of M found in most other programming languages, so that those elements which distinguish M can be recognized as building on the features known to other language users.

Character set

M uses the 7-bit ASCII character set for commands, operators, functions, and variable names. M, however, does permit use of other character sets (e.g., for non-English language applications) in many situations including variable names, data, and a few special syntactical elements.

Operators

■ **Arithmetic:**

+ add
– subtract
* multiply
/ divide
\ integer divide: 13\ 5 = 2
modulo: 13 # 5 = 3

■ **Logical:**

& AND
! OR
' NOT (apostrophe)

■ **Relational:**

= equals (numeric or string)
< less than
> greater than

■ **Unary (force arithmetic interpretation):**

+ –

■ **String: (see below)**
■ **Conditional: (see below)**
These last two classes of operators, less common in other languages, are discussed later.

Command types:

Interestingly, all programming language commands can be grouped into a very few different types. M is unusually simple in this respect, having very few commands. We use a common classification system to list them.

■ **Declarations:** (none in M)

■ **I/O:**
READ
WRITE

■ **Assignment:**
SET
READ
KILL
MERGE (see below)

■ **File manipulation:**
OPEN, USE, CLOSE

■ **Conditional evaluation**
IF
ELSE

■ **Execution Flow Control:**
DO
FOR
GOTO
HALT
HANG
QUIT
JOB (initiate new process; see below)
XECUTE (see below)

■ **Variable Scoping (see below)**
NEW

In addition, M has a few commands used to allow M programmers to interact directly with the system: BREAK, VIEW.

Block structuring, a feature common to most high-level languages, was added to M in the 1990 revision to the standard. This feature is different in several respects from most other high-level languages, however, as noted below.

Variables and Constants:

M provides for variables and for constants, but there are important differences in the nature of M variables as noted later in this overview.

Special Functions and Special Variables:

Like most languages, M provides a standard set of functions and special variables, with some interesting differences noted later.

From this summary, it is clear that M conforms to the general nature of most high-level languages in the important semantic respects required of all computer instruction sets. However, there remain important features that separate M from most other high-level languages, and there are in addition several elements currently not found in any other high-level language. We treat these two groups of distinctive features in the next two sections.

Features present in a few, but not many, other high-level languages

M shares some unusual language elements with languages like LISP and PERL, and has features inherent in many special-purpose database languages not found in general-purpose programming languages. This section considers a number of these language elements.

String Processing:

M was specifically designed to provide powerful string processing capabilities. In this respect, it is perhaps unique in the sum of these features, though parallels for some of these elements exist in many other languages. We consider string operations in their entirety here, recognizing overlap of various elements with various other languages.

- **Operators**

  M offers the following string operators [Chapters 6 and 14]

= String equals
_ Concatenate (underline)
[Contains
] Follows (using code value)
]] Sorts after (using collation algorithm)

- **? Pattern match operator**

A all alpha
U uppercase alpha
L lowercase alpha
N numeric
P non-alphanumeric graphics
C control characters
E any character

M also provides for extensions to this set to accommodate other character sets. The pattern match operation also permits selection of alternate patterns. Pattern match operations prove especially useful for error detection in data input (e.g., a date format of nn/nn/nnnn can be verified with the pattern `?1.2n1"/"1.2n1"/"1(2n,4n)`, allowing for single- or double-digit month and day and either two- or four-digit year entry values, but not three digits).

String Functions

Many high-level programming languages offer some string functions. M is unusually well provided with such functions, which include $EXTRACT, $FIND, $LENGTH, $PIECE, and $TRANSLATE. Although the purpose of many of these functions is intuitively apparent, some features deserve mention here.

- `$LENGTH(VAR,STR)` returns an integer one greater than the number of occurrences of `STR` in `VAR` (e.g., `$LENGTH("3/12/57","/")` returns a value of 3.
- M allows users to SET a $PIECE of a variable even if that variable or piece does not exist. For example, if `X` currently has the value `a/b/c` then `SET $PIECE(X,"/",5)="e"` adjusts the value of `X` to `a/b/c//e` and if `X` did not exist when the command was executed, `X` would have the value `////e`. Similarly, M permits the command SET $EXTRACT to modify or if necessary, create a variable, padding with blanks as required to satisfy the condition specified: `SET $EXTRACT(y,4)="d"` would, if `y` did not yet exist, create a new variable `y` with the current value `"   d"` (three spaces followed by the letter `d`).
- $TRANSLATE can be used in a variety of ways, described in Chapter 6, to adjust the contents of a string. Its general form is

```
$TRANSLATE(var,oldchars,newchars)
```

which replaces every occurrence of each character in oldchars with the correspondingly positioned character in newchars:

```
$TRANSLATE("Jones, David","abcdefg...xyz","ABCDEFG...XYZ")
```

Returns "JONES, DAVID" with the comma and space characters unaffected.

Taken together, these string functions, together with the string operators described previously, represent an exceptionally powerful array of tools for complex character manipulation.

Dynamic code modification

Like LISP, M permits a blurring in the distinction between instructions and data. In the case of M, two language elements are used to permit highly flexible dynamic code modification: the use of indirection, and the XECUTE command. These features can be simply illustrated by the following examples, with user input in **boldface**, system responses in plain font. The system prompt is a '>'.

```
>SET x="WRITE 3*2"
>WRITE x,!  [the exclamation point outputs a linefeed-return]
WRITE 3*2
>XECUTE x
6
>SET y="x"
>WRITE y,!
x
>WRITE @y,![@ is the indirection operator]
WRITE 3*2
>XECUTE @y
6
```

(An attempt to XECUTE y directly would result in an error, since the letter x, while a valid abbreviation for the XECUTE command, has no argument and hence is syntactically invalid.)

Dynamic (run-time) code modification can be used in many AI applications and in the creation of simple menu drivers, as shown by the example in Chapter14, which also illustrates the use of the $TEXT special variable in this context. While it should be used with discretion, it offers an extremely powerful capability for dynamic code execution which is often desired in artificial intelligence applications. (LISP users are very fond of this approach to program design.) This feature also requires that the M interpreter be available at run time in case indirection or the XECUTE command is invoked.

Features rarely found in other programming languages

While the features just described are unusual, there are counterparts of each feature in certain other languages such as PERL, LISP, and PROLOG. There remain, however, a number of features which are considerably less common in other languages. These features are considered briefly in this section, which also contains page references to sections in either Part I or Part II of the text where these features are explained in greater detail.

Single data type: string

M is a nondeclarative language, meaning that variables, even arrays, need not be defined ahead of time. Instead, they are created dynamically, and the data type is assumed to be string. M implementors will usually store numeric data in other forms internally, but this mechanism is transparent to the user, who can perform operations on mixed numeric types without concern. In fact, M will interpret the contents of a variable from left to right, using numeric interpretation where appropriate: `"123abc"*2` will yield `246`, whereas `"abc123"*2` yields `0`.

Hierarchical, sparse arrays (Chapter 11)

One of the consequences of a nondeclarative language is that arrays need not be specified in advance. M takes this feature one step further, allowing arrays to be multidimensional, but sparse. The command:

```
SET var(1996,12,25)="Christmas"
```

will create a single data element, with hierarchical pointers containing no data at the first and second subscript levels. The depth of subscripting can be very large, limited mainly for reasons of practicality (portability requirements do not allow the length of array subscript specifications to exceed 240 characters including the name and separating commas, but it would be rare indeed for any subscript list to approach this limit).

There are some profound implications to this array concept. First, as shown by the example in the previous paragraph, subscript values can take on real-world significance. It is intuitively obvious on inspection that this example stores years in the first subscript, months in the second, and days in the third. Equally self-evident is the fact that, whereas one might not have values for every valid year, month, and day in history, one would not expect to see a value, say, `var(1996,2,31)`, since February does not have that many days. It takes time for programmers used to declarative languages requiring pre-allocation of memory space for all anticipated values to become comfortable with this concept.

A second consequence of the hierarchical, sparse array structure is that subscripts need not be restricted to integer values. Decimal values are perfectly acceptable. In fact, subscripts may even consist of strings:

```
student("123-45-6789")="Evans, Janet"
```

is a perfectly valid M array element, as is:

```
student("Evans, Janet","Major")="Biochemistry"
```

The combination of these features, allowing subscripts to have meaning, allowing non-integer values, and permitting sparse array structures, makes it possible to completely rethink database design, tailoring the design to the real-world characteristics of the data themselves. For instance, it would be logical to store hospital patient data in a structure such as `PAT(ID,Date,Test)=value`, without reserving any space for the many dates and test types which do not exist for that patient.

The third consequence of the use of hierarchical, sparse arrays in M is somewhat less ideal: since there is no predefined sequence of subscripts, the structure of the array is not intuitively apparent. Further, the manner in which one might access the individual subscripts and values must be (and is) provided by special functions in the language. M provides several tools that permit flexible traversal of a hierarchical array. These functions are described in detail in Chapters 11 and 12. Briefly, $DATA provides information on the existence of a specified array node and whether it has descendant nodes attached; $ORDER traverses all subscripts at a specified level of an array; $QUERY permits a depth-first search of an entire array; $GET returns the value, if any, of a specified node; and $NAME, $QLENGTH, $QSUBSCRIPT, and $REVERSE provide further detailed information sometimes helpful in traversing an array. With these functions, it is relatively easy to manipulate arrays in M, although it does require programmer knowledge (unlike the tabular array structures of the relational model database).

In order to permit more flexible manipulation of hierarchical arrays, the MDC adopted the MERGE command, allowing programmers to copy entire subtrees from one variable array to another.

A final consequence of the use of string subscripts is that data are automatically stored in accordance with either the code value of subscript strings (e.g., sorted by alphabetic value), or by a system-defined collation sequence (such as mixing upper- and lower-case letters for Name lists and other indexes). This feature effectively eliminates the need for sorting data elements, since the $ORDER function will retrieve data in the appropriate collation order, regardless of the sequence in which the individual elements were stored.

Persistent, Shared Data (Chapter 12)

One of the most important characteristics of M, available since its inception in the late 1960s, is the fact that data can be stored in a form that makes it both persistent and shared. The command `SET var="hello, world"` creates a 'local' (M usage) variable, specific to a single user session. By contrast, the command `SET ^var="hello, world"` creates a 'global' variable (M usage) that is stored on disk after the session in which it was created terminates. Furthermore, this variable, once created, is immediately available to other users on the system (access authorizations are controlled by system implementation features). We hear a great deal these days about the need for persistent data in programming languages. It is interesting to note that M has had this feature since its inception. In fact, the persistent data stored by M are, in some implementations, accessible to non-M languages, a feature that could greatly simplify database operations in such languages if it were more widely known.

With the availability of shared data built into the language, it is natural to consider the need to provide adequate safeguards for shared use. M handles these safeguards in two ways: through standard features such as the LOCK command and built-in Transaction Processing (Chapter 20); and through implementation-specific definition of groups of users by user code, etc.

Strict left-to-right interpretation of command lines (and the importance of spaces)

One of the more troublesome characteristics unique to M is the fact that all commands are interpreted, one character at a time, from left to right. This feature sounds innocuous, but it leads to some potentially unexpected results. For instance, arithmetic precedence of multiply and divide over add and subtract is not followed in M. The value of `3+2*6-4` is `26`, whereas it would be `11` if normal precedence rules were followed. One can force precedence by using parentheses: `3+(2*6)-4` would yield the result expected in other programming languages. The use of logical operators also requires parentheses to ensure correct results. For instance, the statement `IF a>b&c>d...` is evaluated by M as follows: first `a>b` is evaluated as true or false, with a temporary truth value of, say `t1`. Then `t1&c` is evaluated, with a temporary truth value of `t2`. Finally, `t2>d` is evaluated. The temporary truth values are stored as either `0` or `1`, so any positive value for d would result in a false final answer, which is probably not what was intended (the results are even more complex if d is negative). To obtain the desired result, one should write `IF a>b&(c>d)....`

A second consequence of this strictly left-to-right interpretation results from parsing commands using a state transition diagram approach. A command must be separated from its arguments by exactly one space (multiple spaces may occur between two commands on the same line, but not between a command and its arguments). Further, there cannot be spaces within a series of arguments for a single command. M uses spaces to determine the state of the parser: a space or line start to begin a command line, a space to indicate the end of the command, and a space to indicate the end of the arguments. Since some commands may or may not have arguments (e.g., DO, FOR, IF, and QUIT), their interpretation changes depending on whether they are followed by one or two spaces. IF followed by one space expects the expression to be evaluated as true or false to follow that space. IF followed by two spaces uses the result of the preceding IF statement, and then proceeds to the next command on the line. (QUIT usually has no arguments and hence must be followed by two spaces; it is followed by an argument only when used to return a value from an extrinsic function.) Although this feature simplifies the job of the parser, it causes problems for the programmer, who must sometimes check to find an elusive unwanted second space in a command line in order to have it execute correctly.

Variable Scoping: (Chapter 16)

The terms *local* and *global* have meanings in M that differ from their use in most other programming languages. "Local" M variables are "global" in the sense that this word is used in other programming languages, in that they are available to all procedures during a single user session. They disappear at the end of the session, whereas "global" M variables are "persistent" in the usage of other languages, existing on disk after a session has terminated.

It is counter-intuitive for programmers in other languages to think of all variables created in different procedures to be available to all procedures without specific declarations to that effect. One can readily see, however, that, in the absence of declarations, M would have no way of identifying "public" and "private" variables, so the assumption is made in M that all variables will be available to all procedures.

There is, however, an exception, introduced into the language in the 1990 revision. The NEW command allows M programmers to specify, by inclusion or exclusion, which variables are to be restricted in their use in a given procedure. The statement `NEW a,b,c` at the start of an M procedure stores the current value of those three variables, which will be restored when M QUITs that procedure. Similarly, `NEW (a,b,c)` stores *all variables except* `a`, `b`, *and* `c` until the procedure terminates. (This exclusionary function can cause extensive system overhead and should be avoided whenever possible.) NEW is useful for library functions called by many different programs whose variable names may conflict with names used in those routines. It is also useful to preserve counters in nested iterative loops involving calls to separate procedures, where it is desired to know how many times each loop has been executed. (A common legacy from FORTRAN is to use counters `i` or `j` in FOR loops: `FOR i=1:1 ...`, and when two such loops use the same variable name, the outer value is lost.)

System Interaction with M (Chapter 21)

One feature rarely found in other programming languages is the ability to interact with the operating system directly through language constructs. M began as a language running under a dedicated operating system, so it was not only natural, but essential to provide some system interaction at the language level. Some language elements such as $HOROLOG (which gives information on date and time of day) and $X and $Y (which provide current position on screen or printer) were introduced and standardized early in the evolution of the language. Other system interactive elements such as VIEW and $STORAGE were specified but their precise meaning and values were left to the implementors (who were using many different types of computers whose characteristics might complicate the potential use of these elements). As the language evolved, however, more and more of these features have been standardized, and a wide range of system interactions are now standard across all M implementations that adhere to the language standard. M therefore provides a great deal more control of the environment in which it operates than other languages, enabling the user, for instance, to indicate where in a distributed environment a particular set of routines or data is to be found, and controlling the default character sets to be used. This aspect of the language is somewhat diffuse, and it is also evolving fairly rapidly as the language moves to accommodate greater degrees of flexibility in distributed and international environments.

Chapter 21 deals with many system interactions. Chapter 24 covers the situation of error processing, a situation requiring close interaction with the supporting operating system. For the purposes of this overview, however, it is sufficient to note this distinguishing characteristic so that programmers familiar with other languages will be aware of their existence.

Internationalization

A subset of system interaction, discussed in the same chapter (Chapter 21), allows M to provide support for non-English character sets. This is an extremely powerful and timely extension to the language in the international marketplace. While the features required for true multilingual processing are not yet complete, M far outdistances any other high-level programming language in its ability to incorporate other character sets, different collation algorithms, and string manipulation of those characters.

Summary

From this abbreviated overview of M, it is clear that the language is indeed a powerful high-level language, ideally suited to manipulation of textual data and to many database operations, including the availability of persistent, shared data. Its flexibility lies in part in its simplicity: M has relatively few commands, and it can be easily learned by programmers familiar with other languages. Because it is a standard language, M permits users to port code between operating systems and hardware platforms. It is also a language that can readily interface with other high-level languages. Other chapters in this text present details of the features covered in this section.

Distributed Systems: Multi-tasking, and Multiuser M (Networks, Locks, Transaction Processing, and More)

20

Introduction

Most programming languages offer single-user functionality only, running on a single system. M offers several alternatives. For example, M permits the distribution of activities across distributed systems, and provides the language controls to facilitate communication in a distributed environment. In addition, as noted earlier in this text, M is characterized as a multiuser, multitasking system. Multitasking, accomplished through the JOB command (with support from the ^$JOB structured system variable), allows one user to spawn separate processes that will continue to execute independent of the session that created them. Multiuser implementations allow many people to access the same M system simultaneously, sharing data between users. Although single-user versions of M are available, the language explicitly provides for sharing data between users. In most M implementations, buffers are also shared, a practice that reduces disk I/O but also creates some potential problems in data management. This chapter deals with the kind of situation that arises when an M implementation involves more than one system and when data are accessed by more than one user at a time.

Distributed systems

In keeping with M's capability to interact more completely with the system in which it resides, the problem of distributed M environments was addressed by nonstandard, implementation-specific syntax since the language was first adopted as a standard in 1977. The process of communicating between such systems was standardized, in part, in the 1995 standard by the introduction of the *environment* concept: global variable names, routine names, and certain other language elements that could refer to the location of a process (^$JOB, LOCK, etc.) can include an optional environment specification, embedded in vertical bars.

For example, supposing that one wanted to download a set of data, process it, and return the modified data set to the location where it is archived. The following commands would accomplish such a task:

```
MERGE ^XYZ=^|sysloc|XYZ
...(perform operations on the globals in the current environment)
MERGE ^|sysloc|XYZ=^XYZ
```

(The syntax within the vertical bars is not (yet) standardized; individual implementations may vary as to the precise manner in which different systems are identified.)

This is an excellent example of the use of both *default* and *override* functionalities in M. The use of both options has been accepted in M for reference to location information as shown in this situation. It has not yet been accepted in another important domain: that of internationalization, where default and override functionality combined would be a powerful tool for translation and other multilingual applications.

A second application of the environment override is in executing routines located on other systems. The command `DO ^|sysloc|ROUTINE` will access the code for the named routine from the environment specified by sysloc. It represents yet another way in which M permits programmers to interact directly with, in this case, not only the local system but even with systems or routines that are elsewhere. (Of course, this capability can be applied to multiple work group files on the same system, but its more dramatic application is in the case of reaching out to networked systems.)

Distributed, heterogeneous M systems: the Open M Interconnect

There are many versions of M, implemented by different vendors and running on different machines. It is becoming increasingly important for users to be able to link these systems to each other. At first glance, it may seem that this is not a goal that would be readily embraced by vendors – to permit users to connect to other systems, even M systems, seems to open the door for the purchase of such systems. Many vendors would prefer that their users would remain faithful to a single vendor system.

Unfortunately for vendors, it is often not possible for a vendor to have a monolithic environment, as a great many database vendors have learned. The standardization of the SQL language in the relational database world is a response to precisely this problem: typically, offices, institutions, and other users of database packages are filled with well-established local fiefdoms of different systems whose designers are resistant to change.

For this reason, the MDC (which includes the majority of M implementors) addressed the problem of developing a standard interface protocol for communication between M systems. (The problem of interfacing with non-M systems is addressed in a different way as described in Chapter 22.) The result was approval of a new standard: *ANS X11.2 Communication Protocol – Open MUMPS Interconnect.*

This standard is based on the Open Systems Interconnect model, using layer 5 (session layer) and layer 6 (presentation layer) to define data formats and connections so as to permit standard applications to be performed transparently at the layer 7 (applications) level. The general model is that of a client server, with user sessions representing the clients while the servers control the M global database files.

The purpose of this standard is to permit standard message traffic involving normal operations on global variables to be performed across systems. The actions on nonheterogeneous M systems from the outside include the following:

- **Control Operations:**
  - Connect   create a new session on a remote server
  - Status   request status information from the server
  - Disconnect   terminate a session on a remote server
- **Global Access Operations:**
  - Get   request the value of a global variable ($GET)
  - Define   request the status of a global variable ($DATA in M)
  - Order   retrieve following subscript ($ORDER)
  - Query   retrieve the next subscript in depth-first sequence ($QUERY)
  - Reverse order   retrieve preceding subscript ($ORDER(^gvn),-1)
  - Lock   incremental lock on a global node (LOCK +...)
  - Unlock   decremental lock on global node (LOCK -...)
  - Unlock client   release all locks for single user (argumentless LOCK)
  - Unlock all   release all locks for all users(systemwide un-LOCK)

The latter affects all users on a single system (not all possible users that might be connected to a given server).

- **Global Update Operations:**
  - Set — assign a value to a global variable (SET)
  - Set piece — assign value to a piece of a global variable (SET $PIECE)
  - Set extract — assign value to positions within a global variable (SET $EXTRACT)
  - Kill — kill a global variable

The precise details of the Open M Interconnect are not presented here, as the level of detail for each type of message is beyond the scope of this type of text. However, a few generalizations about this standard are appropriate in this section.

The first component necessary for linking different systems to each other (especially when they are systems supported by different vendors) is some standard nomenclature registry for the systems. While the specific names are not defined in the X11.2 standard, the MDC does serve as an agent to register systems that expect to use the OMI standard. In this context, the MDC has established a prefix for each major vendor and reserved numbers for the addition of other vendors in the future. The details of this system are not presented here.

A second principle that emerges from the definition of the OMI is that, while OMI does provide for all common operations on a global database, it does not necessarily do so in the most efficient manner possible. This is the compromise that makes OMI more attractive to individual vendors. While they can implement the X11.2 standard to permit communication with external systems, they can at the same time implement their own internal communication protocols for operations on vendor-homogeneous globals, even in a distributed environment. Optimization techniques that perform intelligent analyses of the operations requested can profoundly improve the speed of database operations. OMI does not specify any such optimization techniques, leaving this type of performance issue to be dealt with by the vendors. In this manner, it is possible for vendors to adhere to the OMI standard while at the same time providing more efficient communication between systems over which they have control.

The OMI standard is continuing to evolve, and several new features have already been adopted for incorporation into the next standard. However, these details, like the specifics of the protocols themselves, are not covered in this text.

Multitasking: the JOB command and $JOB special variable in M

One of the common activities performed by computer programs is to output hard copy to a printer. Printing often takes a long time, especially if special fonts are used on laser printers. If the user had to wait for completion of this task, it would mean losing time from other tasks that could be performed on the same computer. Today's word processing packages routinely invoke a *background task* when print jobs are requested; these tasks may slow up the user's other programs, but they do not completely prevent the user from doing other tasks.

Suppose, for example, that we have a routine job, one that is supposed to be executed daily, printing the major inventory changes that have taken place in a warehouse during the previous 24 hours. A routine to perform this function has been created and given the name INVNTORY. Since the application in question is used in a warehouse that may process hundreds of transactions daily, the list of inventory changes and possible reorder flags may be long, requiring significant processor time.

One way to minimize the effect of this printout delay time is to assign the output to a printer as a background task, jut as today's word processors do. In order to do so (assuming that the routine to be invoked is named INVNTORY), the user should type

```
JOB ^INVNTORY:PRNTR
```

When this command is executed, the MUMPS interpreter first looks to see if a routine INVNTORY exists in any network member's routine library. If so, the routine is invoked at that site and the interpreter returns control to the user console without checking again to see if the printer in question is performing as expected.

The JOB command invokes *a new process* that need not (or indeed cannot) be synchronized with the parent spawning process. In our example, the device referenced by the variable PRNTR is assigned the task of running the routine INVNTORY, but no further messages are sent regarding the status of its execution.

Obviously, each time such a job is specified, an additional user partition is opened and left open until the job is completed. The JOB command permits use of the *timeout* feature described in relation to several other commands, giving the user an escape if the device requested is not available.

It is possible for a MUMPS user to initiate several jobs, although each one will require one partition in the computer's memory. Multiuser implementations make use of the $JOB special variable to keep track of the different jobs executing at a given time. These implementations provide system-specific commands to enable a user to review which jobs are currently active on the system.

Once a job has been initiated, it is not easy to abort its execution. The MUMPS standard does not address mechanisms for halting a job spawned by another process. However, some implementations do provide utilities or other mechanisms whereby jobs can be aborted, either by the user or by a systems supervisor.

Recent additions to standard M, discussed in the next chapter, provide even greater flexibility in the specification of JOBs created by a user.

Data integrity in M

The concept of persistent data, rare in other languages but available since the first version of M was implemented in 1968 (!), carries with it a second concept not found in other high-level languages: shared data. When an M global is created, it is immediately available for use by other users on the same system (and in the same user group as defined by the implementation). Shared data is a necessary and powerful component of most database applications, but it also opens the door to problems that might occur when two people attempt to access the same data at the same time.

Consider the following scenario:

Time step	User 1	User 2
1	get acct A inf.	(no action)
2	add $300 to A	get acct A inf
3	store A	subtract $500 from A
4	(no action)	Store A

In this case, Acct A would have no record of the $300 added to the account, only the $500 taken out by User 2. The record put in User 2's workspace is the original value retrieved by User 1. When User 1 updates, this information is overwritten subsequently by User 2's modification, and the value is lost. This type of lost transaction is typical of the pitfalls of shared database systems, and it is this type of error that must be avoided.

Studies have shown that, in typical large databases with many simultaneous users performing different types of transactions on the database, the probability of two users trying to access the same record at the same time is relatively small: on the order of 1%. However, when such situations do arise, they can be very serious, and it is essential that the database maintain the integrity of its data through various means, some of them discussed in this chapter.

Although database experts will be familiar with some of the terms, concepts, and solutions presented in this chapter, we will include some basic information that makes it easier to understand the manner in which M solves shared data integrity.

LOCK mechanisms in M

The easiest way to avoid loss of updates on a database is to LOCK the data element while it is being updated. Locks are found in most database systems (although they are generally not available in useful form in most general-purpose operating systems), and M has had a LOCK command since before the time that it was adopted as an ANSI standard. To avoid the problem cited earlier in this chapter, it would be sufficient to use the following code:

Time Step	User 1	User 2
1	Lock Record A	Idle
2	Update A	Lock Record A (deferred)
3	...other actions	...waiting on User 1 to release A
4	Release A	Lock is activated
5	Idle	Update A
6	Idle	Release A

The net effect of this locking procedure is to defer User 2's access to the common record until it has been released by User 1. In effect, this results in *serializing* the operations of User 1 and User 2, as though they had not overlapped in time at all. The concept of serialization is important in more complex operations on shared databases, and this example illustrates how it can be accomplished to resolve a simple concurrent access conflict. The M code used to accomplish User 1's tasks above would be the following:

```
LOCK ^acct("A")
SET ^acct("A")=^acct("A")+300
LOCK
```

The LOCK command with no arguments simply releases all LOCKs held by that user at the time. In fact, the action taken by the LOCK command is first to release existing locked records, then to perform the lock requested. This approach works well if only one record is involved. What would happen, however, if a database operation required transfer of funds from one account to another, and the user wanted to lock both records. The command

```
LOCK ^acct("A"),^acct("B")
```

looks as though it ought to do the job. However, this is an example of the use of a command to perform two LOCKs: this command line is equivalent to

```
LOCK ^acct("A") LOCK ^acct("B")
```

which, as we have already seen, would result in record A being released before B is LOCKed. The way around this dilemma is to use parenthesized LOCK arguments:

```
LOCK (^acct("A"),^acct("B"))
```

will in fact lock both records so that they can be modified together. Any subsequent use of the LOCK command in its simple form will result in both of these records being released prior to performing any other LOCK function.

There are two features of the M LOCK command that are not intuitively apparent. The first relates to the way in which the LOCK command actually works. All computer operating systems make use of *buffers* to store data retrieved from disk. These buffers are used to update data, and eventually they are written back to disk. While a block of data is in a buffer, however, there are actually two copies of that data in the computer, since the disk version is only copied into the buffer. In a multiuser system, these buffers are shared by the different users, and the lock mechanisms are maintained in the buffers with the data itself. The operating system will not permit access to disk versions of a data element when it already resides in a buffer. (M treats this situation slightly differently as we will see in a moment.)

Some database systems offer two types of lock options: a *read lock*, and a *write lock*. The read lock guarantees that no one will change that data element while it is being examined (not modified) by a user. It is possible for more than one user to obtain a read lock on a data element. The operating system provides multiple users access to the shared buffer containing that data element, but it does not permit any user to modify its contents. By contrast, a write lock can only be issued to one person, and no one is permitted to obtain a read lock on that data element until the write lock is released. This mechanism ensures that the integrity of data will be preserved, but also it makes certain that no one is looking at what might be an obsolete version of a data element.

M differs slightly from other database systems in that it does not specifically offer both types of lock. There is, however, a mechanism sometimes referred to as a "shop standard" (according to Ed de Moel): to obtain a *write lock* on a data element, you would type the command LOCK +^XYZ(9,10,11); to obtain a *read lock* on the same node, you would instead type LOCK +^XYZ(9,10,11,$JOB). Since this is in effect one node deeper that the desired node, and the $JOB of each user's workspace is unique, this permits more than one user to obtain such a LOCK. If someone has obtained a *write lock* on the node without the $JOB subscript, no one else would be permitted to obtain read locks on that node. Conversely, if a user has already obtained a *read lock* on ^XYZ,(9,10,11,$JOB), then no one would be permitted to obtain a *write lock* on that node.

In addition, M *does* allow a user to obtain a data element from disk even if it already exists in a buffer, LOCKed by another user. This is considered by many to be a flaw in the design of M, since the LOCK mechanism, guarding the buffered copy of the data element, can be bypassed simply by not requesting a LOCK. The weakness is easily avoided by requiring all programmers in a given environment to adhere strictly to the use of LOCKs whenever data are shared, but the potential for inadvertent or other corruption of data integrity remains.

The second feature that makes LOCKs in M different from those in relational databases is that a LOCK will lock a node and all elements below that node, remembering that M stores data in a sparse hierarchical structure where data elements may be "children" of other data elements. Let us assume that User 1 has LOCKed ^acct("A",3,5). Requests by User 2 to LOCK other elements of the same database would have the following results:

Example	Command Line	Result
1.	LOCK ^acct("B")	action allowed (no conflict)
2.	LOCK ^acct("A",3,7)	action allowed (no conflict)
3.	LOCK ^acct("A",3)	action blocked
4.	LOCK ^acct("A",3,5,11)	action blocked

Example 3 is not permitted while User 1 has ^acct("A",3,5) LOCKed because the nodes covered by User 2's request include User 1's node. Example 4 is blocked for the inverse reason: User 1's scope of influence includes the node requested by User 2. In general, when using the LOCK command in M, it is best to specify as precisely as possible the element(s) needed, so that the LOCK will conflict with as few other requests as possible. It would be pointless, for example, to LOCK ^acct in order to operate only on record A, and all other users would be blocked from the ^acct global while such a LOCK was in effect. It is worth noting at this point that few so-called general-purpose operating systems provide the degree of granularity to permit locking at the record level, much less dealing with hierarchical nodes and their descendants. This incompatibility between general-purpose operating systems and database requirements often forces the designers of database packages to develop their own complete protection mechanisms, separate from those of the operating system [e.g., Stonebraker, 1986].

Another situation can arise which can cause serious system problems, if a user who has LOCKed a global node for some reason leaves his terminal unattended with the LOCK in effect or exits in an abnormal fashion without clearing the LOCK (normally, when a user executes a HALT command in M, all LOCKs are released automatically). If another user wants to access a node that is included in the scope of an existing LOCK operation, the user could wait indefinitely for the node to come available. This situation can be avoided in M by use of the `timeout` option provided in M for the READ and LOCK commands. If a user types the command `LOCK ^acct("A"):20`, M will attempt to LOCK that node for a total of 20 seconds. If the LOCK is unsuccessful within that time period, M automatically goes on to the next command in the user's routine. The special variable $TEST is set to `True(1)` if the LOCK is successful, `False(0)` if it is not. For example:

```
LOCK (^acct("A",3),^acct("A",72)):25
IF DO
. ;update as needed
ELSE  DO  QUIT;execution of routine terminated
.  ;notify user that update not permitted
; (code continues only if update is successful)
```

(Note the *two spaces* after both the ELSE and the argumentless DO commands.)

The timeout provision of the LOCK command protects a user against all possible events that might hang the program at a LOCK request.

Incremental form of LOCK command

So far, we have seen that it is possible to lock more than one node in a single LOCK command. This is a valuable feature, but it does not always conform to real-world situations, where one needs to move through data, checking on valid conditions, and then add to the LOCKs that are present. Recognizing this need, the MDC in 1990 approved an extension to the LOCK command, making it possible to incrementally add or subtract LOCKs to a user's list of LOCKed elements. The syntax of this type of usage reads as follows:

```
LOCK (^acct("A",3),^acct("B",21)
... (perform some operations)
LOCK +^acct("A",72)
```

```
... (continue processing)
LOCK -^acct("B",21)
...(continue processing)
LOCK(release all locks)
```

This sequence of events permits the user to verify that the conditions are appropriate for a given update, and to perform LOCKs as needed, releasing records for use by others when they are no longer required. The ability to perform both incremental and decremental locks is a precursor to the concept of *transaction processing*, which will be discussed in the next section. If multiple users are accessing the same database, some care is required to guarantee that data are not corrupted by the failure to coordinate locks. It has been shown [Eswaran, et al., 1976] that a *two-phase locking protocol* can guarantee that multiple transactions will be completed without interfering with each other (i.e., that the transactions behave as if they were serialized rather than concurrent). This concept of serializability can be achieved by a rather simple but ingenious rule: any user can obtain incremental LOCKs on the database, but, once the user releases any element (a decremental LOCK in M), then no further incremental LOCKs are permitted. Eswaran proved that this simple rule guarantees serializability. It is not difficult to apply this restriction to programs, so that the integrity of a database is preserved. This concept must be implemented through programmer discipline (as must the use of LOCKs in M), but it is worth knowing about.

There is one important caveat with this concept: in today's distributed computing world, the distance in time and space between different transactions acting on the same database are sometimes sufficiently great that a two-phase lock approach would be unworkable. In general, nice as this scheme may be in a local environment, it will break down in most distributed environments and it will also break down when there are multiple long transactions that are required to wait on each other.

Transaction processing

Many database operations involve multiple steps and multiple data records. Funds are transferred from one account to another. Course grades are submitted in one list and subsequently used to update transcripts of each student in each course. Sales invoices involve multiple items, each of which must be used to update the inventory status of that item. Sometimes, the ultimate outcome of a group of operations is not determinable until information has been collected from multiple sources. Real estate transactions often are contingent on a series of conditions, some of which are in part negotiable, and the entire "transaction" may or may not go to completion depending on what can be done to adjust various factors to achieve a satisfactory conclusion.

The term *transaction processing* in database terminology refers to a collection of database operations that should be considered as a single unit, regardless of how many separate steps are involved. A transaction is in effect encapsulated, with a formal start, a series of actions, and a final decision as to whether the entire transaction can be considered to have been successfully completed. If the transaction completes successfully, then it can be *committed*, meaning that the provisional changes made in buffers can now be transferred to disk for permanent storage. On the other hand, if some sequence of events prevents the successful completion of the transaction, then *all* changes to the database must be *rolled back* to their status before the transaction was initiated.

The basic concept of transaction processing, therefore, involves a *start*, an *encapsulated set of operations*, and either a *commit* or a *rollback*. Transaction processing is important in most databases, but until the adoption of the 1995 M standard, there was no explicit provision for transaction processing in M. At first glance, this might seem a relatively small gap in an otherwise powerful language, but one story in the archives of the M language should help explain why this concept is essential. About ten years ago, a firm contracted with a software supplier to conduct a controlled study on the creation and operation of a complex information system. The study compared the use of M with another programming option, and maintained careful records of development time, volume of storage, size of code required, speed of execution of various modules – in short, they compared the relative cost of the M vs. the "other" solution to their complex database problem. The study showed that M significantly outperformed its competition in every criterion mentioned above as well as many others. This is gratifying to those who claim that M is efficient from start to finish. What is less gratifying is that the firm, once it had completed the study, selected the "other" solution simply because it offered transaction processing, whereas M did not. That fact led one M implementor to develop a nonstandard form of transaction processing shortly thereafter, and it also served as the impetus for the MDC to expedite the incorporation of transaction processing into the language, a feature that was incorporated into the 1995 standard. Since M is widely used in financial applications these days, it is obvious that this feature must be available, and M users need to know how to make it work.

Let's begin with a simple example. We want to transfer funds from `^acct("A")` to `^acct("B")`, ensuring that the transaction goes to completion. Here is some M code that would accomplish this task:

```
transfer1;transfer funds between two accounts;rfw;10/96
   TSTART
   NEW a,b,amt
   READ !,"Enter account from which funds will be taken: ",a
```

```
READ !,"Enter account to which funds will be credited: ",b
READ !,"Enter amount to be transferred: ",amt
SET ok=0
LOCK (^acct(a),^acct(b)):60
IF  DO
. IF amt>^acct(a) write !,"Insufficient funds in ",a QUIT
. SET ^acct(a)=^acct(a)-amt, ^acct(b)=^acct(b)+amt
. SET ok=1
IF 'ok TROLLBACK  QUIT  ;two spaces required after TROLLBACK
TCOMMIT
QUIT
```

This program gets the accounts and amount to be transferred, checks that sufficient funds are available, and completes the transfer. If it is not possible to obtain both locks or funds are insufficient, the transaction is aborted; otherwise, the transaction is committed, and the local variables a, b, and amt are returned to their previous values, if any.

This example can be modified in several ways to improve its generality. For instance, it is quite possible that the values used in the transaction would require more extensive and specific verification. To facilitate the generality of the routine `^transfer`, it would be better to set the local variables outside the routine itself. To illustrate the effects of using local variables created outside the routine, let us assume that, if insufficient funds are available in acct a, the routine will transfer what funds are available, notifying the user that the amount has been reduced. Here is a second example using this logic:

```
transfer2;transfer funds, second example
   TSTART(a,b,amt,ok)
   SET ok=0
   LOCK (^acct(a),^acct(b)):30
   IF '$TEST GOTO end
   IF ^acct(a)<amt DO
   .  SET amt=^acct(a)
   .  WRITE !,"insufficient funds. Only ",amt," available."
   .  READ !,"continue? (Y/N): ",yesno
   .  IF "Nn"[$EXTRACT(yesno) GOTO end
   SET ^acct(b)=^acct(b)+amt,^acct(a)=^acct(a)-amt,ok=1
end;
   IF 'ok TROLLBACK  QUIT
   TCOMMIT
   QUIT
```

(Note again, *two* spaces after the TROLLBACK argumentless command.)

Adding the parenthesized arguments to TSTART has the effect of restoring the values of all local variables named to their original values, regardless of actions taken on the global variables modified by the transaction. In the previous example (transfer1) the user would know how much money had been taken from ^acct(a) and might take other steps to achieve his original goals. For very complex transactions, the syntax TSTART * restores the values of all local variables at the conclusion of the transaction.

The two examples given above will result in a rollback if it is not possible to lock the global variables required for the transaction. Since, as noted before, conflicts in LOCKing globals occur very rarely and are not likely to last very long, it might be desirable to make a second (or third, etc.) attempt to complete the transaction. The next example shows how the TRESTART command and the special variable $TRESTART might be used to provide this functionality (details of the transaction are omitted to simplify the example).

```
TSTART *
(transaction code comes here)
IF ok=1 TCOMMIT  QUIT
IF $TRESTART>3 WRITE !,"Transaction aborted." TROLLBACK  QUIT
HANG 20 TRESTART
```

This code assumes that the local variable ok will be set to 1 if the transaction has been completed successfully. Each time the routine comes to this segment of code, if the transaction was not completed as desired, the TRESTART command will go back to the beginning of the transaction (after a 20 second delay to allow conflicting user transactions to go to completion), increasing the value of the special variable $TRESTART by 1. After the third attempt, the program will finally give up, rollback the transaction, and terminate. Incidentally, the default action taken at the conclusion of a TSTART segment of code is to execute an implicit TROLLBACK, so that command is not strictly required in this example, but good coding practice would include it to make the action explicit.

The TRESTART option is only available if TSTART has an argument (one or more variables named or the use of an asterisk to preserve all local variables).

A further variation on the transaction processing code is to require that the transaction is serialized – that is, to ensure that the transaction interacts with other transactions in a manner that ensures their actions are performed as if they had been done in serial fashion. This option may be rather complex to implement, but M makes it very easy for the user to require that serializability is enforced. The command TSTART * SERIAL invokes this option. Furthermore, when the SERIAL option is invoked, LOCKs need not be included in the code embedded in the transaction. M guarantees that appropriate locks are obtained in order to guarantee serialized processing of multiple transactions.

The final option available in transaction processing as defined in the 1995 standard is to permit embedding additional levels of transactions within a single transaction. While it is not likely to be a frequent occurrence, it may sometimes be useful to access code itself containing transactions, and embedding such transactions within the umbrella transaction. The final action taken will either commit or roll back the overall transaction, including actions taken within the invoked transactions. M uses the special variable $TLEVEL to ascertain whether one or more transactions are involved. M would generate an error message if $TLEVEL is zero and a TCOMMIT is encountered. If a TCOMMIT is invoked within a transaction invoked within another transaction, the values will be accepted and $TLEVEL would be reduced by 1. When a TCOMMIT results in reducing $TLEVEL to zero, the entire modifications resulting from the complete transactions are committed and global variables modified accordingly. This feature lends itself to modular programming, permitting one transaction-based code segment to call another, thereby separating related but distinct functions. One final point should be made with respect to the levels of TSTART and its corresponding TCOMMIT: these two commands must be at the same level with respect to DO commands. For example the following code is illegal:

```
TSTART
   ;(some code here)
   DO lab1,lab2
   QUIT  ;routine execution ends here
lab1;
   ;(some processing)
   QUIT  ;(return to DO)
lab2;
   ;(more processing)
   TCOMMIT  ;(illegal at this level, since
   QUIT  ;(return to DO)
   ;end of routine
```

Instead, the TCOMMIT must be after the DO has terminated:

```
   TSTART
   ;(some code here)
   DO lab1,lab2
   TCOMMIT  ;proper location for TCOMMIT
   QUIT  ;routine execution ends here
lab1;
   ;(some processing)
   QUIT  ;(return to DO)
lab2;
   ;(more processing)
   QUIT  ;(return to DO)
   ;end of routine
```

The inclusion of transaction processing in M has ensured the ability of this language to compete with other database systems in financial and other markets. It seems likely that this part of the standard will continue to evolve, with the likely addition of new features to further enhance this important functionality.

Summary

This chapter illustrates a number of features that separate M from other high-level programming languages and provide additional power not often found in general-purpose operating systems. The ability of a single user to invoke multiple tasks represents one such strength. Equally or perhaps more importantly, adding the use of persistent, shared variables makes it possible for the language to serve as a stand-alone vehicle involving multiple users simultaneously accessing the same database. This capability has further evolved to permit users to perform all these operations in a distributed environment involving not only different systems, but, with the use of the Open M Interconnect, different vendor implementations of M.

Taken together, these functions represent a remarkably coherent system for the management of data over a wide range of hardware configurations and vendor implementations. No other high-level language even approaches the power of M in these respects.

References

Eswaran, K.P., Gray, J.N., Lorie, R.A., and Traiger, I.L. (1976), "The notions of consistency and predicate locks in a database system," *CACM* Vol. 19:11.

Stonebraker, M., editor (1986). *The Ingres Papers: Anatomy of a Relational Database System*, Addison-Wesley, Reading, MA.

21 Interacting with the Operating System (Structured System Variables, Internationalization, and More)

Overview

One of the unique features of M, compared with other high-level programming languages, is its built-in capabilities to interact directly with the operating system. Other languages have the ability to open and use files using library functions, and of course this capability is also available in M. However, no other high-level language offers such a rich assortment of special variables, functions, and other elements that make direct interaction with the system more convenient and flexible than is normally the case in programming languages. This characteristic stems in part from M's origins running under a dedicated operating system, but it has been extended in ways that make this interaction considerably more powerful and offers some important possibilities for extension into new application areas such as support of non-English applications and databases. This chapter reviews many of the features that facilitate this interaction, and it sets the stage for some other chapters that extend this concept even further. The chapter recapitulates some information spread through a few other parts of the text and also presents some new concepts introduced in the 1995 standard.

A brief historical recapitulation

The first M standard already had a number of language elements that enabled M programmers to communicate directly with the operating system. Features such as the special variables $HOROLOG (date and time information), $TEST (truth value to measure success of IF, READ, OPEN, and LOCK commands), and $X and $Y (cursor position information) typify the sorts of things that were standardized in the first ANSI-approved version of M (these functions are described in Chapters 14 and 7, respectively). The special variable $STORAGE (information about workspace available) was approved as a standard language element, but its specific interpretation was left to the implementor (see Chapter 17). M also provided the VIEW command and the $VIEW function, intended to provide the user with information about the system, but once again, their exact meaning was left to the implementor (see Chapter 17).

With the passage of time, the MUMPS Development Committee began to re-examine the need for standardizing more systems interaction. More users were moving back and forth between different implementations of M, often linking them in a distributed environment. In addition, the use of M around the world was leading to pressure to fully support character sets other than ASCII. Gradually, some general concepts emerged, from which came a new approach to the definition of systems parameters. The process is continuing, especially with respect to internationalization (see below), but the basic approach is now in place.

Some basic system interactions

The 1995 standard introduced a number of new elements to M that further aid the programmer in interacting with the system. This section covers the elements, old and new, that have been added to the language to make a programmer's life easier in finding out more about the operating system under which M is running.

Input and output devices

The 1977 M standard introduced the special variable $IO to indicate the currently active device to which I/O is directed. The meaning of the values associated with $IO were left to the implementor, and, with the exception of a fair degree of acceptance of the value 0 to indicate the principal device (e.g., keyboard/screen), the other values were not standard. The MDC has taken great pains to avoid any backward incompatibilities with earlier definitions in the standard, so it was not possible to modify the meaning of $IO by fiat. Instead, the 1995 standard allows the use of $IO to refer to different device identifiers (strings are permitted, and used in at least one implementation) as in the past, but it also introduces a new special variable, $P[RINCIPAL], to signify the principal I/O device. From now on, in any standard M implementation, the command USE $P will switch device I/O to the device selected as principal when the M session is initialized (usually keyboard and screen, but sometimes another configuration where appropriate).

Another feature that was introduced in 1995 as a standard is $D[EVICE], which gives specific information about the status of the current device. This concept originated from the idea of "mnemonic space," another term used by the MDC which, according to Ed de Moel, current chair of the MDC (De Moel, 1996, personal communication),

"is best described as a library that contains certain functions to control a certain class of devices (yes indeed, sounds a lot like a class library, doesn't it?)..."

The status options identified with $DEVICE derive from the binding of M with the ANSI standard X3.64, the standard for control functions for I/O devices. The values allowed are as follows (assuming that `$DEVICE(device-expr)` is pointing to a specific device:

`+$DEVICE(deviceexpr)`	=	0	no error conditions noted
`+$DEVICE(deviceexpr)`	=	1	mnemonic space not found (function not recognized)
`+$DEVICE(deviceexpr)`	=	2	invalid control mnemonic
`+$DEVICE(deviceexpr)`	=	3	parameter out of range
`+$DEVICE(deviceexpr)`	=	4	hardware error
`+$DEVICE(deviceexpr)`	=	5	control mnemonic not available for this device
`+$DEVICE(deviceexpr)`	=	6	parameter not available for this device
`+$DEVICE(deviceexpr)`	=	7	attempt to move outside of boundary – not moved
`+$DEVICE(deviceexpr)`	=	8	attempt to move outside of boundary – moved to boundary
`+$DEVICE(deviceexpr)`	=	9	auxiliary device not ready

This set of options covers a large range of I/O conditions. However, this standardized list would not account for every possible contingency. Hence, the 1995 standard allows two extensions to this table. The general syntax of the options is to list the standard M code first, followed by an optional implementation-specific code and an optional explanatory text. For instance, an implementor might amplify `$DEVICE(9)` as follows:

```
9, 4, printer out of paper
```

which would be more helpful than a simple "not ready" message. This definition, then, provides a reasonable degree of standardization while preserving an open-ended approach to special conditions.

Still another addition to the most recent standard is the special variable $K[EY]. This addresses the interesting problem of trying to figure out what some special keys on today's input devices *really* transmit when they are pressed. Obviously, there is no ASCII character for the four arrow keys, yet they must be sending some kind of code. The function keys are programmable examples of keys that can transmit not just one but a series of character codes that may be interpreted in different ways by different application programs. Faced with this fact, most people would simply give up. Other individuals might write arcane code in the computer's assembly language to ascertain what codes are sent when certain keys are depressed.

M provides a far simpler solution. $KEY stores the *control* character code sequence that terminated the most recent READ command, including introductory characters if necessary. For instance, most Reads require that the user end them with the <Enter> key (code 13). However, a READ x#5 will automatically terminate after the 5th character has been typed. If this string of 5 characters does not contain control characters, the value of $KEY is set to empty. However, if the user happened to want to know what the code sequence is that is transmitted when the up-arrow key is pressed, then a READ x#1 would store the values 27,91,65: <Esc>, <[>, and <A> (assuming that the device is acting like a PC or VT100 terminal). This is a very useful tool for certain situations, and it comes free with every READ command issued in M!

To cite another example, a user is filling out a form and the program accepting the user's input is executing a READ x command. If, at the end of one field, presses the up-arrow key (to return to a previous value). The READ command would terminate, and the value of x would be whatever characters the user has typed prior to the up-arrow, and $KEY would be the control characters for the up-arrow key (<Esc>[A). The programmer, seeing the value of $KEY, could move the cursor to the appropriate field on the screen.

Moving toward distributed system management

There are a number of environments where M is running on a large number of systems linked to each other. Brigham and Women's Hospital in Boston, for example, has several hundred servers and several thousand clients operational at any given time, and the number is growing steadily.

In such a distributed configuration, it is often important to know which system is the one on which the current job is running. Many of us have found ourselves in a situation using the Internet where it was necessary for us to obtain the specific address of our system so as to be able to configure port addresses for certain applications. This is the kind of problem that was recognized by the designers of the latest revision of M, who introduced the new special variable $SY[STEM]. Each implementation registered with MDC is assigned a unique number which can be obtained by the command WRITE

$SYSTEM. As we move to a global integration of these systems, the availability of a unique identifier will become increasingly important.

Codes assigned by the MDC have some additional significance: they also identify the M vendor running on that system. The format for this number is nn,xxx,yyy, with the numbers nn representing the vendor's ID, xxx the implementation or version ID, and yyy representing the installation ID. The vendor ID codes assigned (so far) by the MDC are as follows:

43 Micronetics Design Corporation
44 MGlobal Incorporated
45 PFCS Corporation (formerly Plus Five Computer Systems)
46 InterSystems Corporation
47 Greystone Technology Incorporated

There are no other leading numbers currently assigned, an indication that these are the established M vendors today. (Provision will some day have to be made for the vendors of M systems in Brazil, one of the largest per-capita users of M, and for vendors in other countries, but these vendors evidently have not as yet registered their systems with MDC.)

Date and time revisited

As long as we are talking about widely distributed systems, it might be a good idea to raise the issue of date and time in the M context. It is readily apparent to anyone sending messages on the Internet that time has local and global significance. The $HOROLOG variable, whose second argument is the number of seconds elapsed since midnight at the time the system value is interrogated, needs to be "globalized." The MDC recognizes this need, but to date, they have not incorporated a revision to the language that will solve this important issue. While it would seem a simple matter to add Greenwich Mean Time notation to $HOROLOG's time component, that option presents precisely the type of backward incompatibility that is not acceptable to the MDC. Consider what might happen if $HOROLOG suddenly had a slightly different syntax. The millions of lines of M code that currently depend on $HOROLOG being exactly as it is would have to be re-examined and adapted. It seems almost certain that the next revision of the standard will have the solution to this situation. Several have been discussed by the MDC with no final resolution yet incorporated into the standard. I raise this point here to note that, try as we might, the standard is going to need continuing revision as time goes on.

Structured system variables

So far in this chapter, we have covered several useful special variables, a command, and a function that can be used for systems information. These features grew somewhat haphazardly, with the backward compatibility issue preventing any major revision with a goal of standardization.

The MDC recognized a need to go farther in the direction of providing standardized systems information and, largely through the dedication of the European members of the MDC, a new concept was incorporated into the 1995 standard. The name of this general concept is *Structured System Variables*.

The general purpose of Structured System Variables is to provide systems information on a variety of items. Originally, these items were intended to standardize and expand on legacy systems information functions and special variables. In this chapter, we consider first some of the general-information Structured System Variables, then move on to those that have implications for internationalization.

The 1995 standard specifies that a Structured System Variable may have a series of "subscripts" defined by the standard, providing in effect an array very much like a global variable. These values may be examined and used, but they cannot be changed by the user. (A new set of Structured System Variables affecting the Windows environment can, however, be changed by the user. See Chapter 23 on the M Windows Application Programmer's Interface: MWAPI.)

All Structured System Variable names are prefixed by the characters ^$, as in ^$DEVICE. There are currently seven Structured System Variables defined in the 1995 standard; it seems likely that others will be added as the language continues to evolve.

^$D[EVICE]

The purpose of ^$DEVICE is to provide information about devices: their existence (as known to the M system), their characteristics, and their availability. The list will probably not include all items sometimes referred to as devices in M; files external to M are opened as devices, and it would not make sense to list files that might be opened as devices. Strictly speaking, an M implementation should be aware of devices opened in the M environment. The standard does not require implementors to list all devices available to the host operating system, but it allows them to do so optionally. Many implementors do provide, through ^$DEVICE, information obtained from a host operating system regarding other devices available that might be used in the M environment.

^$DEVICE stores information about individual devices in a hierarchical sparse array with two levels of subscripting. The first subscript identifies the device, while the possible values of the second subscript are limited to strings that identify characteristics of that device (currently, only "CHARACTER" is standardized). The simplest way to get a list of all devices and their characteristics would be to execute the following small routine:

```
devlist;1996.Aug;rfw
   SET (dev,chars)=""
   FOR  SET dev=$ORDER(^$DEVICE(dev)) QUIT:dev=""  DO charlist
   WRITE !!,"End of device list."
   QUIT
charlist;
   WRITE !,"DEVICE: ",dev
   FOR  SET chars=$ORDER(^$DEVICE(dev,chars)) QUIT:chars=""
...  DO charout
   QUIT
charout;
   Write !?10,char,?20,^$DEVICE(dev,chars)
   QUIT
```

As one might expect, the names and characteristics of devices that might be available to an M system are much too varied and subject to change to attempt to predict what types of devices might be present. The information stored in ^$DEVICE is, therefore, not controlled by the standard. However, the small M routine written above would work on *any* standard M implementation adhering to the 1995 standard.

^$JOB

Since M permits users to spawn new JOBs, the new standard uses ^$JOB to provide the user with information about all JOBs that are currently active on the system. Each JOB has a unique number in that environment, so it is possible to use a loop like the first FOR loop in the previous example to get the numbers of each active JOB.

As in ^$DEVICE, ^$JOB uses the second-level subscript to provide further information about the JOB. However, in this case, implementors are not free to use terms of their own choosing, since the standard reserves all nonempty strings for its own use. The 1995 standard has thus far identified only one term, CHARACTER, which is to be used to list the "Character Set Profile" active for that JOB. We will discuss Character Set Profiles when we get to internationalization. For now, however, it is clear that this Structured System Variable is due to be expanded in its definition. Watch for the next standard!

Another factor that affects information available in ^$JOB relates to the *default environment* concept, which is discussed in a separate section below.

^$LOCK

Since M is implicitly a shared environment (though single-user versions exist), the use of LOCKs is essential if we are to ensure data integrity. The LOCK command now allows users to incrementally lock and unlock global variables and nodes (with all their descendants). Hence, it is often important to know what variables are currently locked. This information may prevent the occurrence of unpleasant situations such as the classic "deadly embrace" database condition, where two users own one lock and wish to lock the item owned by the other user (see Chapter 21).

^$LOCK provides a list of the names of global variables that are currently locked. The following command lines will retrieve that list:

```
WRITE !,"List of locked global names"
SET lname=""
FOR  SET lname=$ORDER(^$LOCK(lname)) QUIT:lname=""  WRITE !,lname
...?20,^$LOCK(lname)
```

The standard states that the name and "operational characteristics" of the locked variable will be available in this Structured System Variable. Presumably implementors will store this information as the value at the node ^$LOCK(lname).

^$SYSTEM

Earlier in this chapter, we saw that $SYSTEM is a unique identifier for each M system registered with the MDC. ^$SYSTEM is intended to provide additional information about that system. This Structured System Variable uses $SYSTEM as the first subscript under ^$SYSTEM. The second level of subscripting is intended to provide additional information about the system. Unlike the specification for ^$JOB, however, the MDC allows implementors to provide their own descriptor information about the system, provided they prefix all such characteristics with the letter Z. (All other non-empty strings are reserved by the MDC for future extensions.) The only term so far defined by the MDC at this level of subscripting is CHARACTER, which takes the same meaning (character set) as in $JOB. Once again, we defer discussion of that term to the section on internationalization later in this chapter.

Given this information, if you wanted to know something about your system, you could, if you knew the ID of your system, use the following code to find out what your version of M can tell you about your system:

```
SET char="Z")
FOR  set char=$ORDER(^$SYSTEM($SYSTEM,char)) QUIT:char=""  WRITE
... !,char,!?10,^$SYSTEM($SYSTEM,char)
```

There are three other Structured System Variables to be covered: ^$CHARACTER, ^$GLOBAL, and ^$ROUTINE. We will defer consideration of these terms until we have set the stage by talking about internationalization.

Default environments

Before moving on, we need to cover an extremely important concept that is introduced at the end of the 1995 standard's coverage of Structured System Variables: default environments. This term requires some background explanation. As you know by now, M is implicitly a multiuser environment. That means that two or more users may share the same globals, routines, and, when necessary, secure locks on globals. It is also true, however, that most M systems allow different *groups* to share these resources without being aware that other groups exist on the same system. This is a condition that is hidden from the user, who only knows that he can use the globals and routines which are a part of his *default environment*, defined by the system manager through the assignment of user codes to different groups.

In the past, users were not able, using standard M syntax, to access information not contained in their default environment. As databases get more complex, and especially as they get more distributed, it has become necessary to re-examine the default environment concept. There are many reasons for wanting to gain access to different environments. A database application program may need to be used in conjunction with several data sets. The code need not change, but if the default environment of the database (i.e., the globals in which the data are stored) is redefined, the code could run *without change* simply by redefining the default environment. Another example would be during development of an application package. Until the programmer is convinced that the new routine(s) are correct, he will want to continue using the old code. As soon as the new code is satisfactory, all he has to do is redefine the default routine environment, and the new routines, with the same names as the old ones, are substituted, leaving the old ones in place for backup or other reasons.

Default environments are therefore important, especially to M users who enjoy a shared environment of routines and globals, and who need to be able to lock global values at various times to ensure data integrity.

The key functionality that is required for this concept to work effectively is for the *user* to be able to reset the default environments for these components of M. The standard provides precisely this kind of user control through the $^JOB Structured System Variable. For the Structured System Variable `^$JOB(processid)`, where `processid` is (one of) the user's JOBs, the 1995 standard allows the user to redefine default environments for the following specific elements:

```
^$JOB(processid,"GLOBAL")
^$JOB(processid,"LOCK")
^$JOB(processid,"ROUTINE")
```

This control is important in a great many applications. One might be when a user spawns a separate JOB which should run using different defaults from those of the user's regular environment (testing new code, examining a different department's files, etc.). In this case, the user may use ^$JOB to determine the `processid` of the job he created, then use the SET command to redefine appropriate default environment(s) for that JOB.

We review this concept in some detail because we will return to the important concept of default environments in several other contexts, notably internationalization and networking. Resetting a default is an important part of M's power not reflected in other high-level languages.

Internationalization

What does all this have to do with internationalization? A great deal, as a matter of fact. But in order to get into this area, we have to understand a little background so as to place in perspective the leading role that M has taken in the field of internationalization.

History of internationalization efforts

Commercial computers and programming languages got their start in English-speaking countries. Consequently programming languages use English words as the basis for their syntax. Although it might have happened that other spoken or written languages might have been used as the basis for a programming language, it is interesting to note that this has not happened. Although there exist some front-end processors that permit use of non-English terms as substitutes for the original English commands, no compilers have yet been written based on a non-English natural language.

The character sets used in computer processing also have a heritage of English. The 7-bit ASCII code, for example, does not provide for any characters with diacritical markings. Since, however, computers are now used for virtually every written language (Mongolian appears to be an exception, in that it is only written vertically), some accommodation has been necessary to provide for non-English data. The ANSI and ISO SQL3 standards groups have wrestled with this issue, providing extensions that accommodate non-English database processing. To date, however, programming languages have been very slow to take up the challenge of providing an effective internationalized programming environment. M is a marked exception to this generality. Beginning with a 1984 meeting in Japan of international users of the M language, the MDC, spearheaded by its membership from Japan and Europe, began to investigate ways in which M could be extended to provide a truly multilingual environment.

Nonstandard internationalization steps had been taken even earlier. Several nonstandard version of M exist that provide bilingual language support for English plus one other language. Such systems have been developed for several western European languages, Japanese, Chinese, and Russian, to mention a few widely used examples. While these versions provided some experience to enable the MDC to begin specification of features leading to internationalization, they were incompatible with each other and the data generated by one vendor could not be automatically adapted for use by another.

The MDC decided that several basic functionalities were required if M is to become truly international. Subcommittees of the MDC developed a number of language concepts which have been incorporated into the 1995 standard.

Functional Requirements of Multilingual Support

If programming languages are going to provide full support for non-English languages, they must contain several important characteristics (Walters, 1994):

- **Character sets**

  Users should have access to more than one character set. The characters should be supported by appropriate methods for input, storage, and display in ways that are acceptable for users of that character set, including provisions for more than one language making use of that character set.

- **Cultural Conventions**

  Users should be able to view automatically data displayed in forms compatible with local cultural usage. Appropriate forms for different cultural assumptions for presenting date (12/31/96, 31/12/96, 96.12.31, Heisei 8.12.31, etc.) should be available, as should those for numerics (1,000.56 vs. 1.000,56), postal codes, and other common culturally distinct notations.

- **Character Manipulation**

  It should be possible to perform operations such as language-specific pattern match, collation, and other string operations on the various character sets. Collation in particular represents a complex problem with sometimes more than one solution for a single country (telephone books and dictionaries do not follow the same rules in many countries, including English-speaking ones).

- **Programming Language Syntax**

  A programming language should support non-ASCII character sets as data. Ideally, it should also allow other character sets to be used for labels, variable names, and, where appropriate, operator syntax such as pattern match options.

- **Multilingual Environment**

  It should be possible to define *default* environments that embrace the appropriate adjustments for a given written natural language—character set, collation, pattern match, display conventions, and so on. It should also be possible to *override* these specifications temporarily as needed to provide mixed character strings, automated multilingual translation, and other features in which more than one character set is to be used in a single application.

- **Operating System Support**

  Users should be able to interact with the operating system with commands and responses in their own native language

This list, perhaps incomplete, suggests that true multilingual support is a complex issue. The 1995 M standard provides a few of the features described above, but clearly it does not yet provide for all of them.

Structured system variables and internationalization

^$CHARACTER

With this background, we return now to the remaining Structured System Variables, beginning with ^$CHARACTER. Although ASCII is by far the most widely used character set, there are a great many other standardized character sets. Most of them are 8-bit characters; some are 14-bit, others 16-bit. With few exceptions, most character sets retain at least partial compatibility with 7-bit ASCII (since so many I/O devices have certain hard-wired features based on ASCII control characters). The ISO family of standard character sets, 8859-1, 8859-2, ... 8859-9 (the last I heard), are defined as follows (Clews, 1988):

ISO 8859 part 1: Latin alphabet no 1 (western European languages)
ISO 8859 part 2: Latin alphabet no 2 (eastern European languages)
ISO 8859 part 3: Latin alphabet no 3 (Afrikaans, Maltese, Turkish, etc.)
ISO 8859 part 4: Latin alphabet no 4 (Scandinavian languages)

ISO DIS 8859/5: Latin/Cyrillic 8-bit character set (Russian, etc.)
ISO 8859 part 6: Latin/Arabic character set
ISO 8859 part 7: Latin/Greek character set
ISO 8859 part 8: Latin/Hebrew character set

(I believe a part 9 has been created especially for the Turkish language, but I do not have a specific reference for this or other 8859 character sets.)

In addition to this group of standards for many languages of the world, other standards exist for the oriental languages (Chinese, Japanese, and Korean). These character sets require a great many more characters and hence use two-byte codes.

In recent years, a group of US computer manufacturers have pushed strongly for the adoption of a 16-bit multilingual character set referred to as UNICODE (Unicode, 1990). If accepted, UNICODE would provide a single character set for almost all of the written languages in the world (its universal acceptance remains uncertain at this time). Various committees are at work on other multibyte, worldwide character sets, such as ISO DP10646, which uses a four-byte code. The status of all of these developing standards is unclear at present, but what seems likely is that, within a decade, there will be one more standard and generally accepted multilingual character sets available on most computers.

^$CHARACTER was defined at a time when these factors were known but, as is still the case, uncertain. Rather than adopt, for example, the UNICODE approach, the MDC decided to allow different character sets to be allowed for use in M. The first subscript for ^$CHARACTER, then, is the character set, referred to as *charset* in M's metalanguage terminology. Charset identifies a *character set profile* for a specific character set. (There could be more than one character set profile if, for instance, the profile were used for two languages whose character sets are the same. The names of these profiles are reserved for future definition by the MDC. A character set profile consists of several elements. The first deals with **INPUT.** Since it seems likely that the "QWERTY" type keyboard will be used for some time to come, it is likely that some form of input conversion process will be required to accommodate different character set profiles. If no algorithm is specified for a character, the character as input is accepted without any transform taking place.

As one should expect, the second feature in a character set is **OUTPUT**, which in most character set profiles is the mirror image of input (the character displayed is the one entered). There are exceptions: ligatures, double characters (e.g., 'll' or, until recently, 'ch' in Spanish), but the general process is the same.

The third component of a character set profile is **IDENT**, which is used to identify which character codes are allowed in names of labels and other identifiers. In ISO 8859-1, for example, there are diacritical characters used in many western European languages, but none of these languages requires all of these diacritical characters. It is both convenient and a good error detection approach to limit the characters allowed in the character set profile only to those required by the language.

Another probable extension to English text processing in M deals with the pattern match operator, which is one of the most powerful features of M's string processing capabilities.

Since, for example, diacritical characters such as é, è, and ê are not defined as A (alpha) or L (lowercase alpha), a character set profile for the French language would want to make sure that these characters are included in these two *patcodes*. To take another example, Japanese has two phonetic alphabets: hiragana and katakana, in addition to the "logographs" referred to as kanji characters. An appropriate extension to the *patcodes* for Japanese might provide for each of these sets of characters new *patcodes*, perhaps using a code for one of these characters as the patcode itself.

Finally (as far as provided for in the 1995 standard), the character set profile includes the term **COLLATE**. The standard collation sequence in M follows the ASCII code values for letters and other graphic characters. This code value will automatically sort alphabetic text in its correct collation value, provided that only uppercase or only lowercase characters are used. If, however, mixed upper and lowercase characters are used, then the $ORDER function will return all uppercase characters before the lowercase characters. This example shows that, even in English, a collation algorithm is needed to provide 'perfect' sorting.

Collation algorithms in other languages are a great deal more complex, some of them requiring as many as five passes through the text before the algorithm is complete. It is clear, therefore, that a collation algorithm is needed for all character sets. It is also true that many languages will need more than one such algorithm for different applications, and it is equally true that a character set like 8859-1 (western European languages) will need to have a number of character set profiles to accommodate its use in different languages such as French, German, and Spanish.

With a complete character set profile, it is possible to provide a number of the important requisite functions for internationalization. It remains for different language groups to define such character set profiles and submit them to the MDC for approval. To date, three character set profiles have been accepted by the MDC. The first is the M standard character set, which includes a collation rule that defines M collation to consist of a sequence in which the empty string comes first followed by data stored as 'canonic' numeric values (numbers with no leading or trailing insignificant zeros), followed by characters according to their ASCII code value. The second is the ASCII character set, which is identical to that of charset M, except that it collates all characters according to their ASCII code values.

The third character set profile approved by the MDC was submitted by the Japanese MUMPS Development Coordinating Committee (MDCC-J). The original text of this character set profile is in Japanese; however, key points made in that document are reproduced as "Annex H," an informational annex not formally a part of the M Standard. The profile calls for use of the Japanese character set JIS X0208 – 1990, identifies some additional patcodes to be used as described earlier, and specifies a collation algorithm based solely on the code values of each of the characters in that (2-byte, 14-bit standard).

We can safely assume that character set profiles will be developed by M users in other countries in time for approval as a part of the next standard. However, it is important that the process has been defined and, more important, already utilized, putting M significantly ahead of other programming languages, none of which have even begun to address these issues.

^$GLOBAL

Now that we have covered the concepts inherent in ^$CHARACTER, we can turn to ^$GLOBAL, whose meaning depends on this background. For any global named in an M system, ^$GLOBAL provides information about the character set used for that global and the collation algorithm specified. The first subscript of $^GLOBAL is the global name. Under each name, the standard defines two subscripts: CHARACTER, which defines the character set profile used for the global, and COLLATE, which provides information about the collation algorithm. Even though the character set profile includes a specification of the collation algorithm, this subscript will reproduce that information independent of the character set profile.

An easy way to get a complete listing of all globals with their character set profiles and collation algorithms is by using the following lines of code, which is essentially the same as shown by De Moel (1995, p. 36).:

```
WRITE !,"Global variable information",!!,"Global name: "
WRITE ?15,"Char set profile",?35,"Collation Algorithm"
SET gname=""
FOR  SET gname=$ORDER(^$GLOBAL(gname)) QUIT:gname=""  DO
 . WRITE !,gname
 . WRITE !?12,^$GLOBAL(gname,"CHARACTER"))
 . WRITE !?30,^$GLOBAL(gname,"COLLATE")
 . QUIT
```

Remember, M does not allow the user to change the specifications of a global that already exists, nor does M permit users to create a new global with a user-specified character set profile. However, remember too that M allows users to establish different *default* values character set profiles to be attached to ^$JOB. Using this technique, users need to set the character set profile of a job (probably at the beginning of the job, so that no incompatibilities could be created), then create the global to which they wish to assign those values, and then insert data into the global.

The ^$GLOBAL table of values, once created, are not destroyed by KILLing the global. The values originally assigned remain in effect in case new values are assigned to the same global name. It is not necessary, or possible, to reuse an old global name with a new character set profile.

^$ROUTINE

As in the case of ^$GLOBAL, ^$ROUTINE provides information about what routines are stored in the user's directory. It also allows the user to determine which character set profile is associated with which routine. The program used to obtain this information would look almost identical to the $GLOBAL above, except that the subscript COLLATE is not provided for ^$ROUTINE.

The use of ^$ROUTINE relates to several situations. If a user knows that an application is to be used in several countries, each involving different character set profiles, then he could create customized versions of certain routines such as report generators, which identify specific global variables and routines appropriate for that country. The routines could all be stored in the same computer, but access would be by JOBS that have set the default environment to the target routines and global database with the appropriate character set profile.

What's missing in M's internationalization?

A comparison of the functions provided by the Structured System Variables ^$CHARACTER, ^$GLOBAL and ^$ROUTINE with the ideal features needed for truly multilingual computing shows that M has made substantial progress in that direction. Many of the elements needed, including character sets, collation, manipulation of non-English text strings, default environments, and systems interaction can be accommodated through the 1995 standard. No other high-level programming language comes close to matching those capabilities. In essence, the bilingual capabilities are provided, and in time the character set profiles for other languages will presumably be defined, submitted, and incorporated in more and more M implementations.

The most important missing element is the ability to provide truly multilingual functionality. Bilingual (i.e., English and one other language at a time) functionality seems to be in place. However, there is already a need for dealing with mixed strings, comparing strings from different character sets and in different languages, and storing multilingual data. In the broadest sense, the ability to *override* default specifications as well as to create new defaults is going to be necessary for M to achieve the multilingual functionality that is nearly in its grasp at this time.

Summary

Because of its origins running under a dedicated operating system, M has always provided more user access to systems information than other high-level languages. Those features have been significantly expanded, moving from implementation-specific elements to standardized, generic approaches to systems interaction and, at the same time, opening the door to support of non-English data processing. Given the concerns for backward compatibility, it is remarkable that so much progress has been made. For someone like myself, who has espoused truly multilingual computing for the past ten years and more, the process has not been as rapid as I might have preferred. I can say, however, that the progress has been substantial, and I believe the model for completing the job is available in other recent developments of the language. It will be interesting to see how rapidly the MDC is able to progress in this direction, now that so may important elements are already in place.

References

Clews, J. (1988), *Language Automation Worldwide*, SESAME Computer Projects, Harrogate, North Yorkshire, England.

De Moel, E. (1996), *M[UMPS] by Example*, M Technology Association, Silver Spring, MD.

Unicode Consortium, The (1990), *The Unicode Standard: Worldwide Character Encoding, Version 1.0, Volume 1*, Addison-Wesley, Reading, MA.

Walters, R. F. (1994), "Internationalization of M: Progress and Responsibilities," *Proc. MUMPS Users' Group Japan 19th Ann. Meeting, Izumo, Japan*, pp. 3–13.

Interfacing M to Other Standards

22

Introduction

As powerful as M might be, there are many reasons why it makes sense not to make it all things to all people. One of the more powerful features of M is its simplicity: the language elements can be summarized on a single page, and it is recognized as an easy language to learn at a novice level. It makes more sense, therefore, to link the powerful features of M with the best elements of other complementary languages and standards, so that the details best solved in other languages are incorporated into M in a way that allows M programmers to get the best of both worlds.

Over the past two cycles of revising the M standard, the MDC has taken on the formidable task of relating M to other standards. This is a slow process, often made more difficult by the "moving target" aspect of evolving standards. The benefits, however, are considerable. By linking M to such well-known languages as SQL (the Structured Query Language of the relational database world), it is possible to use SQL constructs to perform relational operations on M globals, thereby linking the hierarchical and relational models to form a significantly more powerful final result. The results of the MDC efforts in this regard are impressive. Several important standards are directly linked to M, either in the main standard (ANSI X11.1) or, in some cases, by the adoption of ancillary standards (e.g., X11.3: GKS Binding and ANS X11.4: X Window System Binding). Other documents are under consideration at this time. This chapter is devoted to consideration of these efforts to link M to other important standards in order to enhance M's utility in a variety of settings.

This should be a two-way street; programmers in languages such as C should be able to access M data for use in the C environment. While this feature is important, it is not the main focus of this chapter. Instead, we will concentrate on the ways that M can make use of other standards in order to enhance its own capabilities.

A word or two about standards organizations. There are a large number of both national and international standardization bodies concerned with a wide range of issues. In the computer world, these issue include hardware specifications, character sets, network communication protocols, and programming languages, to mention only a few. The committees are organized into major committees, special ad hoc work groups, and a wide variety of other formats. Some of the more active committees (like the MDC) meet several times a year for four to five days. The MDC is unusual among these organizations for a number of reasons. Its membership, for one thing, is unique, consisting of implementors, software vendors, users (including a significant representation from government organizations), academics (I was active for the first 20 years of MDC's existence, and other faculty types remain active today), and a healthy and actively contributing contingent from other countries. Many, perhaps most, of the other standards groups are dominated by vendors, a fact that may affect their decisions.

This chapter presents a sampling of the techniques used to interface M to other standards. The examples selected are intended to be illustrative of principles, not to cover exhaustively the individual interfaces. From this sampling, the reader should gain insight into the ways that this process is likely to continue to evolve.

M's use of the ASCII character set

Standards exist at all levels of computer hardware and software. In order to make use of these standards, M has adopted several different approaches to defining appropriate interfaces. The most direct, explicit link takes the form of direct reference to other standards within ANSI X11.1: The M Standard. The single most important link for the M language definition is to ANSI X3.4–1990 (ASCII Character Set). This standard is introduced on page 1 of the standard (along with two others referenced below), and the characters forming that standard are used to define the syntactical elements used in M. Although M provides for non-ASCII characters to be recognized and used in M programs and data, there are strong ties between M and ASCII that stem back to the prestandard origins of the language, nearly thirty years ago.

Interfacing M to other character sets

While M can work effectively within the ASCII character set for English language applications, many countries require characters not available in the ASCII code set. It is important, therefore, to provide for the use of these non-ASCII character sets in an open-ended manner so that, as the need arises, new character sets can be incorporated.

The 1995 M standard has indeed allowed for standard incorporation of non-ASCII characters. Through the use of the Structured System Variable ^$CHARACTER, and the specific attributes CHARACTER and COLLATE of ^$GLOBAL, M can deal with characters and coding sequences other than ASCII. The mechanism whereby other character sets are accepted as valid within the M standard is through a *character set profile*. The 1995 M standard lists three character set profiles: M, ASCII, and JIS90. The latter character set is the one used in Japan, fully defined in the documents JISX0201–1990 and JISX0208–1990. Portions of those definitions are incorporated in Annex H of the M standard, which also contains the rules for pattern codes, names, and collation sequences using these characters. The MDC has already approved a character set profile to be used with ISO-8859-1 (ISO-LATIN-1), the 8-bit character set used for many European languages, and it is expected that additional character sets will also be approved in the next revision of the standard.

Device control mnemonics: M's interface to ANSI Standard X3.64

Two other ANSI standards are also referenced on the first page of the M standard. They are ANSI X3.135–1992 Information Systems – Database Language SQL, and ANSI X 3.64–1979 R1990 (ANSI Terminal Device Control Mnemonics). The interface between M and SQL is covered in a later section of this chapter. Control mnemonics, however, provide an important extension to M, defined in the 1995 standard. This is a good place to start when we look at ways that M can be extended without reinventing the wheel.

Before the 1995 standard, M generally reserved device control to implementors. The OPEN and USE commands were accepted as part of the first standard in 1977, but the manner in which they referenced devices was not standardized. As a result, code using device controls had to be modified for each implementation. While device control still has some elements that have not been completely standardized, an important area of device control operations has been incorporated into the 1995 standard through reference to the control mnemonics of X3.64.

Computers require a wide range of auxiliary devices to communicate with the outside world. Hard copy printers and screen displays are two important families of devices which vary widely in the way in which they permit computer bits to be converted to visible displays. The features available vary within these families of systems, and their capabilities are continuing to expand. However, in broad terms, there are groups of functionalities that can be ascribed to families of display devices. In order to secure wider acceptance of these devices, hardware vendors found it convenient to agree on some standard features, such as positioning of a cursor, provision for tabs, scrolling, status information, and editing characters. ANSI's X3.64 was created to standardize many of those functions. The intent was not to force manufacturers to implement the functionality in the same way, but rather to provide a mechanism whereby programmers could use the same code to invoke those features. The codes required were compiled into a set of *control mnemonics*, which would be recognized by all devices adhering to this standard and which would result in the same or comparable end results in each device capable of responding to this function. Of course, no single display device can respond to all of the control mnemonics defined in that standard. A black and white printer will never generate other colors, nor will a monochrome screen. The intent of the standard is to make it possible for code to be used on all devices capable of common actions without changing the control mnemonics required.

There are several families of control mnemonics used in the X3.64 standard. They include codes to control cursor movement, scrolling, graphic renditions, editing functions, font selection (type of font and point size), line spacing, character justification and spacing, and definition of device mode (editing, control, positioning, and other). In addition, there are codes that return status information about the device, and others that specify various types of device area qualification such as whether and what kind of data can be typed in a defined area (numeric, alpha, graphics, none, justification, filling, etc.). The complete set of control mnemonics accepted by M are given in Section 3 of the 1995 M standard. This section also defines the manner in which M interacts with these mnemonics. This text does not attempt to cover all these operations (an amplified explanation of each is found in De Moel's *M By Example*), but a few examples should illustrate the value of using X3.64 control mnemonics with M.

The underlying syntactic binding between the M standard and ANSI X3.64 involves extensions to the OPEN, USE, and WRITE commands. If X3.64 control mnemonics are to be used in conjunction with a device, the extended M syntax adds a second set of possible *mnemonicspecs* that define which control mnemonics can be manipulated by the USE command.

```
OPEN device:parameters:20:"X3.64"
```

stipulates that M is to attempt for up to 20 seconds to open the device named, and assign it values defined in the parameters following the first colon; and it defines the *menmonicspecs* available for manipulation by the USE command to be those available in the X3.64 standard. Later, we will see that M's interface to the GKS (Graphical Kernel System) can also be specified by an argument in this position of the OPEN command.

The USE command has been similarly modified, using a set of parameters following a second colon in the argument list of this command. For instance `USE device::"X3.64"` will similarly make available the control mnemonics of that standard, even if it was not specified in the original OPEN command. It might be necessary to switch from X3.64 to some other control mnemonics (GKS, for example), and M allows users to accomplish this change with the USE command.

The WRITE command has also been extended with the very simple syntactic device of adding a '/' before the control mnemonic to be used in conjunction with the WRITE statement. The following code illustrates one example, assuming that a VT100-compatible terminal is specified by the variable 'device' in a previous OPEN command.

```
USE device::"X3.64"
WRITE /CUP(12,34),"Hello, world"
```

will move the cursor to line 12, column 34, and write `Hello, world` approximately centered on the screen (which in a VT100 contains 24 lines).

The next example relates to the manner in which cursor position is managed in M. $X and $Y allow only integer arguments, measured in terms of a fixed pitch font position. In today's world, most fonts (including the non-program fonts used in this text) are proportional-spaced fonts, where each letter has a different width. $X and $Y might have been modified to accommodate decimal values, but the MDC recognized that this might lead to ambiguous interpretations, and therefore it would be preferable to find another solution to the cursor position problem. The ultimate solution was to bind M to ANSI X3.64, which had developed general, standard solutions to cursor positioning.

The X3.64 standard can be used to help a user manipulate several different fonts, including those with proportional spacing. WRITE /FNT(font,size) enables the user to switch from the primary default font (FNT(0) to any of 9 other alternate fonts, and to specify the point size with the second parameter in the FNT parameter list.

Having selected the font, the programmer can then use normal WRITE commands to output text. In order to determine the actual position of the cursor on the display device, X3.64 provides a function that will return the current position of the cursor. The following code illustrates how an M programmer can obtain this information:

```
WRITE /CPR READ xxx
```

The control mnemonic causes the cursor position information to be returned to the current device. When M completes the READ xxx statement, the value of xxx is the empty string, but the cursor position information is stored in the special variable $KEY, which can then be used to ascertain the position of the cursor. The values returned by X3.64 are expressed in integers and "decipoints." According to X3.64, a decipoint is 1/720th of an inch, or 0.0353 millimeters. A word processing package in M could make use of this information by calling a function each time a letter is written to the screen to determine if the cursor is reaching the end of the line, and if so, use a wraparound routine to erase a partial word at the end of a line, go to the next line, and copy the partial word before proceeding.

Binding M to the Graphical Kernel System (GKS)

This approach, using a standard specifically designed to manipulate display device characteristics together with M's programming power, is a great deal more reasonable than extending M to provide the same functionality. The same approach has been used to solve another problem in the use of graphic displays. Today's computers are capable of displaying a great deal more than simple ASCII text. This field is exploding, with ever more sophisticated graphic features appearing on devices that are becoming cheaper and more widespread each year.

M's involvement with graphic displays started in the mid 1980s. Another committee of ANSI had been working on graphical standards, resulting in the adoption of ANSI X3.124–1985: Computer Graphics – Graphical Kernel System (GKS) Functional Description. This standard was widely used in the 1980s, with bindings defined for FORTRAN, C, and other high-level languages. Members of the MDC felt that it would make sense to bind M to the GKS standard, and worked on a binding mechanism that was finally approved in conjunction with the 1995 standard. The document defining the binding to the GKS standard is ANSI X11.3 M[UMPS]– GKS Binding. This document was approved as a standard separate from the X11.1 standard, but it carries the same weight as that (and other) X11 standards related to the M language. Since GKS seems to be less important today, we will not dwell on the details of its binding to M. A brief example is included here, kindly provided by Ben Bishop, a member of MDC who has been active in the GKS binding process.

GKS uses the concept of a "workstation," including the display devices, input devices such as keyboard and mouse, and other input and output devices as may be available. Communication between a workstation and GKS is through GKS primitive messages to the workstation, to perform certain operations or return information. The following framework of an M device supporting the GKS *mnemonicspace* was provided by Mr. Bishop:

```
OPEN GKSDEV:::"GKS" ;open the device with GKS functionality
USE GKSDEV::"GKS" ;identify device as GKS type
;
WRITE /GOPKS("error.fil",10240) ;open GKS with error file and
;                       state buffer size
;
WRITE /GQLVKS ;inquire what 'level' GKS exists
READ ERROR,LEVEL ;look for error flag and GKS level
IF ERROR GOTO OPENFAIL ;abort if error returned
;
;open a workstation channel to this device for OUTPUT
WRITE /GOPWK("WORK1",255,"OUTPUT")
WRITE /GACWK("WORK1") ;activate the workstation
;
; ... insert drawing commands here (not shown)
;
WRITE /GDAWK("WORK1") ;deactivate workstation
CLOSE /GCLWK("WORK1") ;close workstation
WRITE /GCKLS ;close GKS interaction
CLOSE GKSDEV ;done
```

This framework shows the manner in which calls to GKS can be used in M to generate GKS graphics. Since the GKS standard is undergoing revision (it is over ten years old at this time), we will not go into any further details. The fact that this binding exists is important, however, as an example for future bindings to as-yet-undeveloped standards which may evolve (including the new GKS standard). The M standard has defined the *mnemonicspace* GKS for use with the OPEN and USE commands, and X11.3 defines the *control mnemonics* of that standard as ones that can be used in M to achieve a wide range of graphic visualization effects. Hence:

```
OPEN device:::"GKS"
```

or

```
USE device::"GKS"
```

will instruct M to accept all WRITE /[*controlmnemonic*] commands in the context of the GKS standard.

This is an important extension of the concept introduced in X3.64 binding, and it paves the way for future links between M and other evolving standards. Readers interested in using GKS should refer to X11.3 for details. It does seem probable that a new binding to some other standards may be adopted in a future M standard. The two most likely candidates in the graphics domain are either the revised GKS standard currently in its final approval process, or Open GL, a *de facto* standard developed by Silicon Graphics Corporation and widely used by many in the graphics communiuty. Clearly, binding to some graphics standard makes sense in extending the power of M in that area.

M binding to the X Window System: the use of external references

A second approach to interfacing M with the outside world is provided by the syntax of the M *External reference* syntax, specified in Section 8.1.6.3 of the 1995 X11.1 standard. Simply stated, the use of *any* program external to the current M environment may be defined by the use of an ampersand (&) followed by the program name, which may be optionally preceded by the name of the library in which the program is to be found. For instance:

```
DO &library1.prog2
```

will invoke prog2, found in `library1`. In the case of an external function, which will return a value, the ampersand is preceded by a '$'. Arguments may be passed to either external programs or external functions.

The X Window System is a windowing system designed originally for the UNIX environment (now available on several other platforms) and a trademark of the Massachusetts Institute of Technology. It is a multi-layered architecture, with different levels being considered for standardization by different ANSI and IEEE committees. At the lowest level is the *X protocol*, which is being studied by ANSI X3H3.6 for adoption. Next comes the code library *XLIB*, and above that *XTOOLKIT*. Both of these levels are included in FIPS 158. Layered above these are the two packages *Motif* and *Motif Resource Manager*, occurring in a single layer that has been adopted as a *de facto* standard by the Open Software Foundation, which owns the trademark on these names. IEEE 1295.1 was in the process of balloting on this as a new standard at the time that M's draft standard was out for approval. In effect, M has adopted a new standard X11.4 X Window System Binding, even before that system has completed a rather complicated standardization process through several different channels. The importance of the X Window System is too great to allow this interface to be delayed, especially in view of the fact that the formal binding will not be affected by minor changes in these standards. More important is the formalization of links to the X Window System so that M programmers can take advantage of the various layers of its windowing functionality.

Window environments are present on all the major operating system platforms. The X Window System runs primarily on UNIX, but also on some other platforms (Open VMS, a PC version, etc.). It is complex; computer science majors rarely are exposed to its inner workings, and students who have learned it estimate that it took several months of concentrated effort to become adept at using it. The payoff is great in terms of being able to do some very powerful things with Windows and with the connection of multiple systems using these protocols. In this text, we consider only the broad components of binding M to the X Window System.

Binding to the X Window System involves the use of both external functions and external programs. The syntax of a number of components in the interface is controlled by the conventions of the X Window System. In that system, programmers write code in C, and hence they must be concerned with multiple data types: char, double, float, int, long, short, signed, unsigned, (or a data type with the nonspecific denotation *xtype*, accepted as valid in the X Window System).

There are five libraries of programs required to bind M to the X Window System: XLIB, XTOOLKIT, XMOTIF, XMOTIFRM, and XMUMPS, which provides certain functionality needed to perform many functions in this environment. The naming conventions of these libraries use a case-sensitive notation. For instance, there is an XLIB function called XStoreColor, which requires that the S and C be uppercase and the others be lowercase.

■ The general naming conventions are as follows

`XLIB:` *XA[Aa]*

`XTOOLKIT:` *XtA[Aa]*

`XMOTIF:` *XmA[Aa] or XwmA[Aa]*

`XMOTIFRM:` *XrmA[Aa] or MrmA[Aa]*

`&XMUMPS:` one of the following specific names:

`$&XMUMPS.Allocate(xdeclaration)`	*[memory allocation]*
`&XMUMPS.Copy(xname1,xname2)`	*[copies window data structure]*
`&XMUMPS.Deallocate(xname)`	*[returns allocated memory]*
`$&XMUMPS.GetValue(xmember)`	*[returns numeric value of element]*
`$&XMUMPS.SetValue(xmember,expr)`	*[modifies value of element]*
`&XMUMPS.SetString(xmember,expr)`	*[modifies (string) value of element]*

`$&XMUMPS.GetString(xmember)`	*[returns (string) value of element]*
`$&XMUMPS.Exit([intexpr])`	*[notifies M to exit X Window env]*
`$&XMUMPS.RegisterEventHandler(lbexpr)`	*[used with &XTOOLKIT]*
`$&XMUMPS.RegisterCallback(lbexpr)`	*[translator for labels in &XTOOLKIT]*
`$&XMUMPS.RegisterWorkProc(lbexpr)`	*[another label translator]*
`$&XMUMPS.UnregisterEventHandler(xpointer)`	*[disables label translation]*
`&XMUMPS.UnregisterCallback(xpointer)`	*[disables label translation]*
`&XMUMPS.UnregisterWorkProc(xpointer)`	*[disables label translation]*

(Details of these functions are found in the descriptions of the X Window System definitions.) By combining the X Window System library routines (accessed using their terminology) with routines specific to M for the purposes of providing appropriate interface information in both directions, M programmers are able to take full advantage of the many features available through the X environment.

The next section illustrates a slightly different use of the general external reference syntax to provide an interface to a different standard.

Embedded SQL: another approach to binding M with other standards

The relational model was first described by E. F. Codd in 1970. It gradually gained acceptance, not only in the academic community (it was the first database model with a formal definition that could be treated analytically). Codd and his associates at IBM developed a research version of the relational model which was ultimately marketed as DB2. The Oracle Corporation also developed a relational model for mainframes, from which it moved to mini and ultimately microcomputers and many different platforms. INGRES appeared as a relational model in the UNIX world. And, as microcomputers grew in importance, almost all database packages developed for the PC world were relational (e.g., dBase and DATAEASE). By the late 1980s, virtually all desktop computer packages were based on the relational model, and it even began to replace the more traditional IMS hierarchical-based system of IBM mainframes. There are dozens of software vendors who have their own version of the relational model. Individual departments in many organizations purchased database packages for their internal use, running them on desktop computer systems without coordinating the purchase with other departments in the same organization. When efforts were made to coordinate these databases, there was a need to transfer data between different packages. While database vendors might have wished that they could persuade entire organizations to settle on their product, it was already too late. Instead, the vendors were told that they *must* find ways to transfer data between database packages marketed by other vendors.

This situation gave rise to a new effort in database standardization. The relational model provided a formal basis for general agreement on the definition of files and their attributes. It also set the stage for definition of a common set of operations that could be performed on these files or "relations." Early in the evolution of the relational model, IBM developed a database language called Structured Query Language, or SQL. By the early 1980s, SQL was fairly widely known. With the advent of the multiple relational model database packages for personal computers, all vendors developed their own languages, but in most cases these languages had enough in common with SQL that the possibilities of developing a standard were promising.

As the need for data exchange between different vendor packages grew, so did the recognition that some standard was required. An ANSI committee, X3H2: Databases, took on the task of defining a language, based on SQL, that would provide the communication link between different relational database packages. As one might expect, the original version of SQL, adopted as an ANSI standard in the 1980s, was a somewhat limited subset of the ideal capabilities of a complete database language. The committee continued to meet, however, and it was at about this stage that representatives of MDC began to participate. The second SQL standard, adopted in 1992 by both ANSI and ISO (ANSI X3.135, and ISO/IEC 9075), defined SQL2, a standard that was considerably expanded over its predecessor and one that was developed in coordination with M, among other high-level programming languages. The two standards — 1992 SQL and the 1995 M standard — cross-reference each other in ways that make both standards aware of the capability of *embedding* SQL statements in M routines. Annex D of M X11.1 (1995) reproduces portions of ANSI X3.135 which refer directly to M.

Since M is based on a hierarchical rather than a relational file structure, it might seem strange, or at least incompatible, to attempt to interface the two languages. In fact, the relational file design can be considered a subset of the hierarchical model. (The reverse of this statement is technically correct: it is possible to represent hierarchical data in a relational model by using a series of tables linked by primary and foreign keys. However, the result tends to make for inefficient retrievals.) To illustrate the differences in these structures, consider the following example. Suppose we have a database which contains personal identification information about sales personnel and also contains information about the sales made each month by each employee. In a typical M database design, we might have two different designs for this information (assume that the details of each invoice are stored in a separate file).

One design would use a single subscript level for each individual, with data stored at that node:

```
^emp(id)="Jones, John^346 B St^Arlington^MA^02198^617-349-1982"
^sales(id,date)="invoice1^invoice2^invoice3..."
```

A second option might be to use more than one level of subscript:

```
^emp(id,"name")="Jones, John"
^emp(id,"street")="346 B St"
^emp(id,"city")="Arlington"
^emp(id,"state")="MA"
^emp(id,"zip")="02198"
^emp(id,"phone")="617-349-1982"
^sales(id,date,invoice1)=""
^sales(id,date,invoice2)=""
^sales(id,date,invoice3)=""
...
```

These two sets of data would be stored in a relational model as two relations:

```
Employee:
      ID    Name     Street   City     State  Zip     Phone
Sales:
      ID    Yr       Month    DayInvoice_number
```

The "primary key" of Employee is ID; the primary key of Sales has to include ID and invoice number (date might optionally be included as well), in order to have a unique identifier for each row.

Retrieving information from this data set in M would require writing appropriate combinations of $ORDER and the output WRITEs to get the desired data. In SQL, one could get a list of all sales in November made by a given salesperson by writing the general SQL statement

```
SELECT Invnumb from Sales
            Where ID = "39867"
            and DATE is >"96/Oct/31" and Date is <"96/Dec/1"
```

(The specifics of the date arithmetic may vary, but SQL does permit manipulation of dates in a meaningful way.) People familiar with SQL would not be comfortable writing M code to achieve these results, and indeed it would take more commands to accomplish the given task. The point is, however, that it is perfectly easy to represent relational tables using one or more M file designs. It should therefore be relatively easy to use SQL syntax to allow specification of this type of retrieval within a routine written in M.

In order to permit a direct link between M and SQL, the MDC defined an embedded SQL code segment as beginning with &SQL (followed by the SQL statements and terminated with a final). &SQL is a specific reference to an *externid*, that is, a reserved identifier linked to the SQL standard. It sets the stage for use of this concept in linking to other standards. Within the parentheses, the syntax of commands follows SQL2 conventions. Specifically, this means that, whereas in M commands are either restricted to a single line or preceded by an argumentless DO with added linestarts, SQL statements can cover several lines as allowed by the SQL syntax. In order to accomplish the retrieval specified above, one could write the following code:

... M commands ...

```
&SQL(SELECT Invnumb from Sales
        Where ID = "39867"
        and DATE is "Nov" )   note final closing parenthesis
```

... continue with M commands ...

From the user's point of view, this is a relatively easy way of accomplishing the retrieval task by using code typical of SQL statements. Behind the scenes, however, a number of things have to take place in order for this embedded code to work.

The &SQL(...) syntax is unlike that used to interact with the X Window System standard, since the code may be stored in the same routine which invokes it, whereas a true "external ref" is usually stored elsewhere. Some vendors have implemented this feature by translating the SQL code into M and inserting the M code in place of the SQL statements; others rely on external SQL compilers. (In fact, the SQL standard does not define the manner in which SQL is to be interfaced to other standards, a decision left to implementors and third-party vendors.) SQL is a compiled language that includes declarations. M is interpretive, with no declarations involved. In order for a routine written in M to include SQL code, the SQL portion (at least) must be *precompiled*. Furthermore, the SQL precompiler must be provided with sufficient information to ascertain which fields will be found in what part of the M hierarchical file structure. This requirement further makes it necessary to have a package that identifies database elements in terms of their location in the database. The design of the M precompiler is left to the implementor; usually it means that certain rules of database creation must be followed in order to permit M to map its global files to fit the relational model.

SQL has been successfully embedded in M in several implementations. Users should be aware, however, that there are sometimes unexpected performance idiosyncrasies that arise depending on the way in which the SQL code is written.

Linking M to *de facto* standards

Although many formally approved standards exist, there are just as many other conventions which have been accepted by a large segment of the computer community as *de facto* standards. These standards have gained wide enough acceptance that they are adhered to even though they have never been approved by standards bodies. Earlier in this chapter we referred to the *Open GL* graphics *de facto* standard. Because of its widespread acceptance, this approach, developed intially by Silicon Graphics, may be a good choice for interfacing with M. Another example is Microsoft's *Open Data Base Connectivity (ODBC)*, which has gained support in part because of the size and influence of its developer, Microsoft. Several M vendors support ODBC links to their database. These are only two examples of what will undoubtedly be a mechanism for the gradual introduction of interfaces to other languages and systems, standard or *de facto* standard through usage.

Summary

M is a powerful language with many unique and versatile capabilities. It is not, however, capable of performing all things for all people. (One of the German members of the M community tells of a German term: *eiernlegende Wollmilchsau*, which translates into an egg-laying, wool-bearing, milkgiving pig, the ultimate in being all-purpose in its field.) The best way to provide the specific functionality for those areas in which M cannot currently provide solutions is to permit simple, flexible interfaces that can be standardized, so that M programmers do not need to develop unique or multiple solutions when programming for different environments and vendor implementations of M.

In this chapter, we have seen a number of different approaches already used by M to interface with other standards (and with some *de facto* standards that are likely to be accepted formally as standards in the future). Explicit references, such as those to ASCII, represent one way in which interface can be accomplished. In some cases, the syntax of the language has been extended (e.g., by adding a WRITE /... to the language for certain operations that would be awkward or impossible to define in a standard way using M alone). Other approaches make more oblique references to standards by using external references.

Each of these methods was designed carefully to be open-ended. Each technique can be used to solve interface problems with other *classes* of standards, and it is likely that several additional bindings between M and other standards will appear in the next M standard, and that some of the existing bindings will be further extended to accommodate greater functionality. This process will probably not end in the foreseeable future.

At the same time, some efforts are being made to facilitate the reverse process — accessing M through other languages. For instance, it would be beneficial to many other high-level languages to make use of M globals, providing persistent data without requiring those languages to be modified. Several vendors promote this type of interface between their M implementations and other languages or packages residing on their database. It may not be necessary at this point to define closer ties with access to the M language as well as its data, but that time may well arrive in the not-too-distant future. M users should be sensitive to the need to promote this concept among their non-M programmer friends.

M and Windows Environments

23

Background

The 1995 M standard is 97 pages long. *X11.6: M[UMPS] Windowing Application Programmer's Interface* is 120 pages long. Most manuals found in computer bookstores dealing with programming in windows environments are several hundred pages long. In this text, the windows component of M is covered in this single chapter. Obviously, it is not possible to cover it all in that short a space. Instead, we will try to present enough of the concepts associated with windows programming so that readers will understand the M approach to windows programming, and so that they may also understand that several alternatives exist when it comes to interfacing M with the windows environment. A large portion of this chapter is derived from the ideas of others who have been active in the use of windows in the M environment. I am particularly indebted to Gardner Trask and Bill Yaksick, who provided the examples used to illustrate these concepts.

In this chapter, we will use the term "windows" to refer to a general set of windows applications Graphical User Interfaces (GUIs); Windows (with a capital W) for Microsoft Windows; Macintosh Windows for the Macintosh equivalent; and X Window System, or X Windows for short, for the UNIX equivalent.

When M first appeared on the computer scene, almost all interaction with computers was done in batch mode, with large, droppable stacks of punched cards serving as input and, hours and many cups of coffee later, printed output appeared which was often measured by "side inches" rather than the number of pages produced. M seemed pretty innovative in those days, giving users a chance to receive instant feedback from the computer for lines of commands as soon as they were entered. Early user interactions devised by M programmers were based on programmer-controlled dialogues, in which users had to respond to one question at a time as they scrolled past on the screen.

A number of things have changed since these not-so-good old days. Computer operating systems developed time-share systems which permitted direct communication with the computer, then moved to personal computers that were single user, providing even more user independence. In the 1980s, the concept of windows emerged, first on the Macintosh, then on UNIX and PC systems. Some of the old methods persisted, but the "new generation" of computer users came to expect and insist on different modes of interaction with the computer.

This change goes much deeper than the style of user-computer interaction. There are in fact profound factors at work that are affecting our attitudes on many things, computers among them (and to some extent computers have caused these changes). One major change is that learning is no longer assumed to stop at the end of one's formal education (grade school, college, wherever one stops "going to school"). Instead, people today realize that they will have to develop lifelong learning habits if they are to stay competitive in today's rapidly changing society.

In turn, this shift in the characteristics of learners today affects the way in which material should be presented to the learners. Whereas we have managed somehow to force our children to sit through lock-step instruction, lectures, artificial deadlines, and all the other components that can be summed up as "linear learning," we cannot hope to force adults into the same mold. An adult learner wants to be in control of the learning process, both in terms of content and schedule. The importance of "certification" — the diploma, certificate, or even course grade — is waning in favor of more realistic, self-determined measures of appropriate learning achieved.

The desire to participate in nonlinear learning is not new, nor is it restricted to adults. Teenagers channel surfing on TV are not doing so (solely) to annoy their parents, but because they truly enjoy keeping track of several things at once, and *they* want to be in control of what they watch, see, and learn. What has happened is that technology has at last made nonlinear, user-controlled learning possible. No longer are we required to put up with learning that is little more than "teaching," with no regard for the learner.

These changes affect us in many ways, but clearly, designing user interfaces for computers is going to require emphasis on two major guidelines: nonlinear design and user control. As more people get used to working with the World Wide Web and hypertext formats, they will begin to insist on designs that allow them to find material the way *they* want to, not according to the guidance of an instructor or programmer.

Windows is an outgrowth of this set of events. In some ways, it has contributed to the change in user attitudes toward computer programs. The M community, which consists of people who use computers a significant portion of most days, is fully aware of the need to design user interfaces to match the nonlinear, user control philosophy. The question that remains is how best to accomplish this task in the M environment.

This chapter shows that there are in fact several alternative approaches to the design of an application involving both windows and M. To understand how these approaches have evolved, we need to consider some additional factors of a historical nature.

Windows and more windows

I can remember visiting Xerox's Palo Alto Research Center (PARC) in the early 1970s, and seeing some of the precursors of what evolved into the windows approach we take for granted today. The mouse and a screen with more than one task running at the same time were features of those early systems. Alan Kay, then a researcher at Xerox PARC, went on to help with the evolution of Apple's Macintosh, which started the trend to windows environments. The UNIX and PC environments followed along in time, and the paradigm was firmly entrenched as the most appropriate user interface for many applications and environments.

Since M runs on all three of these platforms (as well as others), programs written in M may have to be portable across two or more of these platforms. That is not to say that all M applications must run on all systems, only that, from the MDC point of view, it is inappropriate to restrict the design of windows interfaces to one or another of these platforms. This decision affected the way the MDC approached windows design for use with M.

Typical windows-based applications in M

M applications are almost always concerned with manipulating data. Computation plays a minor role in M solutions to problems. Instead, users typically enter large volumes of data, and then seek to retrieve and manipulate the data in ways that will be productive and efficient.

Several different types of operations are required in such applications. First, there is the collection of data, an ongoing process that never stops in an active database application. This includes initial data entry, error detection and correction, updates, and deletions. The second task centers around the storage and manipulation of the data. Finally, applications of this type require data retrieval in many forms ranging from on-line, interactive queries to scheduled, time-consuming reports generated at regular intervals in the operations cycle for which the application was designed.

From the point of view of the M programmer, the middle step of this process (data storage and manipulation) is almost certainly going to involve M. Its global arrays are the heart of such a database system, and both storage and manipulation of the data properly belong in the domain of the M language.

Before the windows environments came along, input and queries, including report generation, were also considered to be best done in M. That assumption is open to question in today's world. Prior to MWAPI (M Windows Application Programmer's Interface), input in M did not keep pace with the competition. Unfortunately, many, perhaps most, M database applications were designed with either scrolling dialogue entry systems or somewhat primitive, programmer-controlled screen forms. Report generation, while still a strength of M for complex retrievals, has also proven difficult for naive users to master – whereas relational model databases with SQL offer more user-friendly output formats (for simple queries and reports). We will not consider the output component of this model, since window systems do little to enhance report generation. However, the input side of databases requires more scrutiny.

With the advent of windows, M lost some of its competitive edge over earlier database packages. Since it did not readily interface to the existing windows environments, application programmers had to attempt to work around this limitation in a variety of ways.

For this reason, the MDC decided that one of its highest priorities for the 1995 standard was to develop effective interfaces to the windows environment. Two paths were taken to achieve this interaction: one which involved creation of M Windows Application Programmer's Interface capabilities within the M language (the *MWAPI* method); the second, an indirect approach that enhances M's ability to interface with other languages. Both of these approaches have their advantages. Both have their strong adherents and, as it happens, equally strong opponents. We will present both approaches, together with some of the arguments used by each to support these two viewpoints. The answer clearly is not one-sided: there are times when one solution appears to be preferable to the other. In this chapter, we will present the MWAPI methodology in greater detail. M interfaces to other programming languages are covered in greater detail in Chapter 22, but some examples using this approach are presented here for purposes of comparison.

An overview of windows programming

Basic design

The windows paradigm has evolved in methods that are remarkably similar in all three environments that we will be considering in this text (Macintosh, PC, and UNIX). In fact, the similarity caused Apple to sue Microsoft for precisely that reason, and even though Apple lost its case, it is clear that the parallels are numerous.

There are several distinct operations that go to make a complete windows application. They include:

- Configuration of the display that is presented to the user. This step includes design of the windows: their size, location on the screen, color, font, and other formatting decisions;
- Selection of user interface tools to allow the user to take desired actions associated with the application; and
- Interface with the data management system supporting this application.

These activities require markedly different skills, so it should not be surprising to see windows applications with strengths in some design features and weaknesses in others.

Hardware and operating system components

A user interface in the windows environment assumes the following basic (hardware and operating system) environment:

- A monitor capable of displaying several windows simultaneously;
- A keyboard input device;
- A mouse with at least one button; and
- An operating system or layer above an operating system that can manage these devices.

Access to other hardware devices, such as printer and network connectivity, voice input/output, and other devices, may be required for certain applications. Touch screens, digital tablets, and other special-purpose systems may also be incorporated in some windows applications.

Design philosophy

The windows approach to user interaction assumes that *the user, not the program, is in control.* This assumption requires that windows systems have certain nonlinear approaches to user input. While the programmer may exert some control by requiring, for example, completeness in data entry before accepting the user's input, there is no control over the sequence in which different tasks are performed. This is a different approach compared to legacy systems in which the programmer had complete control over user actions.

A second important design criterion of windows-design systems is their dependence on primitive functions supplied by the windows environment. In most cases, these primitives are sufficient for the purpose at hand. If they are not, then it becomes necessary to adopt a far more painstaking and detailed approach to windows design – one that we will not consider in this chapter. (In my research on distance learning, we found that the fonts available in standard windows support tools were insufficient for language learning involving mixed strings from different character sets in the same window. We therefore had to "go deeper" into the windows system to generate these capabilities, which also meant providing the common tools which could not be called at that level.)

MWAPI provides the basic calls to windows environments to support windows configuration, user interaction, and interaction with the underlying (M) database. The complete specifications of these tools are cases too detailed to cover completely in this chapter. However, the basic elements described above are separated and discussed in the sections that follow. The steps outlined below are comparable to those required in other windows-design languages; readers are invited to refer to some other windows programming environments to compare their methods with those provided in M. As we will see, Structured System Variables provide the major tool whereby M programmers can control each of these processes.

Structured System Variables, discussed in Chapter 21 provide M programmers access to systems-level information. They are used in the same context in the windows environment, but in this case, unlike those discussed earlier, they can be SET or even KILLED by the user.

General screen layout

M provides for two levels of screen configuration. The first is managed by the Structured System Variable ^$DISPLAY. Each process running under M with windows has at least one ^$DISPLAY available. In most cases, ^$DISPLAY is related to a single screen, and the parameters associated with it depend on the characteristics of that screen. Different users on the same system each have individual instances of ^$DISPLAY, to which each user has access (i.e., no user can view the status of another user's screen attributes).

In some cases in which multiple displays may be available (such as the use of special displays for medical images), a single user may have two or even more instances of ^$DISPLAY. We do not consider those cases in this chapter.

At this, the highest system configuration layout, it is possible to define a number of different attributes, using reserved terms addressing each of these attributes. They include the following groupings.

- **Systems information:**

  PLATFORM (name and version number of platform)

- **Devices available:**

  KEYBOARD

  PEN

  PTR (pointer, such as a mouse)

- **Scaling information:**

  UNITS (sizing units: pixel, point (1/72"), char)

  SIZE (horizontal and vertical size in UNITS)

- **Color information:**

  BCOLOR (background color)

  COLOR (windows application area color)

  FCOLOR (default foreground color for gadgets)

  COLORTYPE (gray scale, mono, or color)

  SPECTRUM (number of grayscales or colors available)

- **Font information:**

  TYPEFACE (fonts, faces, and point sizes available)

- **Interaction information:**

  CLIPBOARD (contents of clipboard)

  FOCUS (identifies the window [and gadget] to which keyboard and pointer actions are directed)

Most of these attributes (with the exception of FOCUS) are usually provided by the system as default values. They can, however, be overridden if appropriate, and additional implementation-specific values can be added. For instance, the standard currently defines values for PLATFORM to include the following choices:

MAC (Macintosh)

MSWIN (Microsoft Windows)

PM (Presentation Manager)

X/MTF (XWindow/Motif)
X/OPNLK (XWindow/Open Look)
implementation-specific

Similar options, not covered in this chapter, are available for other attributes, and the implementation-specific option is usually available, allowing for technological growth, with the assumption that other attributes and values may be added in future revisions of this standard.

Screen details

Once the general features of the display are established through ^$DISPLAY, the next level deals with the definition of individual elements on that display (we will assume it is a single screen). Most windows applications consist of one or more (usually more) windows, in which are one or more gadgets: items that allow the user to interact with the windows environment. Figure 23.1 illustrates most of the types of elements that might be used in a single window. (Timer attributes cannot be illustrated graphically, but they are discussed below.)

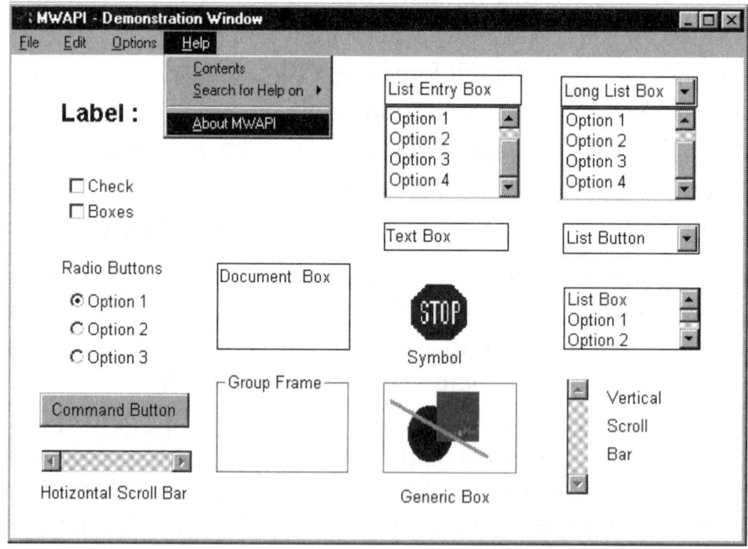

FIGURE 23.1: *Typical Components of a Window (from Trask, 1994a)*

Some window elements are positioned in a predefined location on the window, e.g., menu bar and title, and window-level scroll bars (not shown in this example). Others can be moved around within the window. This window is obviously much more crowded than would ever be the case in a real application, but it does serve to illustrate the types of features available. Designing a "good" window is a skill that can be learned only through practice, an iterative process that requires frequent user feedback.

^$WINDOW attributes

With Figure 23.1 as a model for the components of individual windows, we can turn next to the manner in which the second Structured System Variable, ^$WINDOW, can be defined. The first point to be made is that the hierarchical structure of M makes it possible to introduce the concept of *inheritance*, a feature usually associated with object-oriented programming. Windows can be considered as subclasses of Displays, and the idea of inheritance of certain attributes is useful, allowing for consistency and simplifying the programmer's task. In addition to allowing windows to inherit certain characteristics from ^$DISPLAY, the MWAPI environment also allows windows to inherit attributes from "parent" windows, thereby extending the subclass inheritance concept. M also allows windows to define their own characteristics, overriding the inherited characteristic. As a consequence of this approach, KILLing an override definition of some attribute will result in return to the default value, if one exists.

This concept of inheritance, with override permitted, is an excellent example of the default-override approach to programming that has found its way into M in several areas, such as networking and, with time, internationalization (where override has not as yet been specified).

^$WINDOW has many attributes that can be defined. The list that follows omits those that can be inherited from ^$DISPLAY.

- **Systems information:**
  ID (internal identification number of window)
  DISPLAY (the device where the window appears)
  PARENT (identifies parent window, if any)
  TYPE (specifies type of window: MTERM or APPLICATION)
  ICON (identifies icon to use if iconified)
- **Screen identifying information:**
  TITLE (title of text)
  ITITLE (title of icon)
- **Sizing information:**
  POS (defines original position, in units)

TIED	(indicates if position is tied to parent window)
SIZE	(in units, not usually inherited)
RESIZE	(indicates whether user can resize window)
SIZEMIN	(minimum resize allowed for this window)
SIZEWIN	(window frame height and width, in units)

- **General attributes:**

DEFBUTTON	(specifies default push button for window)
FFACE	(font face to be used for gadgets in window)
FSIZE	(font size for gadgets in window)
FSTYLE	(font style for gadgets in window)
MENUBAR	(identifies menu bar to be displayed at window level)
SCROLL	(indicates whether horizontal or vertical scroll bars present)

- **Interaction information:**

VISIBLE	(indicates whether window is visible to user)
ACTIVE	(indicates whether window, elements, and descendants are active)
ICONIFY	(if true, enables user to iconify window)
NEXTG	(action taken if window (not gadget) receives focus)
MODAL	(disable PARENT, ANCESTOR, APPLICATION)

Two items require clarification in this list. Most windows are APPLICATION type, which can contain elements like gadgets. MTERM windows are used as terminal emulation areas which can accept M commands, but do not contain elements like gadgets.

MODAL windows, when visible, can disable other windows. If MODAL is defined as PARENT, only its parent is disabled; if ANCESTOR, all parents in the subclass hierarchy are disabled; if APPLICATION, all windows except itself are disabled.

MWAPI gadgets

Once a window has been defined with its basic components, the programmer can place a variety of different elements in that window in addition to the fixed-position items described above. There are 14 different types of gadgets defined in the 1995 standard, as listed below, grouped by common characteristics:

- **Inactive gadgets:**

LABEL	(text appearing in the window)

SYMBOL	(image appearing in a window)
FRAME	(a rectangular outline around a group of gadgets)

- **Buttons:**

BUTTON	(a push button that can be "clicked" to cause an event to occur)
LISTBUTTON	(a push button associated with a list of options; user can select one)
RADIO	(a set of related items, only one of which can be selected at a time)

- **Boxes:**

GENERIC	(a box in which user can draw text, figures, etc.)
CHECK	(a check box that can be turned on or off)
LIST	(a list box, allowing selection of more than one item)
LONGLIST	(similar to list box, but designed for very large lists of items)
TEXT	(a box allowing entry of a single line of text)
DOCUMENT	(a box allowing entry and editing of several lines of text)
LISTENRY	(allows editing of a selected entry on a list)

- **Sliding bars:**

SCROLL	(a scrolling device allowing user to move slider along bar horizontal or vertical)

There are a great many attributes that can be assigned to these different gadgets. Those that can be inherited from the ^$WINDOW in which they occur are not discussed further. Other attributes specific to one or more of the gadgets listed are as follows:

- **Cosmetic:**

TBCOLOR	(title background color)
TFCOLOR	(title foreground color)
TFFACE	(title font face)
TFSIZE	(title font size)
TFSTYLE	(title font style)
TPOS	(title position)
FRAMED	(frame around gadget)

- **Display control:**

INSELECT	(insertion point for new text)
TOPSHOW	(display value in top line of gadget)
SCROLLBY	(scroll increment when user scrolls)
SCROLLDIR	(orientation of scroll bar: horizontal or vertical)

SCROLLRNGE	(value range of scroll bar)
ROWCOL	(specifies arrangement of radio button set)

- **I/O:**

CHARMAX	(maximum characters in text)
SELECTMAX	(maximum concurrent selections allowed in list)
CANCHANGE	(users can change values)
DRAWTYPE	(defines type of draw commands)
DRAW	(defines draw commands allowed)

- **Interaction information:**

CHANGED	(flag set if value of gadget changes)
CHOICE	(choices for radio buttons, etc.)
EVENT	(defines events that can happen to gadget)
NEXTG	(defines next gadget to get focus)
RESOURCE	(specifies an image to display)
CANCEL	(do not perform focus, change or unfocus event)

Not all of these attributes can be applied to all gadgets. The table on page 311 places an 'x' in each position where the attribute applies to the gadget listed. The gadgets are listed in the order presented above, with abbreviation indicting the name of the gadget.

^$EVENT

In order to process the interaction with the user, MWAPI provides a third Structured System Variable called ^$EVENT. There are a number of different classes of events that might occur. The general categories of events are:

Window State Events	(CLOSE, MIN, RESIZE, etc.)
Pointer events	(PDOWN, PMOVE, CLICK, etc.)
Keyboard events	(KEYDOWN, KEYUP, FKEYDOWN, FKEYUP)
Focus events	(FOCUS, UNFOCUS)
Select events	(SELECT, DESELECT)
Longlist Box events	(GOBOTTOM, GODOWNBIG, etc.)
Help events	(HELP)
Timer events	(TIMER)

These events are not applicable to all window types or gadgets; the standard lists a table of those cases where the particular events apply.

	CKB	DOC	GEN	FRM	LAB	LBX	LBT	LEB	LLB	PSH	RAD	SCR	SYM	TXT
ACTIVE	x	x	x			x	x	x	x	x	x	x		x
BCOLOR	x	x	x	x	x	x	x	x	x		x	x		x
CANCEL	x	x	x			x	x	x	x	x	x			x
CANCHANGE		x				x	x	x	x					x
CHANGED	x	x				x	x	x	x		x	x		x
CHARMAX		x						x						x
CHOICE						x	x	x	x		x			
DRAW			x											
DRAWTYPE			x											
EVENT	x	x	x			x	x	x	x	x	x	x		x
FCOLOR	x	x	x	x	x	x	x	x	x		x	x		x
FFACE		x	x			x	x	x	x		x			x
FRAMED		x	x		x						x			x
FSIZE		x	x			x	x	x	x		x			x
FSTYLE		x	x			x	x	x	x		x			x
ID	x	x	x	x	x	x	x	x	x	x	x	x		x
INSELECT		x						x						x
INTERVAL														
NEXTG	x	x	x	x	x	x	x	x	x	x	x	x		x
POS	x	x	x	x	x	x	x	x	x	x	x	x	x	x
RESOURCE										x			x	
ROWCOL											x			
SCROLL		x												
SCROLLBY												x		
SCROLLDIR												x		
SCROLLPOS									x					
SCROLLRNGE									x			x		
SELECTMX						x			x					
SELECTVAL		x						x						x
SIZE	x	x	x	x	x	x	x	x	x	x	x	x		x
TBCOLOR		x				x	x	x	x		x			x
TFCOLOR		x				x	x	x	x		x			x
TFFACE	x	x		x	x	x	x	x	x	x	x			x
TFSIZE	x	x		x	x	x	x	x	x	x	x			x
TFSTYLE	x	x		x	x	x	x	x	x	x	x			x
TITLE	x	x		x	x	x	x	x	x	x	x			x
TOPSHOW						x		x	x					
TPOS						x		x	x		x			x
TYPE	x	x	x	x	x	x	x	x	x	x	x	x	x	x
UNITS	x	x	x	x	x	x	x	x	x	x	x	x	x	x
VALUE	x	x				x	x	x	x		x	x		x
VISIBLE	x	x	x	x	x	x	x	x	x	x	x	x	x	x

^$EVENT contains information about the most recent event that has occurred. The programmer must react to those events in the order they are received.

Timer events allow the programmer to set time limits on certain anticipated actions, and to take alternative actions if the expected event does not occur within that time.

Programming in MWAPI

This introduction to the functions available through MWAPI illustrated a comprehensive set of tools that can be used to interface with windows environments on several platforms. The code written by the programmer would not have to change to target a different platform, since these tools are platform-independent. This is a major strength of the M approach to windows, but it should be noted that other languages suitable for windows application development have also developed platform-independent approaches (e.g., PERL).

The options available to an M programmer wishing to develop a windows application include (a) using MWAPI and M for the complete application package; (b) using M to call functions in other languages for windows development, but relying on M to access its globals; and (c) using another language for windows development and calling M globals from that other language. We will illustrate the first two of these options later in this chapter; the third is less relevant to this chapter, since it deals only with M data, a subject covered elsewhere in this text.

The best way to start to program a windows application using M and MWAPI (after the design phase is over) is to create a set of globals containing the basic definitions used in MWAPI, and then, using the MERGE command, copy those definitions into the Structured System Variable ^$WINDOW with the same application name as in the global. In the concluding section of this chapter, we illustrate this process.

The most effective way to evaluate the use of MWAPI vs. the use of another language controlled by M for the windows-related functions is to give an example of each. I am indebted to Gardner Trask, who published the "calculator" example reproduced below in *M Computing* (Trask, 1994b), and to Bill Yaksick, who reproduced the same example (with slight embellishments) using Visual BASIC and M. In the next section, we examine these two options, and the comments of each of these individuals on his approach to the problem.

A Windows example: a Windows calculator (the MWAPI approach)

Figure 23.2, taken from (Trask, 1994b), illustrates a calculator created in a generic windows environment, using the MWAPI approach to the problem. It runs without change on all machines for which M and Windows are available. Trask executed his design by first creating a set of global data defining the different MWAPI components, then wrote M code to copy the global data into a ^$WINDOWS environment, after which he wrote the M code to run this application. The globals and M program are reproduced in Appendix A at the end of this chapter.

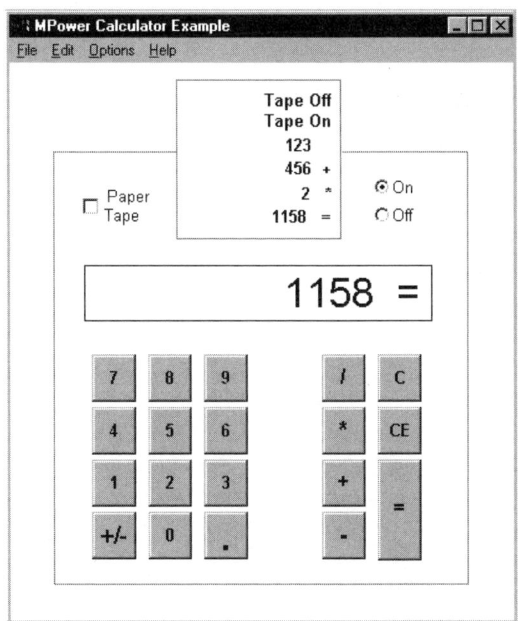

FIGURE 23.2: *Calculator Example Generated by MWAPI*

This illustration contains a number of the general features available in Windows, and has some interesting components permitting calculations and optional paper tape simulations, etc. Persons unfamiliar with the details required to generate such an example may be somewhat daunted by the length of the code required for this case; however, by use of M editors and the MERGE command, it is relatively simple to create globals that contain much of the "boilerplate" necessary in such an application. Mr. Trask's papers, referenced at the end of this chapter, give reasons why he believes that MWAPI is an efficient approach to Windows generation and maintenance. Among them are portability, ease of programming entirely in the M environment, the ability to use M structures for data, and the concept of reusable code for similar applications.

Another Windows example: a calculator (M-Visual BASIC approach)

So as to present a balanced view of the options available to M programmers wishing to program in the Windows environment, we present next a similar example created by William Yaksick, an M systems consultant from Cool, California (lovely name!). Mr. Yaksick examined the articles written by Mr. Trask, and produced the following example for purposes of comparison.

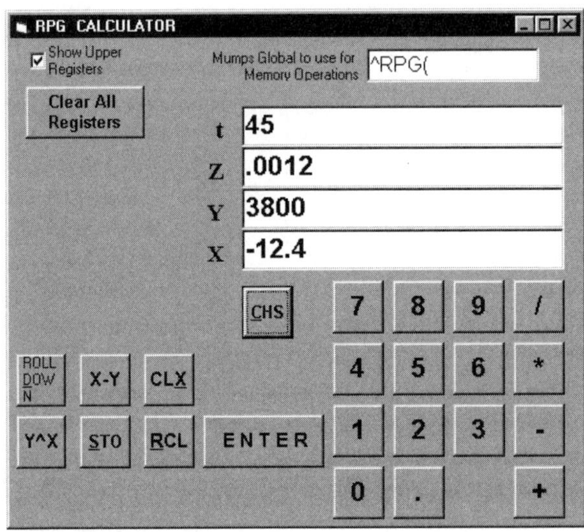

FIGURE 23.3: *RPG Calculator Written with M and Visual Basic (Yaksick, 1996)*

Mr. Yaksick wrote the following notes to accompany his example:

> This RPG Calculator mimics an HP 10C. Function keys have been added to demonstrate how M can be called to perform functions that may be easier to add in M than VB (due to our common ability to "think" in M more clearly than in VB). Where robust applications will typically make "calls" to M, in this example, all M code is contained in the VB window.
>
> The 10C's 10 memory registers have been implemented (STO-3 will store the X register into memory location 3, RCL-3 will retrieve the value). To avoid colli-

sion with existing globals, the user may specify the global structure in which to store the memory registers. Specifying an incomplete GVN such that GVN_integer_")" is valid: ^MYRPGSTORE("SUB1", (with trailing ",") will work.

Some of us think mousing a 10-key pad is silly: so numeric keys and <ENTER> have been implemented, Alt keys work in the windows style. I didn't bother with a square root key: try Y to the X power with X=0.5. Uncheck "Show Upper Registers" to hide t, Z & Y."

Yaksick, 1996

Code for this example is provided in Appendix B at the end of this chapter.

The example provided by Mr. Yaksick is aimed specifically at the Microsoft Windows environment. It would not be portable to other systems. However, as noted by Mr. Yaksick, he has minimal need for such portability, since his consulting involves only Microsoft Windows GUI design, even though M globals may reside on other servers.

From this example, you can see that, individual styles set aside, the same end can be achieved with both methods. M can also be interfaced with a number of other application languages and packages (e.g., Delphi) to achieve comparable results. In addition, a number of new portable languages have appeared on the Internet in recent years, notably PERL and Java, so the relative uniqueness of M's portability argument loses some strength. The fact remains, however, that M programmers will definitely find it easier to write their code in M, partially or entirely, rather than have to learn a new language just for the windows environment. The M community is by no means uniform in insisting on one of these choices; the preference depends on experience and familiarity with different environments, the need for portability, and individual programming styles.

Summary

The examples and code presented in this chapter serve to introduce the concepts of Windows Application Programming. Those wishing to confine their programming environment to the M world will be able to do so just about as comfortably as those happy to accept solutions requiring different languages. The choice is yours: M can provide either a complete or a complementary solution. Most of us would prefer at the least to retain M's persistent global data, and this option is available whichever choice you adopt.

References

Trask, G. S. III (1994a), "The M Windowing API: The Tools," *M Computing*, Vol 2:2, pp. 47–52.

Trask, G. S. III (1994b), "The M Windowing API: Windows, Ho!" *M Computing*, Vol 2:4, pp. 41–50.

Yaksick, William (1996) personal communication to the author, Aug. 20, 1996.

Appendix A: MWAPI Code for Calculator Example

MPower Calculator code

```
MPower   ; MPower Calculator code - Gardner S. Trask III (07-13-93)
         ; Copyright 1994 - MPower Computer Consultants
         ;all rights reserved
A1       ;
         KILL ^$WINDOW("MPower")
         SET $zt=ERRExit"
         SET newflag=1
         MERGE ^$WINDOW("MPower")=^MPower("MPower")
         DO clrtape,tapebox,clear
         ESTART
         ;
GSTExit  ;
         ;general call for ESTOP
         ESTOP
         QUIT
ERRExit  ESTOP
         QUIT
         ;
GSToff   KILL ^$WINDOW("MPower")
         GOTO GSTExit
         ;
GSTNum   ;
         ;add number to display
         DO getdisp
         DO getkey
```

```
            ;
            IF key="." DO
            .QUIT:dval["."
            .SET dval=dval_"."
            .Do putdisp
            ;
            IF key="+ - /" DO
            .SET dsign=$SELECT("-":"+",1:"-"
            .DO putdisp
            ;
            IF key>"0" DO
            .IF newflag SET dval=key,dsign="" DO putdisp QUIT
            .IF +dval>0!(dval[".") SET dval=dval_key
            .ELSE  SET dval=key
            .DO putdisp
            ;
            IF key=0 DO   ;order of logic is important here
            .IF dval["." SET dval=dval_0 DO putdisp QUIT
            .IF newflag SET dval=0,dsign="" DO putdisp  QUIT
            .IF dval=0 QUIT
            .SET dval=dval_0
            .DO putdisp
            ;
            SET newflag=0
            QUIT
            ;
GSTOper     ;process for operator key-clicks
            DO getkey
            IF key="C" DO clear QUIT
            IF key="CE" DO cleare QUIT
            IF key="=" DO equal QUIT
            DO oper
            QUIT
            ;
getkey      ;get keyclick title value
            SET key=$EVENT("ELEMENT")
            SET key=$PIECE(key,",",2)
            SET key=^$WINDOW("MPower","G",key,"TITLE")
            QUIT
            ;
clear       ;clear key
            SET dsign="",doper="C",dval=0,newflag=1
            SET msign="",moper="C",mval=0
            IF tapeon SET tapeval="0 C" DO puttape
            DO putdisp
            ;
cleare      ; clear entry
```

```
         SET dsign=msign,doper=moper,dval=mval DO putdisp
         SET newflag=1
         QUIT
         ;
oper     ;operator manipulation
         set moper=$SELECT(moper="C":"+",moper="=":"+".1:moper) ...
         ... DO calc IF $GET(zdflag) QUIT
         IF tapeon SET tapeval=dsign_dval_" "_$SELECT(moper="C":""...
         ...,moper="=":"",1:moper) DO puttape
         SET (mval,dval)=$EXTRACT(rval,1,15),(msign,dsign)=rsign
         SET (moper,doper)=key
         SET newflag=1
         DO putdisp
         QUIT
         ;
equal    QUIT:newflag
         SET nmoper=moper DO calc IF $GET(zdflag) QUIT
         IF tapeon DO
         .SET tapeval=dsign_dval_" "_moper DO puttape
         .SET tapeval=rsign_rval_" "_key DO puttape
         .SET tapeval="" DO puttape
         SET newflag=1
         QUIT
         ;
calc     ; calculate new values
         DO getdisp SET zdflag=0
         SET mem=$SELECT(msign=" ":"",1:msign)_mval
         SET disp=$SELECT(dsign=" ":"",1:dsign)_dval
         IF moper="/",(disp)=0 DO zdivide SET zdflag=1 QUIT
         SET result=msign_mval
         IF nmoper="+" SET result=mem+disp
         IF nmoper="-" SET result=mem-disp
         IF nmoper="*" SET result=mem*disp
         IF nmoper="/" SET result=mem/disp
         IF nmoper="=" SET result=disp
         SET rsign=$SELECT(result<0:"-",1:"")
         SET rval=$SELECT(result>0:+result,1:result*-1)
         QUIT
         ;
getdisp  ;get value in display
         SET old=^$WINDOW("MPower","G","TEXT1","VALUE")
         SET y=$LENGTH(old) FOR i=1:1:y QUIT:$EXTRACT(old)'=" "...
         ...SET old=$EXTRACT(old,2,y) ;strip leading spaces
         SET dsign=$EXTRACT(old) IF dsign'="+",(dsign'="-" ...
         ...SET dsign=" ",old=" "_old
         SET old=$EXTRACT(old,2,$LENGTH(old)
         SET doper=$EXTRACT(old,$LENGTH(old))
```

```
          SET dval=$EXTRACT(old,$LENGTH(old))
          SET dval=$EXTRACT(old,1,($LENGTH(old)-2))
          QUIT
          ;
putdisp   ;display value
          IF newflag,(dval'=0),(doper="C") SET doper=""
          IF newflag,(doper="=") SET doper=""
          SET xval=dsign_$EXTRACT(dval,1,15)_" "_$SELECT($LENGTH...
          ...(doper):doper,1:" ")
          SET ^$WINDOW("MPower","G","TEXT1","VALUE")=$JUSTIFY(xval,20)
          QUIT
          ;
tapebox   ;
          SET teapon=+$GET(^$WINDOW("MPower","G","CHECK1","VALUE"))
          SET tapeval="Tape "_$SELECT(Tapeon:"On",1:"Off") DO puttape
          QUIT
          ;
clrtape   ;
          KILL $WINDOW("MPower","G","LIST1","CHOICE")
          QUIT
          ;
puttape   ;
          NEW x
          SET x=$WINDOW(^$MPower","G","LIST1,"CHOICE","")
          SET x=x+1
          SET ^$WINDOW("MPower","G","LIST1,"CHOICE",x)=$JUSTIFY
          ...(tapeval,25)
          SET ^$WIDOW("MPower,"G","LIST1,"TOPSHOW")=x
          QUIT
          ;
zdivide   ;
          MERGE ^$WINDOW("zero")=^MPower("zero")
          QUIT
          ;
zdbut     ;
          KILL $^WINDOW("zero")
          DO cleare
          QUIT
          ;
notyet    ; callback for unimplemented features
          QUIT
          ;end of listing MPower
```

Gobal Variables Used to Generate ^ $WINDOW("MPower")

```
^MPower("MPower","G","BUTTON1","EVENT","SELECT")        GSTNum^MPower
```

```
^MPower("MPower","G","BUTTON1","POS")                    79,320,PIXEL
^MPower("MPower","G","BUTTON1","SIZE")                   39,41,PIXEL
^MPower("MPower","G","BUTTON1","TITLE")                  1
^MPower("MPower","G","BUTTON1","TYPE")                   BUTTON
^MPower("MPower","G","BUTTON10","EVENT","SELECT")        GSTNum^MPower
^MPower("MPower","G","BUTTON10","POS")                   129,369,PIXEL
^MPower("MPower","G","BUTTON10","SIZE")                  39,41,PIXEL
^MPower("MPower","G","BUTTON10","TITLE")                 0
^MPower("MPower","G","BUTTON10","TYPE")                  BUTTON
^MPower("MPower","G","BUTTON11","EVENT","SELECT")        GSTNum^MPower
^MPower("MPower","G","BUTTON11","POS")                   180,370,PIXEL
^MPower("MPower","G","BUTTON11","SIZE")                  39,41,PIXEL
^MPower("MPower","G","BUTTON11","TFSIZE")                25
^MPower("MPower","G","BUTTON11","TITLE")                 .
^MPower("MPower","G","BUTTON11","TYPE")                  BUTTON
^MPower("MPower","G","BUTTON12","EVENT","SELECT")        GSTOper^MPower
^MPower("MPower","G","BUTTON12,"POS")                    281,221,PIXEL
^MPower("MPower","G","BUTTON12,"SIZE")                   39,41,PIXEL
^MPower("MPower","G","BUTTON12","TITLE")                 /
^MPower("MPower","G","BUTTON12,"TYPE")                   BUTTON
^MPower("MPower","G","BUTTON13,"EVENT","SELECT")         GSTOper^MPower
^MPower("MPower","G","BUTTON13,"POS")                    280,272,PIXEL
^MPower("MPower","G","BUTTON13,"SIZE")                   39,41,PIXEL
^MPower("MPower","G","BUTTON13,"TITLE")                  *
^MPower("MPower","G","BUTTON13,"TYPE")                   BUTTON
^MPower("MPower","G","BUTTON14","EVENT,"SELECT")         GSTOper^MPower
^MPower("MPower","G","BUTTON14,"POS")                    280,320,PIXEL
^MPower("MPower","G","BUTTON14","SIZE")                  39,41,PIXEL
^MPower("MPower","G","BUTTON14","TITLE")                 +
^MPower("MPower","G","BUTTON14","TYPE")                  BUTTON
^MPower("MPower","G","BUTTON14","EVENT,"SELECT")         GSTOper^MPower
^MPower("MPower","G","BUTTON15,"POS")                    281,373,PIXEL
^MPower("MPower","G","BUTTON15","SIZE")                  39,41,PIXEL
^MPower("MPower","G","BUTTON15","TFSIZE")                25
^MPower("MPower","G","BUTTON15","TITLE")                 -
^MPower("MPower","G","BUTTON16","TYPE")                  BUTTON
^MPower("MPower","G","BUTTON16","EVENT,"SELECT")         GSTOper^MPower
^MPower("MPower","G","BUTTON16,"POS")                    332,219,PIXEL
^MPower("MPower","G","BUTTON16","SIZE")                  39,41,PIXEL
^MPower("MPower","G","BUTTON16","TITLE")                 C
^MPower("MPower","G","BUTTON16","TYPE")                  BUTTON
^MPower("MPower","G","BUTTON17","EVENT,"SELECT")         GSTOper^MPower
^MPower("MPower","G","BUTTON17,"POS")                    332,271,PIXEL
^MPower("MPower","G","BUTTON17","SIZE")                  39,41,PIXEL
^MPower("MPower","G","BUTTON17","TITLE")                 CE
^MPower("MPower","G","BUTTON17","TYPE")                  BUTTON
^MPower("MPower","G","BUTTON18","EVENT,"SELECT")         GSTOper^MPower
```

```
^MPower("MPower","G","BUTTON18,"POS")                    333,319,PIXEL
^MPower("MPower","G","BUTTON18","SIZE")                  39,41,PIXEL
^MPower("MPower","G","BUTTON18,"TFSIZE")                 25
^MPower("MPower","G","BUTTON18","TITLE")                 =
^MPower("MPower","G","BUTTON18","TYPE")                  BUTTON
^MPower("MPower","G","BUTTON19,"EVENT,"SELECT")          GSTNum^MPower
^MPower("MPower","G","BUTTON19"POS")                     81,370,PIXEL
^MPower("MPower","G","BUTTON19,"SIZE")                   39,41,PIXEL
^MPower("MPower","G","BUTTON19,"TITLE")                  + / -
^MPower("MPower","G","BUTTON19,"TYPE")                   BUTTON
^MPower("MPower","G","BUTTON2","EVENT","SELECT")         GSTNum^MPower
^MPower("MPower","G","BUTTON2","POS")                    131,321,PIXEL
^MPower("MPower","G","BUTTON2","SIZE")                   39,41,PIXEL
^MPower("MPower","G","BUTTON2","TITLE")                  2
^MPower("MPower","G","BUTTON2","TYPE")                   BUTTON
^MPower("MPower","G","BUTTON3","EVENT","SELECT")         GSTNum^MPower
^MPower("MPower","G","BUTTON3","POS")                    180,319,PIXEL
^MPower("MPower","G","BUTTON3","SIZE")                   39,41,PIXEL
^MPower("MPower","G","BUTTON3","TITLE")                  3
^MPower("MPower","G","BUTTON3","TYPE")                   BUTTON
^MPower("MPower","G","BUTTON4","EVENT","SELECT")         GSTNum^MPower
^MPower("MPower","G","BUTTON4","POS")                    81,269,PIXEL
^MPower("MPower","G","BUTTON4","SIZE")                   39,41,PIXEL
^MPower("MPower","G","BUTTON4","TITLE")                  4
^MPower("MPower","G","BUTTON4","TYPE")                   BUTTON
^MPower("MPower","G","BUTTON5","EVENT","SELECT")         GSTNum^MPower
^MPower("MPower","G","BUTTON5","POS")                    129,270,PIXEL
^MPower("MPower","G","BUTTON5","SIZE")                   39,41,PIXEL
^MPower("MPower","G","BUTTON5","TITLE")                  5
^MPower("MPower","G","BUTTON5","TYPE")                   BUTTON
^MPower("MPower","G","BUTTON6","EVENT","SELECT")         GSTNum^MPower
^MPower("MPower","G","BUTTON6","POS")                    179,272,PIXEL
^MPower("MPower","G","BUTTON6","SIZE")                   39,41,PIXEL
^MPower("MPower","G","BUTTON6","TITLE")                  6
^MPower("MPower","G","BUTTON6","TYPE")                   BUTTON
^MPower("MPower","G","BUTTON7","EVENT","SELECT")         GSTNum^MPower
^MPower("MPower","G","BUTTON7","POS")                    82,220,PIXEL
^MPower("MPower","G","BUTTON7","SIZE")                   39,41,PIXEL
^MPower("MPower","G","BUTTON7","TITLE")                  7
^MPower("MPower","G","BUTTON7","TYPE")                   BUTTON
^MPower("MPower","G","BUTTON8","EVENT","SELECT")         GSTNum^MPower
^MPower("MPower","G","BUTTON8","POS")                    129,221,PIXEL
^MPower("MPower","G","BUTTON8","SIZE")                   39,41,PIXEL
^MPower("MPower","G","BUTTON8","TITLE")                  8
^MPower("MPower","G","BUTTON8","TYPE")                   BUTTON
^MPower("MPower","G","BUTTON9","EVENT","SELECT")         GSTNum^MPower
^MPower("MPower","G","BUTTON9","POS")                    179,221,PIXEL
```

```
^MPower("MPower","G","BUTTON9","SIZE")                      39,41,PIXEL
^MPower("MPower","G","BUTTON9","TITLE")                     9
^MPower("MPower","G","BUTTON9","TYPE")                      BUTTON
^MPower("MPower","G","CHECK1","EVENT","SELECT")             tapebox^MPower
^MPower("MPower","G","CHECK1","EVENT","DESELECT")           tapebox^MPower
^MPower("MPower","G","CHECK1","POS")                        69,119,PIXRL
^MPower("MPower","G","CHECK1","SIZE")                       20,22,PIXEL
^MPower("MPower","G","CHECK1","TITLE")
^MPower("MPower","G","CHECK1","TYPE")                       CHECK
^MPower("MPower","G","LABEL1","FCOLOR")                     30,30,30
^MPower("MPower","G","LABEL1","POS")                        92,110,PIXEL
^MPower("MPower","G","LABEL1","SIZE")                       38,16,PIXEL
^MPower("MPower","G","LABEL1","TITLE")                      Tape
^MPower("MPower","G","LABEL1","TYPE")                       LABEL
^MPower("MPower","G","LABEL2","POS")                        92,132,PIXEL
^MPower("MPower","G","LABEL2","SIZE")                       168,123,PIXEL
^MPower("MPower","G","LABEL2","TITLE")                      Tape
^MPower("MPower","G","LABEL23","TYPE")                      LABEL
^MPower("MPower","G","LIST1","CHOICE")
^MPower("MPower","G","LIST1","POS")                         149,31,PIXEL
^MPower("MPower","G","LIST1","SIZE")                        168,123,PIXEL
^MPower("MPower","G","LIST1","TITLE")
^MPower("MPower","G","LIST1","TYPE")                        LIST
^MPower("MPower","G","RADIO1","CHOICE")
^MPower("MPower","G","RADIO1","CHOICE",64)                  On
^MPower("MPower","G","RADIO1","CHOICE",64,"ACTIVE")         1
^MPower("MPower","G","RADIO1","CHOICE",96)                  Off
^MPower("MPower","G","RADIO1","CHOICE",96,"ACTIVE")         1
^MPower("MPower","G","RADIO1","EVENT","DESELECT")           GSTOff^MPower
^MPower("MPower","G","RADIO1","EVENT","SELECT")             GSTOff^MPower
^MPower("MPower","G","RADIO1","FCOLOR")                     0,0,0
^MPower("MPower","G","RADIO1","POS")                        335,106,PIXEL
^MPower("MPower","G","RADIO1","SIZE")                       65,48,PIXEL
^MPower("MPower","G","RADIO1","TITLE")
^MPower("MPower","G","RADIO1","TYPE")                       RADIO
^MPower("MPower","G","RADIO1","VALUE")                      64
^MPower("MPower","G","TEXT1","FFACE")                       SYSTEM
^MPower("MPower","G","TEXT1","FSIZE")                       20
^MPower("MPower","G","TEXT1","POS")                         85,173,PIXEL
^MPower("MPower","G","TEXT1","SIZE")                        296,34,PIXEL
^MPower("MPower","G","TEXT1","TITLE")
^MPower("MPower","G","TEXT1","TYPE")                        TEXT
^MPower("MPower","G","TEXT1","UNITS"                        CHAR
^MPower("MPower","G","zFRAME1","POS")                       23,71,PIXEL
^MPower("MPower","G","zFRAME1","SIZE")                      398,360,PIXEL
^MPower("MPower","G","zFRAME1","TITLE")
^MPower("MPower","G","zFRAME1","TYPE")                      FRAME
```

```
^MPower("MPower","M","File","CHOICE",1)                        &Quit
^MPower("MPower","M","File","CHOICE",1,"ACTIVE")               1
^MPower("MPower","M","File","CHOICE",1,"EVENT","SELECT") notyet^MPower
^MPower("MPower","M","File","CHOICE",1,"EVENT","SELECT","ENABLE") 1
^MPower("MPower","M","File","ID")                              17
^MPower("MPower","M","File","UNITS")                           PIXEL
^MPower("MPower","M","File","VISIBLE"
^MPower("MPower","M","Help","CHOICE",1)                        &About Calculator
^MPower("MPower","M","Help","CHOICE",1,"ACTIVE")               1
^MPower("MPower","M","Help","CHOICE",1,"EVENT","SELECT") notyet^MPower
^MPower("MPower","M","Help","CHOICE",1,"EVENT","SELECT","ENABLE")  1
^MPower("MPower","M","Help","ID")                              18
^MPower("MPower","M","Help","UNITS")                           PIXEL
^MPower("MPower","M","Options","CHOICE",1)                     &Binary
^MPower("MPower","M","Options","CHOICE",1,"ACTIVE")            1
^MPower("MPower","M","Options","CHOICE",1,"EVENT","SELECT")notyet^MPower
^MPower("MPower","M","Options","CHOICE",1,"EVENT","SELECT","ENABLE")  1
^MPower("MPower","M","Options","ID")
^MPower("MPower","M","Options","UNITS")                        PIXEL
^MPower("MPower","M","Options","VISIBLE")
^MPower("MPower","M","MAIN","CHOICE",1)                        &File
^MPower("MPower","M","MAIN","CHOICE",1,"ACTIVE")               1
^MPower("MPower","M","MAIN","CHOICE",1,"SUBMENU")              File
^MPower("MPower","M","MAIN","CHOICE",2)                        &Options
^MPower("MPower","M","MAIN","CHOICE",2,"ACTIVE")               1
^MPower("MPower","M","MAIN","CHOICE",2,"SUBMENU")              Options
^MPower("MPower","M","MAIN","CHOICE",3)                        &Help
^MPower("MPower","M","MAIN","CHOICE",3,"ACTIVE")               1
^MPower("MPower","M","MAIN","CHOICE",3,"SUBMENU")              Help
^MPower("MPower","MENUBAR")                                    Main
^MPower("MPower","POS")                                        137,0,PIXEL
^MPower("MPower","SIZE")                                       468,431,PIXEL
^MPower("MPower","SIZEMIN")
^MPower("MPower","SIZEWIN")                                    476,477,PIXEL
^MPower("MPower","TITLE")                                      MPower Calculator
^MPower("MPower","TYPE")                                       APPLICATION
^MPower("zero","G","BUTTON 1","EVENT","SELECT")                zdbut^MPower
^MPower("zero","G","BUTTON 1","POS")                           121,79,PIXEL
^MPower("zero","G","BUTTON 1","SIZE")                          80,40,PIXEL
^MPower("zero","G","BUTTON 1","TITLE"                          O.K.
^MPower("zero","G","BUTTON 1","TYPE")                          BUTTON
^MPower("zero","G","LABEL 1","POS")                            84,29,PIXEL
^MPower("zero","G","LABEL 1","SIZE")                           170,20,PIXEL
^MPower("zero","G","LABEL 1","TFSIZE")                         10
^MPower("zero","G","LABEL 1","TITLE")                          Cannot Divide by Zero
^MPower("zero","G","LABEL 1","TYPE")                           LABEL
^MPower("zero","G","SYMBOL 1","POS")                           41,21,PIXEL
```

```
^MPower("zero","G","SYMBOL 1","RESOURCE")          M.WARN
^MPower("zero","G","SYMBOL 1","TYPE")              SYMBOL
^MPower("zero","POS")                              183,166,PIXEL
^MPower("zero","SIZE")                             319,153,PIXEL
^MPower("zero","SIZEMIN")
^MPower("zero","SIZEWIN")                          327,180,PIXEL
^MPower("zero","TITLE")                            WARNING !!!
^MPower("zero","TYPE")                             APPLICATION
```

Appendix B: RPG Calculator Using M and Visual BASIC

The code for the RPG calculator follows. This is the actual Visual Basic form file RPG.FRM: the M code is toward the bottom.

```
VERSION 4.00
Begin VB.Form CALC
   Caption         =   "RPG  CALCULATOR"
   ClientHeight    =   6585
   ClientLeft      =   1695
   ClientTop       =   1755
   ClientWidth     =   8610
   Height          =   6990
   KeyPreview      =   -1  'True
   Left            =   1635
   LinkTopic       =   "Form1"
   ScaleHeight     =   6585
   ScaleWidth      =   8610
   Top             =   1410
   Width           =   8730
   Begin VB.CommandButton cmdENTER
      Caption         =   " E N T E R"
      Default         =   -1  'True
      BeginProperty Font
         name            =   "Arial"
         charset         =   0
         weight          =   700
         size            =   11.25
         underline       =   0   'False
```

```
      italic        =  0   'False
      strikethrough =  0   'False
   EndProperty
   Height      =  615
   Left        =  3000
   TabIndex    =  34
   Top         =  5280
   Width       =  1455
End
Begin VB.TextBox txtGVN
   BeginProperty Font
      name          =  "Arial"
      charset       =  1
      weight        =  400
      size          =  12
      underline     =  0   'False
      italic        =  0   'False
      strikethrough =  0   'False
   EndProperty
   Height      =  390
   Left        =  4920
   TabIndex    =  32
   Text        =  "^RPG("
   Top         =  240
   Width       =  2055
End
Begin VB.CommandButton cmdRCL
   Caption          =  "&RCL"
   BeginProperty Font
      name          =  "Arial"
      charset       =  1
      weight        =  700
      size          =  11.25
      underline     =  0   'False
      italic        =  0   'False
      strikethrough =  0   'False
   EndProperty
   Height      =  615
   Index       =  0
   Left        =  2160
   TabIndex    =  31
   Top         =  5280
   Width       =  615
End
Begin VB.CommandButton cmdSTO
   Caption    =  "&STO"
   BeginProperty Font
```

```
         name          =   "Arial"
         charset       =   1
         weight        =   700
         size          =   9.75
         underline     =   0   'False
         italic        =   0   'False
         strikethrough =   0   'False
      EndProperty
      Height      =   615
      Index       =   0
      Left        =   1320
      TabIndex    =   30
      Top         =   5280
      Width       =   615
   End
   Begin VB.CheckBox chkSHOW
      Caption     =   "Show Upper Registers"
      Height      =   495
      Left        =   840
      TabIndex    =   29
      Top         =   120
      Width       =   1815
   End
   Begin VB.CommandButton cmdCLEAR
      Caption     =   "Clear All Registers"
      BeginProperty Font
         name     =   "Arial"
         charset  =   1
         weight   =   700
         size     =   9.75
         underline=   0   'False
         italic   =   0   'False
         strikethrough=   0   'False
      EndProperty
      Height      =   615
      Left        =   840
      TabIndex    =   24
      Top         =   840
      Width       =   1455
   End
   Begin VB.CommandButton cmdEXP
      Caption     =   "Y^X"
      BeginProperty Font
         name     =   "Arial"
         charset  =   1
         weight   =   700
         size     =   11.25
```

```
            underline     =   0   'False
            italic        =   0   'False
            strikethrough =   0   'False
         EndProperty
         Height       =   615
         Left         =   480
         TabIndex     =   23
         Top          =   5280
         Width        =   615
      End
      Begin VB.CommandButton cmdROLLDOWN
         Caption      =   "ROLL &DOWN"
         Height       =   615
         Left         =   480
         TabIndex     =   22
         Top          =   4560
         Width        =   615
      End
      Begin VB.TextBox txtT
         Alignment        =   1  'Right Justify
         BeginProperty Font
            name          =   "Arial"
            charset       =   1
            weight        =   700
            size          =   15.75
            underline     =   0   'False
            italic        =   0   'False
            strikethrough =   0   'False
         EndProperty
         Height       =   480
         Left         =   4200
         TabIndex     =   21
         TabStop      =   0   'False
         Top          =   960
         Visible      =   0   'False
         Width        =   3855
      End
      Begin VB.TextBox txtZ
         BeginProperty Font
            name          =   "Arial"
            charset       =   1
            weight        =   700
            size          =   15.75
            underline     =   0   'False
            italic        =   0   'False
            strikethrough =   0   'False
         EndProperty
```

```
      Height       =   480
      Left         =   4200
      TabIndex     =   20
      TabStop      =   0   'False
      Top          =   1440
      Visible      =   0   'False
      Width        =   3855
   End
   Begin VB.TextBox txtY
      BeginProperty Font
         name          =   "Arial"
         charset       =   1
         weight        =   700
         size          =   15.75
         underline     =   0   'False
         italic        =   0   'False
         strikethrough =   0   'False
      EndProperty
      Height       =   480
      Left         =   4200
      TabIndex     =   19
      TabStop      =   0   'False
      Top          =   1920
      Visible      =   0   'False
      Width        =   3855
   End
   Begin VBX.MVB MVB
      Code         =   ""
      ExecFlag     =   0  'Quiescent
      Interval     =   1000
      Left         =   120
      NameSpace    =   ""
      P0           =   ""
      P1           =   ""
      P2           =   ""
      P3           =   ""
      P4           =   ""
      P5           =   ""
      P6           =   ""
      P7           =   ""
      P8           =   ""
      P9           =   ""
      PLIST        =   ""
      TimeOut      =   20000
      Top          =   1440
      VALUE        =   ""
   End
```

```
Begin VB.CommandButton cmdPLUS
   Caption          =   "+"
   BeginProperty Font
      name          =   "Arial"
      charset       =   1
      weight        =   700
      size          =   15.75
      underline     =   0   'False
      italic        =   0   'False
      strikethrough =   0   'False
   EndProperty
   Height      =   615
   Index       =   1
   Left        =   7440
   TabIndex    =   18
   Top         =   5520
   Width       =   615
End
Begin VB.CommandButton cmdMINUS
   Caption          =   "-"
   BeginProperty Font
      name          =   "Arial"
      charset       =   1
      weight        =   700
      size          =   15.75
      underline     =   0   'False
      italic        =   0   'False
      strikethrough =   0   'False
   EndProperty
   Height      =   615
   Index       =   2
   Left        =   7440
   TabIndex    =   17
   Top         =   4800
   Width       =   615
End
Begin VB.CommandButton cmdMULT
   Caption          =   "*"
   BeginProperty Font
      name          =   "Arial"
      charset       =   1
      weight        =   700
      size          =   15.75
      underline     =   0   'False
      italic        =   0   'False
      strikethrough =   0   'False
   EndProperty
```

```
      Height      =   615
      Index       =   3
      Left        =   7440
      TabIndex    =   16
      Top         =   4080
      Width       =   615
   End
   Begin VB.CommandButton cmdSIGN
      Caption          =   "&CHS"
      BeginProperty Font
         name          =   "Arial"
         charset       =   1
         weight        =   700
         size          =   9.75
         underline     =   0   'False
         italic        =   0   'False
         strikethrough =   0   'False
      EndProperty
      Height      =   615
      Index       =   1
      Left        =   4080
      TabIndex    =   15
      Top         =   3360
      Width       =   615
   End
   Begin VB.CommandButton cmdCLX
      Caption          =   "CL&X"
      BeginProperty Font
         name          =   "Arial"
         charset       =   1
         weight        =   700
         size          =   11.25
         underline     =   0   'False
         italic        =   0   'False
         strikethrough =   0   'False
      EndProperty
      Height      =   615
      Index       =   2
      Left        =   2160
      TabIndex    =   14
      Top         =   4560
      Width       =   615
   End
   Begin VB.CommandButton cmdDIV
      Caption          =   "/"
      BeginProperty Font
         name          =   "Arial"
```

```
         charset       =  1
         weight        =  700
         size          =  15.75
         underline     =  0   'False
         italic        =  0   'False
         strikethrough =  0   'False
      EndProperty
      Height        =  615
      Index         =  3
      Left          =  7440
      TabIndex      =  13
      Top           =  3360
      Width         =  615
   End
   Begin VB.CommandButton cmdPLUSMINUS
      Caption           =  "X-Y"
      BeginProperty Font
         name          =  "Arial"
         charset       =  1
         weight        =  700
         size          =  11.25
         underline     =  0   'False
         italic        =  0   'False
         strikethrough =  0   'False
      EndProperty
      Height        =  615
      Index         =  1
      Left          =  1320
      TabIndex      =  12
      Top           =  4560
      Width         =  615
   End
   Begin VB.CommandButton cmdPERIOD
      Caption           =  "."
      BeginProperty Font
         name          =  "Arial"
         charset       =  1
         weight        =  700
         size          =  15.75
         underline     =  0   'False
         italic        =  0   'False
         strikethrough =  0   'False
      EndProperty
      Height        =  615
      Index         =  2
      Left          =  5640
      TabIndex      =  11
```

```
      Top          =   5520
      Width        =   615
   End
   Begin VB.CommandButton cmd9
      Caption          =   "9"
      BeginProperty Font
         name            =   "Arial"
         charset         =   1
         weight          =   700
         size            =   15.75
         underline       =   0   'False
         italic          =   0   'False
         strikethrough   =   0   'False
      EndProperty
      Height       =   615
      Index        =   9
      Left         =   6360
      TabIndex     =   10
      Top          =   3360
      Width        =   615
   End
   Begin VB.CommandButton cmd8
      Caption          =   "8"
      BeginProperty Font
         name            =   "Arial"
         charset         =   1
         weight          =   700
         size            =   15.75
         underline       =   0   'False
         italic          =   0   'False
         strikethrough   =   0   'False
      EndProperty
      Height       =   615
      Index        =   8
      Left         =   5640
      TabIndex     =   9
      Top          =   3360
      Width        =   615
   End
   Begin VB.CommandButton cmd7
      Caption          =   "7"
      BeginProperty Font
         name            =   "Arial"
         charset         =   1
         weight          =   700
         size            =   15.75
         underline       =   0   'False
```

```
      italic        =   0   'False
      strikethrough =   0   'False
   EndProperty
   Height       =   615
   Index        =   7
   Left         =   4920
   TabIndex     =   8
   Top          =   3360
   Width        =   615
End
Begin VB.CommandButton cmd6
   Caption          =   "6"
   BeginProperty Font
      name          =   "Arial"
      charset       =   1
      weight        =   700
      size          =   15.75
      underline     =   0   'False
      italic        =   0   'False
      strikethrough =   0   'False
   EndProperty
   Height       =   615
   Index        =   6
   Left         =   6360
   TabIndex     =   7
   Top          =   4080
   Width        =   615
End
Begin VB.CommandButton cmd5
   Caption          =   "5"
   BeginProperty Font
      name          =   "Arial"
      charset       =   1
      weight        =   700
      size          =   15.75
      underline     =   0   'False
      italic        =   0   'False
      strikethrough =   0   'False
   EndProperty
   Height       =   615
   Index        =   5
   Left         =   5640
   TabIndex     =   6
   Top          =   4080
   Width        =   615
End
Begin VB.CommandButton cmd4
```

```
      Caption          =   "4"
      BeginProperty Font
         name          =   "Arial"
         charset       =   1
         weight        =   700
         size          =   15.75
         underline     =   0   'False
         italic        =   0   'False
         strikethrough =   0   'False
      EndProperty
      Height      =   615
      Index       =   4
      Left        =   4920
      TabIndex    =   5
      Top         =   4080
      Width       =   615
   End
   Begin VB.CommandButton cmd3
      Caption          =   "3"
      BeginProperty Font
         name          =   "Arial"
         charset       =   1
         weight        =   700
         size          =   15.75
         underline     =   0   'False
         italic        =   0   'False
         strikethrough =   0   'False
      EndProperty
      Height      =   615
      Index       =   3
      Left        =   6360
      TabIndex    =   4
      Top         =   4800
      Width       =   615
   End
   Begin VB.CommandButton cmd1
      Caption          =   "1"
      BeginProperty Font
         name          =   "Arial"
         charset       =   1
         weight        =   700
         size          =   15.75
         underline     =   0   'False
         italic        =   0   'False
         strikethrough =   0   'False
      EndProperty
      Height      =   615
```

```
      Index        =   1
      Left         =   4920
      TabIndex     =   3
      Top          =   4800
      Width        =   615
   End
   Begin VB.CommandButton cmd0
      Caption           =   "0"
      BeginProperty Font
         name           =   "Arial"
         charset        =   1
         weight         =   700
         size           =   15.75
         underline      =   0   'False
         italic         =   0   'False
         strikethrough =   0   'False
      EndProperty
      Height       =   615
      Index        =   0
      Left         =   4920
      TabIndex     =   2
      Top          =   5520
      Width        =   615
   End
   Begin VB.CommandButton cmd2
      Caption           =   "2"
      BeginProperty Font
         name           =   "Arial"
         charset        =   1
         weight         =   700
         size           =   15.75
         underline      =   0   'False
         italic         =   0   'False
         strikethrough =   0   'False
      EndProperty
      Height       =   615
      Index        =   2
      Left         =   5640
      TabIndex     =   1
      Top          =   4800
      Width        =   615
   End
   Begin VB.TextBox txtX
      Alignment         =   1  'Right Justify
      BeginProperty Font
         name           =   "Arial"
         charset        =   1
```

```
      weight       =   700
      size         =   15.75
      underline    =   0   'False
      italic       =   0   'False
      strikethrough =  0   'False
   EndProperty
   Height       =   480
   Left         =   4200
   TabIndex     =   0
   TabStop      =   0   'False
   Top          =   2400
   Width        =   3855
End
Begin VB.Label Label5
   Alignment    =   1  'Right Justify
   Caption      =   "Mumps Global to use for Memory Operations"
   Height       =   375
   Left         =   2640
   TabIndex     =   33
   Top          =   240
   Width        =   2175
End
Begin VB.Label Label4
   Alignment         =   1  'Right Justify
   Caption           =   "t"
   BeginProperty Font
      name           =   "Times New Roman"
      charset        =   1
      weight         =   700
      size           =   14.25
      underline      =   0   'False
      italic         =   0   'False
      strikethrough =  0   'False
   EndProperty
   Height       =   375
   Left         =   3720
   TabIndex     =   28
   Top          =   1080
   Visible      =   0   'False
   Width        =   255
End
Begin VB.Label Label3
   Alignment         =   1  'Right Justify
   Caption           =   "Z"
   BeginProperty Font
      name           =   "Times New Roman"
      charset        =   1
```

```
      weight        =  700
      size          =  14.25
      underline     =  0   'False
      italic        =  0   'False
      strikethrough =  0   'False
   EndProperty
   Height      =  375
   Left        =  3600
   TabIndex    =  27
   Top         =  1560
   Visible     =  0   'False
   Width       =  375
End
Begin VB.Label Label2
   Alignment        =  1  'Right Justify
   Caption          =  "Y"
   BeginProperty Font
      name          =  "Times New Roman"
      charset       =  1
      weight        =  700
      size          =  14.25
      underline     =  0   'False
      italic        =  0   'False
      strikethrough =  0   'False
   EndProperty
   Height      =  375
   Left        =  3600
   TabIndex    =  26
   Top         =  2040
   Visible     =  0   'False
   Width       =  375
End
Begin VB.Label Label1
   Alignment        =  1  'Right Justify
   Caption          =  "X"
   BeginProperty Font
      name          =  "Times New Roman"
      charset       =  1
      weight        =  700
      size          =  14.25
      underline     =  0   'False
      italic        =  0   'False
      strikethrough =  0   'False
   EndProperty
   Height      =  375
   Left        =  3600
   TabIndex    =  25
```

```
         Top          =   2520
         Visible      =   0    'False
         Width        =   375
      End
   End
   Attribute VB_Name = "CALC"
   Attribute VB_Creatable = False
   Attribute VB_Exposed = False
   Option Explicit
   Dim NEWFLAG As Boolean  'next numeric keystroke is a new number
   Dim RAISE As Boolean    'raise stack before entering number
   Dim MEM As Integer      'memory operation in progress
   Dim TEMP As String
   Private Sub DropStack()
       txtY = txtZ
       txtZ = txtT
       NEWFLAG = True
   End Sub
   Private Sub FuncKeyHit(KEY As String)
       MEM = 0         'cancel memory op, expecting a number
    Select Case KEY
       Case "+"
           MVB.P1 = txtX
           MVB.P2 = txtY
           MVB.Code = "S P0=P1+P2"
           MVB.ExecFlag = 1
           txtX = MVB.P0
       Case "-"
           txtX = txtY - txtX
       Case "/"
           If txtX = 0 Then
               MsgBox "Divide by Zero"
               Exit Sub
           End If
           txtX = txtY / txtX
       Case "*"
           txtX = txtY * txtX
       Case Else
           Exit Sub
       End Select
       DropStack
       NEWFLAG = True
       RAISE = True
   End Sub
   Private Sub NumPress(KEY As String)
       If MEM = 1 Then 'store X register in ^GVN(KEY)
           MEM = 0
```

```
            MVB.P1 = txtGVN & KEY & ")"
            MVB.P2 = txtX
            MVB.Code = "S @P1=P2"
            MVB.ExecFlag = 1
            cmdENTER.SetFocus
            Exit Sub
        End If
        If MEM = 2 Then 'recall ^GVN(KEY), put in X register
            MEM = 0
            MVB.P1 = txtGVN & KEY & ")"
            MVB.Code = "S P2=$g(@P1)"
            MVB.ExecFlag = 1
            txtX = MVB.P2
            cmdENTER.SetFocus
            Exit Sub
        End If
        If NEWFLAG Then
            If RAISE = True Then RAISESTACK
            txtX = KEY
        Else
            txtX = txtX & KEY
        End If
        RAISE = False
        NEWFLAG = False
        cmdENTER.SetFocus
    End Sub
    Private Sub RAISESTACK()
        txtT = txtZ
        txtZ = txtY
        txtY = txtX
    End Sub
    Private Sub chkHIDE_Click()
        MEM = 0
        If chkHIDE Then
            txtY.Visible = 0
            txtZ.Visible = 0
            txtT.Visible = 0
            Label4.Visible = 0
            Label3.Visible = 0
            Label2.Visible = 0
        Else
            txtY.Visible = 1
            txtZ.Visible = 1
            txtT.Visible = 1
            Label4.Visible = 1
            Label3.Visible = 1
            Label2.Visible = 1
```

```
    End If
End Sub
Private Sub chkSHOW_Click()
    MEM = 0
    If chkSHOW Then
        Label1.Visible = 1
        Label2.Visible = 1
        Label3.Visible = 1
        Label4.Visible = 1
        txtT.Visible = 1
        txtZ.Visible = 1
        txtY.Visible = 1
    Else
        Label1.Visible = 0
        Label2.Visible = 0
        Label3.Visible = 0
        Label4.Visible = 0
        txtT.Visible = 0
        txtZ.Visible = 0
        txtY.Visible = 0
    End If
End Sub
Private Sub cmd0_Click(Index As Integer)
    NumPress (0)
End Sub
Private Sub cmd1_Click(Index As Integer)
    NumPress (1)
End Sub
Private Sub cmd2_Click(Index As Integer)
    NumPress (2)
End Sub
Private Sub cmd3_Click(Index As Integer)
    NumPress (3)
End Sub
Private Sub cmd4_Click(Index As Integer)
    NumPress (4)
End Sub
Private Sub cmd5_Click(Index As Integer)
    NumPress (5)
End Sub
Private Sub cmd6_Click(Index As Integer)
    NumPress (6)
End Sub
Private Sub cmd7_Click(Index As Integer)
    NumPress (7)
End Sub
Private Sub cmd8_Click(Index As Integer)
```

```
    NumPress (8)
End Sub
Private Sub cmd9_Click(Index As Integer)
    NumPress (9)
End Sub
Private Sub cmdCE_Click(Index As Integer)
End Sub
Private Sub cmdCLEAR_Click()
    MEM     = 0
    txtX    = 0
    txtY    = 0
    txtZ    = 0
    txtT    = 0
    NEWFLAG = 0
    RAISE   = 0
End Sub
Private Sub cmdCLX_Click(Index As Integer)
    txtX    = 0
    NEWFLAG = 1
End Sub

Private Sub cmdDIV_Click(Index As Integer)
        FuncKeyHit ("/")
 End Sub

Private Sub cmdENTER_Click()
    MEM = 0
    If txtX = "." Then Exit Sub
    txtT = txtZ
    txtZ = txtY
    txtY = txtX
    NEWFLAG = True
    RAISE = False
End Sub
Private Sub cmdEXP_Click()
    MEM = 0
    If txtX = 0 And txtY = 0 Then
        MsgBox "Exponeniation Error"
        Exit Sub
    End If
    MVB.P0 = txtY
    MVB.P1 = txtX
    MVB.Code = "S P2=P0**P1"
    MVB.ExecFlag = 1
    DropStack
    txtX = MVB.P2
    RAISE = True
```

```
    NEWFLAG = True
End Sub
Private Sub cmdMINUS_Click(Index As Integer)
    FuncKeyHit ("-")
End Sub
Private Sub cmdMULT_Click(Index As Integer)
    FuncKeyHit ("*")
End Sub
Private Sub cmdPERIOD_Click(Index As Integer)
    MEM = 0
'allow decimal point only if there is NOT one
    If RAISE Then RAISESTACK
    If NEWFLAG Then txtX = "."
    MVB.P1 = txtX
    MVB.Code = "I P1'[""."" S P1=P1_""."""
    MVB.ExecFlag = 1
    txtX = MVB.P1
    RAISE = False
    NEWFLAG = False
End Sub
Private Sub cmdPLUS_Click(Index As Integer)
    FuncKeyHit ("+")
End Sub
Private Sub cmdPLUSMINUS_Click(Index As Integer)
    MEM = 0
    TEMP = txtX
    txtX = txtY
    txtY = TEMP
End Sub
Private Sub cmdRCL_Click(Index As Integer)
    MEM = 2  'begin a memory RECALL operation
End Sub
Private Sub cmdROLLDOWN_Click()
    MEM = 0
    TEMP = txtX
    txtX = txtY
    txtY = txtZ
    txtZ = txtT
    txtT = TEMP
End Sub
Private Sub cmdSIGN_Click(Index As Integer)
    MEM = 0
    txtX = txtX * -1
End Sub
Private Sub cmdSTO_Click(Index As Integer)
    MEM = 1  'begin a memory STORE operation
End Sub
```

```
Private Sub Form_KeyDown(KeyCode As Integer, Shift As Integer)
    If KeyCode = 13 Then
        KeyCode = 0
        cmdENTER_Click
    End If
End Sub
Private Sub Form_KeyPress(KeyAscii As Integer)
    If KeyAscii >= 48 And KeyAscii <= 57 Then
        NumPress (KeyAscii - 48)
    End If
    If KeyAscii = 46 Then cmdPERIOD_Click (0)
    If KeyAscii = 47 Then cmdDIV_Click (0)
    If KeyAscii = 42 Then cmdMULT_Click (0)
    If KeyAscii = 43 Then cmdPLUS_Click (0)
    If KeyAscii = 45 Then cmdMINUS_Click (0)
End Sub
Private Sub Form_Load()
    MEM  = 0
    txtX = 0
    txtY = 0
    txtZ = 0
    txtT = 0
    NEWFLAG = True
End Sub
```

Error Handling in M

24

Overview

I once read a text on numerical analysis that began "there are errors, and there are blunders; this book is concerned with the former." Unfortunately, life is not quite that simple in programming. There are indeed errors (e.g., relating to precision of calculations) that occur in computation, and there are blunders relating to improper syntax and incorrectly entered data. But there are also many other inappropriate conditions that arise in dealing with programs operating on databases, large and small. Logical inconsistencies, a data element that does not fall into the expected pattern, an unexpected conflict in the requirements of two users, a system not available when needed – these and many other problems arise to haunt the programmer. And, true to Murphy's law, they usually arise at the most unwanted times when deadlines must be met or dire consequences will result.

Most programming languages do not provide much in the way of support for these kinds of problems. Solving them usually involves artificial subterfuges, such as putting in temporary debug statements to write out the contents of certain variables or otherwise determine, somehow, what is going wrong. M is different in this respect. Chapter 17 describes the use of the BREAK command in M, which enables users to put in break points as a means of examining the state of affairs during run time. (Unlike the 'break' command in C, the M BREAK transfers control to the user until a command is issued to return to program execution immediately after the BREAK command. See Chapter 17.) Most implementations of M had a variety of implementation-specific ways of handling different types of errors conditions. The MUMPS Development Committee wrestled for many years during the 1980s and early 90s trying to standardize error handling. A number of elements of error handling are now incorporated into the standard. The process cannot be considered perfected yet, but the provisions already adopted are in many respects open-ended, reserving certain areas for further standardization while allowing implementors and even programmers to adopt error handling techniques suitable for their needs.

In this chapter, we touch on the rather complex subject of error handling. Many of the ideas are based on the work of Roger Partridge (e.g., Partridge, 1992), to whom I am indebted for assistance in the presentation of material with which I am not completely at ease. Ed de Moel, Chair of the MUMPS Development Committee at the time this text was revised, also provided useful insights both through his book *M[UMPS] by Example*, from which I have reprinted an example, and by his helpful comments on drafts of this chapter (Roger Partridge also offered helpful comments).

Syntactical errors

There are several ways that errors might be classified. Strictly compiled languages sometimes subdivide errors as arising either at "compile time" or at "run time." This distinction blurs in M, since dynamic code modification can generate errors at run time that are identical to ones identified during compilation. A more robust classification might be to group syntactical errors (which could occur at run time through use of the XECUTE command in M) as one set, and then to subdivide nonsyntactical errors into appropriate subgroups. This other set would include data-generated errors and logical errors, to mention two important categories.

If we hear someone say (as I once did), "I knowed she seed me because she retched out and wove at me," we may understand the message while wondering perhaps at the level of education of the speaker. Unfortunately, computers are by no means as understanding as humans and might respond to that sentence with four separate error messages (assuming it is processing verbs, not the noun equivalents with no semantic meaning). M implementors have adopted a number of ways of handling this type of error. The most frustrating is the simple message "Syntax Error," which leaves to the user the task of trying to figure out what is incorrect in the offending command line. In the early days of the M standard (i.e., the late '70s and early '80s) implementors were conscious of the evolving state of the language and hence reluctant to incorporate into the standard error messages that might require change with new directions of the language. However, with time the specificity of implementor-specific error messages has grown, and most vendors now provide quite detailed information on the syntactical problem encountered.

The MUMPS Development Committee decided that it would be helpful if implementations used the same error messages to respond to some of the more common errors, including some syntactical ones, encountered in M code. They therefore developed a series of messages, each identified by the letter 'M' followed by one or two digits, to use when these sorts of errors are encountered. For instance, if the user types the pattern match expression `IF x?5.3N ...`, M would respond with the error message ,M10, (invalid pattern match range). Note the commas on each side of the number: these are required by the standard, so that it will be possible to identify uniquely codes M1 and, for example, M10 using the M contains operator '[' to test the message number. The 'M' preceding the error message number indicates that this is a message defined in the M standard. A complete list of error codes defined in the 1995 standard appears at the end of this chapter.

To date, only a few syntactical errors of this type have been standardized. Here is an example of one of the most common errors in writing M code. The following two lines are often used to produce a sorted list:

```
SET x=""
FOR i=1:1 set x=$ORDER(^stud(x)) QUIT:x="" DO output(i)
```

The second line has a single space following the expression `x=""` which makes M assume that DO is an argument associated with the QUIT command. Since QUIT in this context cannot have an argument, the error message ,M16, (Argumented QUIT not allowed), would be invoked. Adding a second space before the DO command would produce valid syntax for this line.

There are many types of syntactical errors that can occur, and only a few have thus far been standardized. All M implementations will identify syntactical errors, but for the indeterminate future, they may not respond with the same error messages, and we may continue to see Syntax Error show up on our screens.

The M standard provides two additional ways in which error codes may be defined. A code beginning with the letter Z indicates that the error code was defined by the implementor. Z-letter extensions are common in many portions of the M standard, allowing for operations not yet standardized to be performed without violating the standard. In addition, the 1995 standard allows programmers to define error codes, specifying that they must begin with the letter U. Thus there are three sets of error codes: Mnn, Znn, and Unn, that could occur during execution of M code. The next question is how to deal with these codes.

Simple run-time error handling in M: $ECODE and $ETRAP

Syntactical errors may occur when a program is compiled prior to execution, during the typing of a command line during direct-mode execution, or as a result of conditions arising during execution of the code. If this type of error is encountered when a program is filed, the system will report the error and usually give the user an opportunity to go back and fix the code before it is stored. This process is no different from compilation with any high-level language.

In any programming language, many errors might occur after a routine has been compiled. The question then arises, how is one to deal with these errors? Again, solutions vary, but in most programming languages, the responsibility of run-time error handling is left to the user and the operating system. In other words, there are few standardized ways of dealing with these problems. At the very least, it is important to know what type of error occurred, and of equal importance is to know where in the execution of the code the error originated.

In the latest revision of the standard, M provides some useful tools to help programmers with this process. The first standardized element is the special variable $EC[ODE]. During normal execution of M, $ECODE has an empty value, signifying that no error has occurred. When some sort of error does occur, the system will assign a value to $ECODE. That value may contain one or more error codes, delimited by commas, with a comma preceding the list. For example, if a user types `SET result=a*b` and either `a` or `b` has not been defined, $ECODE will be assigned the value ,M6, (undefined local variable).

So far, these features give the user no more control over error conditions than would exist in other languages. However, the M standard has also provided another special variable, $ET[RAP], which can be defined by the user and can contain code to be executed when $ECODE is assigned a non-empty value. Suppose, for instance, that an M routine is calculating the average number of sales by salespersons for each department in a store. A portion of the code might read:

```
SET salesavg=sales(dept(i))/reps(dept(i))
```

where the program is looping through the different departments in a store. This program might work well until the Accounting department is encountered. Since there are (probably) no sales representatives in Accounting, the value for reps(dept(i)) would be 0, and a zero divide condition would occur. $ECODE would be set to ,M9, (divide by zero). If the programmer had anticipated a possible situation where this condition might occur, she might have defined $ETRAP as follows:

```
SET $ETRAP="WRITE ""No Reps in "",dept GOTO ^ERRALERT"
```

(assuming that no other kinds of errors are likely to occur). If, during execution, a department without sales representatives was encountered, the code stored in $ETRAP would automatically be invoked, transferring control to the program called ERRALERT, which could take whatever actions were required to notify the programmer and allow her to rectify the situation. The GOTO command above assumes that the programmer would invoke code that makes a note of the erroneous information (and perhaps corrects it right then), resets $ECODE to the empty string (so that the error condition no longer pertains), and then resumes execution at an appropriate place in the original code. This is one case where the use of a GOTO might be preferable to a DO command. In either event, it is necessary to reset $ECODE to the null string so that normal execution can proceed. If, however, other errors are anticipated, then $ECODE should be left as is, allowing a more complete analysis of the error condition(s), since a non-empty string value for $ECODE in effect freezes the process stack, allowing for more complete analysis, and normal execution cannot resume until $ECODE is assigned the empty string.

The example given above may be slightly contrived, but it illustrates a degree of programmer control over error conditions. The important point to emphasize is that M *automatically* inserts the code contained in $ETRAP immediately after an error is encountered, and implicitly transfers control to that code followed by a line that QUITs the executing program (in case $ETRAP contains no code).

As a second example, let us assume that a programmer is dealing with a very large database which contains some incorrect values that are hard to detect (such as a trailing space in a name which causes incorrect matching to its dictionary equivalent). In this case, neither standard M nor implementor-specific M error trapping will detect the problem. The programmer must find these offending items, sometimes embedded deep in another data structure. One way to catch these offending elements would be as follows. Suppose the programmer defines $ETRAP as follows:

```
SET $ETRAP="WRITE !,name,""has invalid spaces"",!" GOTO ^NAMECHK
```

and also inserts the following code in the data processing routine:

```
IF name?.E1." " SET $ECODE=",U14,"
```

as one of the user-defined error codes. In this case, when an invalid name is found, execution will transfer to the routine ^NAMECHK, which might note the error and even fix it, then return to an entry point that allows continued processing of the data file. If execution continues, the routine ^NAMECHK must reset $ECODE to the empty string so that it will not immediately invoke the $ETRAP command line again.

This example illustrates a semi-automated process for handling a certain class of error codes. There are other ways in which this situation might be handled, but the example is typical of some situations where multiple errors might be detected and processed without restarting the program each time a single error is encountered.

The example also illustrates a difference of opinion within the MDC. Some members would prefer to provide the ability to return, after processing an error, to the command immediately following the one executed at the time the error occurred (even if that command is in the middle of a command line). Others feel that this level of granularity would be difficult to achieve, and are willing to settle for resumption at the start of a specified line. The latter position is the one available in the 1995 standard; it seems unlikely that it will change in the near future.

Error handling in a complex execution flow control environment

The examples cited above assume that the error condition has occurred in an environment in which it is not necessary to know whether the offending routine has been invoked by others or by a recursive iteration which eventually produces an error. In fact, errors arising in complex execution flow control situations occur more often than the simple examples shown in the previous section, and the need to unravel this execution process is often crucial to proper identification of the error condition.

The 1995 M Standard provides tools that allow programmers to obtain details about the execution stack and conditions that might have been created during execution. These tools include the following two special variables:

- $ST[ACK]an integer value representing the depth of nesting of DO or XECUTE commands plus calls to extrinsic functions
- $ES[TACK]an integer representing the depth of the error trapping stack. $ESTACK can be reset to 0 via the NEW command, so that it does not always coincide in value with $STACK.

and the following function (some people might prefer to call this a special array variable):

- $ST[ACK]() returns information from the error trap information stack (see below)

Since confusion may arise between the special variable $STACK and the function $STACK(), we will always identify the function as $STACK(), omitting parentheses only when we are talking about the special variable $STACK.

The use of the special variable $STACK will allow the user to determine at what exact point during execution an error condition exists. One example might be an error condition arising during recursive calls to a routine. The user would like to know at what depth in the recursion the error took place. (Sometimes, a recursive call turns out, through a logical error, to be an infinite loop, in which case the stack level would be very much larger than anticipated.)

The 'function' $STACK() is intended to provide additional information that will help the user understand how an error condition has arisen. Typically, a user would want to know things such as the system status, depth of nesting, command used to get to that level, the actual line of code causing the problem, and the error code generated at the time the error took place. M provides all of these capabilities through the $STACK() function, and even a little more. However, the method for retrieving this information is somewhat involved, so let's take it one step at a time.

$STACK() can have either one or two arguments. Let's look at the one-argument form first. The first argument of $STACK() can be –1, 0, or a positive integer that can be between 1 and one less than the value of the special variable $STACK.

When the user invokes $STACK(–1), M will return the highest value of $STACK at which an error was encountered, or else, if no error has occurred (i.e., $ECODE has an empty value), then $STACK(–1) returns the value of $STACK, the current depth of nesting during normal operation.

In evaluating $STACK(I), where I can be a positive integer up to the value of $STACK–1, M returns one of three values:

- If the stack level came from a DO or XECUTE, $STACK(I) returns the command.
- If the stack level resulted from an extrinsic function, then $STACK(I) returns the string $$.
- If the stack level was reached because of an error condition, $STACK(I) returns the error code that caused $STACK to reach that level.

Finally, if the user invokes $STACK(0), then the M standard provides for a return value that can be implementation-specific, with the intent that the implementor provide useful information as to how the code was invoked. The intent is that the implementors may have several different values, depending on things such as a distributed M configuration, client-server architecture, or any of a host of other characteristics that might need unraveling to help the programmer solve his error condition. Rather than specify all of these possible scenarios, and knowing that many of them would only be applicable to a specific implementation, the MDC members responsible for the creation of this function wisely decided to leave the specifics to the implementor, while still preserving a measure of standardization in the more predictable situations.

As you can see, M provides a little more detail than one might require in many debugging situations, by giving implementors a free hand to deal with unusual situations. This approach has characterized the evolution of M, as you may have noticed in several other contexts. In fact, standardizing error handling in any form required a long, drawn-out series of careful negotiations before a valid subset of all error handling options was adopted for incorporation into the standard.

In the next set of cases, we consider $STACK(I,code), where code can be one of three values: ECODE, PLACE, or MCODE. Now we are getting to the remaining "wish list" of values that might help a programmer with an error problem. These codes return values as follows:

- ECODE returns the complete list of any ecodes encountered at this level.
- PLACE returns the location (place) of the command at the I-th level of execution:
  - If I is not equal to $STACK and $ECODE is the empty string, Stack(I,PLACE) returns the last command executed.
  - If I=$STACK but $ECODE is the empty string, $STACK(I,PLACE) returns the command currently being executed.
  - If $ECODE is non-empty, $STACK(I,PLACE) returns the line just *before* the position that caused $ECODE to acquire a non-empty value, followed by an integer representing offset into that line.
- MCODE returns the value of the XECUTE command, if that command was used in this situation, or else the line (label + offset) defined by PLACE or, if that is not available, an empty string.

This series of options completes almost all of the tools provided by the 1995 M standard to help programmers resolve error conditions. The number of options and the complexity of the possible results are too varied to try to give a whole series of examples. Instead, I present below, with permission from Ed de Moel, an adaptation of the example in his text *M[UMPS] By Example* in which he has managed to use $STACK, $ESTACK, $STACK(), $ECODE, and $ETRAP. This example is only the first of several in De Moel's book, which I recommend to anyone seriously interested in pursuing the details of error handling in M. A few annotations are provided with and following the code and its output. The example is intended to allow a user to track different states of some of the error handling values described in this chapter.

```
demoelex ;error handling sampler; demoel;6/95
         ;reprinted by permission of Ed de Moel
START    ;
     WRITE !,"start error demo routine"
     WRITE "  $STACK = ",$STACK,"  $ESTACK = ",$ESTACK
     SET $ECODE="",shown=0
```

```
        DO L1;first DO for process stack
        ;routine returns here to exit at end if exit is normal.
        ...It is not executed in this example
        WRITE !,"end of demoelex","  STACK = ",$STACK
        WRITE ", $ESTACK = ",$ESTACK
        QUIT   ;end of routine
L1      ;first level DO called
        WRITE !,"Now at label L1,"," $STACK = ",$STACK
        WRITE ", $ESTACK = ",$ESTACK
        SET $ETRAP="WRITE !,""Error trap from L1 ("",$STACK,
        ...""/"",$ESTACK,"")."" DO E1 DO SHOW($STACK)"
        DO L2
        ;Once again, this code is not executed because exit is abnormal
        SET shown=0
        WRITE !,"Note The error has ended here."
        WRITE !,"next, let's generate a user-defined error."
        SET $ECODE="User defined error."
        WRITE !,"Now returning from L1,"," $STACK = ",$STACK
        WRITE ",$ESTACK = ",$ESTACK
        QUIT;exit L1 procedure under normal execution
        ;
L2      ;use NEW to reset special error variables
        NEW $ESTACK,$ETRAP
        WRITE !,"Now at label L2 with NEWed $ESTACK and $ETRAP"
        WRITE !?15,"$STACK = ",$STACK,",$ESTACK = ",$ESTACK
        SET $ETRAP="WRITE !,""Error trap from L2 ($STACK ="",
        ...$STACK,"" $ESTACK = "",$ESTACK,"")."" DO E2
        ...SET:'$ESTACK $ECODE="""" DO SHOW($STACK)"
        DO L3
        WRITE !,"Now leaving procedure L2,"
        WRITE " $STACK = ",$STACK,",$ESTACK = ",$ESTACK
        QUIT;exit L2 procedure
        ;
L3      ;
        WRITE !,"Now at label L3,","$STACK = ",$STACK
        WRITE ", $ESTACK = "$ESTACK
        ;Error occurs when XECUTE-ing next line
        SET x="WRITE !,""Now comes the error:"" SET z=1/0"
        SET y="EXECUTE x"
        SET a="EXECUTE y";note: several levels of XECUTE here
        ...change stack values
        XECUTE a
        ;The error has just occurred, so the following code is
        ...not executed
           WRITE !,"Now leaving procedure L3","   $STACK = ",$STACK
           WRITE "   $ESTACK = ",$ESTACK
           QUIT;exit procedure L3
```

```
        ;
E1      ;user defined error
        WRITE "E1 ",$ECODE,! DO TRACE QUIT
        ;
E2      ;
        WRITE "E2 ",$ECODE,! DO TRACE QUIT
        ; end of user defined error procedures
TRACE ;
        NEW max,i,k,here
        QUIT:shown
        SET max=$STACK(-1),here=$STACK
        FOR k=0:1:max DO
        . WRITE !,"$SELECT(here=k:" * ",1:"  "),
        ...$JUSTIFY(k,2),": ",$STACK(k)
        . FOR i="PLACE","MCODE","ECODE" WRITE !?29,I," = ",$STACK(k,i)
        . QUIT
        SET shown=1
        QUIT;end of TRACE procedure
SHOW(n);
        WRITE !,"In SHOW, n= ",n,!?5,"$STACK = ",$STACK
        QUIT;end of Show procedure
```

This example illustrates a variety of cases which shed some light on the way that the error handling features discussed up to this point operate. It is liberally sprinkled with WRITE commands so that the reader can see exactly how different cases are handled. Here is how the output of the program would look:

```
DO START

Start error demo routine,   $STACK = 1, $ESTACK = 1
Now at label L1, $STACK = 2, $ESTACK = 2
Now at label L2 with NEWed $ESTACK and $ETRAP
            $STACK = 3, $ESTACK = 0
Now at label L3, $STACK = 4, $ESTACK = 1
Now comes the error:
      (with the occurrence of the error, control transfers
      ...execution to $ETRAP in procedure L2)
Error Trap from L2 ($STACK = 7, $ESTACK = 4). U2 ,M9,
      (,M9, is the standard M "Divide by 0" error code)
      (control passes to TRACE procedure)

      0:       (no implementor-specific code shown here)

            @ +1(at start of routine: @ shows it was invoked
               ...by direct command)
```

```
DO START

   1:  DO
         START+4^demoelex +1
         DO L1
   2:  DO
         L1+4^demoelex +1
         DO L2
   3:  DO
         L2+5^demoelex +1
         DO L3
   4:  DO
         L3+7^demoelex +1
         XECUTE a
   5:  XECUTE
         @  +1(@ shows xecute-originated command)
         XECUTE y
   6:  XECUTE
         @  +1
         XECUTE x
   7:  XECUTE
         @  +30(character position of SET command causing error)
         WRITE !,"now comes the error" SET z=1/0
         ,M9,(Divide by zero error code)
   8:  DO
         E2^demoelex+26(character position of DO command)
         E2 WRITE " U2 ",$ECODE,! DO TRACE QUIT
 * 9:  DO(end of stack +1, therefore an asterisk printed)
         TRACE+3^demoelex+14(character position of DO command)
         FOR k=0:1:max DO

In SHOW, N=7, $STACK=8
Error Trap from L2 ($STACK = 7, $ESTACK = 4). U2 ,M9,

In SHOW, N=6, $STACK=7
Error Trap from L2 ($STACK = 7, $ESTACK = 4). U2 ,M9,

In SHOW, N=5, $STACK=6
Error Trap from L2 ($STACK = 7, $ESTACK = 4). U2 ,M9,

In SHOW, N=4, $STACK=5
Error Trap from L2 ($STACK = 7, $ESTACK = 4). U2 ,M9,

In SHOW, N=3, $STACK=4
```

At this point, $ETRAP ends and execution of the SHOW procedure terminates.

This example is the first of several in De Moel's excellent book. They warrant attention by anyone wishing to take full advantage of the error handling features of the 1995 M standard. For the purpose of this text, however, the example shown gives enough of a flavor of the process to allow the user to understand how error handling works.

Error handling with extrinsic functions

Extrinsic functions in M are functions not included in the standard. They may be user- or system-supplied M subroutines or even procedures external to the current M environment. In terms of error handling, however, they are somewhat different in that the process stack in M is saved when the extrinsic function is called, and restored on return. The result of an extrinsic function is provided by an argument associated with the QUIT from the routine (if it is an M routine). When an error occurs during execution of an extrinsic function, it is important that this condition be detected, returning an empty string from the function.

As a final (to date, at least) component of the tools provided by standard M for error handling, the special variable $QUIT has been defined. The value of $QUIT is 0 if the current execution level was started with a DO command, and QUIT is set to 1 if the current execution level was started with an extrinsic function call.

M's error handling makes use of this special variable to ensure that an empty value is returned from an extrinsic function in which an error occurred. It accomplishes this task by implicitly inserting two lines of code into the execution flow. The first line contains any code supplied by the value stored in $ETRAP, as described earlier in this chapter. The second line consists of the following code:

```
QUIT:$QUIT "" QUIT
```

In other words, if $QUIT is true (i.e., an extrinsic function has been invoked), return with an empty value for that function. Otherwise execute a normal QUIT.

Summary

Error handling is complex. Different M implementors adopted a variety of strategies to help programmers deal with error conditions, many of which were incompatible with those adopted by other implementors. It took a long time and some real persistence on the part of a few individuals (notably Harlan Stenn) in the MDC to achieve standardization of the error handling process to the degree described in this chapter. There are no standard techniques for displaying the contents of local variables when an error condition arises; this feature might be reconsidered for adoption, but at present the need for this functionality is minimal, since all implementors have this feature available in one form or another.

It would take many pages more to describe all possible outcomes of error handling. Such detail goes beyond the scope of this text. Readers are encouraged to refer to De Moel's *M[UMPS] By Example* for more detailed coverage of a complex issue.

References

De Moel, E. (1995), *M[UMPS] by Example*. Available on-line:

`http://world.std.com/~demoel/mdc/index.html#m2`

Partridge, R. (1992), "Error Processing," *MUMPS Computing*, Vol 22:2, pp. 51–55.

Appendix: Standard Error Codes in M (1995 Standard)

Note: No values have been specified for codes M25 or M34. These values are reserved by the MUMPS Development Committee for later definition.

M1 naked indicator undefined
M2 invalid combination with P *fncodatom*
M3 $RANDOM seed less than 1
M4 no true condition in $SELECT
M5 *lineref* less than zero
M6 undefined *lvn*
M7 undefined *gvn*
M8 undefined *svn*
M9 divide by zero
M10 invalid pattern match range
M11 no parameters passed
M12 invalid *lineref* (negative offset)
M13 invalid *lineref* (line not found)
M14 *line* level not 1
M15 undefined index variable
M16 argumented QUIT not allowed
M17 argumented QUIT required
M18 fixed-length READ not greater than zero
M19 cannot copy a tree or subtree into itself
M20 *line* must have *formalist*

M21 algorithm specification invalid
M22 SET or KILL ^$GLOBAL when data in global
M23 SET or KILL ^$JOB for nonexistent job number
M24 change to collation algorithm while subscripted local variables defined
M26 nonexistent *environment*
M27 attempt to rollback a transaction that is not restartable
M28 mathematical function, parameter out of range
M29 SET or KILL on *ssvn* not allowed by implementation
M30 reference to *glvn* with different collating sequence within a collating algorithm
M31 *controlmnemonic* used for device without a *menmonicspace* selected
M32 *controlmnemonic* used in user-defined *mnemonicspace* which has no associated line
M33 SET or KILL ^$ROUTINE when *routine* exists
M35 device does not support *mnemonicspace*
M36 incompatible *menmonicspace*
M37 READ from device identified by the empty string
M38 invalid *ssvn* subscript
M39 invald $NAME argument
M40 call-by-reference in JOB *actual*
M41 invalid LOCK argument within a TRANSACTION
M42 invalid QUIT within a TRANSACTION
M43 invalid range value ($X,$Y)
M44 invalid *command* outside of a TRANSACTION
M45 invalid GOTO reference
M57 more than one defining occurrence of *label* in *routine*
M58 too few formal parameters

Looking into the Future

25

Overview

The brief history of M presented in Chapter 2 notes that the language continues to evolve. The M standard has been revised and approved by ANSI three times so far: in 1984, 1990, and 1995. The MDC continues to work on new proposals for adoption in the next revision, many of which are already approved and ready to go. This chapter summarizes the known changes already approved, offers a glimpse into areas under active consideration by MDC for approval, and speculates on other factors that may affect the evolution of M into the next millennium.

In the first edition of this book, published under the title *The ABCs of M*, the equivalent chapter (at the end of what is now Part I of this text) spoke of growth as a dominating factor – growth in implementations, users, vertical markets, and visibility. This factor is still important, but in different ways. M has seen a steady growth in its use around the world, though its percentage of the market has perhaps not changed significantly. The number of implementors has diminished, due primarily to acquisitions rather than the disappearance of implementations. The international market is continuing to expand. Acceptance of M as an ISO standard has opened doors for its further growth, which is continuing to take place.

But growth is not the dominating theme in today's evolution of M, nor in fact of the use of computers worldwide. The biggest factor that pervades all of the computer industry is that, as Adam is said to have remarked to Eve, "We are living in a time of profound change." The continued existence of mainframes, minicomputers, long-established operating systems, and even long-established general-purpose and special-purpose programming languages is uncertain. Faced with these imponderables, it is not clear how the M community is going to adjust to these changes, nor how the language will evolve to meet the challenge of change.

The process of change

When M was adopted as a standard language by the American National Standards Institute (ANSI), it entered into a controlled environment as a price for its acceptance. The MUMPS Development Committee (MDC) continues to be the official body responsible for monitoring evolution of the M language and has been given the formal name ANSI X11.1: MUMPS Development Committee. Meeting several times annually, this group prepares new features for submission as addenda to the current standard. A new list of additions to the language already exists and is summarized below. Other documents are in preparatory stages, and other ideas could be considered "likely" but as yet not formulated in sufficient detail to make it into the MDC process as formal documents.

The rules for change adopted by MDC are quite explicit with respect to the steps that a new proposal must go through prior to incorporation in the next proposed standard. According to the bylaws of the MDC, new language elements proposed by non-MDC members may be accepted as "Type C" releases of MDC. These proposals carry no binding obligation on MDC to adopt them at later dates, but they represent a process whereby all M users can have a voice in the evolution of the language. The MDC usually assigns these new proposals to a subcommittee for study and minutes of the subcommittee reflect actions taken on each of these proposals.

The next level of approval specified by the MDC is a "Type B release," meaning that it is recommended for inclusion in the next revision of the standard, but it is not yet formally adopted. Subsequently, and usually after a period of testing by vendors who have implemented this feature, it will be proposed for adoption as a "Type A release," which means that it will be proposed for adoption in the next standard. Type A releases are rarely rescinded or modified (only one such release was subsequently removed from Type A status), which means that, often, implementors anxious to get a jump on the new standard will begin implementation of Type A releases before the next standard is approved.

Once a new standard is ready for approval, it undergoes the *canvass method* of approval specified by ANSI. This entails mailing out notifications of the proposed change to all who, in the judgment of the MDC and ANSI, might be affected by the adoption of the new standard. These individuals, institutions, or groups are invited to participate in the canvass, and, if they choose to do so, they are sent the draft standard and given a period (approximately 90 days) in which to vote for or against the proposed standard. Objections are considered, and the correspondence associated with the objection is mailed to all those participating in the canvass, offering them an opportunity to change their vote based on this correspondence. The draft standard, together with all documents generated by the canvass process, are then submitted to ANSI, which then decides whether to approve or deny the new standard. An appeals process exists if objectors feel that there are grounds for review of the ANSI decision, but eventually the decision becomes final. Submission to ISO has become the next step in this process since ISO approval of M in 1992. This process involves submission of the ANSI standard to ISO using what is called the *fast track* method, in which ISO representatives vote on the standard as approved by ANSI, without forming a separate ISO study group to make its own recommendations.

This deliberate and very specific review process ensures a careful evaluation of new language features prior to their incorporation into the standard. One of the important factors affecting evolution of the language is the desire to retain compatibility with existing language features. For example, only one function in M has been removed over time: the $NEXT function, which was replaced by $ORDER ($NEXT did not lend itself to the use of string subscripts and was completely superseded by $ORDER), and that process took over a decade of notification of its impending removal before it disappeared in the 1995 M standard.

This process continues even as a standard is in the canvass process. The MDC continues to meet, and there already exists a significant list of elements approved for incorporation into the next standard. The most current information on the status of new language elements is found on the MDC World Wide Web home page:

```
http://www.radix.net/~demoel/mdc
```

which is maintained by the MDC Chair, Ed de Moel.

New language elements already approved for the next standard

As this text goes to press, the MDC has already approved nearly 70 changes to the M standard. These include items such as the incorporation of new operators, reinterpretation or revision of the interpretation of existing language elements, the addition of a *library document* to M (standardizing a number of library functions for the language), and actual new language elements. The following list, provided by the current MDC Chair, Ed de Moel, presents the flavor of these proposed changes, omitting specific details.

- **New operators:**

  M currently includes two operators which require two characters: the *exponention* operator ** and the *sorts after* operator]]. New two-character operators approved for adoption include the *less than or equal* operator <= and the *greater than or equal* operator >= and the *xor* operator !!. The first two of these operators can be used in conjunction with the *not* operator: '<= and '>=.

- **M library functions**

  In addition to approving the process whereby library functions can be standardized (and defining the use of the term 'standard' in library documents), the MDC has also approved a number of specific library functions, identified as such by insertion of a reserved name such as $%ABS. They include several types of mathematical functions:

  - general functions ($%ABS, $%EXP, $%LOG, $%SQRT, *etc.*)
  - trigonometric functions ($%SIN, $%COS, *etc.*)
  - hyperbolic functions ($%SINH, $%COSH, $%ARCTANH, *etc.*)
  - complex mathematical functions ($%CADD, $%CDIC, $%CLOG, *etc.*)
  - matrix functions ($%MTXADD, $%MTXINV, *etc.*)

  Other library functions already approved include $%PRODUCE and $%REPLACE. The new function $%REPLACE is an extension of $TRANSLATE that replaces one or more strings of characters with another string (rather than a character-by-character replacement as in $TRANSLATE). This function goes through the input string only once; it does not revisit any characters that have been included in the replacement. $%PRODUCE is an iterative replacement of a string that examines the output from the first iteration and repeatedly applies the same transformation rule until no target strings matching the replacement rules remain in the string.

- **New commands**

  In a continuing effort to standardize elements associated with interface to the operating system, the MDC has approved the two new commands RSAVE and RLOAD to handle the saving and loading of routines, respectively. Also approved are KV[ALUE], which KILLS a value at a node but leaves its descendants, and KS[UBSCRIPTS], which KILLs subscripts and leaves the value at a node.

- **New special variable**

  A new special variable, $REFERENCE, has been added to the language. It contains the complete expanded version of the last global reference (as an aid to the use of the naked indicator).

- **New structured system variables**

  The structured system variable `^$DEVICE` has been further defined to incorporate:

  - `^$DEVICE(device,"MNEMONICSPACE")`
  - `^$DEVICE(device,"MNEMONICSPEC")`

  A document has also been approved guiding future submissions of changes or additions to structured system variables.

  Provisions for specification of character set profiles and collation have also been defined. The definitions of ^$GLOBAL and ^$JOB have also been clarified or slightly extended.

- **Revisions and extensions to related standards**

  The Open MUMPS Interconnect document (ANSI X11.2) has been extended, reworded, and improved in several ways, including providing for internationalization of M, specification of WRITE to a device across a network, specification of the JOB command, and other refinements to that standard.

  MWAPI (ANSI X11.6) has undergone revision and a new version has been proposed.

- **Revisions, clarifications, and extensions to existing language elements**

  A number of changes have been approved which serve to strengthen or clarify existing language elements. Among those affected are the *pattern match* operator, the commands CLOSE (with $IO), DO, GOTO, JOB, KILL, SET $EXTRACT, and TSTART; the functions $FNUMBER, $ORDER, and $QUERY (reverse operation allowed); the special variable $TEST (used with the NEW command); and the initial values of special variables $DEVICE, $KEY, $IO, $TEST, $X, and $Y.

- **Internationalization**

  In an effort to make further headway in providing for internationalization, a number of steps have been taken. Most important among these, as already referenced in Chapter 21, is the specification of *override* syntax in dealing with mixed character strings. Other elements occurring in several components of the language include character set profile specification and collation clarification. While these additions do not complete the process, they represent an important step in the right direction.

- **Interfacing M**

  Several clarifications relate to the use of M in conjunction with other languages. Embedded program syntax and parameter passing are the two most important of these, although the OMI revisions are also related to this area.

- **Error handling**

  A number of new error messages are defined and others clarified.

- **Syntax and portability extensions**

  Two extensions to syntactical provisions have been added to the language. Names may now be up to 31 characters in length for portability purposes. This is a very important addition to the language, in that the name limitation of 8 characters is a restriction that is both incompatible with many other programming languages and unnecessarily restrictive in today's complex world. The uniqueness of a longer name will open the door for many improvements in connotation and readability of M code.

The second syntactical change is that spaces will be permitted at the end of a line (a feature that was ambiguous before). While not a major addition, it often happens that a user will inadvertently type extra characters, and this could, in some implementations, have led to syntax errors that are hard to track down.

In addition, the portability requirements allow for 510, rather than 255 characters in a string (subscripts are left at the 255-character limit). This is a limit that is less often encountered, but it does recognize the need for longer text strings in some situations.

Looking over this list, one realizes that a great deal has gone on since the "1995" standard was finalized, which actually took place early in 1994. It is equally probable that a number of other areas will receive further attention in the months and years ahead prior to submission of the next standard. A few important areas likely to receive attention are discussed in the next sections.

Object-oriented M

The concept of object-oriented languages has appeared on the computing scene in the last 10 years with important effects on concepts of programming and languages. C++ , the object-oriented extension to C, is an excellent example of the pervasive influence of this new approach to programming. M is in many respects ideally suited to the concept of objects, and there are strong proponents of adopting M to become fully object-oriented. A subcommittee of the MDC has been wrestling with the problem for several years. Their results are by no means final as yet; in fact, there remain controversies as to whether there will be a new, separate OO-M language or whether the necessary changes can be incorporated into the current standard without violating backward compatibility principles of the language evolution process. One thing does seem clear: the potential for M to adopt object-oriented concepts is strong, and the perceived need is growing. It would be presumptuous to predict an outcome, but some extensions to the current standard relating to object-oriented features seem to be a likely element in the next few years.

Internationalization

The pressure to continue to make progress in internationalization remains. Although M is far ahead of all other programming languages in this regard, much remains to be done. With the active support and assistance of international members of the MDC, this area is likely to continue to receive a high priority in the short-term future.

Interface to other standards

M made important strides in interfacing to other languages. With the ice broken, it seems natural that new interfaces will be defined, most of them based on the existing approaches already defined through existing interfaces. It is likely, for instance, that a new graphic standard will emerge and when it does, M will move rapidly to interface to it. Other areas are slightly less predictable, but there are several where interface is essential. The SQL standard, for example, continues to evolve, and changes in that standard may require revisiting the manner in which M interfaces to it. Other new standards are emerging, and they too will have an impact in this aspect of the MDC's workload.

Large objects

The need to deal with large objects such as image files or complete documents in one form or another needs to be addressed through M. How this question is eventually resolved is not certain, but it appears likely that some effort will be made in this direction.

It would appear, then, that the changes already visible on the horizon – adopted, under consideration, or seemingly probable – will provide an ongoing agenda for the MDC well into the next century.

Summary

Change is inevitable and necessary; without it, many forms of life would wither and die. Languages, too, continue to change, and computer languages must adapt to changing environments and pressures. M will continue to evolve, perhaps quite rapidly in the next few years. The pressures for acceptance of the features described in this chapter translate into pressures to evolve, slowly, in coordination with other standards in the years to come. The process of change, once adopted on an international level, will necessarily slow in response to the need for broader input from international representatives.

Readers of this text should by now be convinced that the M language offers unique and exciting alternatives to program development. The language has made important contributions to computer language evolution in the last 30 years, and it appears poised to play an important role for the next decade or two. Whatever else happens, the evolution of M will continue to be interesting to observe and exciting to participate in. Perhaps it is for this reason that it has been said that once exposed to M, it is hard not to be converted to a "believer," and once converted, it is hard not to become either a missionary or a zealot in supporting its cause. This author has been accused of being a zealot (with good justification). If this text serves its purpose well, some readers may themselves be persuaded to join the ranks of active supporters of the M movement.

Answers to Selected Exercises

This section contains some suggested solutions to certain exercises found at the ends of the chapters describing M language features. The simpler exercises (i.e., those providing practice in entering different forms of variables or exercising M operators) are not treated in this section. Furthermore, there are many correct answers to certain exercises, and the ones listed below are only one correct alternative.

Chapter 4

■ Exercise 4

There are several ways to set about solving this exercise. First, in order to obtain the correct answer, it is not necessary to know the exact time, down to minutes and seconds. However, we will go ahead and get the complete answer to illustrate the use of M arithmetic operators.

The exercise gave a total number of elapsed seconds since the start of a month. That number can be converted into elapsed minutes and hours as follows:

```
SET TIME=1190647 (starting figure in seconds)
SET MINS=TIME\60 (integer number of 60-second units in TIME)
SET HOURS=MINS\60 (integer number of 60-minute units in MINS)
```

With these values, it is possible to calculate the final answer:

```
SET DAY=HOURS\24
SET HOUR=HOURS#24
SET MIN=MINS#60
SET SEC=TIME#60
```

If you have done these problems correctly, you should be able to obtain the following results:

```
WRITE DAY
13 ;(this means that 13 days have elapsed; it is now the 14th)
WRITE HOUR
18
WRITE MIN
44
WRITE SEC
7
```

This would mean that you might be eating supper, dinner, high tea, or whatever other meal is served around 6:44:07 P.M. on the 14th day of the month.

Although the calculation of days is not needed in M, since there is another function which you will learn later for that purpose, the ability to calculate hours, minutes, and days will prove valuable in many practical situations.

Chapter 6

■ Exercise 1

```
SET BONMOT="This is the first day of your life as an M Programmer"
WRITE $EXTRACT(BONMOT,$LENGTH(BONMOT)/2)
```

(The answer should be "y.")

■ Exercise 2

```
SET NAME="Lori G. Rennick"
```

■ *Solution 2a*

```
SET FNAME=$EXTRACT(NAME,1,$FIND(NAME," ")-2)
SET MI=$EXTRACT(NAME,$FIND(NAME," "))
SET LNAME=$EXTRACT(NAME,$FIND(NAME,". "),99)
WRITE FNAME,!,MI,!,LNAME
```

The answer should read:

```
Lori
G
Rennick
SET LASTFIRST=LNAME_", "_FNAME_" "_MI_"."
```

This use of $EXTRACT with a nested use of $FIND is typical of many M programs. It would be possible to create some temporary variables, but this is a cleaner, more efficient method. Notice, however, that the solution would have to be modified if the middle initial were, in fact, two or three characters (e.g., McD) or if there were more than one initial.

- ***Solution 2b***

```
SET FNAME=$PIECE(NAME," ",1)
SET MI=$PIECE($PIECE(NAME," ",2),".",1)
SET LN=$PIECE(NAME," ",3)
```

(The rest of the solution is the same as for 2a.)

This solution also used an expression nested inside another; only in this case it is using $PIECE inside $PIECE. The second line's internal $PIECE retrieves the characters G, which are then used as the string from which to extract the G by the external $PIECE expression.

This solution is more robust, but it would still have problems with several separate middle initials. You may want to think about how to find the last name in a string as an added brainteaser.

- **Exercise 3**

```
SET DATE="March 12, 1957"
SET MONTH=$EXTRACT(DATE,1,3)
SET DAY=$EXTRACT($PIECE(DATE," ",2),1,2)
SET YEAR=$PIECE(DATE," ",3)
SET NEWDATE=MONTH_"/"_DAY_"/"_YEAR
```

The nesting in this case combines $PIECE with $EXTRACT to retrieve first the characters 12 and then take the first two characters of that string for the solution of the exercise. It also would be possible to use two nested $PIECE functions in this case. How would you do it?

- **Exercise 4**

```
SET M="March"
SET TMP=$EXTRACT(M,2),M2=$CHAR($ASCII(TMP)-32)
SET TMP=$EXTRACT(M,3),M3=$CHAR($ASCII(TMP)-32)
SET TMP=$EXTRACT(M,4),M4=$CHAR($ASCII(TMP)-32)
SET TMP=$EXTRACT(M,5),M5=$CHAR($ASCII(TMP)-32)
SET M=$EXTRACT(M)_M2_M3_M4_M5
```

The clue to this solution lies in the ASCII character code values for uppercase and lowercase. If you look at Table 3.1, you will see that all the uppercase characters come first and that they are in sequence, with no intervening characters. Similarly, the lowercase characters are also in sequence. Hence subtracting the difference in code values will work for any letter of the alphabet The last line takes the individual characters and concatenates them into the answer.

- **Exercise 5**

```
SET SENTENCE="Now is the time for all men to aid their country."
SET P1=$EXTRACT(SENTENCE,1,30)
SET SPACES=$LENGTH(P1," ")  ;(spaces=8 in this case)
SET P!=$PIECE(P1," " 1,7) ;P1 is now "Now is the time for all men"
SET P2=$PIECE(SENTENCE," ",8,99) ; P2 is now "to aid their country."
```

In this case, since the sentence is less than twice 30 characters, it is not necessary to repeat the process of extracting the next set of words to fit a 30-character line.

- **Exercise 6**

```
SET MONTH=" <use whatever month you want to>"
SET MNEW=$TRANSLATE(MONTH,"abceghilmnprstuvy","ABCEHILMNPRSTUVY")
```

This solution assumes the first letter is capital, the others lowercase. This is why some letters were omitted (since they do not appear in the names of months). What letters would you have to add if the first letter were also lower case?

- **Exercise 7**

```
SET NAME="Richard"
SET NICKNAME=$TRANSLATE(NAME,"Richard","Dick")
```

In this case, having a third expression shorter than the second expression will result in eliminating all characters after the fourth letter in the second expression. This is a rather contrived solution, since it is so specific to this particular name. Later in this text we will show you ways to generate dictionaries where you can store a long list of names and their respective nicknames.

Chapter 7

■ Exercise 2

```
READ !,"Please enter the current month: ",MONTH
READ !,"Next, please enter the current day of the month: ",DAY
READ !,"Finally, please enter the year (4 digits): ",YEAR
SET D="/"
SET $PIECE(DATE,D,1)=MONTH,$PIECE(DATE,D,2)=DAY
SET $PIECE(DATE,D,3)=YEAR WRITE !!,DATE
```

This solution is a typical example of prompts used in M programming. It is visually more pleasing to use both uppercase and lowercase letters in writing prompts, and this convention is followed throughout this text. Also notice that there is always a space at the end of the prompt. If no space were present, the characters typed by the user would follow immediately, creating a confusing line on the display screen.

■ Exercise 3

■ *Solution 3a*

```
READ !,"Enter a single word of any length (no spaces):",GOODWORD
WRITE !,?40-($LENGTH(GOODWORD)/2),GOODWORD
```

The secret to this solution is finding the length of the word, dividing it in half, and then starting that many characters before the center of the line (column 40) by using the ?nn format control in the WRITE expression. Notice that the entire expression "40-($LENGTH(GOODWORD)/2)" is used as the format control.

■ *Solution 3b*

```
READ !,"Enter title of paper: ",TITLE
SET PAGE=12 (or some other number)
WRITE #,TITLE,?72,"Page",PAGE
```

You may find that instead of clearing your screen, your implementation outputs some strange characters and then prints the title. If this happens, you need to check with your implementor to find out how to reset the control characters used to clear the screen.

■ Exercise 4

```
READ !,"Enter a number with integer and fractional components: ",N1
READ !,"Enter a number with integer and fractional components: ",N2
READ !,"Enter a number with integer and fractional components: ",N3
READ !,"Enter a number with integer and fractional components: ",N4
```

```
READ !,"Enter a number with integer and fractional components; ",N5
WRITE !?40,$JUSTIFY(N1,10,2)
WRITE !?40,$JUSTIFY(N2,10,2)
WRITE !?40,$JUSTIFY(N3,10,2)
WRITE !?40,$JUSTIFY(N4,10,2)
WRITE !?40,$JUSTIFY(N5,10,2)
```

Note: These WRITE statements could be combined into one WRITE.

Chapter 8

■ Exercise 1

```
   READ !,"Enter your age in years: ",AGE SET VOTER="N" SET:AGE>17
...VOTER="Y" READ:VOTER="Y" !,"Are you registered to vote? ",YN
```

This solution strings several commands on one line and uses postconditionals for both SET and READ. It would be possible to use IF statements, but the postconditional is a more compressed way of testing the desired conditions than, for example, `IF AGE >17 SET....`

■ Exercise 2

```
READ !,"Enter your age in years: ",AGE
SET AGEGRP=$SELECT(AGE<20:"Juvenile",AGE<65:"Adult", 1:"Senior Citizen")
```

This solution is almost identical to the example in the chapter on grades. M works from left to right and picks the first true solution. If AGE is greater than 64, the $SELECT function defaults to the Senior Citizen result.

■ Exercise 3

```
   READ !,"Please type in all you can remember of the start of Lincoln's
...Gettysburg address",!,GTBRG
```

▪ *Solution 3a*

```
SET LINE1=$EXTRACT(GTBRG,1,30) WRITE !,LINE1
IF $LENGTH(GTBRG>30) SET LINE2=$EXTRACT(GTBRG,31,60) WRITE !,LINE2
IF $LENGTH(GTBRG<60) QUIT
ELSE△△SET LINE3=$EXTRACT(GTBRG,61,99) WRITE !,LINE3
```

This is one way to break up a long text, but if you run this solution, you will see that the text gets broken at the end of the first 30 characters, regardless of whether it is at a word boundary. Of course, a better solution is needed. The next version provides an improved way to solve this problem.

■ ***Solution 3b***

```
SET TMP=$EXTRACT(GTBRG,1,30) ;use a temporary variable for clarity
SET LINE1=$PIECE(TMP," ",1,$LENGTH(TMP," ")-1)
SET TMP=$EXTRACT(GTBRG,$LENGTH(LINE1)+2,$LENGTH(LINE1)+31)
SET LINE2=$PIECE(TMP," ",1,$LENGTH(TMP," ")-1)
SET START=$LENGTH(LINE1)+$LENGTH(LINE2)+3) (temporary value)
SET TMP=$EXTRACT(GTBRG,START,START+29)
SET LINE3=$PIECE(TMP," ",1,$LENGTH(TMP," ")-1)
```

This solution uses nested functions, with $LENGTH inside $PIECE. The $LENGTH function takes advantage of the two-argument form of that function and gives a count of how many spaces are found in the first 30 characters of the user's input. You may want to try this part of the answer separately: Set a string equal to some combination of characters with repeating spaces for slashes or some other delimiting character) and then use $LENGTH of that string, using the delimiter as the second argument. The third line uses nested $LENGTH functions to take the correct length of line 1 (stopping at the last space in the first 30 characters) and adds 31 characters to that value. It is necessary to start with the second character after LINES, since the first is a space. The following lines merely repeat this approach, in case the user remembered more than expected of Lincoln's speech.

Chapter 9

■ **Exercise 1**

```
SENIOR;RFW:9/87;QUESTIONNAIRE
      Read !,"Please enter your age in years: ",AGE
      GOTO:AGE<65 CONTINUE
      READ !,"Are you a member of the Senior Citizen's Club (Y/N)? ",YN
      IF YN["Y" GOTO CONTINUE
      READ !,"Please give us your phone number: ",PHONE
CONTINUE ;more code could follow
      QUIT  ;END OF ROUTINE
```

This example of the use of GOTO is not all that bad in programming form, since it skips around a short sequence if the user has already provided a phone number in a previous session (the assumption being that the club has phone numbers for all members). The fourth line is an example of the use of the contains operator to check the user's answer. It will work for any uppercase answer that contains the letter Y, such as YES, Y, AYE, or even OH MY YES. However, it won't work for lowercase letters. You might think about how to solve the lowercase letter problem. There are some examples of its solution later in this text.

■ Exercise 2

```
VET   ;RFW; 9/87; CLINIC ADMIT
      WRITE !,"Welcome to Dog's World Veterinary Clinic."
      WRITE !!,"Is your pet a",!?5,"1. Dog,"!?5,"2. Cat, or"!?5,"3.
   ...Other species?"
      READ !!,"Please enter 1, 2, or 3: ",ANS
      GOTO DOG:ANS=1,CAT:ANS=2,OTHER:ANS=3,EXIT
DOG   ;Insert some doggy questions
      GOTO EXIT
CAT   ;insert some feline questions
      GOTO EXIT
OTHER ;
      READ !!,"Please enter what kind of pet you have: ",TYPE
      WRITE !!,"We'll try to add a form for "TYPE," soon."
      WRITE !,"Please bear with us."
      GOTO EXIT
EXIT  ;END OF ROUTINE
```

This solution is far from elegant, since it uses GOTO in a rather awkward form. As noted in the text, the use of a DO is better, but for the sake of providing practice, it uses the GOTO command.

■ Exercise 3

```
TOSSPOT ;RFW; 9/87; COIN FLIP GAME
      WRITE !,"This is a coin-toss betting game (for fun only)."
      SET PURSE=10
BETS  WRITE !!,"You have $",PURSE
      READ !!?5,"Place your bet (even dollar amount, 0 to quit): ",BET
      IF 'BET WRITE !,"Don't spend it all at once. Bye now." QUIT
      IF BET>PURSE WRITE !!,"Sorry. you don't have that much." GOTO BETS
      DO FLIP
      SET PURSE=PURSE+WIN IF PURSE GOTO BETS
      WRITE !!,"You seem to have lost it all."
      WRITE !?5,"Better luck next time." QUIT
FLIP ;
      READ !!,"Call it: HEADS or TAILS (H/T): ",HT
      SET HT=$SELECT($EXTRACT(HT)="H":0,1:1)
      SET FLIP=$RANDOM(2)
      IF FLIP=0 WRITE !,"HEADS IT IS."
      ELSE  WRITE !,"It's TAILS."
      WRITE:FLIP=HT !,"You win ",BET
      WRITE:FLIP='HT !,"sorry, you lose ",BET
      SET WIN=$SELECT(FLIP=HT:BET,1:-BET)
   QUIT
   ;END OF ROUTINE
```

This is actually a fairly enjoyable routine to play with. I had fun running it several times when I created it (of course, I also had to make a few adjustments to correct some syntax and some logic before I put it into the text). It also could serve as a model for other game-type routines. You might consider writing one that plays blackjack, but if you do, you will find that it takes quite a bit more code to make sure that you have removed cards from the deck once they have been played. If you were to assume that each hand was dealt from a new deck, the problem would really not be all that bad. Perhaps you might want to try that, or try some form of dice game. The trick is to use $RANDOM in a fashion that will pick a valid choice from the numbers available to you. In dice games, it's easy. In card games, you have to create a variable with 52 values, and use $RANDOM to select one of those 52 choices. Anyway, now that you see how easy it is to write one game program, you may want to try some others.

- **Exercise 4**

```
WORDS ;RFW; 9/87; WORD GAME
      FOR I=0:0 READ !,"Type a sentence (null to quit): ",SENT
      QUIT:SENT=""  DO CALC
      QUIT  ;exit routine here
CAL ;
      WRITE !?5,"It has ",$LENGTH(SENT," ")," words."
      QUIT  ;return to FOR loop
      ;END OF ROUTINE
```

There are a good many word games that could be devised, but those requiring dictionaries of stored words would have to be programmed using techniques introduced in later chapters.

Chapter 10

- **Exercise 1**

There are four routines in this package, as specified.

```
PRMAIN ;RFW;9/87; PAYROLL MAIN PRG
      WRITE !,"This package calculates payroll information."
      READ !,"Please enter month for this transaction(3 ltr caps): ",MONTH
PRNEXT ;loop for each employee
      IF MONTH["JAN" DO ^PRINIT
      READ !,"Enter employee ID number (null to quit):",PREMPNO
      READ !,"Enter wages earned this month: ",PRSAL
      DO ^PRDEDUC
      DO ^PRWRCK
      QUIT
      ;END OF ROUTINE
```

```
PRINIT;RFW;9/87; INITIALIZE VALUES
     SET (PRSSEC,PRSSCUM,PRSTATE,PRSTCUM,PRFED,PRFEDCUM)=0
     SET (PRHLTH,PRCHAR,PRCUM)=0
     QUIT
     ;END OF ROUTINE

PRDEDUC ;RFW;9/87; CALC DEDUCTIONS
     SET PRCHAR=25,PRHLTH=120
     SET PRSSEC=PRSAL*.08,PRSSCUM=PRSSCUM+PRSSEC
     SET PRFED=PRSAL*.18,PRFEDCUM=PRFEDCUM+PRFED
     SET PRSTATE=PRSAL*.05,PRSTCUM=PRSTCUM+PRSTATE
     SET PRCURDED=PRCHAR+PRSSEC+PRFED+PRSTATE+PRHLTH
     SET PRNET=PRSAL-PRCURDED
     SET PRCUM=PRSAL+PRCUM
     QUIT  ;END OF ROUTINE

PRWRCK ;RFW;9/87; WRITE CHECK, STUB
     WRITE #,"PAYROLL STATEMENT FOR ",PREMPNO," MONTH OF ",MONTH
     WRITE !!,"GROSS SALARY FOR MONTH: ",PRSAL,?50,"CUMULATIVE TO
     ...DATE: ",PRCUM
     WRITE !!?20,"DEDUCTIONS",!!?5,"ITEM",?15,
     ..."THIS MONTH",?40,"TOTAL THIS YEAR",!!
     WRITE !,"FED WITHOLDING: ",?20,$JUSTIFY(PRFED,15,2),?40,
     ...$JUSTIFY (PRFEDCUM,15,2)
     WRITE !,"STATE WITHOLDING:",?20,$JUSTIFY(PRSTATE,15,2),?40,
     ...$JUSTIFY(PRSTCUM,15,2)
     WRITE !,"SOCIAL SECURITY:",?20,$JUSTIFY(PRSSEC,15,2),?40,
     ...$JUSTIFY(PRSSCUM,15,2)
     WRITE !,"HEALTH INSURANCE",?20,$JUSTIFY(PRHLTH,15,2)
     WRITE !,"CHARITY DEDUCTION",?20,$JUSTIFY(PRCHAR,15,2)
     WRITE !,"______________________________________",!,"TOTALS"
     WRITE !,"CURRENT DEDUCTIONS:",?20,$JUSTIFY(PRCURDED,15,2)
     WRITE !?25,"NET AMOUNT:",?40,$JUSTIFY(PRNET,15,2)
     WRITE !!,"BANK OF LAKE WOEBEGONE",?50,MONTH,", 1987"
     WRITE !,"PAY TO THE ORDER OF:",PREMPNO,?65,
     ...$JUSTIFY(PRNET,14.2)
     WRITE !?10,"$",PRNET," EXACTLY"
     WRITE !?50,"Signed E. Scrooge, Treasurer"
     QUIT
```

Although these routines are fairly long, the only really new element in them is the use of execution flow control to direct where execution will continue at certain points. You may wish to study this example and possibly look at some other financial problem that you would want to solve. Please bear in mind, however, that the solutions provided up to this point in the text do not store answers on disk. This is a feature that you will need for real applications, and it is one that we will take up in Chapter 12. It won't be hard to fix programs written up to now so that the values will be stored, but you should be aware of that limitation.

Chapter 11

The exercises in this chapter will also benefit from revision after you have studied the material in Chapter 12. However, it is easy enough to revise them, and the practice of working with arrays is the main point you are learning in this chapter's exercises.

- **Exercise 1**

```
GRADES ;RFW;9/87;COLLECT STUDENT GRADES
      WRITE !,"This program creates an array of student scores."
      WRITE !,"We would like to have 20 or more scores to generate"
      WRITE !,"output for the next problem."
      SET MAX=0,MIN=999,SUM=0
      FOR I=1:1 DO ENTRY QUIT:ID =""
      SET I=I-1,AVG SUM/I
      WRITE !!,"List of grades entered:"
      SET XT=""
      FOR I=1:1 SET X=$ORDER(STUD(X)) QUIT:X =""  WRITE!,X,?10,STUD(X)
      WRITE !!,I," Student scores entered."
      WRITE !,"The average score is ",AVG
      WRITE !,"High score is: ",MAX," Low score is:",MIN
      QUIT  ;exit routine
   ENTRY ;
      READ !,"Enter student id (1st letter of last name plus 3 digits;
      ...null to quit)" ",ID
      QUIT:ID =""
      READ !,"Enter score (between 0 AND 100): ",GRADE
      SET SUM=SUM+GRADE
      SET STDN(ID)=GRADE
      SET:GRADE>MAX MAX=GRADE
      SET:GRADE<MIN MIN=GRADE
      QUIT ;END OF ROUTINE
```

The first interesting point to note in this solution is the open-ended `FOR I=1:1 DO ...` line (the sixth line in the routine). This line will execute until the user presses the *<enter>* key without typing any other characters. It is essential to have the `QUIT:ID =""` at the end of this line, or else it would never terminate. However, the benefit of being able to accept any finite number of values is quite useful in many programming situations, so this approach is often used.

The line using the $ORDER function is one more example of this extremely common line of M code. You should actually memorize this line or the logic it contains so that you can do it quickly and easily yourself. Remember the *two* spaces after the `QUIT:X =""`, though, because otherwise you will get a syntax error. In the section called `ENTRY` are two lines used to store MIN and MAX. You may want to study them just to be sure you see why it is that they work as desired.

The rest of this routine is fairly straightforward, as long as you understand the way in which the `ID` number is used as an index (subscript) for the array `STUD`. You should study this use to be certain that you thoroughly understand how it works.

- **Exercise 2**

```
HISTOGR ;RFW;9/87;CREATE HISTOGRAM OF GRADES
     SET X=""
     FOR I=1:1 SET X=$ORDER(STUD(X)) QUIT:X =""  DO HIST1
     WRITE !!,"Histogram of grades",!
     FOR I=1:1 SET X=$ORDER(DIST(X)) QUIT:X =""  WRITE!,X,?10,DIST(X)
     QUIT  ;exit routine
HIST1 ;
     IF $DATA(DIST(STUD(X)))=0 SET DIST(STUD(X))="*" QUIT
     SET DIST(STUD(X))=DIST(STUD(X))_"*"
     QUIT
     ;END OF ROUTINE
```

The most interesting part of this exercise is the section beginning with the label `HIST1`. In the first line following that label, the function $DATA is required to tell whether a value already exists for that grade. If a value does not exist, `$DATA(STUD(X))` will be zero, and the remainder of the line inserts an asterisk at that point. This line is required, because the line following it would generate an error the first time, since it uses the current value at that point and no such value exists the first time through. This type of solution is common in M, demonstrating the effectiveness of the use of the $DATA function.

- **Exercise 3**

```
STDNAME ;RFW; 9/87; NAME SORT OF STUDENTS
        SET X=""
        FOR I=1:1 SET X=$ORDER(STUD(X)) QUIT:X =""  DO NAME
        FOR I=1:1 SET X=$ORDER(STDNAM(X)) QUIT:X =""  WRITE !,
        ...STDNAM(X),?10,X
        QUIT  ;EXIT ROUTINE
  NAME ;
     WRITE !,"Please enter name of student whose ID is ",X
     READ !,"Name: ",NAM
```

```
SET STDNAM(NAM)=X
QUIT
;END OF ROUTINE
```

This exercise is one of the most useful you have worked with so far in the text. It is indeed a common occurrence in programming that you have to create a cross-reference of one kind or another, and listing students (or any other groups of individuals) by number as well as by name is something that must be done in many situations. Once you are done, you will have two arrays, one, STUD, sorted by ID, and the other, STDNAM, sorted by name. There are several different ways in which cross-reference dictionaries can be generated, but this is a good example in which the name is not known beforehand.

Chapter 12

- **Exercise 1**

```
GRADES2 ;RFW; 9/87; COLLECT STUDENT GRADES
   WRITE !,"This program creates an array of student scores."
   WRITE !,"We would like to have 20 or more scores to generate"
   WRITE !,"output for the next problem."
   SET MAX=0,MIN=999,SUM=0
   FOR I=1:1 DO ENTRY QUIT:ID=""
   SET I=I-1,AVG=SUM/I
   WRITE !!,"List of grades entered:"
   SET X=""
   FOR I=1:1 SET X=$ORDER(^STUD(X)) QUIT:X =""  WRITE !,X,?10, ^STUD(X)
   WRITE !!,I-1," Student scores entered."
   WRITE !,"The average score is: ",AVG
   WRITE !,"High score is: ",MAX," Low score is," ",MIN
   QUIT  ;EXIT ROUTINE
ENTRY ;
   READ !,"Enter student id (1st letter of last name plus 3 digits;
   ...null to quit): ",ID
   QUIT:ID =""
   READ !,"Enter score (between 0 AND 100): ",GRADE
   SET SUM=SUM+GRADE
   SET ^STUD(ID)=GRADE
   SET:GRADE>MAX MAX=GRADE
   SET:GRADE<MIN MIN=GRADE
   QUIT  ;END OF ROUTINE
```

As promised in the previous chapter, here is a fix that makes that program one you can actually use, since the values created for ^STUD will be stored on disk until you decide to remove them, using the KILL ^STUD command. Now that you know how to modify routines to create permanent disk-resident values, you can do a great many more useful tasks. You may even want to look back at some of the problems you solved before to see if you want to modify them as well.

- **Exercise 2**

```
DICTNARY ;RFW; 10/87;CREATE DICT OF TERMS
        READ !,"This program creates sorted dictionaries of terms."
        WRITE !,"The terms are stored in subareas of interest."
        WRITE !?5,"The areas currently included are:"
        SET X="" FOR I=1:1 SET X=$ORDER(^DICT(X)) QUIT:X =""
        ...WRITE !?10,X
        READ !,"Please enter the area for which you wish to
        ...add terms: ",AREA
        QUIT:AREA=""
        IF '$DATA(^DICT(AREA)) WRITE *7,!,"This is a new area.
        ...Please enter"
        READ !?10,"a short definition (or null to abort): ",
        ...DEF QUIT:ADEF =""
        SET ^DICT(AREA)=ADEF
   DEFINE ;
        READ !,"ENTER NEXT TERM (NULL TO QUIT): ",TERM
        GOTO:TERMS="" LIST
        READ !,"Enter definition of term: ",DEF
        SET ^DICT(AREA,TERM)=DEF GOTO DEFINE
   LIST ;
        READ !!,"Would you like terms listed? (Y/N) ",YN
        QUIT "yY" '[YN
        SET X =""
        FOR I=1:1 SET X=$ORDER(^DICT(AREA,X)) QUIT:X =""
        ...WRITE !,X,?20, ^DICT(AREA,X)
        WRITE !!,I-1," terms entered in area ",AREA," so far."
        QUIT  ;END OF ROUTINE
```

This is a routine that I wrote one time (in slightly modified form) when I needed to make a list of the names of variables in a large package. I have used it countless times in countless slightly different forms since then. It is one of the most useful and yet simple examples that I know to illustrate the value of M programming techniques over those of other languages. To do the same thing in almost any other language would require many more lines of code, especially for the sorting part of the solution (the fourth line after LIST).

Chapter 13

■ Exercise 1

```
DICT2 ;RFW; 10/87;CREATE DICT OF TERMS
     READ !,"This program creates sorted dictionaries of terms."
     WRITE !,"The terms are stored in sub-areas of interest."
     WRITE !?5,"The areas currently included are:"
     SET X="" FOR I=1:1 SET X=$ORDER(DICT(X)) QUIT:X=""  WRITE !?10,X
     READ !,"Please enter the area for which you wish to add terms:
     ...",AREA
     IF '$DATA(^DICT(AREA)) READ !,"Please enter short definition of
     ...subject area",ADEF SET^DICT(AREA)=ADEF
     QUIT:AREA =""
DEFINE ;
     READ !,"ENTER NEXT TERM (NULL TO QUIT): ",TERM
     GOTO:TERM="" LIST
     READ !,"Enter definition of term: ",DEF
     SET ^DICT(AREA,TERM)=DEF GOTO DEFINE
LIST ;
     READ !!,"Would you like terms listed? (Y/N): ",YN
     QUIT:"yY"'[YN
     READ !,"Output to printer or screen (P/S): ",PS
     IF "Pp"[$EXTRACT(PS) OPEN 1 USE 1 ;UCD MicroM printer device
     SET X=""
     FOR I=1:1 SET X=$ORDER(^DICT(AREA,X)) QUIT:X=""  WRITE !,X,
     ...?20,^DICT(AREA,X)
     WRITE !!,I-1," terms entered in area ",AREA," so far."
     CLOSE 1 ;release printer
     QUIT  ;END OF ROUTINE
```

This variation of the dictionary program illustrated in the solutions to the previous chapter's exercises is almost identical except for two aspects. First, in the lines just above DEFINE, it gives a way to describe the separate dictionaries that are to be created and hence it is a little more user friendly than the previous exercise. Second, it allows for use of the printer. This exercise was created on UCD MicroM, where the device number of the printer is 1. You will probably have to use another number if you are using another version of M. Check your documentation to see what device number to use for your implementation.

■ Exercise 2

```
CAPITALS ;RFW; 10/87; CREATE CAPS GLOBAL
     OPEN 3:("C":"STATES.DAT") ;use file created in STATES
     FOR I=1:1 USE 3 READ X QUIT:X?1"***".E  SET:X'="" ^CAPITAL($PIECE
```

```
     ...(X,"/",2))=$PIECE(X,"/",1)
     CLOSE 3
     OPEN 2:("C":"CAPITALS.DAT")
     SET X="" FOR I=1:1 SET X=$ORDER(^CAPITAL(X)) QUIT X=""  USE
     ...2 WRITE X,"/",^(X),! USE 0 WRITE !,X,?15,^(X)
     USE 2 WRITE "****" CLOSE 2:0
     USE 0 WRITE !,"Done"
     QUIT  ;END OF ROUTINE

STATES ;RFW; 10/87; STATES, CAPITALS, SIZE
     WRITE !,"This routine asks for Information about states,"
     WRITE !,"their name, size and capitals. Accuracy is optional"
ENTRY ;
     READ !,"Enter state name: ",ST IF ST="" GOTO PRINTOUT
     READ !,"Enter name of capital: ",CAP
     SET ^STATE(ST)=CAP GOTO ENTRY
PRINTOUT ;
     OPEN 2:("C":"STATES.DAT")
     SET X="" FOR I=1:1 SET X=$ORDER(^STATE(X)) QUIT: X =""  WRITE
     ...!,X.?15,^(X) USE 2 WRITE X,"/",^(X),! USE 0
     USE 2 WRITE !,"*****"; END OF LIST MARKER
     CLOSE 2:0
     QUIT ;END OF ROUTINE
```

Once again, these two exercises use device numbers and device parameters specific to UCD MicroM. You will need to check your documentation if you are using another version so as to be able to define the correct values for that system.

Chapter 14

■ Exercise 1

```
SCREEN ;RFW; 10/87 SCREEN MOVE DRIVER
     ;accepts following characters:
     ;<tab>=next field <->=previous field
     ;<^>=top of form <@>=bottom of form
     ;<#>=designate field number (with nn)
SC1 ;
     READ !,"Enter control character: ",*CTL
     IF CTL=9!(CTL=35)!(CTL=64)!(CTL=94)!(CTL=45) GOTO SC2
     QUIT
SC2 ;
     DO SCTAB:A=9,SCBACK:A=45,SCBOT;A=64,SCTOP:A=94,SCNUM:A=35
     GOTO SC1
SCTAB ;call next field subroutine
```

```
   QUIT
SBACK ;call previous field subroutine
   QUIT
SCBOT ;call bottom subroutine
   QUIT
SCTOP ;call top of form subroutine
   QUIT
SCNUM ;call field number subroutine
   QUIT
   ;END OF ROUTINE
```

This sample routine is incomplete, but it has the makings of being an extremely useful utility. To complete it, however, you have to find out exactly how your computer (or terminal) controls the functions called for. If you learn how to do each of them, you can flesh out the skeleton of this routine and have a set of screen utilities that will be really useful.

It is important to remember, however, that these screen functions may vary from one terminal to another within the same implementation of M. Hence, even though you solve it for one device, you may not have the solution for another. This is one of those annoying areas where standardization would be helpful but has not yet occurred.

- **Exercise 2**

```
SCREEN2 ;RFW; 10/87; SCREEN CONTROLS
      ;sequences to control screen controls for IBM PC/
      ;assumes system booted with CONFIG.SYS containing
      ;instruction DEVICE=ANSI.SYS
HOME ;
      WRITE *27,"[2J"
      WRITE *27,"[1m"
      QUIT
DIM ;
      WRITE *27,"[0m"
      QUIT
CURS ;move cursor to loc Y=DY,X=DX (set before called)
      WRITE *27,"["DY,$C(59),DX,"H"
      QUIT ;END OF ROUTINE
```

As noted, this solution works for the IBM PC, but it may not work even on that system if you have EGA cards or other enhancement features. The lack of standardization is indeed a problem, but it is worth the trouble to find out how to modify the routine for specific devices, since these utilities are extremely useful.

- **Exercise 3**

This exercise does not have sample answers. If you would like more information on the British postal code example listed in the text, see the examples following Chapter 15.

- **Exercise 4**

```
HOROLOG ;RFW; 10/87; CALC $H FROM DATE
      WRITE !,"This routine accepts a date (MM/DD/YY), then calculates"
      WRITE !,"the date portion of $HOROLOG."
      READ !!,"Enter a date after 1900 (MM/DD/YY): ",DAT
      SET M=$PIECE(DAT,"/",1),D=$PIECE(DAT,"/",2),Y=$PIECE(DAT,"/",3)
      SET YR=21549+(Y*365)+(Y-1/4)
      SET DAYS="0,31,59,90,120,151,181,212,243,273,304,334"
      SET MB=$PIECE(DAYS,",",M) ;days up to start of current month
      IF (Y>3),(Y#4)=0,M>2 SET MB=MB+1 ;leap yr after 1903,
   ...month after Feb
      SET H=YR+MB+D WRITE !,"First part of $HOROLOG is ",H
      SET TIME=$PIECE($HOROLOG,",",1)-H/365
      WRITE !,"The time elapsed since that date is ",$JUSTIFY(TIME,
   ...10,2)," Years."
```

This exercise works backwards from the example given in the chapter. However, it is a useful one, since you can do valuable calculations of time intervals if you have values stored in the $HOROLOG format. There are no examples of date calculations, but, for instance, it would be a fairly simple matter to calculate a person's age by converting the date of birth to $HOROLOG value and then subtracting that value from the current value of $HOROLOG (the first piece of that variable) and dividing by 365. You could even refine it to exact age (years, months, and days), but that would be considerably more tricky, since the months and days depend on which month an individual was born in as well as the current date.

- **Exercise 5**

```
APTS2 ;RFW; 10/87; GET APT INFO
      ;modified from example APTS in chapt 10
      WRITE #,"This routine is used to get all apartment dweller names"
      WRITE !?10,"in a city. You will be asked for the"
      WRITE !?20,"Street Name. Then, for each street, for the"
      WRITE !?20,"Street Number of the Apartment. Finally, for each"
      WRITE !?20,"Apartment, you will be asked to enter the"
      WRITE !?20,"Apartment Number and tenant's name."
      WRITE !!,"The street names, street numbers and apartment numbers"
      WRITE !,"need not be entered in any order"
```

```
STREET ;
      WRITE !,$PIECE($TEXT(INFO+1),";",3) READ APSTRNM
STRNUM ;
      WRITE !,$PIECE($TEXT(INFO+2),";",3) READ APST
      GOTO:APST"" STREET
      FOR I=0:0 WRITE !,$PIECE($TEXT(INFO+3),";",3) READ APN QUIT:
      ...APN="" DO APNAME
      GOTO STRNUM
APNAME ;
      WRITE !,$PIECE($TEXT(INFO+4),";",3) READ APNAM
      SET APT(APSTRNM,APST,APN)=APNAM
      QUIT
INFO ;text messages follow
      ;;Enter name of next street (null to quit):
      ;;Enter street number of apartment unit (null to quit):
      ;;Enter apartment number (null to quit):
      ;;Enter name of tenant:
      ;END OF ROUTINE
```

This exercise is one that uses the $TEXT function to generate some prompts. It is a common technique in M programming, because it makes it possible to generalize menu-driven questionnaires. In its current form, it is quite useful. However, we will see that the same approach can be made quite a bit more elegant with some added capabilities described in Chapter 18.

Please notice also that this routine could be changed to make the storage of the values permanent by changing the name of APTS to ^APTS.

Chapter 15

- **Exercise 1**

```
SALUPDT ;RFW;3/88;UPDATE SALARY
      READ !!,"This routine allows you to update salaries for
      ...selected employees."
NXTSAL ;
      SET (ID,SAL,CHG)=0,OP=""
      READ !!?5,"Enter Employee ID no (null to quit): ",ID
      QUIT:ID'?1N.E  ;ID number starts with a digit
      READ !?5,"Enter current salary: ",SAL
      READ !?10,"Next, enter amount to add or subtract: ",CHG
      READ !?15,"Finally, enter a + to increase, - (minus) to decrease
      ...salary:",OP
      IF SAL'?1.N!(CHG'?1.N)!("+ -" 'OP) WRITE *09,!"Invalid entries"
      GOTO NXTSAL
      SET UPD="SET ^SALARY("""_ID_""")="_SAL_OP_CHG
      XECUTE UPD
```

```
WRITE !!."The salary of ",ID," has been changed to: ",^SALARY(ID)
GOTO NXTSAL
;END OF ROUTINE
```

This exercise builds an executable line of code which is then used as an M command and is executed in the fourth line from the end. The creation of such lines is a bit tricky, especially making sure that the right number of quotation marks is used. When writing this sort of code, it is a good idea to write out the desired final result and then build it a piece at a time to be sure that the logic is accurate before inserting it into the routine. The nice thing about M is that you can indeed test individual lines in this manner as you create routines, instead of having to combine many lines into a compiled version before you know what logic errors have been made.

- **Exercise 2**

```
GAMES ;RFW; 10/87; GAME MENU DRIVER
   FOR I=1:1 SET P=$PIECE($TEXT(CHOICE+1),";",4) QUIT:P=""  WRITE !,P
   WRITE !!!"Choose a number (1-",I-1,"): " READ OPT
   QUIT:OPT'?1N
   IF OPT,OPT<I DO @$PIECE($TEXT(CHOICE + OPT),";",3)
   GOTO GAMES
DUNGEON ;
   WRITE !,"dungeon routine."
   QUIT
ADVEN ;
   WRITE !,"adventure routine."
   QUIT
LIFE ;
   WRITE !,"life routine."
   QUIT
CHOICE ;
   ;;DUNGEON;1 Dungeons and dragons
   ;;ADVEN;2 Adventure
   ;;LIFE;3 Life matrix
```

This is of course an incomplete routine, and we do not recommend that you try to write a new version of Dungeons and Dragons. However, you could by now write several games in addition to those which have been used as examples earlier in the text, and you could then modify this routine to be a menu program giving the user a choice as to which game to play. You may want to experiment with interfacing this routine, suitably modified, with the TOSSPOT example, and perhaps add a word game that uses a dictionary, now that you have also learned to create dictionaries. For example, you could write a HANGMAN example in which you store a sizable number of good HANGMAN words and then let the computer pick one at random for the user to guess. The point is, you have by now learned enough to do some really fun and practical things with M!

- **Exercise 3**

```
CRCAL ;RFW; 10/87;CREATE CALENDAR MATRIX
      FOR I=1:1:12 READ !,"Enter 3 ltr abbrev for month: ",M,!"Days in
      that month: ",D SET^CAL(M)=D
      SET X="" FOR I=1:1:12 SET X=$ORDER(^CAL(X)) WRITE !,X,?10,^CAL(X)
      QUIT
CALENDAR ;RFW; 10/87; GET DAYS IN MONTH
      READ !,"Enter three letter (caps) abbrev for month: ",M
      QUIT:M'?1U.E
      SET M="^CAL("""_M_""")"
      IF $DATA(@M) WRITE !,M," has ",@M," days."
      ELSE  WRITE !!,*9,"no month with that abbreviation."
      GOTO CALENDAR
      ;END OF ROUTINE
```

This is a fairly straightforward exercise, with the only tricky part being the use of indirection in the fourth line after the label CALENDAR. You should study that line to be sure you understand it. Otherwise, the routines are quite simple.

- **Exercise 4**

```
PATTERN ;RFW; 10/87
      SET P="1.2A1.2AN1"" ""3AN"
      READ !,"Enter a legitimate British zipcode: ",ZIP
      QUIT:ZIP'?1A.E
      IF ZIP?@P WRITE !,"That's an ok brit zip. try again."
      ELSE  WRITE !,"Sorry, not legal brit zip. try again."
      GOTO PATTERN
```

Pattern matching is a fascinating field, and this small exercise gives you some idea of the flexibility of the pattern approach. The added feature of having indirection available (line 5 of this routine) merits some study. The most valuable use of this form of matching is in error checks. Because such error checks can be made very sophisticated in M, the language has a well-deserved reputation for being among the most powerful available for careful input verification.

Chapter 16

Note: The answers to this section were provided by Bruce Douglass, using an M implementation with NEW available. The listing, with comments, is reproduced below to give an example of a different programming and documenting style.

- **Exercise 1**

```
AVG   ;BD; 03 Jan 88, 12:00:50 PM
      ; Chapter 16 -- Exercise no 1
      ;
      ;
      ; Using the local array X provided, write a procedure
      ; to calculate the AVERAGE of the values therein.
      ;
      ;
      ;--- Delete all local variables ---
      KILL
      ;--- Initialize input array ---
      ;
      FOR I=1:1:7 SET X(I)=$PIECE("7,13,4,11,14,9,6",",",I)
      ;
      ;--- Display ---
      WRITE !!,"Input array:"
      FOR I=1:1:7 WRITE ?13,"X(",I,")=",$JUSTIFY(X(1),3),!
      WRITE !!,"Variables present before call to procedure:",!
      WRITE ; (Note implementation-specific way of viewing local variables.)
      ;
      ;
      ; Compute and Print Average
      ;
      DO AVERAGE
      ;
      ;
      ; See if the 'NEW' command worked
      ;
      ;
      WRITE !!,"Variables present after return from procedure:",!
      WRITE
      ; (SUM, MEAN, K, N should all be deleted)
      QUIT
      ;
      ;
      ; PROCEDURE Compute and Print Average of X
      ;
      ;
AVERAGE NEW SUM,N,K,MEAN
      SET K="",(SUM,n)=0
      ;
LP    SET K=$ORDER(X(K))
```

```
      IF K="" GOTO PRNT
      SET SUM=SUM+X(K)
      SET N=N+1
      GOTO LP
      ;
PRNT IF N<1 WRITE !!,"Count < 1 -- No average." QUIT
      SET MEAN=SUM/N
      WRITE !!,"Average of ",N," elements=",MEAN
      WRITE !!,"Variables present while in procedure:" '!
      WRITE
      QUIT
      ;END OF EXERCISE
```

■ **Exercise 2**

```
DATCALC ;BD; 03 Jan 88, 02:50:29pm
      ; Chapter 16 -- Exercise no 2
      ;
      ;
      ; Use of procedure with a parameter to convert a date of
      ; form mm/dd/yy to $HOROLOG format and display results
      ;
DAT WRITE !!,"Enter date, mm/dd/yy :,"
      READ DT
      IF DT="" QUIT
      ;
      ; --- Convert display form to $HOROLOG form --
      ;
      DO DDAT(DT)
      GOTO DAT
      ;
      ;
      ; PROCEDURE Convert mm/dd/yy to $HOROLOG date
      ;
DDAT(DS)
      IF DS'?1.2N1"/"1.2N1"/"1.2N WRITE " use form : mm/dd/yy" QUIT
      ;
      NEW M,D,Y,YR,MB,DOLH
      ;
      ; --- Separate month, day, year --
      SET M=+$PIECE(DS,"/",1)
      SET D=+$PIECE(DS,"/",2)
      SET Y=+$PIECE(DS,"/",3)
      ;
      ; --- Check for reasonable values --
      IF D<1 WRITE " day < 1 " QUIT
      IF M<1!(M=12) WRITE " month not in [1,12]" QUIT
```

```
IF (Y#4),M=2,D>28 WRITE " only 28 days in Feb this year" QUIT
IF Y=0,M=2,D>28 WRITE " only 28 days in Feb, 1900" QUIT
IF D>!$PIECE("31,29,31,30,31,30,31,31,30,31,30,31",",",M)
...WRITE " day exceeds end-of-month" QUIT
;
; --- Base day count ---
SET YR=21549+(Y*365)+(Y\4)
IF Y>3,(Y#4)=0 SET YR=YR - 1
SET MB=$PIECE("0,31,59,90,120,151,181,212,243,273,304,
...334", ",",M)
;
; --- Leap years. this century only (1900–1999) --
IF Y>0,(Y#4)=0,M>2 SET MB=MB+1
;
; --- Final value--
SET DOLH=YR+MB+D
;
WRITE " => ",DOLH
QUIT
;END OF EXERCISE 2
```

■ **Exercise 3**

```
DAT2 ;BD; 03 Jan 88, 02:52:51 pm
      ; Chapter 16, Exercise no 3
      ;
      ;
      ; Use extrinsic function with a parameter to convert a date
      ; of form mm/dd/yy to $HOROLOG and display results.
      ;
      ;
DAT WRITE !!,"Enter date, mm/dd/yy : "
      READ DT
      IF DT ="" QUIT
      ; --- Convert display form to $HOROLOG form ---
      WRITE !?25,"$HOROLOG date=",$$DDAT(DT)
      GOTO DAT
      ;
      ;
      ; Extrinsic FUNCTION: Convert mm/dd/yy to $HOROLOG date
      ;
      ;
DDAT(DS)
      ; --- Return 1 if error --
      NEW DOLH
      SET DOLH=1
      IF DS'?1.2N1"/"1.2N1"/"1.2N WRITE " use form: mm/dd/yy" GOTO XIT
```

```
      ;
      NEW M,D,Y,YR,MB,DOLH
      ;
      ;--- Separate month, day, year--
      SET M=+$PIECE(DS,"/",1)
      SET D=+$PIECE(DS,"/",2)
      SET Y=+$PIECE(DS,"/",3)
      ;
      ;--- Check for reasonable values ---
      IF DO<1 WRITE " day < 1 " GOTO XIT
      IF M<1!(M>12) WRITE " month not in 11,12]" GOTO XIT
      IF (Y#4),M=2,D>28 WRITE " only 28 days in Feb this year" GOTO XIT
      IF Y=0,M=2,D>28 WRITE " only 28 days in Feb, 1900" GOTO XIT
      IF D>$PIECE("31,29,31,30,31,30,31,31,30,31,30,31",",",M)
      ...WRITE " day exceeds end-of-month" GOTO XIT
      ;
      ; --- Base day count ---
      SET YR=21549+(Y*365)+(Y\4)
      IF Y>3,(Y#4)=0 SET YR=YR-1
      SET MB=$PIECE("0,31,59,90,120,151,181,212,243,273,304,334",
      ...", ",M)
      ;
      ;-- Leap years, this century only (1900–1999) --
      IF Y>0,(Y#4)=0,M>2 SET MB=MB+1
      ;
      ; --- Final value ---
      SET DOLH=YR + MB + D
      ;
XIT QUIT DOLH
      ;END OF EXERCISE 3
```

These routines were written on an M implementation with the language extensions discussed in this chapter.

It would be a good idea to compare them with the solutions given for exercises in earlier chapters (and with the large example given in Chapter 18). This code is typical of a programmer who has considerable experience in developing applications as well as utilities for M products. As such, it merits careful study and comparison with the (less polished) examples given for other chapters. Some of the points to look for are the overall appearance, the use of comments, and the consistency in choice of variable names. Each M programmer will develop his or her own style, but discipline, consistency, and clarity are goals to be aimed for by all programmers.

Index

P62. concatenate : _ (underline)
P91 : comment : ; (semi colon)
P91 : space rules.
P94 : Postconditional expression : (colon)
(Note: Can't use it with: IF, ELSE, FOR)

up to 255 char for command line

special characters P79

! : move to nex line
: move to new page
?n : start at the n column

} combined with write command

special variables : P83 $X ; $Y ;
P96 $TEST ;

argumentless command :

P36 IF
P37 ELSE

} alternatives Form of IF
else: always argumentless